Je puis une plume et j'aurais surpris de qui m'a dit
que j'avais quitté à Quyini. —

Mon cher Menotti —

Voici pour vous une occasion d'une pros un
Ouvrir! S'il le faut la lettre ci-inclus à ton père pour
retentissante

A. D. —

J'irai à Garibaldi —

Dimi —
J'aurai de tranchées la tête dans toute la
Garqui, grand enthousiasme m'emportons
D'hommes

Vous vous que j'aille vous en Cha
France Je vous choisirai Cela en chasera

General Giuseppe Garibaldi

ON BOARD THE EMMA

Adventures with Garibaldi's "Thousand" in Sicily

BY ALEXANDRE DUMAS

Translated
and with an introduction
by
R. S. GARNETT

London
ERNEST BENN LIMITED
1929

First Published in
1929
Printed
in
Great Britain

A FEW WORDS TO THE READER FROM THE TRANSLATOR

"Le plaisir de rire n'est pas un des moindres besoins de l'homme."
(Le Père Porée.)

"*The life of Dumas is not only a monument of endeavour and success, it is a sort of labyrinth as well. It abounds in pseudonyms and disguises, in sudden and unexpected appearances, and retreats as unexpected and sudden, in scandals and in rumours, in mysteries and traps and ambuscades of every kind.*"[1]

So writes the critic W. E. Henley. Let us glance inside the "labyrinth." In 1832, when Dumas was thirty years of age and already famous as the author of "Henri III et sa Cour," of "Christine" and of "Antony," and as the capturer of a powder magazine at Soissons—a feat which his d'Artagnan would have envied—he got into a serious scrape with the Government. His king, his friends, and his doctor united in saying, "Leave the country for a time: you have been imprudent from the political standpoint; any other than you would have been arrested. Go away, and let the clouds roll by."

The doctor, who had been treating him, as so many had then to be treated, for the cholera,—the doctor, I say, added: "Try Switzerland." So Dumas ran round to a publisher to propose a few volumes of travels in Switzerland.

"In Switzerland?"

"In Switzerland."

"*Diable!* No!"

"Why, no?"

"You certainly did say Switzerland."

And that was all that Dumas could extract from the publisher, for truly, even in 1832, Switzerland seemed to be an exhausted subject. It was, however, to that country that Alexandre went; and in a few months' time, with his health, which never again failed him, restored, he contributed some chapters from his note-book to *La Revue des Deux Mondes*. They astounded everyone alike: Dumas, the dramatic poet, was, in them, found to be an amusing writer! When the book itself came out [2] it was such a great success that the author, with his inborn insatiable thirst for travel and adventure, had a vision in which he saw himself exploring and writing about the entire old

---

[1] "Views and Reviews," by W. E. Henley, London, 1890.

[2] "Impressions de Voyage," 2 vols., Paris, 1833–34. A new edition has just recently been published.

world! Burning with enthusiasm, he hastened to Lamartine, whose famous "Voyage en Orient" he had devoured, and asked him to sketch out an Itinerary. Lamartine, impressed and kindly, called in the two *savants*, Amadée Jaubert and Alex. de Laborde, to his assistance, with the result that the three collaborators produced the marvellous Itinerary which I give in the Appendix.[1]

Alexandre thereupon sought out the Minister of Public Instruction, and having secured his support, wrote the following "Prospectus," in which, perhaps "by request," he made no mention of the poet and the *savants*.

Prospectus.[2]

10th October, 1834.

"An idea has struck us as being great and national; and it is this:

"Not only France, but Europe, has no book of travels describing the Mediterranean region from the poetical, historical and scientific point of view.

"Many, such as Chateaubriand, Champollion and Volney, have carefully perused some pages of this great work wherein is inscribed the history of the world in its entirety; but nobody has read it continuously from Homer to Byron, from Achilles to Bonaparte, from Herodotus to Cuvier.

"We are going to attempt an expedition in the cause of art and science, in an age when, we are told, politics have stifled art and science. To those who accuse our age of being materialistic and hostile to poetry, we would say that at least we have a government which is helping us.

"We are going to visit Corsica, Sardinia, Italy, Sicily, Greece, Turkey, Asia Minor, Palestine, Egypt, the Coast of Africa, the Barbary States, and Spain—that is to say, the world of Napoleon, Augustus, Constantine, Christ, Sesostris, Mahomet, Hannibal, and the Cid.

"Our narration—as may be supposed, when we mention such names—will be less a record of a voyage than a universal history. We shall take the human story from its Genesis, watch the exodus from the ark, descend the mountains of Armenia with our three ancestral brothers who have peopled the earth. We shall search in the dust of the nations to which they gave birth, and in the ruins of the cities which they built. Nothing that was great will escape our notice.

"In poesy we shall start with Homer, and, passing through Virgil and Dante, we shall end with Chateaubriand.

"In religion we shall have Moses for Prophet, Christ for God, and Mahomet for Reformer.

"In history we shall follow in the footsteps of the phalanxes of Alexander, the legions of Cæsar, the armies of Charlemagne, the crusaders of Saint Louis, the fleets of Charles V, and the grenadiers of Bonaparte.

"In geography Herodotus will describe to us the world as known to the Greeks, and Strabo the world as known to the Romans.

"In architecture Egypt will show us its mosques, Greece its temples, Italy its basilicas. We shall seek the mythic relationship which exists, in the faiths of all epochs, between monuments and the mystic rites that are performed therein, and

---

[1] Dumas improved it into the Itinerary which he gives "as having been drawn up" in Chapter VII.

[2] This Prospectus, which so perfectly reveals Dumas, is not given in any of his biographies. It was brought to light by M. Marius Bernard, the author of "Autour de la Méditerranée, la Terre Sainte et l'Egypte" (Paris 1895–1901), who in that magnificent work accomplished what Dumas, but for his joining Garibaldi, would himself have done. A volume of Dumas' manuscript, in my possession, bears the title "Autour de la Méditerranée."

we shall see emerge the ruins of three beliefs, Saint Sophia of Constantinople with the Greek cross, and Saint Peter's of Rome with the Latin Cross.

.   .   .   .

"All the cities which, in turn, have been queens will pass before us, discrowned: Rome with the *fasces* of the Consuls, the diadem of the Cæsars, and the papal tiara. Syracuse with her sleeping volcano, her harbour half silted up, and the paving of her streets, still bearing ruts left by the chariots which traversed them two thousand years ago. Venice with her two-fold Council of Three and Council of Ten, her Bridge of Sighs, and her Giant's Staircase. Athens with her double aspect—ancient and modern: the courtesan laid to rest in the tomb with the mirror of Aspasia, and the virgin that issued forth from it bearing the yatagan of Botzaris. Constantinople with her Crescent and Cross; in one hand the sceptres of her emperors, in the other the horse-tail standards of the pachas: Jerusalem with the blood-stained Calvary, the bereaved Mother, and the empty tomb. Thebes, the living, so deserted: Thebes, the dead, so thickly populated. Alexandria with her triple souvenir of Alexander, Pompey, and Bonaparte. Carthage with the cradle of Hannibal and the Tomb of Saint Louis; and finally Granada with her Generalife and her Alhambra—that marvellous palace built by the Peris on the land of the faëry."

Having issued this poetic document to the public, which, to its shame be it said, was unresponsive, together with the announcement that letters of credit had been accorded to the explorers by the President of the Council of Ministers and by the Ministers of Marine and of Foreign Affairs, Dumas entered into a contract with Louis Godefroy Jadin, the painter. Jadin agreed to accompany Alexandre on the voyage—a necessarily modified one—and to supply him with a certain number of sketches and drawings with which to illustrate his book. On the 15th October, 1835 the two men set off; but Dumas, who had thought of so much, had not thought of Gregory XVI, or rather of the watchfulness—for let me not call it malice—of one or two of the temporal advisers of His Holiness,[1] and, as he mentions in an early chapter of this book, when in the full course of a second attempt to accomplish his voyage, he was arrested and conducted to one of the frontiers of the Pontifical States. Fortunately he had visited Sicily and Calabria. The result was that Alexandre returned to Paris conquered, for the time being. But, as he himself says, he was a tenacious man. . . .

Such, in outline, was the great idea that sprang into Alexandre's brain in 1834, and was still there in 1858, when, being universally known as the author of the "Impressions de Voyage," "Monte-Cristo" and "Les Trois Mousquetaires"—both of which had appeared in 1844–45—and of many other romances almost equally famous—and having managed to keep in his pocket a few hundred thousand francs out of the millions he had made—this, in truth, was the most extraordinary feat of all—he decided, when he should return from

[1] Gregory XVI and Dumas understood each other perfectly well later on, and had much liking for each other.

Russia and the Caucasus, whither he was just proceeding, to have a yacht built at Syra, to be called the *Monte-Cristo*, on which to attempt the accomplishment of his vision, and afterwards to sail to America. (You will be told by Alexandre how the Greek-built '*Monte-Cristo*,' after an interval of misadventures, became the Liverpool-built '*Emma*.') Jadin was as much his friend as ever, but, unlike him, had grown older. Dumas, agreeing with his Abbé Faria in "The Count of Monte-Cristo" that "the young are not traitors," called around him, or rather selected from the crowd that was always at his table, some young men, and the one and only young woman (for him),—and set sail with them, "ink, paper and pens not being forgotten."

But the Fates had decided otherwise. Whilst his many adventures incident to his preparations were happening, our hero had met Garibaldi, who in former days, in South America, had read certain of our author's romances. It is not to be doubted that the chivalrous deeds of some of their characters had taken root in the soldier's mind. Dumas, the son of a great soldier, on his part, had written as far back as the year 1849, in his political journal, *Le Mois*, in whole-hearted admiration of the heroic deeds of Garibaldi at Monte-Video. Without having seen Garibaldi, he had divined his noble character perfectly. In January 1860 they, as I have said, had met—it was at Turin—and had fallen into each other's arms, Garibaldi finding, as Michelet had said, that Dumas was elemental—"one of the forces of Nature." As the result of the meeting, Dumas had begun to write—or rather to translate and edit—the General's "*Mémoires*" when the *Emma* left Marseilles on the 9th of May, 1860, to sail to the East.

BUT—I must use the word so disliked by Dumas and his Duc de Richelieu, who considered it "ever the harbinger of some folly"—but, I say, on the way to the East is the port of Genoa. The *Emma* put in there; Dumas found notes from Garibaldi for his assistance in regard to the second volume of the "Mémoires," and inspired by his telegram to "rally where you hear my guns," he decided to follow him and the "Thousand" to Sicily, whither they had just sailed on the historic Enterprise.

So much for the genesis of this work; and now for its literary history.

No one with any knowledge of Alexandre will imagine that his paper and pens were being taken for nothing. He had, in fact, arranged with Mirès of *Le Constitutionnel* for the publication there of his voyage, which later was, of course, to form further volumes of his brilliant series "Impressions de Voyage," some volumes of which in those days almost rivalled the popularity of the romances. Now Mirès, a gentleman of Hebraic origin, was, above all things, anxious about his circulation. When he heard that his author at the outset of his voyage had joined Garibaldi, "that filibuster, that pirate," he intimated to Dumas' representative in Paris that as Alexandre had changed his plan, he would follow suit and change his.

The fact was, that *Le Constitutionnel* was not only the delight, the refreshment, the solace of all the *bourgeois* readers of France, but also their guide, counsellor and (financial) supporter. To have daily thrust before their eyes the *actes et paroles* of Dumas, when in concert with a filibuster who might at any moment bring down the funds and "upset everything," was a thing unthinkable. But the author of "Antony" had another friend in the world of journals, the great Émile de Girardin of *La Presse*, who, by no means a *persona grata* with Napoleon III, actually approved of Garibaldi and his Cause of Italian Unity, and who, indeed, had given Alexandre a revolver wherewith to shoot any one he fancied. So Alexandre sent Girardin a number of excellent "letters from the seat of war." It was a great score for *La Presse*. No one could properly complain of getting news, of course—"what else were journals for?" Mirès told himself that he had been an ass. And, indeed, no sooner had Garibaldi's enterprise succeeded than many people "came round." It is true that some among Dumas' fashionable friends, habitués at the Elysée Palace especially, never forgave him; and, what was far worse, some of his *compagnons de voyage* left him *en route*, probably not because they disapproved of Garibaldi and his Cause, but because they disliked the change of plan.

The success of the war letters signed "A. Dumas" was great, and very soon they reappeared, with additions, in the Œuvres Complètes, in the volume entitled "Les Garibaldiens: Révolution de Sicile et de Naples" (1861). It is a strangely made book. It begins with a chapter, evidently concocted, in which Dumas relates his arrival in the *Emma* at Genoa. "Twelve days ago," he says, "I arrived at Genoa on my *goelette* the *Emma*, whose appearance in port produced—thanks to the reputation made for her—a sensation calculated to arouse the jealousy of the squadron of the Vice-Admiral Le Barbier de Tinan, who is cruising hereabouts." No explanation is given of how Dumas obtained the *Emma*, or from whence she had sailed, why she had come to Genoa, or with whom, or where she had been going. The book, moreover, is eloquent in its "blanks" and rows of dots betokening omissions and bewildering leaps in point of time. Its contents were, in fact, hastily put together from the manuscript to harmonise with the title "Les Garibaldiens." Dumas' personal adventures were omitted unless they happened to be relevant to the title.

You now know, reader, far, far more than all the writers on Dumas have related. The *Emma*, to them, has been a mystery. In the words of her owner (anent the "mystery" of Providence allowing the Queen of Naples and Lady Hamilton to exist), any of them might have written "Mystère je dis, mystère je répéte, et encore je dis mystère." The sudden irruption into Sicily of the author of "Les Trois Mousquetaires" on board his yacht the *Emma*, equipped for eighteen months, with a band of joyous young men and a charming young lady attired as a midshipman, has been often misunderstood. Some writers who have read, in contemporary books by Garibaldians, of Alexandre's ample provision of champagne, Bengal lights, and catherine-wheels—to say nothing of his "midshipman"—have not unnaturally assumed that he took them as *munitions de guerre*. I must admit that he was capable of so doing; and indeed, a charming lady, young men, champagne and Bengal lights proved to be delightful additions to his campaign. If you are not an 'Alexandrian,' remember that Sicily is a poetic land, and that had Dumas not been there, the revolution—although without its most original assistant— would nevertheless have been made to the accompaniment of music, song and laughter, with much dancing.

But beneath all this joyous expansion on our author's part, there was a very ardent desire to be of service to Garibaldi's Cause, that of Italian Unity—a desire which, it may be said, he amply gratified in the sequel. Dumas, as he himself says, had "the cult of liberty." He hated oppression, cruelty, stagnation, and priestcraft. It is true that, as he also tells you, he had *une affaire de famille* as an additional reason for detesting the Bourbons of Naples; for had not King Ferdinand had his father, General Alexandre Dumas, poisoned when lying as his prisoner in a loathsome dungeon? But, apart from this circumstance, Dumas, with Mr. Gladstone, echoed, as you shall see, the invective against the Bourbonian tyranny: "This is the negation of God erected into a system of government."

Alexandre Dumas—a phenomenon rather than a man—was in advance of his time, for many things that he said and did, which provoked the scorn and derision of his contemporaries, seem perfectly natural to-day. Capital punishment revolted him; cruelty in any shape revolted him; jealousy revolted him; love of money for money's sake revolted him; trampling on the fallen revolted him. He could not help doing good. ("I belong to that class of imbeciles which does not know how to refuse," is his humorous explanation.) All his life through he was succouring, nursing, helping, and, to do these things, working sixteen hours a day in the garret of his house. And yet in the popular estimation he was considered luxurious. It was clearly because he was one of what he calls "the dynasty of Dumas" that he "went in" for some artistic display. To him, his father the General, he himself, and his son the dramatist, were a family of giants; and giants are not nourished and housed and clad as are men.

Garibaldi and Dumas were, in their different ways, geniuses—or let me call them big children who were naïve, natural, and delightful. Poets, or as you may prefer to call them, dreamers, they each accomplished the "impossible." Each started his career almost friendless; each had an excellent mother, however,—and each battled against incredible difficulties. Each was misunderstood, calumniated; each has left an imperishable name, Garibaldi by his deeds, Dumas by his writings.

This introduction might be almost indefinitely prolonged, for our author, from the very imperfections of his original character—the result, in part, of his mixed race—furnishes an almost inexhaustible theme; but, happily for the reader, I am convinced of this—that this book can well be left to speak for itself. Those, in fact, who like Dumas have here set before them a rich feast of wit and humour, with some more solid dishes which need no seasoning; while those who do not like him will assuredly not take the book up. It is true that Alexandre will attract another class of readers—namely, those who, while wishing him well as a beloved friend of Garibaldi, will send for this book because of its strong Garibaldian interest. I consider that they will be wise in so doing; for, in translating Dumas' manuscript—from which I have often looked up expecting to see him, and he *has* seemed to be talking and laughing beside me—I have enjoyed the company of the Dictator also: Dumas not only understood him perfectly, but in his narrative makes him come alive.

R. S. GARNETT.

NOTE.—For the information of those readers who do not know "Les Garibaldiens" either in French or in English (a translation issued in 1861 is to-day a very scarce book). I have placed asterisks in the Contents against the chapters not contained in that work. I have described the manuscript elsewhere (in *The Times Literary Supplement* of 21st February, 1929), and have since been so fortunate as to discover that Dumas added to it and published, or intended to publish, the whole in a Journal which has disappeared, no writer on Dumas being cognisant of its contents. Happily, Dumas' additions have been recovered by me. I can claim, therefore, to have translated a book which the author desired the public to have. I have added some explanatory footnotes throughout the text. My introduction and the said notes would necessarily have had to be much more extensive but for the labours of Mr. G. M. Trevelyan, to whose most excellent and, thanks to the new and cheap editions, very accessible books, "Garibaldi and the Thousand," and "Garibaldi and the Making of Italy," I refer such of my readers as do not possess them. Apparently the book of 1861 met with some criticism, for Mr. Trevelyan, in alluding to it, says, "Dumas was not nearly so inaccurate as English contemporary writers said." The fact is that Dumas' reputation as a romancer misled his critics. The more the Garibaldian portion of this book—and it treats of the whole of the Sicilian campaign—is studied, the more will its general accuracy be manifested. The appendix contains some curiously illuminating documents which I have dug up in the course of my editorial duties. I wish here to record my grateful thanks to my wife for her translation of Méry's poem, which so perfectly and happily presents the Dumas of 1860; to William Heinemann Ltd. for their permission to use Swinburne's fine centenary sonnet; and to my friend and old school-fellow, Mr. Richard Williamson, for his cheerfully given and unwearied assistance with my work. My friend Mrs. Andrew Lang has kindly read some of my translation in its manuscript stage, and, in so doing, has corrected some errors.

CONTENTS

The asterisks indicate those chapters which are not to be found in "Les Garibaldians" published in 1861. In a few instances Dumas in his MS. does not give chapter headings, and in such cases the Translator has supplied them.

LIST OF ILLUSTRATIONS

THE CENTENARY OF ALEXANDRE DUMAS

Sound of trumpets blowing down the merriest winds
   of morn,
  Flash of hurtless lightnings, laugh of thunders loud
    and glad.
Here should hail the summer day whereon a light
   was born
  Whence the sun grew brighter, seeing the world
    less dark and sad.
Man of men by right divine of boyhood everlasting,
  France incarnate, France immortal in her deathless
    boy,
Brighter birthday never shone than thine on earth,
   forecasting
  More of strenuous mirth in manhood, more of
    manful joy.
Child of warriors, friend of warriors, Garibaldi's
   friend,
  Even thy name is as the splendour of a sunbright
    sword :
While the boy's heart beats in man, thy fame shall
   find not end :
  Time and dark oblivion bow before thee as their
    lord.
Youth acclaims thee gladdest of the gods that gild
   his days :
Age gives thanks for thee, and death lacks heart to
   quench thy praise.

A. C. SWINBURNE.

ON BOARD THE *EMMA*

CHAPTER I

IN SEARCH OF A YACHT

Marseilles, 1st May, 1860

IT was about a year ago that, on my return from the Caucasus, some friends of mine united in giving me a dinner at the Restaurant de la Madeleine, and Méry,[1] at dessert, improvised this poem:

> Hear me! I come to hymn a man of fame;
> But, sirs, I fear to tell you of his name,
> Cæsar or Alexandre? We keep, 'midst friends,
> Such information till the banquet ends,
> I will not name him. If any man there be
> Who will insist, let him withdraw with me,
> I'll whisper the disclosure of to-day
> As a State secret ere he goes away.
>
> Well might our hero say with Horace old,
> "My work is ended and my story told.
> Behold my monument. Now for repose!
> While others idled, on to each day's close
> I worked. My pen I drove with ceaseless cheer
> Through all the changing seasons of the year,
> Since that far moment when my bashful youth
> Laid on a famous tomb its verse uncouth."[2]
> And we, his friends, reply, "With teeming pen
> He entertained th' entire world of men.
> He followed every manner of the stage,
> Restored to life the Greek, the Roman age;
> Enlivened with his fire and poesy
> Heroes of fable and of fantasy;
> Woke History slumbering 'neath the weight of years,
> And gave it life of laughter and of tears;
> A man of every age and every race,
> He drew the modern world with ancient grace;
> For our delight created with a glance
> A new world of the stage and of romance.
> As o'er his furnace there he bends at ease,
> Romance's Vulcan, Invention's Hercules,
> Singer and tale-teller unmatched of men,
> Graving his parchment with a deathless pen,
> Say, 'He has earned full respite. Our athlete
> Now lays him down to rest, his work complete.
> 'Tis time his friends assembled with their praise,
> Cushions for wearied limbs, and crowns of bays.' "

---

[1] Joseph Méry (1798–1865), the poet and novelist, had a wonderful gift of improvisation, of which this poem is but one of many examples. His imagination was only surpassed by that of Dumas.

[2] The poet is right: my first verses were an Elegy on the death of General Foy, to whose recommendation I owed the position which provided me and my mother with our means of subsistence. (Author's note.)

"Elégie sur la morte du Général Foy" par Alex. Dumas, Paris, 1825.

While round his door our vigil thus we keep,
Fearful to break the silence of his sleep,
A message comes, dated I know not whence—
An unknown land, long leagues and oceans hence.
The vanished Titan, tireless, fresh and young,
Has scaled the rock whereon Prometheus hung,
Shoots vultures like the pigeons at a fair,
To avenge the ancestral poet martyred there.
The Caucasus has called! When night descends
(Night that alone his ceaseless journeying ends),
He takes his pen, his desk a rugged stone,
Nought caring for a morrow all unknown,
And verses writes, translates a poem, sings,
Till his glad hearers' acclamation rings.
With practised hand two promised tales he ends,
And, for a rest, writes letters to his friends.
Next, he explored the far and favoured zone
Where Caspys pours an ocean of his own;
Persia, who in her garden still displays
Flowers, and birds, and Poesy's golden rays:
Shores where the Euxine waves essay the breach,
Lucullus raised the cherry and the peach,
And Mithridates learned the toilsome way
Which brought to Rome the dread Avenger's sway.
And ranging, checked by no fatigue or pain,
Through town and desert, mountain, valley, plain,
From the wild Bedouin's black nomad tent,
Forward the traveller unwearied went,
Burnt with the sun, refreshed with cooling slumber,
Still adding to his volumes without number,
Young with the spell of that horizon wide,
Where Æson erst regained his manhood's pride.

Nor yet believe his labours at an end.
See, *Henri Trois!*[1] A new beginning, friend!
Arrived at Paris, he fresh ventures sees
And spreads once more his sail before the breeze.
He had beheld of old that mountain drear
Where fable lightens history austere,
But steam too swiftly bears with peerless might
The dizzy pilgrim in its hasty flight.
He would behold again Sigea's strand
Where waves sigh "Ilium!" as they kiss the land,
Where the blue ripple, in the days of yore,
To Ida's foot the Grecian army bore.
He would behold once more our Mother Greece,
The land of Art's full sunshine and increase,
The land of Homer's and of Virgil's story,
That still affords a glimpse of all their glory.
And as a scion of Alexander's name,
He wished to tread the Mole of Afric fame,
In Egypt, which still guards in her oasis
Lore of the Mages, secrets too of Isis;
Where, in the graves of mummies, wisdom sleeps,
And for a future age its treasure keeps:
Where the great Sphinx accords to all who come
A needed lesson—for she still is dumb.

---

[1] "Henri III et sa Cour," Dumas' first dramatic triumph, produced at the Théâtre Français, the 10th February, 1829.

Doth he arrive, or if his journey ends,
We greet our poet with the warmth of friends.
Coming, he brings to all who hear a strain
Keyed to the harmony of every brain,
Tales without stint for everyone who reads,
Plays, grave and gay, of all an actor needs,
Still piling high (just now three courses set)
The pyramid that lacks its apex yet.
Goes he, on his swift bark we will indite
The verse which Horace did for Virgil write;
From far his course we'll follow on the wave,
Prayers for his glad returning he shall have,
That Orient sunshine may his travels bless,
(Yon sun that aye to bards brings happiness),
And should he come once more, our cups are crowned;
For him the health, for him the cheer goes round;
Glad we will render thanks for all he gives,
And own him Master, even while he lives.[1]

This, then, is what Méry would wish me—Méry, my old and cherished friend to whom I read my first poetic drama "Christine,"[2] thirty-four years ago. From that day we have walked together along the road, often rugged and seldom strewn with rewards, one never overshadowing the other, the clouds in the sky never finding reflection in our hearts, and the storms which burst over our heads never able to separate us.

Well, the day for starting on the promised voyage has been delayed by circumstances beyond my control—a year has divided my journey across the uncivilised world from my peregrinations across the civilised one; during this year I have continued the never-ending toil of my life—that which most astonishes my lazy *confrère* Méry— the work of a literary man. I have published twenty volumes, I have left fifteen ready for the press,[3] I have written six plays, three of which are at this moment in course of rehearsal, and here I am at Marseilles again, having confided the care of my fortunes and of my reputation to the public with all my usual confidence. Here I am ready to embark on my yacht, which is not precisely like Virgil's, but which will bear off, be certain, my dear Méry, a friend not less faithful than was Horace.

And now, how has my first yacht, built at Syra by a Greek, become a yacht built at Liverpool by an Englishman?

To those who insist on knowing all, I am going to narrate the little history. It will fill two or three chapters, but they will make curious and instructive reading.

---

[1] The original text will be found in the appendix. This translation is by Mrs. R. S. Garnett.

[2] Produced at the *Odéon*, the 30th March, 1830.

[3] Volumes according to Dumas' Computation. About 70 pages of his folio size sheets went to a volume. Some four to six of these constituted one volume of the Oeuvres Complètes in the standard "Lévy" collection.

One day I read in a book of About's that small vessels are built at Syra at half the price charged for them in France, and, moreover, are more suitable than French boats for the navigation of the waters of the Archipelago.

This advertisement, if I may so term it, lodged in a corner of my brain. One of those small vessels became necessary to me.

When I left for Russia, I drew up my itinerary accordingly—Berlin, St. Petersburg, Moscow, Kazan, Saratof, Astrakan, Derbend, Bakou, Tiflis, Trebizond, Constantinople, Athens, and Syra.

So all this long itinerary had in reality but a single object—to reach Milo, where the swineherd of Ulysses was born.

I got there after nine months of travelling, a matter of 4500 leagues. M. Rally, the Bavarian Consul, whom I can never sufficiently thank for the trouble taken in assisting me to accomplish this fantasy, summoned to his own house the best shipbuilder of the island—Paghaïda.

We agreed on the price at 17,000 francs. It was just half of what had been asked of me in France.

This was a happy beginning, which justified my friend About.

I left behind at Syra the son of the best pilot of the Archipelago—that is, of old Dimitri Podimatas, who was decorated with the Legion of Honour for having saved a French vessel at Navarino, I think it was. I had run against him, when he was out of work, on board the *Sully*, on which I had made the journey from Trebizond to Constantinople. Captain Daguerre, an expert in such a matter, had recommended him, and I took him into my service.

His Christian names were Baptème Apostoli, the latter that of one of the most likeable characters in my romance "John Davys."[1] As I am a man of first impressions, this coincidence decided me.

The *Monte-Cristo* was to be built in fifty days. I had the promise of Paghaïda, who had never broken his word, or so he assured me; but Paghaïda had forgotten Lent. Lent came, the Greek workmen, more devout than laborious, knocked off work for fifteen days, and my fifty days became sixty-five.

Then broke out the war against Austria. Modern Greeks, like those of old, are great newsmongers. Paghaïda, when news is concerned, is as eager for it as a modern Greek, and an ancient one also. Instead of proceeding to his workshop, he resorted to the parliament house of his little town. There, were discussed the affairs of Europe neither more nor less than in the time of Demosthenes.

Everyone recognised that he envisaged the Italian question under its true aspect. But the *Monte-Cristo* was delayed for ten days, which, added to the sixty-five which had already elapsed, made seventy-five.

[1] "Aventures de John Davys."   Paris, 1840.

On the seventy-fifth an important question presented itself. The *Monte-Cristo*, built in a Greek shipyard, could not become the property of a Frenchman. This no one had thought of mentioning to me, yet it was of importance, seeing that it was I who had commissioned the vessel.

They now wrote to inform me of the difficulty. I admit that I was upset by it. Nevertheless, as there was but one means of getting out of the hole, I employed it. It was to write to M. Rally, who had already given so many proofs of his kindness, to take the vessel over in his own name, and, declaring that he had received all the rent in advance, to lease it to me for a term of ninety-nine years. During the time intervening between 1858 and 1957 I should have done for the yacht, or the yacht would have done for me. M. Rally accepted, and became owner. But the negotiation had consumed twenty-five days—nine for my letter to get to Syra, seven for M. Rally to decide, nine for his letter of decision to reach me—total twenty-five, which, added to the seventy-five, made one hundred days. Now this was just double the time agreed on. It resulted that the *Monte-Cristo*, which ought to have been launched towards the beginning of April, was placed on the water towards the end of June.

But this was not all.

I had carefully inquired the time it would take the *Monte-Cristo* to come from Syra to Marseilles, and I had been told that under the worst conditions twenty or twenty-five days would suffice.

On the 15th July I received news of my vessel. With her captain and four sailors on board, she had left Syra on the 5th July. So, adding the five days which had already elapsed of Julius Cæsar's month to the extreme duration of the voyage—that is to say, twenty-five days—the *Monte-Cristo* would not reach Marseilles until the 30th.

I wrote to Marseilles that my yacht ought to arrive by the 30th at the latest, begging my correspondent to advise me by telegraph immediately she was signalled.

The month of July, as also the month of August, went by without any telegram coming; at last on 1st September I was informed of the arrival of the *Monte-Cristo*.

I left at once for Marseilles, and found my craft at anchor near Fort St. Nicholas. In spite of the promise of Paghaïda, who ought to have made the *Monte-Cristo* the best sailing craft of the Archipelago, she was a sufficiently creditable-looking vessel with a large beam, a wall of defence against the tempests of the Cape of Good Hope, and the direct descendant of one of the thousand ships which had brought the Greeks to the siege of Troy and had taken ten years to bring Ulysses from Pergamus to Ithaca.

She was reassuring as regards solidity, but disquieting as regards velocity.

Furthermore, she arrived ballasted with stones collected on the shore of Milo, and utterly devoid of fittings.

Paghaïda, who ought to have fitted her, had fancied that this work would be better done in France than at Syra, and had not judged it convenient to deal with this insignificant detail.

It resulted that the first moment that the yacht could be ready for the water would be the 1st October—that is, just when one leaves that element for the winter.

I decided, therefore, that the *Monte-Cristo* should remain just as she was until February 1860, that then the workmen should be put on her, and that towards the end of April, like the child of the "Last Judgment" of Michael Angelo, who wished to re-enter the womb of his mother, she would return on her route and seek the East.

In the meantime I was advised to have her brought to Paris to be decorated.

All my friends, who, in a moment of enthusiasm, had promised to lend me their united aid towards the comfort and embellishment of my yacht, would hold scrupulously to their word when she was near them. I should have been at an expense of 2000 francs in and about the transit of my vessel, but, on the other hand, once the expense was incurred I should save 10,000 francs by the presence of the *Monte-Cristo* at the Quai d'Orsay.

The hope of effecting this saving seduced me. I instructed Podimatas to undertake the journey by the Straits of Gibraltar; but he judiciously made reply that, having taken two months from Syra to Marseilles, he would by no means promise to take less than six months from Marseilles to Havre.

He stated that in the present condition of the *Monte-Cristo*, with a shifting ballast, the first tempest that came along would make her founder, or the first gale blow her to America.

The former supposition postponed my journey to the Greek Kalends; the latter, which was even greater, put in question the safety of five men.

It was decided, therefore, that we should try to get the *Monte-Cristo* up the Rhone, from the Rhone passing into the Saône, and from the Saône into the Burgundy canal, and from the canal of Burgundy into the Seine.

It was a great relief to my conscience when I learnt of the practicability of this transit—it is true that it meant a biggish hole in my purse, for 2000 francs were required from me.

A week later I received a letter announcing that, soundings having been taken, the *Monte-Cristo* was fifty centimetres too deep to pass the shallows of the Rhone.

The matter became one which needed, but did not reach, a decision.

The Rhone refused us a passage, but the Southern canal offered us one. We registered two and a half metres deep; the Southern canal was three throughout. So there was no trouble; we should pass into the ocean by the Gironde—so I was told; we should thread our way out of the Gulf of Gascony; we should double Cape Finisterre; and we should arrive triumphantly at Havre.

Only 800 francs were asked for the journey. This meant a saving of 1200 francs and a real advantage to me.

It is these advantages that have so often ruined me, and will continue to ruin me.

I consulted Podimatas. He in his turn consulted two men; the majority considered the project possible.

I sent the 800 francs to Podimatas, who accompanied his receipt with the announcement of his departure for Cette.

Three days later I received this despatch—

"Impossible to pass Pont d'Agos, the yacht is thirty centimetres too wide; what are we to do (*que faire*)?"

So the *Monte-Cristo* drew too much water to pass up the Rhone, and was too wide for the canal to accommodate. Decidedly she was a difficult vessel to please, was this craft of mine.

I telegraphed in reply—

"Return to Marseilles, *parbleu.*"

The word *parbleu* was indicative of a slight impatience, but for some months past my friends had had more than a fondness for saying—

"My dear fellow, you have made a great mistake in having a yacht built at Syra; at half what she has cost you could have bought one already made at Constantinople, Malta, or Marseilles."

And I now began to feel all the justice of this reasoning, which naturally put me in a bad humour, as proving that I had made a mistake.

Relatively to the situation that occasioned it, the word *parbleu* was, it will be conceded, a very mild one—so mild, indeed, that Podimatas did not even observe it.

He returned to Marseilles with the yacht, and I arrived there almost at the same moment.

I had to make an important decision.

In consideration of coming to Paris, which the men had never seen, and of spending the winter there, they were willing to accept half-pay.

I proposed to them that they should remain at Marseilles until the spring, on the same conditions as regards pay.

They replied that they preferred to be discharged.

I had nothing to say against discharging them. I asked Podimatas what compensation I should give the men on doing so.

He replied that I should give them nothing, as it was they who asked for their discharge.

"Nothing" seemed to me to be too little. I asked Podimatas to give them a month's pay. With a month's pay, still according to Podimatas, they ought to be enchanted. So I returned to Paris, with the mental prospect of the whole matter of paying off the crew being soon accomplished.

A fortnight later, when I believed the men to be *en route* for Greece, I received a letter from M. Becker, my correspondent at Marseilles.

It appeared that the paying-off was attended with great difficulties.

The same men, whom, still according to Podimatas, I had the right to retain or send away as I wished, even without compensation, now demanded three months' pay by way of compensation.

It was I, in my turn, who asked my correspondent—"What am I to do?"

"Pay," answered he; "the fact that your vessel was built at Syra places you under the jurisdiction of the Greek Consul, and naturally the Greek Consul, placed between the interests of his fellow-country-men and yourself, will find you in the wrong."

How a Consul—that is to say, a man of justice—could find me in the wrong when I was in the right, because they were Greeks and I was French, was what I did not understand.

The problem having to be resolved, I consulted my friends, who contented themselves with replying—

"We told you that you made a mistake in building a craft at Syra instead of having one constructed at Malta, Constantinople, or Marseilles."

It was the fable of the teacher and the children—while I was drown-ing, a lecture was being read me; I found the lecture ill-timed. Nevertheless I sent 660 francs to Marseilles.

But during the debate a month had gone by; and three months to pay in advance now made four months, in all 880, and not 660 francs that I owed to my crew.

I increased the credit of Podimatas to the sum of 880 francs, utter-ing an oath as they flew away, but saying to myself: "Good, I will work another hour a day," which accordingly I did, believing myself this time disembarrassed of my crew.

I was in error.

A week later I received a letter from my correspondent to the effect that two of my men had left, their pay in their pockets, without making any difficulty; but that the two others required, in addition to three months' pay, to be repatriated at the cost to me of seventy francs more.

And, faithful to his position as a native of Marseilles, and as a poet, he ended his letter with this quotation by the author of "Tancrède" :—

" *Atous les cœurs bien nés que la patrie est chère!*"

I was in an ill-humour at the moment—one of my friends, to whom only an hour before I had remarked that I was relieved of my crew, had answered me with the eternal refrain—

"All the same, instead of having a vessel built at Syra, I, in your place, would have bought one at Constantinople, Marseilles, or Malta."

Then my friends were more and more in the right, and I was more and more in the wrong.

So I contented myself by replying to my correspondent—

"My dear Sir,—I am at the end of my money, and, above all, of my patience; let the two men go to——"

It was a little abrupt, but what do you expect? The most placid man has moments of impatience.

My correspondent answered—

"Quick, quick, quick, authorise me by telegraph to pay seventy francs to each of your men, or the Greek Consul will have the *Monte-Cristo* sold."

The *Monte-Cristo* to be sold for 140 francs!—the sum claimed by men to whom I had already paid 440 francs more than I owed them! That appeared to me unfair. I consulted a friend experienced in such matters.

"What do you expect?" said he to me; "your opponent is not your fellow-countryman, but a foreigner, a Greek Consul, and his fellow-countrymen will, as a matter of course, have to be found in the right as against you; so pay the 140 francs demanded, and pray God that this may be the last demand."

"But is it not hard to have to submit to be plucked in this scandalous manner?"

"What do you expect, my dear fellow? Instead of having a vessel built. . . . Pay, pay, my dear fellow, *pay!*"

So I sent the 140 francs, begging my correspondent, M. Becker, to obtain from my men, who included Podimatas, a formal receipt in discharge, so as to secure me from any fresh extortion.

M. Becker replied by sending me the receipt in discharge from my two men, but telling me that Podimatas could not send me one, for the reason that I was far from being out of debt towards him.

A shiver ran through my body. What could I possibly owe Podimatas? On leaving Syra he had received 2000 francs from M. Rally. I had the receipt. I had sent him 800 for the journey up the Southern canal that he had not made; 880 for the disembarkation of the four men, of whom he had paid off only two; finally 140 more to repatriate the two fanatics; in all, 3820 francs, when, on my own calculation, board included, I did not owe to him and to his men for pay, disembarkation, and repatriation, more than 2680 francs.

As full of confidence in my own cause as Raoul, the Huguenot, was in his, after self-examination of my conscience I wrote—

"Let Podimatas send me his account."

By return of post I received the account of Podimatas—it amounted to 2160 francs, with postage to pay in addition.

One of the most striking items of this account was 400 francs for stones collected on the shore of Milo for the ballast of the vessel.

The 1760 remaining francs were for purchases and repairs made before the departure from Greece and since the arrival in France.

I wrote to M. Becker—

" Can you understand this account?"

He replied—

"I understand absolutely nothing, except that you have committed an error in having a craft built at Syra instead of buying one already constructed at Marseilles, Malta, or Constantinople."

If he had thus answered me orally, I should have stopped him in his first word, but he was replying in writing, and I was obliged to read to the end.

This obligation put me in such a bad humour that I wrote—

"This is to inform you that in a week's time I will proceed to Marseilles, and I will have the account of Podimatas examined."

To which letter my correspondent rejoined with his customary logic—

"By whom will you have the account of Podimatas examined? Your vessel is Greek, you will go before the Greek Consul, the Greek Consul will decide against you."

For a moment I longed to answer—

"*Eh bien,* be it so; if he decides against me, I will not pay."

But I reflected that if the Greek Consul had threatened to have the *Monte-Cristo* sold for 140 francs—I will never say "owing to," but I must say "claimed by" her two sailors—all the more would he have her sold for 2160 francs, which I will never say are "owing to," but I must say are "claimed by" her captain.

I paid the 2160 francs, but found it as difficult of digestion as lead. I went to bed that night with the 400 francs' worth of stones gathered on the shore of Milo weighing on my chest.

Consequently I spent part of the night trying to devise a means of escape from the jurisdiction of Greek Consuls, which seemed to me more arbitrary than the justice of Turkish cadis.

CHAPTER II

IN SEARCH OF A FLAG

WITH the coming of dawn came also my decision. Instead of sailing in Grecian waters flying the Greek flag—a proceeding that seemed to me to be at the same time like a gesture to Greece and a security to myself—instead, I say, of hoisting the flag of Greece, I would nationalise the yacht and navigate her under the pennon of France.

But nothing is more true than "one bill finished with, another begins."

I had inquired as to the possibility of my idea at Syra; I was told that nothing in the world was easier—it would just be a matter of paying the cost of nationalisation—namely, 10 per cent. of the purchase price of the yacht.

The *Monte-Cristo* had cost me 17,000 francs. Ten per cent. of this sum amounts to 1700 francs. Total, 18,700 francs, plus the 3000 or 4000 francs which I was forced to pay—in all, 22,000 or 23,000 francs—24,000, perhaps, on a close reckoning; but, even so, considerably short of the 30,000 quoted to me by Vanes, the shipbuilder, at Boulogne, or the 45,000 by Mazeline, the shipbuilder, at Havre.

It would be in vain for my friends to say, directly I escaped from the Greek Consul, that I had not made a good bargain, and in the end I should be glad that I had followed the advice of About, whom no one will accuse of having any partiality for the Greeks.

At two o'clock I jumped into a cab and called to the driver—

"Ministry of Marine!"

Do not suppose that I was going straight to the Minister. I am not on such terms with my Government; they were all right in the time of my dear friend St. Maur, and in that of the gallant Admiral Jacob; but since the celebrated discussion about the *Véloce*, I am not on terms with any Minister of Marine, whether born or unborn.

No; I was going to seek the good offices of my friend the Abbé Coquereau, the same who, with the Prince de Joinville, brought back Napoleon's remains from St. Helena.

Here I want to say in the most graceful way I can that the Abbé is at once one of the most witty and most erudite of men. How did I become acquainted with the Abbé Coquereau? I am going to tell you.

One day I was dining at the Princesse Mathilde's—her eulogy

also I would write, if she were not a princess—when the conversation turned on the true and the false Apostles.

A discussion on the Councils at Nicea followed.

My antagonist, a cleric, was a stranger to me, and he knew me no more than I did him.

The point in question was keenly debated, and it was agreed that on our leaving the table it should be settled by means of reference to Bouillet's Dictionary.

We left the table. Bouillet's Dictionary was brought and consulted, and it was seen to be so obliging as to be in my favour.

To be in the right against an abbé in a theological discussion was a great triumph for a poet. The Princesse Mathilde took occasion to rally the Abbé Coquereau on his defeat; he, a reverend gentleman, worsted by a heretic in a discussion on the Councils!

The Abbé tried to turn the tables on me.

"A heretic! Princesse," said he; "do not believe it. M. Dumas, on the contrary, is a Christian, and a very good one."

"Oh, M. l'Abbé," said the Princess, "permit me to doubt that, even though you say it."

"If you do not believe me, Princesse, I will give you proof."

"What proof?"

"A letter from M. Dumas preserved by me as an autograph."

"A letter from me," said I in my turn. "I do not recall ever having had the honour of writing to you, M. l'Abbé, yet my memory is a good one."

"The letter, in fact, is not addressed to me," replied the Abbé Coquereau, "but to Mgr. the Bishop of Evreux, to whom at that time I, as Abbé, was attached."

"To Monseigneur Olivier! Yes," said I, with a sigh, "he was a good friend of mine, and he had much affection for me."

Because the last time I saw Monseigneur Olivier was at Dreux at the funeral of the Duc d'Orléans—I had wept for a long time in his arms and on his breast, and certainly, had consolation been possible, his gentle words would have afforded it. But it was not possible; I never speak of the Duc but tears come to my eyes.

No one noticed my emotion.

"Well, Abbé," said the Princess, " what did the letter say?"

"It asked Monseigneur the Bishop to celebrate on a certain day at a certain hour a Mass for a friend of M. Dumas, who on a certain day and at a certain hour was going to be in great danger."

"Is this true?" asked the Princess of me.

"As true as the true gospels of which we were just now speaking."

"Was the Mass said?"

"Religiously."

"And the person who ran the great danger escaped it?"

"Yes, Princesse; thanks be to God."

"What was the danger that the person was in?"

"He was about to fight a duel at Helbron on the Neckar."

"What!" cried the Princess. "It was for my brother that you had the Mass said, Dumas?"

"For your brother, yes, your Highness."

"Come now, M. l'Abbé," cried the Princess, laughing, "you must still admit that you were fairly beaten in the theological argument."

The Abbé made the admission, and held out his hand to me in sign of peace; and since that day, beginning, as we did, as antagonists, we have become the best friends in the world. Therefore, I had most naturally thought of the Abbé in the matter of the nationalisation of my vessel.

Though I do not see him oftener than every second or third year, he held out his hand to me as if we had parted only yesterday.

I told him the object of my visit.

"Nothing could be easier," said he. "I am going to send to the *Directeur des Douanes.*"

"Then I will call again to-morrow or the day after."

"No," said he; "sit down, and we will have a talk while waiting."

I think I have said already that the Abbé Coquereau is a delightful conversationalist. The answer, therefore, did not seem long in coming, but it was the opposite of what was hoped for. Since the Crimean War, to facilitate the transport of foreign ships, the nationalisation of foreign vessels had been authorised, but, only eight days before the inquiry now made for me, a law had been passed putting an end to this facility.

It was necessary, therefore, to give up my idea of nationalising the *Monte-Cristo.*

An idea occurred to me which I mentioned to the Abbé Coquereau. It was to adopt the flag of Jerusalem. As I had the Grand Cross of Jerusalem, the idea was pleasing to me. Furthermore, the flag of Jerusalem is the flag of pilgrims—it bears the red cross, that of the Tancreds and of Godefroy de Bouillon. Its device is that of our old chevaliers: *Dieu le veult.* Again, the flag is neutral, and, as such, respected by all nations enjoying the direct protection of France, and, in consequence, upheld by French Consuls.

I begged the Abbé to ascertain to whom I ought to address myself to obtain the authorisation to navigate under the flag of Jerusalem.

The Abbé ascertained. He was informed that formerly it was France which gave the authorisations, but, the grants having been

frequently abused during recent years, the Government had decided
to divest itself of the right, and to leave its exercise entirely to the
Holy Fathers of the Holy Land, with whom it had formerly jointly
enjoyed it—that consequently I ought to address myself to our Chancellor at Marseilles, M. Famin, who would be in communication
with the Holy Fathers.

An Italian proverb says—

"He who desires goes, he who does not desire sends."

As I desired, I resolved to go. It meant a journey to Marseilles,
but, at the point I had reached, a journey more or less was
nothing.

So I set off for Marseilles, and, having arrived there, I went straight
to M. Famin.

M. Famin told me that the Reverend Fathers of the Holy Land had
had until the past year a representative at Marseilles, but that,
owing to a certain want of sympathy on the part of the French
Government towards their flag, he had some months since removed
to Leghorn.

I had more desire to go to Leghorn than to return to Paris; besides,
thanks to the obliging behaviour of the *Messageries* towards me, the
journey would cost me the price of my food only.

I stretched my legs and found myself on board the *Capitole*. By good
fortune she was sailing the same day, and the next day but one I
awoke in the port of Leghorn.

We had not yet received permission to disembark, which our
Consul at Leghorn had the power to give. Decidedly my lucky star
was shining, for our Consul at Leghorn proved to be an old friend—
Bernard des Suarts. I had known him at Amsterdam, when the
King of Holland had invited me to attend the ceremony of his
coronation.

My first call was on Bernard des Suarts, my first word was to ask
him where I should find the representative of the Fathers of the
Holy Land.

"At Florence," he replied, and he added, " It is a matter of three
hours and a half by the railway."

"And when does the train leave for Florence?"

"Thrice daily, at eight in the morning, at noon, and at four in
the afternoon. You have plenty of time to catch the noon train."

"And am I sure to find the man I want in Florence? for you notice,
my dear friend, that since my visit to the rue Royale, Paris, I have
been pursuing him."

"You are sure to find him; only yesterday I had something from
him."

"And his name is——"

"Le Comte Piccolimini."

"Give me a line to him."

Des Suarts wrote a few lines.

"Here you are," said he.

It was a recommendation to do quickly and in the most convenient way what I desired.

At four o'clock the next day I was at Florence.

At five o'clock Le Comte Piccolimini had the note of des Suarts with my card.

At six o'clock he was at my hotel.

This time I was at the end of my pilgrimage. What I desired, it appeared, was of all things in the world the simplest, and I had nothing to do but pay the sum of 250 francs, when a provisional authorisation would be accorded me. Le Comte Piccolimini undertook to obtain the ratification of the Fathers of the Holy Land later on. Meanwhile I could sail when I chose. The definite authorisation would be sent after me, and await me in some port or other, on some island, or in some continent. Only seven days were necessary for the legalisation of the signature and the fulfilment of some subsidiary formalities. In seven days the patent would be sent to our Consul at Leghorn, who would forward it to me. Meanwhile the Comte gave me a receipt for my 250 francs, without even asking where my vessel had been built—if she were English, American, French, or Spanish.

At eleven o'clock that same night I was again at Leghorn.

The next day I knocked at the door of the Consulate before Bernard des Suarts was awake, but as his *valet-de-chambre* had seen him embrace me, he took it on himself to announce me to his master, who came down at once in his dressing-gown.

"Well," he asked, "are you satisfied with Piccolimini?"

"Enchanted," I replied, and I told him that in a week the provisional patent would be in his hands.

"Where can I send it to you?"

"Keep it until you hear from me. Now that I am in Italy I should not be sorry to make the acquaintance of Garibaldi, whom for the last ten years I have admired without knowing him. Can you tell me where he is?"

"At Genoa or Turin."

"Well, then, keep my patent; perhaps I shall come for it myself."

"You will?"

"Why not? I wish to finish with this devil of a vessel. Perhaps my presence will be necessary to complete matters. Wait for me a little without waiting for ever. If anything should prevent my return, I will write to you."

"And when do you leave?"

"To-day, if I can. Leghorn is not a lively place, as you ought to be aware, since you live in it; you are the only person I know, and I cannot station myself at the Consulate. Please tell me when I can leave for Genoa."

Bernard des Suarts ascertained that the *Quirinal* was in port, and was to leave for Genoa at six o'clock that evening.

"You will lunch with me and start as late as possible."

"I will go at five o'clock, if you like."

"But you will die of *ennui*. I have a lot to do and cannot enjoy your company."

"I shall not be bored, if you give me three things."

"And they are?"

"Paper, pens, and ink."

"You shall have them, and as an extra I will give you the desk of my Chancellor, who is at Elba."

It was all that I wanted. Des Suarts installed me at the desk of his Chancellor, and gave me the necessary articles.

I profited by them to write some fifteen letters—I have always a series of replies on hand which await an opportunity to be written. If the opportunity does not present itself, I let the capital and interest accumulate until the moment arrives when I declare myself insolvent.

At eight o'clock the *Quirinal* weighed anchor, at three o'clock the next morning we were entering the port of Genoa.

Garibaldi was at Turin.

The same evening I was at Turin. The next day I was present at the famous sitting of the Nation in Arms. The day after, I left for Milan to pay a visit to my friend Téléki—another patriot, that is to say, another exile, who was twice condemned to death and who twice saved himself when the rope was round his neck—the first time at Barcelona, the second time at Arad.

Once at Milan I had the idea to try if I could not get as far as Venice—it would be, at all events, an attempt. I had already made one in 1835, and another in 1841—both had failed: the first time I was arrested at Foligno, the second time at Bologna.

The number three is beloved of the gods, and my third attempt was completely successful. I passed like a letter in the post.

It is true that, like "a letter in the post," I was unsealed on the frontier, but they knew how to read on both sides. Nothing was discovered that was dangerous. I continued my journey, aided by a clasp of hands with the Chief of Police.

I saw Venice. Poor Venice!

Two enslaved queens remain to be rescued from the yoke of kings —Venice and Naples: let them hope still; as for us, we pray for them.

I stayed five days in Venice. I paid my call on the Comte de Chambord, who returned it in the person of M. de la Ferron—then I left by the same route by which I had come, and thus, three weeks later, again at Leghorn, I knocked once more at the door of the Consulate.

The Comte Piccolimini had kept his word. The patent was in the hands of my friend des Suarts; only, the name of the captain, which I had not given, was represented by a blank.

I pointed this out to des Suarts.

"Nothing is easier," he replied; "tell me your captain's name and I will fill it in."

"Apostoli Podimatas," I replied.

"But that name seems to me Greek."

"None in the world could be more so. He is as Greek as the Venus of Milo—was born there, in fact."

"But as he is a Greek, he is a member of the Greek Church."

"Probably."

"In that case he cannot command your vessel."

"Why not?"

"Simply because one of the first conditions required of a captain sailing under the flag of Jerusalem is that he is a member of the Catholic Church."

I uttered a cry of real despair. I had gained a flag, but I had lost a captain.

"But tell me, Dumas," said des Suarts, "why the devil, instead of having a yacht built for you at Syra, didn't you purchase one already constructed at Malta, Constantinople, or Marseilles?"

I was so utterly crushed that I let him continue to the end.

CHAPTER III

IN SEARCH OF A CAPTAIN

AFTER so dire a disappointment, such was my need of relaxation that the next morning I found myself—how it came to pass I do not know —on the boat that was leaving for Civita Vecchia. She was the *Capitole*, the same that had taken me to Leghorn the previous month.

You ask me why I was going to Rome?

Was it because of Chateaubriand's saying that in that city, with its prodigious memories, no man is so happy or so unhappy that he cannot there find a bliss or a despair greater than his own?

Not so. I was travelling to Rome to see it over again. If I love the sea as a mistress, I love Rome as an ancestress. How often have I been to Rome? I cannot count the number of times. When I am tired out, exhausted, beside myself with fatigue, I find a pretext for going to Rome; and I go.

When pretexts fail me, I go all the same.

But what do you do at Rome?

Oh, that is easily told. I go to see the Appian Way; I go to see the rolling Tiber; I go to seat myself under one of the arcades of the Colosseum; and I whisper to myself—

"Yes, I must write a history of Rome."

"Why don't you write it, then?"

Because it would be considered too amusing. No one would read it. The public will never be induced to believe that Herodotus, Suetonius, and Walter Scott are historians. You recollect that only lately, when my "Mémoires d'Horace"—a purely historical work— appeared in the *Siècle*, my friend Desnoyers, not wishing that there should be the least doubt of that fact in the minds of his readers— I should say of *my* readers—craved their forgiveness for putting before them such a dull work, and promised, as a compensation, to interrupt my *feuilletons* frequently with others by Messieurs Oscar Conmettare and Philibert Andebrand. At first, I thought his foreword super-fluous, but, with that superior logic that characterises him, M. Lettodey, the manager of the *Siècle*, ended by proving to me that it had produced the most excellent effect. The readers of his journal found themselves amused, when expecting to be bored. The contrary, it appears, is often the case.

In short, I was on the way to Rome on the seventh or eighth occasion. This is not the moment for talking about Rome. But rest assured that when the occasion comes, it shall not escape me.

To-day, I am telling you the story of my yacht, and nothing shall come between me and her.

"But what connection can there be between your yacht and the city of Rome?"

· You are about to learn.

We have an ambassador at Rome. He is the Duc de Gramont. The Duc de Gramont, who was a Guiche before being a Gramont, is one of my oldest friends. His uncle, the Comte d'Orsay, that English-Frenchman whose elegance has become proverbial, and whose wit, like that of the Mortemarts, had currency all over Europe, was the connecting link. It is to the Comte d'Orsay that my "Mémoires" are dedicated.[1]

Our ambassador at Rome being the Duc de Gramont, it was natural that I should pay him a visit, not in his character of ambassador, but in that of friend. His inquiry, what had brought me to Rome, was as natural. I told him, not what I had come to Rome to do—which in truth I did not know—but what I had gone to do at Leghorn. And starting at this point, I laid before him the history of my woes.

"That should be a lesson to you," said he, "for having built a yacht at Syra instead of buying one already constructed at Constantinople, at Malta, or at Marseilles."

I was strongly tempted to stop him in the middle of his sentence, and I should have done so, had he been merely my friend, but as, besides, he was an ambassador, I let him finish.

"Well," said I, poorly concealing my impatience, "nothing would have suited me better than to buy one already built, but there wasn't one to be had."

Now, my denial was a terminological inexactitude, for, attracted by the picturesque idea of having a yacht built for me at Syra, I had never inquired for one ready for the sea.

"Ah," replied Gramont, "so there wasn't one to be had?"

"No," I repeated firmly, "there was not."

"But *I* had one."

"You?"

"Yes, I."

"Where?"

"At Marseilles."

"But not for sale."

"On the contrary, for sale, seeing that I have sold her."

"Ah, so you admit that you have sold her."

"Yes, to one of my friends, the Baron de M——. Oh, my dear fellow,

---

[1] "These Memoirs are dedicated to the Honourable Count Alfred D'Orsay, my fellow-craftsman and my bosom friend."

an entrancing little yacht—the very one you wanted, seventy-eight tons, built at Liverpool, made of mahogany and maple, copper bottomed—in short, a marvel. She cost 110,000 francs."

"But as she was built at Liverpool, how did you become her owner?"

"I nationalised her."

"At the Ministry I was told that doing so was against the law."

"Yes, to-day, but not then."

"I see. But as I am not an ambassador, yachts at 110,000 francs are not for me."

"In the first place, I have not sold her for 110,000 francs; I have sold her for 36,000."

"Never mind, even 36,000 are too much for me."

"Let us consider. What has yours cost you?"

"Seventeen thousand."

"Which you paid to her builder?"

"Yes."

"Just for the shell and the masts."

"Just so."

"What did she cost you for ballasting, and for the voyage to France?"

"Three thousand francs."

"Ah, 20,000 already."

"Yes, but 20,000 is not 36,000."

"Just a moment. You are going to give her a copper bottom?"

"Yes."

"You will ballast with metal?"

"Yes."

"And you will fit, furnish, and ornament her to your taste?"

"Yes."

"Well, consider. She will cost you 20,000 francs, will she not? Let us reckon at the lowest figures: copper bottom, 4000; metal ballasting, 2000; interior fittings, 6000; furnishings and decorations, 6000; compass, chronometer, sextant, etc., etc., 2000; extras another 2000. That makes 20, and 4 are 24, and 2 are 26, and 6 are 32, and 6 are 38, and 2 are 40, and 2 are 42—42,000 francs, say 50, and have done with it."

"*Diable!*" exclaimed I, "but you have made my flesh creep, my friend."

"Oh, check my figures as much as you like, you will find them correct, and . . . all that money to sail on a Grecian transport with the flag of Jerusalem, which is recognised by all nations, it is true, but is respected by none. Accept good advice, sell your *Telemacus* at what you can get for her, and buy the *Emma*."

"The *Emma!* What is the *Emma?*"

"My yacht, the yacht of the Baron de M——."

"But if he has bought her, he is not selling again."

"On the contrary."

"But he will want to make money by her."

"On the contrary."

"Will you explain all this? My head is spinning—it is indeed—with these yachts, these schooners, these *Telemacuses*."

"My good friend, it is all very simple. When the Baron de M—— bought his yacht he was a bachelor."

"Good."

"And he has since married."

"Very good."

"His wife, whom he adores, cannot endure the sea. Consequently, she being upset by the yacht, the Baron has offered her—the vessel, that is—for sale, and at any price to get rid of her."

"What, at any price?"

"Yes, you shall have her for a song."

"A song is not a sum of money."

"Well, for 20,000 francs, for fifteen, for twelve, perhaps."

"Ah, you are taking too much for granted, my dear friend."

"I am telling you the simple truth."

"When can I leave for Marseilles?"

"To-morrow by the direct route—the *Philip Augustus*."

"*Diable*. Philip Augustus was perhaps a great king, but is certainly a bad boat. Adieu."

"What do you say?"

"*Par dieu*. I fly. I am going to buy the *Emma*, and sell the *Monte-Cristo*."

"Very well. You have perhaps not had many good bargains in your life, but put this one through, and it will make up for the others."

"Thanks."

I embraced our ambassador, and three days later I was at Marseilles. The first words I uttered were—

"Where is the *Emma?*"

"Lying under Fort St. Midas," I was informed.

"Boatman, to the *Emma*," I cried, as I jumped into a boat.

"Ah, a pretty little craft that," said the boatman, with a note of genuine admiration.

"Quickly, then."

Ten minutes more and we slowed up beside a most charming *goëlette*,[1] graceful in her slim lines—elegance and an aristocratic appearance everywhere, a true sea-bird.

---

[1] Dumas invariably calls the *Emma* a *goëlette*, and *goëlette* is a schooner; but it has been thought best to fall in with the many writers who speak of Dumas' "yacht."

I went thoroughly over her, searching into each corner like a Customs house officer. Everywhere she revealed the talent of the English builder, who had succeeded in every detail—comfort above all. She had everything necessary, as a bride has her trousseau—her plate, her linen, her china, her lamps, her nautical instruments, and her carpets. Apart from tastes and fancies of one's own, such as hangings over the mahogany and pictures decorating the maple-wood, she needed nothing. The only thing she could be reproached with was a look of luxury, such as is seen in the faubourg St. Antoine. No other reproach was possible.

"Who has the sale of this yacht?" was my question to the watchman.

"Madame Altaras, 41 rue de Breteuil," was his reply.

I was delighted. The augury was a good one. I much like business between a man and a woman. There is on the one side a coquetry, and on the other a courtesy, which brings them together. Madame Altaras had no coquetry, but otherwise was what I expected—she was entirely delightful. In ten minutes the bargain was concluded—the yacht was mine for the sum of 13,000 francs, payable 3000 down and 10,000 in the course of the next month.

I hastened off, truly delighted to be able to tell my good news to Podimatas. To my exceeding surprise, he received it coldly.

"But, then, who will command your yacht?" he asked me.

"You, *parbleu.*"

He shook his head.

"I cannot," he said.

"Why not? First you could not command the *Monte-Cristo*, now you cannot command the *Emma.*"

"I cannot command the *Monte-Cristo* sailing under the flag of Jerusalem, because I am a member of the Greek Church; I cannot command the *Emma*, a French-English craft, because I am a subject of Greece."

"But whatever your religion, whatever your nationality, you can be my pilot."

"As to that, yes."

"Then all can be arranged. Now how far have we got on with the *Monte-Cristo?*"

"*Dame.* I have pushed the work forward."

"Ah, ah! How much have you done?"

"I have copper-bottomed her; I have made the deck water-tight; I have repaired the hold."

"*Diable!* Spend no more, my good man. You will understand that I do not wish to keep two vessels, since one has all but ruined me."

"What then are we doing with the *Monte-Cristo?*"

"Putting her up for sale."

Podimatas shook his head and scratched his ear.

"Such a pretty boat," he murmured.

"My good man, you look on her as on a woman of your country. To me, she does not look so pretty—to me, she is a regular *patache;* and when I think that, such as she is, she has cost me double what the *Emma* has cost me—for you have expended two or three thousand francs on her, haven't you?"

"Six thousand."

"What? Six thousand!"

"At the least."

"Well, well, at all events she is worth 6000 more than she was."

"Certainly."

"I mean her sale value is."

"Oh, not her sale value, I don't say that."

"What, you don't say that? Let us consider—the *Monte-Cristo* has let me in for 30,000 francs."

"About that."

"Very well, what can I sell her for?"

"Ten or twelve thousand, maybe."

"What? I stand to lose 20,000 francs?"

"Monsieur le Duc de Gramont lost 60,000, and Monsieur le Baron de M——23,000."

It was my turn to scratch my ear. No answer to Podimatas was possible.

I went off to find M. Petit, a shipbroker, to leave my interests in his keeping—that is to say, so far as they concerned the *Monte-Cristo*. M. Petit undertook to sell her, and, greatly relieved in mind, I started for Paris, entrusting the work of the decoration of the *Emma* to a young friend of mine—M. Roux, an architect. It appeared that to make her a perfect gem of a yacht would be a matter of about 2000 francs.

Roux set to work at once. The dining-room was to be hung with the tapestry and the trophies in the shape of weapons brought by me from the Caucasus. The sitting-room was to be painted in the Pompeian style of M. Regnier, one of Gleyre's most distinguished pupils.

As for the paint-work in general, M. Duboscq had claimed the *right* of doing it *gratis*. This reminds me that I had just paid the bill of another painting gentleman, de Lavarenne, a bill rendered at 2700, but reduced to 1500 francs.

It is really incredible how delightful people become towards me, the farther I get from Paris. Abroad, it is even better. I have related how I was received in Russia.[1] Certain warm-hearted friends seem

[1] In his "Impressions de Voyage : en Russie."

to be my unknown ones. "No one is a prophet in his own country." Let me therefore leave my country for others—but it is sad to think of it.

My want was now that of a captain; for consider the position I had occupied: at first I had a captain, but no yacht; then I had a yacht, but no flag; then a yacht and a flag, but no captain; finally I had a yacht and two flags, but no captain. However, at Marseilles I was told not to be anxious, and that captains are always to be got.

So I suffered no anxiety. Heaven has bestowed on me a happy-go-lucky disposition on which anxiety takes no hold. Furthermore, everything seemed at first to be going on excellently. Two days after my arrival I got a letter from my friend M. Becker reporting the sale of the *Monte-Cristo* for 12,000 francs. As this sum was Podimatas' maximum there was nothing to do but accept.

I replied: "Pay for the copper bottom, the caulking, and hand the balance to Madame Altaras on account of the 10,000 francs I still owe her."

Three days later I got a letter telling me that the purchaser, fearing in his turn to meet with the difficulties which had obliged me to sell, had cried off.

I found the news bad, but the reason good. With the Turks, I replied, "God is great."

Eight days later I was informed that a new purchaser at 10,000 had been found, and I was asked for my instructions.

I replied, "Sell, pay for the copper bottom and the caulking, and hand the balance to Madame Altaras."

I believed that all this had been accomplished, when I learnt that the purchaser had cried off, having ascertained that under the flag of Jerusalem he could not trade on the French coast.

Decidedly the *Monte-Cristo* was difficult to sell.

I did not reply. Why add the cost of a postage stamp to all the other expenses?

Eight days later I received this telegram from M. Petit: "I have a cash offer of 9000 francs for the *Monte-Cristo*. Shall I accept?"

I replied with the laconicism, if not the insensibility, of a Spartan: "Sell."

The fact was that if I lost time, and if the same decrease should occur by degrees in the offers, I should end by having money to pay instead of having money to receive.

In the midst of my sufferings arrived a letter bearing the Marseilles postmark.

I confess that at first I lacked courage to open it. At last I broke the seal.

The purchaser had signed the contract, but instead of paying cash as the telegram had stated, he did not wish, observing the nautical code, to pay before the end of two months, seeing that there was a mortgage *à la grosse* given by Podimatas.

This was Hebrew to me. What on earth was a mortgage *à la grosse?* And howsoever it had been made, why and in virtue of what circumstances had Podimatas, whom I had paid with the most exact regularity, borrowed money on the security of my vessel?

The affair seemed to me to demand a journey to Marseilles. It would be the tenth or twelfth within a year. Fortunately, my old friend Enfantin[1]—faithful to our days of companionship in the rue de Montigny—had smoothed the way for me. Without him and without M. Réal, to whom I now offer my hearty thanks, 24,000 francs would have gone in fares.

I had recourse to Enfantin once more, and I left for Marseilles.

I hastened to M. Petit, who, let me record it, helped me not only most kindly, but also most disinterestedly, as, indeed, he did throughout all these long and troublesome negotiations. Indeed, he has declined to accept any remuneration.

M. Petit explained the position to me. Podimatas had borrowed on security of the vessel for the vessel's occasions. As captain, he had the right to do so, in the absence of the owner, in the case of damages needing prompt repair.

I sent for Podimatas, who frankly admitted that the 1000 francs had been necessary not for the occasion of the vessel, but for his own, and that he had pledged the craft to get the money, not daring to ask me for it. My remedy was to stop the sum out of his pay.

I do not know why I have a weakness for Podimatas in spite of his gloomy look, his eyes which never meet your own, and his hat always pulled down over his eyes.

"It is all right," said I to M. Petit. "Add these 1000 francs of Podimatas to the cost of the copper-bottoming and the caulking, and hand the balance to Madame Altaras."

"But," replied M. Petit, "I think I told you that the purchasers do not wish to pay before the 14th of May."

"Yes, no doubt on account of the mortgage *à la grosse* of Podimatas, but since I recognise it and leave the amount of the same in their hands——"

"He can disclose the existence of another mortgage to-day, to-morrow, the day after to-morrow."

"Nevertheless, my dear M. Petit, I must tell you that I had relied

[1] B. P. Enfantin (1796–1864), commonly called *le Père Enfantin*, one of the founders of Saint-Simonism.

on the balance purchase money, small though the amount is, to help towards my debt to Madame Altaras."

"To obtain the balance you must find a surety."

"A surety for what?"

"For the sum which will be paid to you."

"And to what will it amount?"

"To about 1500 francs."

"I will go to find a surety. It will be extraordinary indeed if in Marseilles there does not exist a friend who will go bail for me in a matter of 1500 francs."

I got up to go. But I felt a hand on my shoulder, which pressed me down again.

"*Ah! coquin de bon sort*," said the owner of the hand in an accent of the purest Marseillaise, "it is not worth troubling about such a trifle."

And approaching M. Petit, he added—

"I, Edmond Pireaudeau, am a surety for M. Dumas."

I looked at the man who was doing me this service. He was an entire stranger, and therefore another of the unknown friends of whom I have spoken.

I went towards him and offered him my hand. "It is the least that I owe you," said he. "You have made me laugh so much, without counting that you have made my wife cry like a Magdalen."

Then, turning to M. Petit, "Make out M. Dumas' account," said he. M. Petit made it out.

The result of all the figuring was that after paying for the copper bottoming, the caulking, the mortgage *à la grosse*, there was a balance in my favour of 1534 francs. I had lost about 22,000 francs. But it was my fault. Why had I commissioned a yacht at Syra instead of purchasing one already made at Malta, Constantinople, or Marseilles?

I pocketed my 1534 francs, and, after having thanked my surety, I was about to go when he stopped me.

"Ah! you are not going to get off so easily," said he. "I want to make you a present for your yacht."

"You?"

"Yes, I. Do you think I am unable?"

"No, oh no!"

"I want to give you ship lamps so that the big ships do not run you down. *Peste!* I do not want you to sink. You have made me laugh too much, and my wife cry. Are you going to decline my lamps?"

"No, *sacré dieu!*"

"Very good. Come and see them. And then there is my brother Jean —he is Jean and I am Edmond—who wishes to make you a present."

"What! Your brother Jean wants to make me a present?"

"Yes, he has been thinking of it for a long time. It is a handsome marble table, that he got—I don't know how; and twenty times I have heard him say, 'This marble table would do twenty times better in M. Dumas' yacht than it does in my house.' "

"But, but—I am very much obliged to your brother Jean!"

"Oh! a good lad. And he also has a sabre of which he is always saying, 'If I dared give this sabre to M. Dumas.' "

"Let him give it, let him give it, *pardieu*. I enjoy receiving from those to whom I can return."

"Oh, he will give them with the same pleasure that I myself do, but what you want is to find a good captain."

"I have instructed Podimatas to find one."

"Still your Greek! Misfortune will be yours, my dear monsieur, on account of those Greeks. As an old author of Marseilles says in Latin, 'I fear the Greeks.' "

"*Timeo Danaos.* It is Virgil."

"Virgil; yes, that is the name. Your friend Méry is always talking about Virgil."

"Excuse me, but Virgil was not of Marseilles, he was of Mantua."

"Of Mantua or of Marseilles, it is all one, since he speaks the truth."

"Well, my dear Pireaudeau, allow me to doubt it. I was brought up to admire the Greeks, and my firmest friendships are those formed through admiration. It is for this reason that I am so fond of Hugo and Lamartine."

"That is as it may be, but your Greek devils . . ."

"Listen, my dear monsieur, it is an experiment in chemistry that I am making, and if at the end of my travels I have not obtained a speck of gold, I will say, with you, that they are the worst people in the world."

"Do as you like. You are the master. But here we are! Just go inside and see your ship lamps."

I looked up. We were opposite the shop of M. Stane. I went in.

"Get down M. Dumas' lamps so that he may see them and tell me whether they please him."

M. Stane turned on hearing my name and bowed to me; then, standing on the counter, he got out three splendid lamps—one red, another green, and the third white. Two were for the rigging, the third for the mainmast. The present was worth four or five hundred francs.

"But," I asked Pireaudeau, "what on earth can I give you in return for such a gift?"

"Your portrait with your autograph. Is that too much to ask?"

"No, *sacré bleu*."

"Well, then, I answer for it that my wife will be delighted. You have made her cry so much, and you have made me laugh so often."

What is the reason that people one has made laugh and cry are so grateful? It is this—laughter and tears come direct from God.

I have mentioned that I had entrusted Podimatas with the duty of finding a captain. Like my good friend Pireaudeau, you ask, "Why did you get a Greek to obtain a French captain?"

I am going to tell you.

Podimatas, engaged by me a year ago on board the *Sully*, had come to France on the *Monte-Cristo* in the confidence that he would command her. In consequence of the series of events which I have related, Captain Podimatas now found himself merely a pilot. Well, it seemed to me that if he himself introduced the captain, he would not object to obeying him, and that his pained expression would give place to smiles. I delight in having smiling faces round me. I prefer a day without sunshine to a day without a smile for me.

That evening, Podimatas came to see me accompanied by a captain of experience, in appearance the exact opposite of himself—that is, with a smiling face, an eye that sought your own, a hand that grasped your own. What is more, he was a Breton—that is to say, a fellow-countryman of one of my best friends. Aged thirty-three, he had already been twelve times to America, fourteen times to Constantinople and the Black Sea. He hopes, after our voyage to the East, to take me to America on my *Emma*. God grant it! The name of the man is Captain Beaugrand. I will return to him, dear readers, when I sketch the likenesses of all my travelling companions.

We were just settling the details of the engagement when a commissionaire with a marble table was announced. I had him admitted. Jean Pireaudeau followed timidly behind. I recognised him by his likeness to his brother.

He had had his table carried for him, and he himself bore his sabre —a Russian one taken at Solferino. The table—a magnificent piece of marble with vivid shades—had been found at Panderma in Anatolia.

I thanked him warmly, and took his two hands in mine.

I need hardly add that Edmond Pireaudeau's lamps are fixed to the rigging and the mainmast, and that the sabre and marble table are respectively hung among the trophies of the dining-room and riveted down on the deck.

In return, each of the Pireaudeaus has my portrait, and I am sure that they consider themselves the gainers in this episode.

CHAPTER IV

SOME PLEASANT SURPRISES AT MARSEILLES

Marseilles, 3rd May

I ARRIVED here on 20th April. I have described the journey else-where, and have nothing further to add except that the buffet is execrably bad at Lyons, but excellent at Avignon. There the train stops for five and twenty minutes, but two hours would be required for merely tasting all the fare on the table. Please clearly understand that, for me, the merit of a meal does not consist in the quantity, but in the quality of the dishes; yet the most fastidious gourmet would be well pleased to pay twenty francs in Paris for the dinner costing three francs ten sous that is served at Avignon.

Only those who have travelled much know the importance that meals on the journey assume, and the feeling of despair brought about by a succession of bad dinners. In Italy one gets bad food, in Spain one gets little food, in Russia one gets no food at all!

Nevertheless, it is in Spain and Russia that I have fared the best, for the reason that, knowing that in the former country I should find little to eat, and in the latter nothing at all, I took due precautions, and personally cooked the provisions I had brought with me.

Spanish cooks are without any appreciation of responsibility, and are idle to boot; so that they are quite disposed to allow you to do their work for them. As regards Russian cooks, you will understand that they are completely unknown among the Kerghis, Kalmuks, Tartars, Nogais, and Circassians. The cook of Kazan, where he poisoned you with batavinia and sterlet, disappears only to be found again at Tiflis, where he poisons you with Georgian messes of which I do not know even the name.

But in Italy it is otherwise; because we have called some of our dishes *Cotelettes à la Milanaise, Stuffato à la Napolitaine, Truits à la sauce Genoise,* Italy imagines that she has a *cuisine,* and, obstinately cherishing this idea, she insists on cooking for the traveller against his own desire, not allowing him at any price to cook for himself.

You remember Blin, the best and most fashionable tailor of his day. Well, one day some one asked him:

"Blin, what is your price for a coat?"

"Monsieur knows my price."

"No, I don't, as it is what I am asking."

"It is—145 francs."

"For a coat?"

"Yes, Monsieur."

"But if I supply the cloth?"

"In that case it would not be any dearer."

Well, I declare that in Italy all the times I have been there I should have been happy not only to supply the food, but to cook it myself on condition that it "would not be any dearer."

In Turin, at Feder's, I and my companion, aged fifteen, could not exist for less than fifty francs *per diem*. In Milan, by "special arrangement" at Brusquetti's (hotel du Palais Royal), we expended 560 francs in seven days, and, despite so doing, fared so ill that we usually sent away our dinner almost untouched and went out after nightfall to buy potatoes, which we brought back in our pockets to roast under the cinders and eat with salt.

Let the traveller in Italy, if it be winter time, be on his guard against another kind of robbery. I refer to wood. Wood is very dear in Italy, where forests are unknown. A basketful of wood costs four francs. If you feed your fire yourself a single basket will last all day; but as the hotel-keeper makes a profit per basket of three francs ten sous, his myrmidons have their instructions. While you are out in the daytime they come into your room and pile the wood up the chimney. You return, you find your room warm, but your wood gone. It is the same game at night, when you are asleep—you get up to find no wood. In consequence, when on your departure from the place you scan your bill, you find twelve francs a day charged for wood, whereas if you yourself kept up your fire four francs would be the cost. All this is vastly amusing to you.

You must know that northern Italy—that is to say, Turin, Milan, Venice—appear in the winter to be the coldest places on earth. In Italy every precaution is taken against heat, but not one against cold. The contrary is the case in Russia, where all precautions are taken against cold, and not any against heat. Then, in Russia one sees the cold, but one does not feel it, whilst in Italy, on the contrary, one does not see the cold, but feels it.

We shall not have all these drawbacks to fear. Italy we shall scarcely touch, and then only at the points of which I have not yet spoken. We shall quickly reach Illyria and Epirus. We shall land on all the little historic islands which no one visits, and there we shall eat what our own man cooks, or we shall cook it ourselves.

We shall avoid all the advertised hotels, as well as the official *cicerones*, whenever possible. We shall only enter the towns just to see them. At Athens we shall camp in the gardens of the Academy; at Smyrna, on the banks of the Meles; at Jerusalem, in the garden of Olives, or on Mount Emmaus; in Cairo, at Boulac or near the sepulchre of the Caliphs. In this way we shall benefit by all the picturesque chances that our journey may afford.

On the eve of our departure we mean to devote a special chapter to our programme. When I left two years ago for Russia, my readers will recall that I traced a similar itinerary for their benefit.[1] Whatever have been the difficulties, the obstacles, I might almost say the impossibilities, that I have encountered on my journey, I have surmounted them; the itinerary once traced, I have followed it faithfully.

To-day, we are only concerned with Marseilles, where we have put up at Falquet's (Hôtel du Louvre—on the Cannebière) during the past year—that is, since the hotel has existed. It is there that is to be found, either *à la carte* or *à prix fixe*, the best-served table of all the hotels in Marseilles.

There, one can be accommodated and fare sumptuously for ten francs a day—*déjeuner* and dinner inclusive, and one is better off than at Feder's at twenty-five francs and at Brusquetti's at thirty-five. I therefore cordially recommend the Hôtel du Louvre to those who have confidence in me.

At the moment of leaving Paris, Guerlain gave us a surprise. You all know Guerlain, don't you? One day in some *feuilleton* or other I mentioned the name of this celebrated professor of the art of perfumery; Guerlain has never forgotten this fact; so, having heard that I was on the point of leaving for a voyage to the East, he sent me a case of perfumery with these lines—

"You are leaving for the countries of perfumes. If only for the sake of *esprit national*, show all the distillers of otto of rose that the *rue de la Paix* can sustain the competition of the bazaars of Constantinople, Smyrna, and Cairo."

I opened the case, and found a grand supply of *Eau de Cologne, Eau de Portugal, Eau de l'Impératrice, Essence de Cedrat*, etc., etc.—more kinds of perfumes than I can mention—each kind by the half-dozen bottles; in addition, soaps, cold creams, dentifrices, pastilles which one burns, or which sweeten the air in evaporating.

I gladly accepted the gifts as one accepts things offered in such a kindly way.

But here on reaching Marseilles a number of similar surprises awaited us.

Five or six friends—known or unknown—have sent us presents specially valuable to the traveller; some enclose cards, others are sent anonymously.

In the first place, there have arrived from St. Brie a hundred

[1] "Impressions de Voyage : en Russie."

bottles of *vin de Migraine et d'Hérissé*, with a barrel of excellent *Chablis*.

Folliet-Louis has sent us a hundred and thirty bottles of his best *vin de Crément* and *vin de l'Impératrice*—and one knows what these wines of Folliet-Louis are. Like Guerlain, he might have written—

"You are going to the land of mythology; offer a taste of my nectar to Jupiter."

Greno, who has remembered a promise playfully made of old, has sent along fifty bottles of his best vintages.

M. Bergier, to whom I am all the more obliged since I only know him by name, and since in all probability he knows me only in the same way—M. Bergier has made us a present of sixty bottles of his famous *Hermitage*, which I made Jadin [1] respectfully salute when, twenty years ago, we passed by the little hill that produces it.

Messieurs Picard et Cie., whom I do not know any more than I know M. Bergier, and who do not know me otherwise than M. Bergier knows me, have forwarded to Falquet's for my use twenty-four bottles of Vermouth, which they export to all countries whose gourmands prefer to stimulate their digestive organs rather than burn them with absinthe.

Finally, to drop from the heights of poesy to humble prose, sacks of haricot beans from Trebizond awaited us, sent by an unknown exporter, who, no doubt knowing that I am from Soissons,[2] wished to humiliate me by the comparison, the haricot beans of Soissons being the finest in Europe, but those of Trebizond being the finest in the universe.

To these beans a huge sack of tobacco from Samsoum was added. It is sweet and perfumed, and the only sort which, in the form of a cigarette, I can smoke every second or third day. This tobacco will be the delight of my travelling companions. And I must not forget three or four hogsheads of *Lamalgue*, of *Cassis*, and of *Langlade*, and fifteen or eighteen hundred francs' worth of preserves bought at Appart's, or Carnet and Saussier's—the two best houses in the world for preserves. So you need feel no disquietude about us, seeing that we are sufficiently provided withal to make the circuit of the globe like Captain Cook or Dumont d'Urville.

For the rest, we have found Marseilles half under water,—Marseilles, which the first giraffe that was brought to Europe took for the *faubourg* of Nubia; Marseilles, which Méry called the town of the hydrophobic springs; Marseilles where, as at Cairo, one could count the drops of rain which fall during the year; this very Marseilles,

---

[1] Louis Godefroy Jadin, the celebrated landscape painter.
[2] Dumas was born at Villers-Cotterêts, near Soissons.

since the making of the Canal de la Durance—which cost her thirty-four or thirty-five millions—wallows in a swamp, and weeps like a widow. She had her passage of pigeons, now she has her passage of woodcocks. She has gained in green peas, but has lost in figs.

Marseilles, however, weeps not only tears from her sky, but her own also. Dreadful disasters follow one another with terrible persistency. Two months ago there was the wreck of the *Louise* on the jetty of the port of Bastia. You know the details: in addition to twelve of the crew, five-and-forty passengers out of eighty perished. A week ago, there was the wreck of the *Jason*. Of this tragic affair no details are as yet known, save those in the following telegram—

"Sailed from Marseilles with a general cargo for Suez : was lost on the evening of 11th April.

"Out of twenty passengers, nineteen have been drowned; and out of a crew of eleven, nine have perished. A sailor and a mate are the sole survivors of these."

4

CHAPTER V

IN SEARCH OF A SEQUEL TO "*MONTE-CRISTO*"

Marseilles, 7th May

ANYONE returning to Marseilles after an absence of twenty years would be visiting a place strange to him. The conquest of Algiers, the establishment of relations with Egypt and Constantinople, and the Crimean and Italian wars have made Marseilles as a city second only in the kingdom to Paris. Lyons has lost her crown.

Fortunes are gained with bewildering rapidity. On the day Free Trade was proclaimed in France, an English merchant purchased 18,000,000 francs' worth of wine. The broker's commission amounted to 20,000 francs. On my return from the Caucasus, I was the guest of another broker whose books showed a gross profit of 960,000 francs.

Marseilles herself, like a queen receiving tribute from her subjects, enjoys a rising tide of success no less rapid: to-day a Stock Exchange, to-morrow a Cathedral—these free gifts are hers for the mere acceptance.

I want to speak of the colossal undertakings that are being carried out at Marseilles, believing, as I do, that a certain proportion of my readers will be interested to hear of them.

The Continental *lazaret* was done away with, in the interests of sanitation, and its large site became building land. Reclamations from the sea were also effected, resulting in a considerable gain of ground—not less, in all, than forty hectares.

But all accretions of territory are followed by disputes. I recall to your memory the situation caused in 1831 or 1832 between England and Naples by the island of Julia, which had suddenly appeared out of the sea, to the south of Sicily.

England succeeded. She put the island on her map; then, wishing to have actual, in addition to political, possession, she sent out a Governor and a garrison. When the Governor and the garrison arrived at the spot shown on the map, they failed to find the island: it had entirely disappeared.

Well, the territories of Marseilles which, like the island of Julia, appeared all at once, were simultaneously coveted by the Government and by the Municipal Authority, each of which claimed ownership. Ultimately, a compromise was reached. The accretions of soil became the city's, on condition that she contributed to the cost of the building operations which burdened the Government. Among these operations, were the jetties in the offing, and the Cathedral. But what was needed was ready money to defray their cost.

It was then that one of our ablest and boldest financiers foresaw the future of Marseilles. For 20,000,000 francs Mirès acquired the ground won from the hill and the sea. Further, he came to the financial aid of the building operations.

His workmen attacked a hill which sheltered the port from the Mistral. The Municipal Council became alarmed. "I will build houses higher than your hill," replied Mirès, with the confidence that the possession of money gives; and he built the island of houses, which are but a foretaste of the street he is going to construct.

And the hill was thrown into the sea.

From the view-point of the new port, one is amazed by the immensity of the project which placed the pickaxe in the workers' hands. As yet, the Cathedral at one end of the quay is hardly visible, and the Castle at the other end barely to be seen.

Meanwhile, the work on the docks proceeds, and helps the building of that new quarter of the city which will communicate with Spain, Africa, Asia and America by sea, and with Havre by rail. All this portends a future Liverpool or New York.

Mirès has foreseen the great destiny of the Phocean city and has drawn his plans in due proportion. He does not stop at anything less than destroying the old city, which, to-day, prevents the junction of the two new ones.

The old port had only thirty hectares of water, and 3000 metres of quay.

The auxiliary port, begun under Louis Philippe, continued and completed under the Governments that followed the revolution of 1848, contains, inclusive of the seaward port, eighty-four hectares of water, while it doubles the length of the quays.

The basin of the docks will have not less than sixteen hectares of water. As for the Napoleon basin, in course of construction, it will of itself be larger, both as to length of quay and water surface, than both ports and the basin of all the docks combined.

Finally—for, once a gigantic task is entered on, there is no stopping—finally, there is the idea of continuing the jetties all the way to the hills which form the foreshore, and of thus creating a harbour of more than eighty hectares in size. Then, when these operations are completed, Marseilles will have not less than fifteen kilometres of quay and more than 200 hectares of water.

Marseilles, indeed, next to Paris, is, perhaps, in all the world the city where the most gigantic works are being carried out.

Her canal, planned to bring her the waters of the Durance, has cost not less than 45,000,000 francs. The aqueduct of Roqui-favour, less handsome in appearance, but more massive than the Pont du Gard, leaves the latter far behind. Next to the pyramids of Egypt and the clock-tower of Strasburg, it is the highest building in the world.

Simultaneously, there are being built a Stock Exchange, 100 metres larger than the one in Paris; Law Courts which will be the largest in France; and a Cathedral in the Byzantine style, of which the nave will be as long and as wide as that of St. Peter's at Rome.

At this moment the hammer is attacking the houses which separate the Allées de Meillan from the Cannebière, thus preparing the site of a street which will rival the rue de Rivoli in Paris and the Strand in London.

We have spoken of two new towns, and of the old town which is on the point of destruction. A fourth town is being created at the Catalans on the humble native soil of Mercédès. A road bordering the sea for nearly a league will connect the town of the Catalans with the promenade of the Prado. The palace of the Prince Imperial is rising up, and its first storey will command the four ports. The rue d'Aix is to be widened, and changed into a splendid avenue. Finally, a chapel in marble is being erected on the hill top, consecrated to the miraculous Vierge de la Garde.

Let me add that all these improvements and adornments are not the result of any chance caprice, any change of fortune or fashion; no, for Marseilles alone this wonderful future, with the growth of industry, of trade, and of modern civilisation, was reserved.

Maybe this city of commerce lacked something in the mural crown adorning her head—the jewel of poesy. If so, I have been so fortunate as to be the jeweller who has set it there. One day the idea of the romance of "Monte-Cristo" came to me; and thus Marseilles had at the beginning of her history her legend, and at the end her story of Mercédès and Edmond.

When I visited Marseilles for the first time, in 1834, I asked to see the house of Milo and the bust over its door; the clock tower of Accouls, which was all that remained of the church of Our Lady of Accoas; the old abbey of St. Victor, built at the very spot where Cassius, arriving from the deserts of Thebais, found the relics of the Saint from which it takes its name, and where is worshipped the Black Virgin—the most adored of all the Madonnas of Marseilles, for the reason that it was at her intercession that rain fell in the great droughts; the tower of St. Paul, from the top of which the cannon had replied to the cannon of the Constable of Bourbon; the hôtel de Ville, where stands the statue of Libertat, the liberator of Marseilles, who killed Casaulx; finally, the Château d'If, where are Mirabeau's prison and the remains of Kléber's coffin.

To-day the stranger visiting Marseilles asks to be shown three things —the house of Morrel in the Allées de Meillan, the house of Mercédès at the Catalans, and the dungeons of Dantès and the Abbé Faria.

It goes without saying that although the house of Morrel in the Allées de Meillan, although the house of Mercédès at the Catalans, although the dungeons of Dantès and Faria at the Château d'If have never existed, except as scenery at the Théâtre Historique, the obliging guides, not to disappoint strangers, show them all they wish to see.

Three *concierges*, during the space of fifteen years, have successively retired with a competence which they owe to the persistency of travellers—English ones above all—in visiting the dungeons of Dantès and Faria.

To-day it is not the coffin of Kléber or the prison in which Mirabeau composed his famous "Erotica Biblion" that is asked about—Dantès and Faria have monopolised everything.

It is the privilege of romancers to create characters who slay those of the historians; the reason is that, for the most part, the historians are content to invoke phantoms, while the romancers create people made of flesh and blood.

And so, when I visited Marseilles two years ago, I desired, in my turn, to see the dungeons of Dantès and Faria. That I was within my rights, no one, I hope, will dispute. I had known for some time[1] that Marseilles believed in my romance.

When, in 1848, I was producing the drama of "Monte-Cristo" at the Théâtre Historique, I wrote to Marseilles for a sketch of the Château d'If. I received a very fine one, signed by Crapelet, with these two lines written beneath it—

"The Château d'If, taken from the spot where Dantès was precipitated."

I could not ask for anything better. I could not even have hoped for anything so good.

Those who had witnessed my drama, therefore, saw the Château d'If from the point from which the artist had sketched it—that is to say, from the place where Dantès had been precipitated.

The revolution of 1848 broke out, interrupting the performances in the midst of their career, and many people went to gaze at the Tuilleries from the spot where Charles X. and Louis Philippe had been precipitated, and so the Château d'If and the dungeons of Dantès and Faria were, for the moment, forgotten.

[1] The romance "Le Comte de Monte-Cristo" was published in 1844–45.

But the real misfortunes of the Bourbons, whether of the elder branch or the younger, presently lost interest; and the fabulous adventures of the abbé and the sailor again held sway.

The pilgrimages to Goritz and to Claremont diminished in number; those to the Château d'If increased.

In 1857 I was, as I have said, myself among the visitors.

On stepping into the little boat, casually selected to take me to the château, I had my first surprise.

A boatman with a boat next mine called out—

"I will buy your passengers."

"How much for?"

"Ten francs," said the first.

"Done," replied the second.

And the boatman who had valued us at the exorbitant price of ten francs stepped from his boat into ours.

I looked on the matter as one of pure speculation, and did not concern myself with the reasons that lay beneath it.

We reached the Château d'If.

The *concierge* was an old Catalan who had obtained the coveted post on the plea that she was a countrywoman of Mercédès.

The Franco-Spanish *patois* spoken by her proved that on that point, at least, she had told the exact truth.

She did not even ask me my wishes.

"You have come to see the dungeons of Dantès and the Abbé Faria?" said she, as she took up her keys. "You shall see them."

"Thanks, my good woman," I replied, "but first I would like to see the remains of the coffin of Kléber and the prison of Mirabeau."

She gave me an astonished look, and made me repeat what I had said.

I repeated it.

"I know nothing about them," said she.

My triumph was complete. Not only had I created what did not exist, but I had annihilated what did exist.

"Ah, well," said I, "forward then for the dungeons of Dantès and Faria."

She gave me another look, and with a shrug of her shoulders, as much as to say "You shall see them," she led the way.

I ought to state, in praise of whosoever invented the idea of exhibiting the dungeons, that very clever alterations have been carried out by him to give the legend every appearance of truth. A subterranean passage is shown filled with stones, which, it is true, were added later on, and which prevent any communication with the neighbouring dungeon; but on visiting the latter, one sees the other end of the same passage.

In the early days this passage was accessible, and through it one could get from one dungeon to the other. All visitors of the masculine gender made use of their hands and knees to struggle through it. Some women, English women in particular, followed their example, taking such risks as there were; but when crinolines came into fashion, a female encased in a gigantic cage became wedged in a part too narrow for her, and was obliged to stay where she was, being unable either to advance or retreat.

Her husband, assisted by the *concierge*, pulled her so lustily that he ended by extracting her from the mouse-trap, but she was very much bruised.

Then it was that the municipal authorities interfered, and ordered the passage to be filled up, so as to prevent the occurrence of a like catastrophe.

The office for the dearer tickets lost thereby, for there were two scales of charges: one for those who were satisfied to see only the dungeons, and another for those who wished to get access to Faria's by means of his passage.

As may be supposed, I eclipsed everyone in the multiplicity of questions put to the female guide. I may say that my unconcealed pleasure in hearing her answers encouraged her not to keep anything from me.

She declared that in her young days she had known Mercédès, of whom, indeed, she was a distant family connection. As regards Fernand, she only remembered him vaguely, seeing that he had not reappeared since his departure from the Catalans.

But concerning Mercédès, it was quite another story—she had been there on two or three occasions. In her pilgrimages she was invariably dressed in black, and maintained the strictest incognito; nevertheless my informant had immediately recognised her, and could assure me that my heroine was either still living, or had died but recently.

Seeing her to be so well informed, I asked her if she could give me any tidings of Dantès, or rather of the Count of Monte-Cristo.

For a moment she seemed embarrassed and hesitating, and while she paused I believed that she was going to help me to write the sequel to my romance for which all the world asks me, but which, in all probability, I shall never put on paper.

Contrary to my expectation, she was very much more circumspect about Monte-Cristo than about Mercédès.

"The Count of Monte-Cristo," said she; "about him only one man can give you definite information."

"And who may that man be?" I asked her.

"M. Alexandre Dumas, who was his intimate friend, and with whom he still remains in communication."

This time, I admit, I was beaten, and not hoping to get a better reply I ceased questioning her.

As I was leaving the Château d'If, I gave five francs to the good woman, who begged me to sign the visitors' book. I should have asked to do so if she had not made the request.

I was not content with signing my name. I set it at the foot of a formal certificate which declared that the time-honoured customary recital of the *concierge* concerning Dantès and Faria and Mercédès was the exact truth.

I can only hope that my declaration will not be prejudicial to her interests.

On stepping again on the Cannebière, I turned towards my boatman.

"Now," said I, "my good friend, I want to settle with you."

"To settle with me," said he; "that will not be difficult, I am pleased to say."

"Well, then, first I owe you that purchase money—the ten francs, you remember, and also for the two journeys—to the château and back."

"You owe me nothing whatever."

"What! nothing whatever?"

"No! nothing whatever."

"You are joking."

"Evidently you think I have not recognised you."

"What! you have recognised me?"

"Yes. Just say that you are not M. Alexandre Dumas."

"But I have not the slightest intention of denying it, my good friend."

"Very well, then," said he, with a movement of the shoulder impossible to describe.

"But—but—the fact that I am M. Alexandre Dumas is not a reason for rowing me to the Château d'If for nothing."

"Not only ought I to row you to the Château d'If for nothing, and all the other boatmen to do the like, but we ought to join together and give you a pension; you are the father of us all; you it is who put the bread into our mouths by writing the romance of 'Monte-Cristo'; so you are the cause of our making three journeys instead of one. Everyone wants to go to the Château d'If, and in all weathers. Why, when there is a sea on, and we pretend we do not want to go, the English give us anything up to two louis d'or to row them there.

You pay me? Never! And whenever you are at Marseilles, the boat and its owner will be at your disposal, but on this condition, mind: that you never talk of giving me a sou. Otherwise I am upset. My name is Paulet; my boat is called the *Ville de Paris*. We understand each other—you always have me, and no one else; and never any money, or I shall think that you look down on me."

All this was said so earnestly that it admitted of no doubt as to the sincerity of the speaker.

"Well, well, so be it, Paulet. To-morrow at nine o'clock I shall want you."

"Good, at nine o'clock I will await you with the boat."

"Shake hands, my good Paulet."

"Oh, as to that, with pleasure."

We exchanged a hearty grasp of the hand, and separated.

I wrote at once to Paris for the edition of my works published by Dufour and Mulat—the finest edition, the illustrated one.

The next morning at nine o'clock I was on the Cannebière. Paulet was waiting there. I stepped into the *Ville de Paris*, saying—

"To the Réserve."

The Réserve! That is all we have left, the Château d'If with the legend of Dantès excepted. The Catalans have gone, the Réserve is going. In a year's time the Château d'If will be the sole survivor. It is true that it is a prison, and that prisons live long.

The Réserve was, two years ago, and still is to-day, the restaurant where one enjoys the best *bouillabaisse* in all Marseilles.

I ordered a monstrous one.

When it appeared I invited Paulet to share it with me. He made some difficulty, but yielded to my threat of "No dinner, no boat."

Four days later Paulet received at his address, 25 Cours Liotard, an almost complete edition of my works.

I say "almost complete," for I really do not know of a complete one.

I do not wish to be unfair to Paulet's fellow boatmen, but I may be permitted nevertheless to recommend Paulet to visitors to the Château d'If, and particularly to English people who wish to see it in spite of rough weather, and who pay two louis d'or to accomplish their caprice.

And now let me tell you about something rarer than a boatman's gratitude—the gratitude of a whole city.

To-day I dined with M. Louis Lagarde, the Mayor of Marseilles, in the company of the principal notables of the place. As we were leaving the table to go into the *salon* for coffee, the servants handed each guest a copy of the *Courrier de Marseille*. I only rarely read the Paris journals, still less frequently those of the provinces. Besides, I was at the moment in too good and amusing company to depart from what is almost a habit. I put the journal in my pocket, meaning to look at it later on, but my friend Berteaut, being more impatient, opened his copy, and after an exclamation of astonishment read aloud what follows—

"The most learned member of our staff sends us, just as we go to press, an interesting account of a literary luncheon which was given only a few minutes ago in one of our official *salons*. We stop the press so as to communicate it to our readers.

"The guest of honour was Alexandre Dumas.

"The Amphitryon, dear to the arts and to letters, had grouped round the illustrious romancer all those of our city who are known to appreciate imaginative works. We have neither time nor space to tell now of the sparkling sallies and witty remarks that flew about the room. We confine ourselves to a few incidents.

"First surprise—Alexandre Dumas found under his napkin the freedom of the City of Marseilles. The daughter of Phocea enthusiastically adopted the poet who has made her illustrious.

"Second surprise—at dessert, a *Suisse*, of most imposing appearance and in gold-laced uniform, advanced respectfully, lowering his halberd, and presented to the author of 'Monte-Cristo' on a silver-gilt salver several silver keys and a seal richly chased with a coat of arms. The keys were duplicates of those of the Château d'If. On the seal a skilled engraver showed us the old Gothic citadel in relief on a silver ground.

"A third and last surprise—which came near being ruined—was like the set piece of a display of fireworks. Coffee was being served, when the most absent-minded guest laid hold of a paper carelessly put on the mantelpiece and twisted it up as a light for his cigar, without noticing the revenue stamp affixed to one of its corners. Observing the mistake, Alexandre Dumas twitched the paper out of the imprudent man's hand, and mechanically glanced at it. Suddenly, overcome with emotion, the great romancer threw himself into an armchair, and held out the paper to the company. This stamped paper, saved from the flames, was no other than a deed of gift to the poet of several hectares of land on the heights of the Catalans.

"We learn that Alexandre Dumas, having become our fellow-townsman, is going to build a country house on this picturesque site in which he has placed the preliminary scenes of his finest romance."

As is the case with all journalistic efforts, what Berteaut had read was a mixture of truth and the other thing. Eliminate the silver-gilt salver and keys; eliminate the seal with the Château d'If on it; eliminate altogether the gilt-edged *Suisse* decked with his halberd and bearing seal and keys; reduce the subject of the deed of gift to 300 metres; add official authority to adopt the Château d'If as his coat of arms—and you will be within the limits of the most exact truth.

Reduced to its actual limits, it was yet much, and I cannot be too grateful for the benefaction.

The land transfer negotiated by M. Louis Lagarde was from M. Bordes, the owner of the estate on which the old Catalans village was situated. To-day it is no more, alas! Some of my thanks were due to him, so I said that I desired to go to him that very moment.

In ten minutes two carriages drew up and took us to the Catalans, where M. Bordes has developed a regular town. He must certainly have expected us, for on our arrival divers bottles of champagne were uncorked with a rapidity that betokened preparation.

We then betook ourselves to the site which had been given to me. We consecrated it, after the antique manner, by a libation of a few drops of the nectar of champagne, and the household gods of the future having quenched their thirst, we drank the rest.

Let me give thanks to my adopted mother, the City of Marseilles, thanks to the worshipful Mayor, M. Louis Lagarde, and to M. Bordes above all.

CHAPTER VI

IN SEARCH OF A SERVANT

Marseilles, 8th May

AT last all is in readiness, the victualling of the yacht is proceeding—ink, paper, and pens not being forgotten; and to-morrow, with the help of God, we are to sail.

The crew are eight in number, the passengers eleven—nineteen souls in all.

Let us begin with the crew, and put Captain Beaugrand—to every chief the honour that is due—at the head; next to him is our ex-captain Podimatas, reduced to the grade of pilot; then our mate, François Brémont; then three sailors named Passerat, Calvi, and Fugaison; a lad answering to the name of Thibaut, and a cabin-boy called Schmaltz. And, not the least important, our cook, Jean Boyer, closes the list.

Captain Beaugrand, whose age is about thirty-three, possesses black eyes, white teeth, and an open countenance framed in long hair, curling on his forehead. He is rather under medium height, like most Bretons. His disposition is amiable but firm, he is moreover pleasant-looking and an agreeable fellow to be with.

I have mentioned that I came to know him through Podimatas, whose service in the matter has procured him my forgiveness about many things which, otherwise, he would not have obtained.

Captain Beaugrand ran away to sea—against the wish of his parents, that is—when he was seventeen, and, like the seagulls and sea mews, has only touched land, since then, for the purpose of drying himself. That is to be seen by comparing his existence of thirty-three years with his various voyages—five to North America and the Antilles, two to Brazil, seven to the African coast, two to India, fifteen to the coasts of Italy, one on the Danube, and twenty-two to Constantinople. Nevertheless, he has only been wrecked once, and that on the African coast.

You know Podimatas, or almost know him. He is a little fellow, and as hairy as the wild boar of Calydon, his fellow countryman. His beard covers his face. The doctor vows that he shaves the whites of his eyes only. He is a true sea-bird—a halcyon of Milo. He cannot remember his first day on ship. His earliest recollections are of being cabin-boy on board the *Inflexible Amiral*, of which ship his father was the pilot. He has made only one voyage to Senegal, when in charge of the *Sumatra* of Marseilles, but all the years he was cabin-boy he furrowed the waters of the Archipelago from the south to the north, from the east to the west. Not a creek of Greece, of Asia Minor, of Syria, of Egypt that is strange to him; not a rock of the Cyclades and the Sporades of which he does not know the bearing; not a cape that he has not doubled, not a promontory that he has not coasted, not an isthmus that he has not crossed, not a gulf that he has not explored.

And in spite of all, he has only lost two masts at Gibraltar, a record which augurs well for him as our pilot.

Our mate Brémont, who has the full confidence of the Captain, they having made five or six voyages together, is aged twenty-nine. He was born at Cannes, and was a cabin-boy when eleven. Apprentice at eleven, sailor at sixteen. He has made five voyages to India, four to the Colonies, two to Brazil. For three years he sailed regularly to Turkey. He has been wrecked twice—the first time on the coast of Malabar at Goulido, between Pondicherry and Porto Novo; the second time on board the *Aventure*—cut in two in a collision at night with the *Hermus*. The first time he was rescued by the *Etienne* of Marseilles, the second time by the *Hermus* herself. He is our virtuoso and musician, for he plays the guitar and warbles romantic lays.

In his spare time he makes everything that is asked of him—cartridge cases, serviette rings, *penauds*—we will tell later on what a *penaud* is. He is sail-maker, joiner, tailor; to amuse himself he climbs to the main-mast top with the agility of a monkey and the indifference of a cat. His is the department of the sail store-room, in which half of his body is continually thrust. He knows all the contents of that room, crammed with provisions, barrels of preserves, etc. At the first request, and Heaven alone knows how they succeed one another, he stretches out his arm and produces the required object. I have never known him at a loss. On the day that I am attacked by a fit of laziness, I shall tell him to write my *feuilleton*, and I am certain that he will do it.

He will be excellent (in the Captain's opinion) in the night watches, and in moments of danger.

The three other sailors and the lad have nothing remarkable about them further than zeal for the performance of their duties. It is three weeks since I engaged them, and the Captain has not had any fault to find with them.

The cabin-boy, aged thirteen, deserves special mention. His father was the conductor of a well-known orchestra at Marseilles. On his death, the boy went to the cabin-boys' training school, where I engaged him on the recommendation of the manager. My only fear is that he will be so happy with me that, when I quit the sea, he will want to remain with me on land.

And now for the passengers, who, I have told you, are eleven in number.

You already know four or five of them, at least by name; so let us begin with them.

You know Legray, don't you? He is easily the best photographer in Paris.[1] His science as chemist, his skill as artist means the certainty of our having a splendid series of photographs of scenery and celebrities. He warns me that he will take me two thousand times over.

You know Lockroy, don't you? Formerly an eminent actor, to-day a distinguished dramatist; at all times a man of understanding, taste and intellect, the best adviser in things theatrical known to me. He should, if only out of love of art, open a class in opposition to that of the Conservatoire. Ah, well, my companion is his son,[2] whom I have known from his infancy, and have seen grow up and develop. A pupil of Gleyre's, he is going to seek with me in Nature the continuation of studies seriously begun in the Studio. He is tall, thin, brown-skinned, with dark eyes, and black hair mingled with many a white one at the age of twenty-one. In his case, it is rather a matter of health that I have to improve than an education to complete.

The third is Paul Parfait, the son of my dear good friend, Noel Parfait,[3] of whom you know so much and have so often heard me speak. A year ago, in view of this voyage, we sent the lad to England to our mutual friend, Esquiros. During this year he has learnt English, which he reads fluently and speaks passably well. I say *we* sent him, for he is, in a sense, a son to both of us. I saw him when he was a tiny boy; and the day I saw him I loved him. He will be one of my secretaries on board the yacht. I shall speak of the other presently. To say no more about him, here is his portrait. A fine-looking fellow, with chestnut hair, small expressive eyes, a large nose, thickish lips, somewhat large mouth, which opens to say amusing things, and parts with pleasure to laugh with a captivating *naïveté* at those said by others—in a word, an open, attractive and sympathetic countenance, if ever there was one. In brief, he has his father's heart. I should be sorry to say more, for I should spoil all.

The fourth is a young doctor whose name is Albanel. He has studied medicine, not to practise it, but to know it as a science. We hope not to give him much to do. He has nevertheless a pharmacy and cases of surgical instruments sufficient for the medical and surgical occasions of a regiment about to take the field. During the long periods

[1] The portrait facing this page is from a photograph taken by Legray in 1859.
[2] Etienne Antoine Edouard Lockroy (1838–1913), the well-known designer, writer, and politician. He married the widow of Charles Hugo, a son of Victor Hugo.
[3] He was Dumas' secretary for some years, notably at Brussels, where he copied all the Master's MSS. The son became a well-known writer.

ALEXANDRE DUMAS

of leisure that we shall give him, he will botanise, geologise, and so on with Legray. If our drinking water becomes unpalatable, they have undertaken to purify it with charcoal; if it fails us altogether, the sea water, passing through their still, will become more pleasant to drink than the famous *aqua virgina* of Rome.

It is always good to know that one will not die of thirst.

The fifth[1] (of whom there has been so much talk lately in Paris, and even in Italy, where he accompanied me) should, out of courtesy, for one thing, and for another, by reason of his rank, have been mentioned first, but he will be content, I am sure, with the place I give him, as it brings him nearer to myself—who, in all conscience, and according to the rules of the polite world, must be mentioned the last.

On board, he is usually called "the Admiral," but in spite of this pompous title, he is content to wear the uniform of a midshipman; and observe, please, that this uniform is not official, but carried out to his taste and fancy in violet velvet, with blue and gold lanyards. Such is his best costume. His ordinary attire is sometimes a blouse with a Caucasian belt, sometimes a small jacket worn over an embroidered shirt, both inspired by the portrait of little Edward Hampton by the famous painter, Lawrence. When we travel in Greece, perhaps he will don the still more picturesque costume of the page of Lara, and this he hopes to exchange at Constantinople for that of Gulmare—for, in truth, the Admiral is a very coquettish and capricious individual.

It was for his use especially that the case of perfumery was sent by Guerlain. He hopes to take advantage of his youth and of his smooth chin to get inside the harems, taking with him a quantity of assorted sweetmeats and the like, and to return with details of life therein, which will serve to complete those already supplied by Lady Montagu and Princesse Belgiojoso.

One day I received a letter in a most peculiar caligraphy, couched in the kind of Frankish dialect that is spoken on the shores of the Mediterranean, and which at Algiers is called Sabine. Before attempting the deciphering of this long epistle I looked at the signature, and I read "Théodore Canape": the names were entirely new to me.

It is a habit of mine with letters of the kind to throw them away; for the most part they merely entail loss of time, but on that occasion curiosity got the upper hand.

The writer of the letter stated that he was eighteen years of age,

[1] The beautiful girl named Emilie Cordier, about whose adventures with Dumas so much has been written.

that he was born at Cæsarea in Cappadocia, that he was a Turkish subject, although of Greek birth.

He added that he had read my romance "Monte-Cristo" in a Greek translation, and that he deduced from it that I was very rich and very kind; that he had accordingly raised a subscription from his family which had enabled him to come to France; that although a master of the Greek and Turkish languages, he was anxious to acquire a third one; that this third language was French; and that he relied on me to assist him to complete his education.

I replied that I was too busy to complete his education myself, but that if he would call on me we would consult as to the best means of attaining his ends.

My Greek turned up the next day.

I conversed with him for some time, and, although he was plainly very ignorant, I saw that he was genuinely anxious to learn.

This touched me.

I told him to find a suitable *pension* where he would be among Turks and Greeks, and that I would be responsible for the expense.

In three days he came again. He had found what he wanted, and gave me the address of M. Castagne, No. 8 rue Danois. This gentleman had five or six Turks at his *pension*, and he had undertaken to board my new acquaintance and teach him French within the space of a year at an inclusive charge of ninety francs a month. I did not wish such a trivial sum to cause Théodore Canape to lose the goodly opinion he had brought from Cappadocia to France, and from Cæsarea to Paris. I paid M. Castagne three months' money in advance, and I put two further louis in my aspirant's pocket, at the same time recommending him to study hard and not to come to me if he could well do otherwise. I invited him on his off-days to dine with me whenever he cared to do so.

At the end of fifteen months, during which he had dined with me in the rue Amsterdam on perhaps five or six occasions, Théodore spoke French as well as you or I do.

It must have been then that he told me of his family having sent him the sum of money necessary for his journey home, and that, as he had accomplished his object in coming to the capital of the civilised world, he saw no reason why he should not return to Cappadocia.

I had no reason for opposing, so I gave my consent.

Théodore, with many expressions of his gratitude, departed. He told me that should I ever make the journey to Greece of which I had thought for so long, he, wherever he might be, would come to rejoin me.

It is my custom to place very little confidence in such-like declarations. Speaking generally, one performs good actions, not in the hope of being rewarded by the gratitude of the persons obliged, but because to do good is simply and entirely a matter of temperament; to certain individuals it is as impossible not to do good as for a tree not to put out leaves, or for a stream not to flow. My claim is to belong by temperament to that class of imbeciles which does not know how to refuse.

Three months later I received a letter from Cæsarea. Théodore wrote to me from the chief town in Cappadocia to send me his thanks, joined with those of his family.

According to my habit, I mentally responded, wishing him every happiness. Then I thought no more about him. There are but few persons whom I forget quicker than those whom I have benefited; they are those who have done me ill.

Two years went by. I travelled in Russia, and I returned *viâ* Constantinople. There I spoke to a few people of my intention of having a yacht built in Greece to make a voyage in the Archipelago and on the coasts of Asia.

Then, having thrown these words to the winds, I continued my journey to France.

Two months later my door opened, and Théodore appeared.

At first I did not recognise him: two years had entirely altered him. He had been beardless; now his beard resembled that of the Wandering Jew. He uttered his name on seeing that I had failed to know him.

"What the devil are you doing in Paris?" I asked him. "Have you discovered the existence of another language to learn?"

"No," said he, "but I have learnt that you were leaving for Greece and Asia Minor. I have considered that the time has come for me to save you the expense of a Grecian interpreter and a Turkish dragoman, for I speak both languages, and French as well; so here am I."

"I cannot tell," I replied, "when I shall make this two-fold journey of which you speak, but in the meantime, if you do not know where to stay in Paris, stay here."

Théodore did not know where to lodge, so he stayed with me.

So that is how Théodore Canape finds himself on the list of the *Emma's* passengers.

And now for the other passenger whose odyssey is no less picturesque.

If Théodore comes from the banks of the Halys—that is to say, from the country of St. Basil—Vasili comes from the banks of the Phasis— that is to say, from the country of Medea.

On my return from the Caucasus I was obliged, for want of a steam-boat, to spend a week at Poti. This place, which had by ukase of the Emperor Alexander been proclaimed a town and a seaport, is at once a singular town and a singular seaport. The town, at the time of my sojourn there, consisted of fifteen huts. The seaport consisted of some water with a depth of four or five feet. In consequence, steam-boats anchor two or three miles out from Poti, and a boat drawing two or two and a half feet of water takes travellers from Poti to the steam-boat, or from the steam-boat to Poti. One of the fifteen huts was inhabited by a Jew called Akob. He had partitioned his hut into two parts, and of the half which looked on the street he had made a grocer's shop, with his own lodgings thrown in. Of the half which looked on the yard he had made a hostelry. This hostelry, which consisted of four posts supporting a wooden roof, was, as a favour, let to us for twelve francs a day.

Every morning a sheep was conducted inside.

After the animal had been killed, skinned, and cut up before our eyes, we chose two pieces; of one of them we made our luncheon, and of the other our dinner. One Sunday I expressed a wish for pork instead of mutton—a desire that seemed to me the reverse of extravagant, seeing that the streets of Poti, existing only in the imagination, were nothing but a vast marsh in which wallowed hundreds of hogs which might well have been mistaken for wild boars.

Sad to relate, it was in our landlord's interests to sell us mutton, but it was not in his interests to sell us pork. For this convincing reason he firmly replied that it was an impossibility for him to procure us pork, and that in consequence we must continue to exist on mutton. On hearing this ultimatum I caught up my gun, and aiming while standing in my landlord's very doorway, I discharged a bullet into the hog which most took my fancy.

The animal, forty pounds in weight, fell stone dead. The event caused much local emotion, its owner running up uttering shrill cries. After many lengthy arguments through my Armenian interpreter, it was agreed that I should pay ten francs for the defunct beast: hair and tusks, fat and lean, tripes and entrails—all became my sole undisputed property.

This transaction made me put on my thinking cap. My landlord was selling me the two pieces of mutton for from fifteen to twenty francs—so my luncheon cost, say, eight, and my dinner eight; and here for ten I had a whole hog. The disproportion was the more striking, as the pieces of mutton each weighed between five and six pounds, while my hog weighed forty. My deduction from these facts was that my landlord was an extortioner.

My palate was so agreeably tickled by the change of diet that to make another change in our menu became an obsession with me.

In the course of my walks along the banks of a magnificent lake, I had asked a serving lad if one could not throw some kind of a net into it and catch some fish. The lad's reply was the one I wanted. He promised to help, and ended by hiring a net for a rouble for the following day. He was an expert with the net, and he undertook to sweep in more fish than I could eat while at Poti.

The undertaking was an attractive one, and the stake but trifling. I gave him a rouble, and awaited the result.

The result justified the fisherman. In ten or twelve throws he captured a hundred fish, including a carp weighing thirty-five pounds and a soudak weighing eighteen.

Nor was this all. The fish caught, he gave me most active and intelligent assistance in cooking them, as, indeed, he had assisted me to cook the daily mutton and the Sabbath pork.

Perceiving this, I asked him his name. It was Vasili.

Always intent on my next voyage, I reflected that a lad who killed and cooked a sheep so skilfully, made so-called sausages and a kind of black pudding, who captured a carp of five-and-thirty pounds and a soudak of eighteen, was not a servant to be despised in times when hunting and fishing were necessary pursuits.

After a moment's reflection, I said to him—

"Vasili, would you like to come with me?"

"Where?" he asked me.

"To France."

"Yes," he replied, with the eagerness of all men living under the Russian tyranny to whom a chance of leaving their country is offered.

And so it was agreed: I would take Vasili with me.

The following day the steam-boat, *Grand Duc Constantin*, was signalled. It was then that an important question presented itself—that of a passport. Vasili had none. For a moment I thought that I had solved the difficulty. My passport read: "M. Alexandre Dumas, accompanied by a servant."

Furthermore, one of Vasili's friends offered to lend him a pass. But certain others were jealous of Vasili's good fortune. If he had a friend helping towards his departure, he had also enemies resolved to stop it. Nevertheless, their plots remained in the background up to the moment of leaving.

That moment arrived. We took our seats in the Poti boat for the purpose of reaching the *Constantin*. We arrived, and were received on board with that distinguished Russian courtesy of which I have so often spoken. No remark was made about Vasili, who had modestly obscured himself among the crew. But in an hour's time we saw leaving the bank and directing itself towards us a craft manned by several oarsmen, and containing twelve Russian soldiers and an officer.

This craft evidently had designs on us.

Our vessel, which was getting up steam, quietly waited for it.

For my part, I was as tranquil as the steam-boat—I never dreamt that such a display of force had Vasili for its object.

The officer came on board and asked to speak to the captain. The lapse of a moment occurred, and they both came towards me. They demanded the fugitive, and as they were acting within their rights in so doing, there was nothing to be said: Vasili had to be given up.

He was in despair. He screamed out in Russian, in Georgian, in Armenian, and in Turkish, hoping that I would understand him in one of these four languages:

"I do not wish to stay at Poti in the house of the thief Akob, who made you pay twenty francs for the tenth part of a sheep that cost him seven. Tell me where you are going, and wherever you may be I will rejoin you."

The captain of the steam-boat was so kind as to translate all this to me.

It touched me, and I decided to answer—

"Vasili, I do not know you well enough yet, and have not, at the end of my long voyage, enough in my purse to spare you five hundred francs for the expenses of your journey from here to Paris; but I will make it a possible one, I hope, if your wish to rejoin me is real."

Vasili protested that such was the case.

I tore a leaf from my note-book, and I wrote on it as follows:—

"The bearer is named Vasili. He is in my service, but I have not been able to take him with me for his want of a passport; staying behind with the object of getting one, he is going to rejoin me in Paris. I beg everyone whom he asks in my name—if my name inspires the wish to assist—to help him by all means possible to perform his journey."

Then I signed and dated it.

I said to him, "Take with you this paper, with the help of which you can rejoin me, if you are as intelligent as I think you are."

Vasili had my note translated; and, delighted, contented himself by replying with true Spartan sobriety these two words—

"Be easy" (*soyez tranquille*).

Then, half consoled, he gave himself up to the soldiers.

The boat left for Poti, we left for Batoum, and I was two months without news of Vasili.

At the end of two months my female cook rushed one morning, all in a twitter, into my bedroom.

"Monsieur," said she, "there is a man downstairs who can say nothing but two words: '*Monso Doumas, Monso Doumas.*'"

"It is Vasili!" I replied without a second's hesitation, and I rushed down the stairs, four steps at a time.

And Vasili it was, wearing the same garments and, I must add, almost the same shirt that he had done at Poti.

He had come from Poti to Paris by Trebizond, Constantinople, Smyrna, Syra, Athens, Messina, and Marseilles at the cost of sixty-one francs fifty centimes, advanced to him by M. Eymery, the Turkish Consul at Marseilles, who informed me that he would present a bill for a like amount, payable three days after sight. Certainly, had there been a reproach to make to the poor lad, it would not have been on the score of wasting his money. He had paid nothing whatever on the Russian and French boats; he had stayed for twenty-seven days at Constantinople free of expense; and he had not had to put his hand into his pocket until he got on the railway. The expenses there began: a third-class ticket, fifty-four francs; food, seven francs fifty centimes—total, sixty-one francs fifty centimes. Having no luggage, there was no excess charge.

I began by making Vasili take a bath—not an ordinary affair, but a lengthy and a strenuous one. Then, whilst waiting until his Caucasian clothes were ready, I bought him six shirts, a pair of trousers, and a blouse.

In a week's time, thanks to the patterns brought by me from the Caucasus, Vasili made the greatest sensation in the streets of Paris. By the populace he was considered a Russian prince; by persons of a less enthusiastic temperament an officer of exalted rank. A few, who attempted to surround Vasili with a halo of poesy, said that he was a Naib of Schamyl whom I had taken prisoner.

This curiosity continued to be manifested for a year without Paris being at all sure respecting Vasili's position as regards myself. As long as Vasili did not speak French he did not give himself away, because he was unable to do so. When he later learnt to speak French he gave no information, because he did not wish to do so.

Paris remained in a state of dubiety.

It was only those who came within my walls who had the chance of being sure about Vasili's true position. He went about his duties with so much dignity as to make it thought that the services he rendered me were not those of a servant, but of a friend.

Let me add that Vasili, in contrast with his Eastern indolence and his proneness to allow others to do his work instead of serving me himself, had a quality that made him valuable to me—I could leave my purse in his hands and my wine uncorked. (In this latter connection Vasili is practically a Mussulman.)

At length the time to leave for Marseilles arrived. I sent Vasili and Théodore two days in advance of me as couriers.

They put up at the Hôtel du Louvre, where they announced my coming.

Vasili installed himself in one of the best rooms, donned his finest Caucasian costume, and appeared oblivious of the difference between silver and gold.

The *maître d'hôtel*, observing this, although in some doubt as to the true state of the position, ended by misjudging it. It was to Vasili that he applied for his orders, and to Théodore that he was ready to give them. Vasili was asked whether he desired to be served *à la carte* or at *prix fixe*—the latter is three francs for luncheon and four francs for dinner. Vasili replied that he preferred to have two courses only, provided they were such as he liked, and that, in consequence, he would lunch and dine *à la carte*.

Falquet then asked him if he would sit at the same table with Théodore. Vasili contented himself by replying that in his own country superiors did not sit down with their inferiors.

Falquet did not know what to make of it. Vasili's reply had only told him that there was an inferior and a superior, but which was the inferior, which was the superior?

It was a hundred to one against the inferior being other than the man who wore a black coat, and the superior other than the man who wore a costume embroidered with gold, with arms damascened in silver.

The night of Vasili's arrival at Marseilles was that of a benefit performance at the Opera. Vasili took an orchestra stall, and it goes without saying that he was the lion of the occasion.

In the South, manners are very easy, and they are easier at Marseilles than anywhere else. His neighbour ventured to ask Vasili who he was. He replied that he was a Georgian. Seeing that he had been so indulgent as to reply, he was plied with questions. Another neighbour asked him with what object he had come to Marseilles. He replied that he had come to do some yachting with M. Dumas.

Other questions and answers succeeded.

At the end of the performance the rumour ran through the auditorium that a Georgian prince, being delighted with my conversational powers, was taking me with him on his vessel. I would never accuse Vasili of having himself spread this intelligence, but I believe him capable of allowing it to circulate.

Two days after Vasili, I in my turn arrived.

He saw that my presence made him of less account. He therefore asked me to allow him to superintend the work on the *Emma*. I saw nothing but goodwill in this request, so I granted it.

Vasili went on board and gave his orders as he liked.

Three days later the Captain came to me and, drawing me apart, asked me what was the position of the man who gave orders to everyone, himself included.

Ah! I saw that devil of a Vasili in the man referred to.

"Do you complain of him?" I asked the Captain.

"*Dame!* yes, I do," said he, "for I must say that the gentleman is not always civil."

"It is not surprising; the gentleman is my servant."

The Captain stared at me wide-eyed. He thought that I had misunderstood him.

At that very moment Vasili appeared.

| The Captain nudged me with his elbow, and I made him a sign which signified "wait." Then, turning to Vasili—

"Vasili," said I, "do you know what I have just been saying to the Captain?"

"No, *Monso*," he replied.

"Well, I was saying that, at your first lack of respect towards him, I want him to have you taken by four sailors and pitched into the sea."

"As regards the sailors," I continued, turning to the Captain, "tell them that if Vasili is surly they are to tie him to the mainmast and give him a sound flogging."

Then, turning again to Vasili—

"That is said once for all, Vasili, do you understand?"

It was the first severe word I had said to the poor lad, and so he shed tears as he left us.

But the lesson was learned. Since that moment, Vasili never approaches the Captain without saluting with his right hand raised to his *papak*, and never speaks to the sailors without a smile.[1]

Our two other passengers are Greeks who, while being passengers, attend to matters of account, the sailors' pay, and so forth. I am taking them as far as Cyprus. At the moment, I can hardly say more concerning them; the two men are, in fact, something of a mystery. The elder is called Alexandre Rizos; the younger André Lecutzov. But, as these names are difficult to remember, they are usually called "Faria" and "Dantès" respectively.

If I do not speak of our cook, Jean, it is because I do not now seem to see him as apart from the man whose personality will develop

[1] Eight years later, Vasili was still in Dumas' service.

before his stove. Of this personality I shall treat in due time and place.

Two quadrupeds and a bird also accompany us on our pilgrimage.

The two quadrupeds are a dog and a bitch, answering respectively to the names of Valdin and Cartouche. Not having bestowed these names on them, I accept no responsibility in the matter.

The bird is a canary whose sweet song, in Paris and Lavagna, was enjoyed by me during my long hours of work. Unfortunately, on the third day of my arrival in Marseilles, I bought another canary for him. Since then, he has not uttered a note. Poor Jonas, I greatly fear that I have made a sad mess in my endeavour to marry him happily. I had forgotten to say that his name is Jonas.

CHAPTER VII

OUR ITINERARY

Marseilles, Wednesday, 9th May

WE leave within the hour.

Yesterday, on returning to my hotel, I was told that a friend of mine, on arriving from Paris, had expressed the wish that as soon as I came in I should go to his room. I went to it. On the threshold, I saw with joy that the friend was Roger,[1] our celebrated singer, whom I had not seen since his illness. We embraced, and I was foolish enough not to conceal a tear. You have all heard of Roger's accident.

An hour after it occurred, I was sitting on the steep bank of the Marne, absent-mindedly watching a fisherman taking his nets from the water. A man passed over the ferry with his cart, and stopping opposite the wine-shop, called out to the proprietress—

"What a misfortune, Madame Painblanc! Monsieur Roger has blown off his arm with his gun."

I had not seen Roger for two or three years. We artists are like that. We are as fond of each other as brothers—more so than many brothers—and yet years pass without our meeting, each being the slave of his work. I did not know that he was in Paris, or even in France. Although there are many Rogers, the sound of the name went to my heart.

I sprang to my feet.

"Roger! What Roger? Not Roger of the Opera, I trust?"

"Oh, *mon Dieu!* yes, Monsieur. Unhappily it is."

My head fell on my breast, and I felt dreadfully depressed, as I do each time an unnecessary, brutal, undeserved accident forces me to rail against Providence.

Alas! If ever there was a happy, enviable man, it was he—young, handsome, rich, highly endowed by nature, an artist in every fibre of his being, possessing an adoring, helpful wife, and friends who love him; applauded in France, in Germany, in England: one asked oneself by what chink in the armour that is called "popularity" could misfortune reach him? Oh, Misfortune is the lion of the Gospel of St. John, raging ceaselessly around men, trying to devour them. A narrow gap suffices for him to enter, leap on his prey, and tear it down. A peasant comes to tell Roger of a pheasant seen to come

---

[1] Gustave Hippolyte Roger. He visited England with Jenny Lind and may be said to have sung in most of the capitals of Europe.

down in a coppice; he takes his gun, but a hedge is in his way; he puts his gun down, setting it upright on the other side of the hedge, then gets over, and picks up his gun again without uncocking it; a thorn catches in the tumbler, the charge explodes and mutilates his arm. And here, in a moment, the life of this gifted fellow-creature is in danger.

My first impulse was to jump on a horse and gallop to him: then I thought that the injury was perhaps more serious than reported, and that, while waiting for further news, I could at least hope a little, whereas by going I should find myself the spectator of a worse condition of things than the man's words had disclosed. The same day I learnt that an operation had been successfully performed, that Roger had endured it with an artist's courage—the best kind, for it is a mixture of will-power and resignation.

Then came the inevitable reaction. If I went to visit him, I should find the wounded man in a weak condition and full of regrets. On seeing me his sufferings would increase two-fold. It were best to wait for the healing measure of time. So I waited. Roger's progress towards recovery became satisfactory, and therefore I did not see him again until yesterday.

He had come to Marseilles to give a concert, and while I was with him the *artistes* of the Opera were announced. Led by Monjauze, they came to perform their homage to Roger, like subjects to a king in his progresses. Have I not remarked that in like measure as one leaves Paris behind, so are left petty hatreds and squabbles of cliques?

You know Monjauze, don't you? He is a young, handsome, and charming fellow, who took a part, something like ten years ago, at the *Odéon* in I do not remember which of my plays. One fine day, he realised that, instead of earning three or four thousand francs by talking on the boards, he could earn thirty or forty thousand by singing at the Opera: and as the golden harvest that results from work is, whatever may be said to the contrary, the greatest incitement that the talented comedian can experience, he became a singer. He is, moreover, an artist of fine taste, a collector, collecting precisely what the philistine looks down on—antiques, bric-à-brac, *bibelots*. When he saw the arms I had brought from the Caucasus, he declared that no one but himself should arrange them for me, and it is he, in fact, who has grouped them with excellent taste, and yet in such a way that they can be taken down at will, while at the same time all are in full view. And so it comes about that, without premeditation on my part, my pen has led me to express my thanks to him almost at the moment of my departure. In fact, I write these lines to the accompaniment of the varied sounds caused by the making of our final arrangements, and by the whole population of Marseilles surging on to the deck of the *Emma*.

It must be admitted that I am a tenacious man. In 1834, when my first "Impressions de Voyage"[1] appeared, I was dining one day with my poor friend Lautour Mezeray (who was filling the post of prefect of Algiers at the time of his death), when I spoke of my wish to make the tour of the Mediterranean, and to write, after completing it, the history of its civilisation.

He applauded my idea. "Write the book," said he, "and I will publish it." As always occurs in Paris, there was at first much mocking laughter at my expense. A man who had made a million francs out of my "Christine," "Napoleon," "Richard Darlington," and "Tour de Nesle," thanked me for it by this witty comment—

"Did you know that Dumas had discovered the Mediterranean?" This sally had a long and successful career : indeed, witty fellows repeat it to me even now, six-and-twenty years after its first appearance—a long life, it must be allowed, for a jest to enjoy.

On the day in question, Harel[2] believed that he had got even with me ; others contented themselves with saying : "He is a boaster who pursues a dream. He will not do what no one has done yet." And, indeed, without the aid of the Government and merely with the resources of a literary man, how was I to make such a journey? Chateaubriand and Lamartine have made, one, the journey from Paris to Jerusalem, the other the journey to the East, and each has ruined himself. Yes, it was difficult, but with the aid of God nothing is impossible.

Not being able to accomplish the journey at one stroke I decided to do it in several.

I left in 1834. On this first journey I saw all the South of France, from Cette to Toulon; Aigues-Mortes, Arles, Tarascon, Beaucaire, Nîmes, Marseilles, Avignon, Vaucluse. During a rest of a few days at Toulon at the foot of Fort l'Amalgue in a delightful villa belonging to Dr. Lauvergne—who has since met his death as a philosopher should—I wrote "Don Juan de Marana."[3] This first journey was a small affair, but it was a beginning.

I started again the following year; this time my journey lasted eighteen months. I saw Hyères, Cannes, the Gulf of Jouan, Grasse, Draguignan, Nice, the Corniche, Genoa, Florence, Pisa, Leghorn, Turin, Milan, Pistoia, Perugia, Rome, Naples, Messina, Palermo, Girgenti, Marsala, Syracuse, Catania. I ascended Etna and Stromboli. I visited the Liparian isles, getting as far as Lampedousa. I

---

[1] "En Suisse."   [2] The Director of the *Odéon*.
[3] Produced at the *Porte Saint Martin*, 30th April, 1834.

returned to Reggio. I went up Calabria on foot as far as Pæstum, passing Pizzo, which still bears on the walls of the citadel the marks of the balls which killed Murat. I was arrested for the first time at Naples by His Majesty King Ferdinand. I was going to return by Venice when I was arrested for the second time at Foligno by His Holiness Gregory XVI, was brought by carabineers to Trasimeno, and left on the margin of the lake with the threat of five years in the galleys if I should again set foot in the Roman States.

I returned to France, where galleys of another kind awaited me.

During a calm of a week's duration, which kept me at anchor in the strait of Messina, I had written "Captain Paul."[1]

In 1842, still steadfast in my resolution, I took a boat in the port of Leghorn—a two-oared boat, mind—and with the boat which ought to have sunk ten times but never did sink, I visited Elba, Pianosa, Gorgone, Monte-Cristo, and Corsica. Prince Napoleon shared with me the pleasure and the dangers of these voyages. All recollection of the dangers has gone; but this month of intimacy, probably forgotten by him, is remembered by me.

In 1846 I left for Madrid.

I visited Barcelona, Malaga, Cordova, Seville, Cadiz; I took the strait in my stride, and I was at Tangiers; from Tangiers I went on to Tetuan. I returned to Gibraltar, from Gibraltar I went to Mellila, from Mellila to Djemma-Ghazaouat, from Djemma-Ghazaouat to Oran, from Oran to Algiers.

At Djemma-Ghazaouat I visited the marabout Sid-Ibrahim, of bloody memory. At Algiers I made a pause. I had to visit, in the interior, Blidah, the col de Mouzaïa, Milianeh. Then I forcibly requisitioned the Véloce—or so it was alleged in the Chamber of Deputies. I departed again, I stopped at Djijelli, at Collo, at Stora, at Phillippeville. I went to Constantine, returned to Stora, and then left for Tunis and the Kerkennah. In a day and a half's tramp in the interior I visited the Roman amphitheatre of Djem-Djem.

In the course of my first journey in France I spent 6000 francs; over my second journey in Italy 18,000; over my third journey in Corsica and the isle of Elba 4000; and over the last in Spain and Africa 33,000, from which the 10,000 allocated to me by the Minister of Education should be deducted. Total, 51,000 francs.

The works which were the fruits of these wanderings were—

"The Impressions of France"; "From Marseilles to Florence"; "A Year at Florence"; "The Villa Palmieri"; "The Speronare";

---

[1] Produced at the Panthéon, 12th October, 1838, under the title of "Paul Jones." Dumas' romance "Captain Paul" was inspired by this drama. The source of both drama and romance was "The Pilot," by Fenimore Cooper.

"Captain Arena"; "From Paris to Cadiz"; "The Véloce." That is, about thirty volumes; furthermore, "Don Juan de Marana," written at Toulon, and "Captain Paul," written at Messina. These works brought me a sum which was about twice that of my expenses; so, having made the calculation, I felt assured that, God willing, I should accomplish my desires.

Well, to-day it remains for me to finish what I set out to do: it remains for me to describe Venice, which I have only visited incidentally. It remains for me to see Illyria, the Ionian Isles, Greece, Constantinople—which I saw only when returning from the Caucasus, and of which I have forgotten to speak, because I merely got a glimpse—the shores of Asia Minor, Syria, Palestine, Egypt, Cyrene, Tripoli.

And before I begin, before going any further, I have to offer my thanks to the directors of the Imperial Steamships, who, when they learnt of my project, generously and courteously offered me free passages on their boats for myself and secretary, our board only being charged for.

It was a great deal, but it was not everything we wanted.

To travel on Messageries' boats meant going ashore at Malta, Syra, Alexandria, Beyrout, Smyrna, Rhodes and Constantinople, that is, seeing what everyone has seen previously; it meant being able to give a better, or a worse, description than others have done, but, nevertheless, to give it after those others.

Now, the journey I wanted to make was the one it had been wagered I would not make, the journey that no one had yet made. For all that, we are going, inside ten minutes, to weigh our anchor to undertake it.

Our itinerary has been drawn up.

What I wish to see, and what, above all, I wish to enable you, dear readers, to see, are the places famous in history—and even in myth—the Greece of Homer, of Hesiod, of Æschylus, of Pericles, and of Augustus; the Byzantium of the Latin Empire, and the Constantinople of Mahomed; the Syria of Pompey, of Cæsar, of Crassus; the Judæa of Herod and of Christ; the Palestine of the Crusades; the Egypt of the Pharaohs, of Ptolemy, of Cleopatra, of Mahomed, of Bonaparte, of Mahomet Ali, and of Saïd Pasha.

Well, to visit them all profitably, this is what must be done, and what we shall do. We shall touch at Genoa, Ajaccio, Monte-Cristo, Marsala, Malta, Brindisi, Venice. It is here that our journey proper will begin, here that we shall begin to explore.

We shall depart from Venice; we shall stop at Zara, rendered famous by the history of Villehardoin, who, having set out to deliver

Jerusalem from a pagan Sultan, stayed on the way to dethrone a Christian prince; at Dyrrhachium, where Pompey established his camp before going to meet his defeat by Cæsar at Pharsala; at Apollonia, where Octavius was studying when he learnt the news of the death of his uncle who had left him the inheritance of the world; at Corfu, the ancient Corcyra—to-day an English possession—which in the time of the Trojan War already had its own kings; at that famous Gulf of Actium, which witnessed the defeat of Antony and the flight of Cleopatra; at Leucadia, immortalised by the death of Sappho; at Ithaca, the country of Ulysses, which he had such trouble in regaining after the Trojan War; at Cephalonia, which, after its submission to the Thebans, to the Macedonians, to the Romans, and to the Empire of the Mid-East, was conquered in 1146 by the Normans; at Missolonghi, where Byron breathed his last sigh; at Patras, where the Greeks gained their first victory; at the Gulf of Lepanto where Don John beat Selim II, and where Cervantes lost a hand—happily not the one with which he was going to write "Don Quixote." While in the calm sea which the ancients called the Halcyon Sea, we must cast our anchor at Crissa and then go to Delphi; next, leave the gulf and visit Navarino, where the question of Greek independence was solved; land at Messenia, of which place Sparta was so jealous, and whose misfortunes were able, after 2500 years, to make the reputation of Casimir Delavigne;[1] visit Sparta, where Chateaubriand tried in vain to raise an echo to the name of Leonidas; on leaving the Laconian Gulf, stop at Cerigo, the ancient Cythera; go from there to Argos, to search for the tomb of the Atrides; to Orchomenus, to inquire concerning the traces of Sulla; and to Athens, the capital of the nation which has had the strange privilege of attaining perfection in all things.

Then we shall visit Salamis, the isle of victory; Corinth, the city of courtesans; Ægina, which invented gold and silver coinage; Cos, the country of Simonides, the poet beloved of the gods; Syros, modern Syra, wrested by the Greeks from the Turks; Delos, the isle of Latona; Naxos, where Theseus abandoned Ariadne, whom Bacchus so easily consoled; Melos, to-day Milo, where the lovely armless Venus was found, generally accepted as a triumph of the art of sculpture; Paros, whence sprang a forest of columns and a populace of statues; Ios, where Homer died.

Then, after we have touched at Marathon, the grave of the Persians, we shall pass up the Strait of Eubœa, stop at Thermopylæ, and follow, as far as Thebes, the mountainous ravine where the thousand Thebans found their deaths with three hundred Spartans. We shall

[1] By means of his poem, "Les Messéniennes."

double the point of Pelion, from which Achilles saw the Argonauts depart, the while he wept bitter tears for being yet too young to accompany them; we shall land at Scyros, where Ulysses flashed his dazzling sword in the eyes of the women, sitting among their gauds; we shall try to visit Lemnos (where Vulcan, flung down from Olympus, broke his leg in falling) and to seek, beneath the waves which have engulfed it, the isle of Philoctetes. We shall tarry at Tenedos, not so much to renew our supply of wine as to invoke the memory of the Laocoon; we shall descend upon the Trojan shore, and, guided by the tomb of Ilus, we shall separate the Scamander from the Simois, ancient Ilium from modern Ilium; we shall seat ourselves on the ruins of Pergamus, recalling to memory the lettered kings who invented parchment to give longer life to the works of poets; we shall get towed by some steam-boat, and we shall breast the current of the Dardanelles as far up as the Seven Stadia—that is to say, as far as that part of the strait crossed by Leander in swimming from Sestos to Abydos; we shall turn to our right to salute the entrance of the Granicus, the banks of which witnessed Alexander's first victory; we shall pass through the Cyaneæ, at the risk of the loss of some of our feathers, like the dove which flew in front of the ship of Argus, and thus, in one flight, we shall wing our way to Constantinople.

There we shall stay our steps.

We must see the mosque of Soliman, the castle of the Seven Towers, the Golden Horn, Scutari. We must rest for a moment in this oasis of the coast of Asia before proceeding to be burnt by the devouring sun of Palestine and by the scorching breeze of the Dead Sea.

Then we shall spread the pennon of our yacht to flutter in the wind and we shall pursue our course by the route already traversed; we shall again pass by the tombs of Patrocles and Achilles. As we have visited the battlefield of Pharsala in Thessaly, so shall we visit the battlefield of Philippi in Thrace; we shall cast a glance at Mount Athos, where Alexander thought of erecting a statue, and we shall stop only at Lesbos, where the waters of the Hebrus brought forth the head and the lyre of Orpheus, where were born the two Sapphos, one a beauty, the other a poet; we shall go from there to Chios, which disputed with Smyrna the honour of having given birth to Homer; then we shall touch at Samos, where kings were so happy that they tried to disarm misfortune by throwing their treasures into the sea; to Icarus, which received its name from the son of Dædalus; to Patmos, where St. John saw the terrible spectacle of the pale horse of death; to Rhodes (as fresh to-day as in the time when Cæsar studied oratory there) and its street of horsemen, which is falling in ruins; to Cyprus, where will end the Arabian tale which I have promised to tell you concerning our two Greek sailors. Subsequently we will go to seek, upon the coast of the Caramania, those nameless towns of which the vestiges lay strewn on a hundred leagues of shore; Sour, the ancient Tyre, which provided cedars for the temple of Solomon and purple for the mantle of the Cæsars; Carmel, which I have helped to rebuild, as Amphion built Thebes, with magic words;[1] and at last we shall reach Beyrout, and from Beyrout, Jerusalem.

There one ceases merely to see—one adores.

There name presses on name; Nazareth, Bethlehem, the Jordan, the Dead Sea, Jericho, the garden of Olives, Calvary, Gethsemane—I speak of places; Solomon, David, Jeremiah, Alexander, Pompey, Herod, Cæsar, Jesus, Titus, Constantine, Helen, Godefroy de Bouillon, Soliman, Baudoin, Philip Augustus, Richard Cœur de Lion, Kléber, Chateaubriand, Lamartine—I speak of men.

The history of this little corner called Judæa is just the history of the world.

But it will be necessary to leave it; for we have to see Alexandria, the city of the Caliphs, and the tombs of the Pharaohs.

Then, favoured by the northern breeze, we shall sail up the river whose sources are unknown; we shall see the immense towns that are named Thebes and Karnac; the marvellous isles that are named Elephantine and Philæ. We shall hearken whether the dawn still awakens a sigh in what remains of the statue of Memnon; and we shall seek the South as far as permitted by the sun, river, and—our means.

Finally, perhaps, we shall return by Cadiz, Lisbon, Oporto, Bordeaux, Nantes and Havre.

Is not this journey worth the toil of the last twenty-five years which I have cheerfully undertaken in order to accomplish it?

The anchor is being weighed; the Captain summons me on deck to acknowledge the salutations of our friends and of the population massed on the quays.

The *Emma* obeys the impulsion of the sails.

We are off.

> "Au vent la flamme,
> Au Seigneur l'âme."[2]

---

[1] "Temple et Hospice du Mont-Carmel, en Palestine," par Alex. et Adolphe Dumas, au nom du Comité de Paris. Paris, 1844.

[2] Dumas was very fond of this device, which was to be read on the weathercocks of his "Chateau de Monte-Cristo."

CHAPTER VIII

THE HISTORY OF A NOTARY PRINCE AND OF A SERGEANT KING

15th May

You will understand that since we left Marseilles no very important events have occurred, although, as the date 15th May follows the 9th, the day of our departure, it may suggest the occurrence of some mishap.

No; the delay is caused simply by two difficulties that we have met with more than once—head winds and calms.

These are the drawbacks of the sailing vessel—but must it not be so? As an admirer of Fenimore Cooper, my preference must be forgiven—I prefer a sailing vessel, with all its disadvantages, to a steam-boat, with all its advantages.

Sit down beside me on deck.

We weighed anchor at half-past nine o'clock, and passed before the tower of St. Jean, which the engineers had wished to destroy: everything of a picturesque kind annoys engineers. Bernadoux has saved the poor tower, however.

Thanks, my dear Bernadoux; so many memories disappear under the designs of architects and under the trowels of masons that there is no harm done in leaving some of them.

You tell me that no great harm is done in razing State prisons. I reply that it is not the State prisons it is necessary to raze. I do not mind them when they no longer have any prisoners within their walls.

If the dungeon of Bonivard had been razed, we should not possess one of Byron's finest poems.

It is true that the engineer, if one had allowed him, would have razed the prison of Chillon, as he would have razed the tower of St. Jean.

But by parity of reasoning, you remark, the Bastille would now be standing.

Why not? The Bastille would suit the landscape just as well as the Column of July. That would not have prevented the Bastille from being taken; and I applaud with all my strength when there is question of such doings.

M. Pilloy, the city architect, was in the wrong in wishing to demolish the tower. Architects have a mania for wishing to unmake everything which they could not have made. I believe that there would be more instruction from a *concierge* showing the room of the Iron

Mask, of Pellisson, and of Latude, than from the asphalte which has replaced the foundations of the old castle of Charles V.

I admit that I have seen with profound sorrow the dungeon of the Temple fall, and with a lasting regret the prison of the Abbey.

When I passed before the former I said, "The tenth of August," and the reply came: "Louis XVI." When I passed before the latter I said, "The second of September," and the reply came: "Danton."

Look; you see that window which looks on Friule—*forum Julii*, so the etymologists say—it is that of the dungeon of the poor Duc de Montpensier, who has left such charming "Mémoires" of his captivity, and who has sketched at once so grotesque and so life-like a portrait of the old Prince de Conti.

It was by that window that he tried to gain his freedom, but, losing his foothold, he fell from a height of ten metres and broke his thigh, there upon those rocks.

Groans escaped him, which were heard by fishermen whose boats were moored near the *Réserve;* but during the Reign of Terror it was not always prudent to answer the cries that one heard.

Nevertheless, one man was braver than the others; he was the *patron*, Etienne Imbert. He ran up, and found the young prince lying on the rocks; he lifted him up and bore him to his own boat, and seeing that he was in need of medical aid, sought how to get it.

The port was closed, but this did not daunt Imbert. More than once when the port was closed he had entered and got out. The chains were slack, and two men standing on them depressed them below a sufficient depth of water to admit of a boat passing over them. This means was employed, and the boat passed over the chains.

It so chanced that the shop of a wigmaker named Mangin was still open. The Duc de Montpensier was taken to it; there he was identified. First aid was given, and the next morning he was taken back to the fort.

The governor, an unfrocked priest, was then dismissed, and a new governor named Betemps appointed. He was as good a man as he was a brave one. While strictly guarding the young prince, he showed him every consideration. His wife was as a mother to him. In spite of this fact, when, after the Restoration, Madame Betemps, then a widow and without resources, made application to the Duc d'Orléans —not to the son, but to the father—she could not obtain even an audience of him.

Another memory attaches to the Duc de Montpensier: it is one which survives and is known to all of us.

A charming laundress, named Miette Dantan, worked for the

officers and prisoners. She was perhaps two or three years older than the young prince.

Inside a prison there are no social inequalities. The Duc de Montpensier was attracted by a poor girl, whom, had he been on the steps of the throne, he would not have noticed. An intimacy was formed between the descendant of St. Louis and of Louis XIV., and a daughter of the people. It lasted during the whole of the prince's captivity, and when he left prison for exile, following the treaty concluded with his eldest brother, Miette Dantan was *enceinte*.

She gave birth to a son on whom she could bestow only her own name, but for a Christian name she gave him "Philippe." The boy was therefore called Philippe Dantan.

The Duc de Montpensier, then in America, sent some assistance, for a time, through the medium of the United States Consul; then came the Empire, and the Duc had so many things to occupy him that he forgot the child. And so it came to pass that one saw a boy, in whose veins ran the blood of St. Louis, selling the *Bulletin de la Grande Armée* on the quays; and when there were no Bulletins, offering for the amusement of nurses and children tries for a lottery at a penny a try, the prizes being boxes of wafer pastry.

This most precarious existence lasted until 1815. Then the saintly widow of Philippe Egalité, Princesse de Penthièvre, heard that she had a grandson at Marseilles. She sent for the lad. He was so much the image of his father, of whom she had lost sight at the same age, that she seemed to see him again, and held out her arms to the young man.

From that moment, if not recognised legally, he was at any rate adopted.

His education was taken in hand—a little late in the day. A post was found for him in a notary's office; then a practice was bought for him; and it was this notary who, under the name of Philippe Dantan, gave evening parties at which the highest stakes in Paris were made.

Well, such are the memories evoked by a mere window. Were we to enter the fort, we should find plenty more, and they would not be less interesting than those of the ice-house of Avignon.

Go to Blois and you will be shown the window by which Marie de Medicis escaped. More fortunate than her descendant, the parricide queen did not break anything. Can you explain that? She was guilty, and the Duc de Montpensier was innocent.

Providence is often very absent-minded.

While I have been chatting with you, the yacht has progressed. We have rounded the *Réserve*, fated to disappear so as not to dishonour the vicinity of a palace; we have cleared the old port.

Look at that grey mass with heavy angles which seems part of the cliff, so much so that it appears like a growth on the granite. It is the Château d'If, of which I have spoken so much that nothing more remains for me to tell.

It is different with the isle of Ratonneau—don't look round, it is only Berteaut, who is sea-sick. Poor Berteaut! It is the second time, after an interval of twenty years, that his devotion to me makes him brave the sea—his mortal enemy. Berteaut has never been able to understand the passion of Phœbus for Amphitrite. Berteaut is like that abbé who, not caring for dabs, said that if there were only dabs and himself in the world, the world would soon come to an end!

If there were only Berteaut and Amphitrite in the world, the world would have already ended!

It is different with Ratonneau, I was remarking when Berteaut interrupted us; and in fact I, who have so often spoken of Marseilles, have never said anything about Ratonneau, although, like the Château d'If, it also has its story.

In 1765, under the administration of the Duc de Villars, Governor of the province, a small garrison, renewed each month, was sent to the isle of Ratonneau.

One day, the time came for the soldier Jean Courin, known by his comrades as "Francœur," to fall into the ranks of this monthly garrison.

Francœur had some tendency towards insanity, but it was then manifested by high-spirited outbursts, eccentric enough to excite his friends' laughter, but not so eccentric as to cause him to be sent to the mad-house.

It was at Ratonneau that the sun's rays, falling vertically on Francœur's head, developed his disease.

Scarcely was he on the island than he made the circuit of it and then imagined himself to be its king—an absolute king, a king by right divine, and, in consequence, a legitimate king, neither more nor less than the King of Naples, the Emperor of Austria, and the Prince of Monaco.

He took advantage of a moment when his comrades were absent getting provisions to let down the portcullis of the drawbridge, close the door and the posterns of the citadel, load the cannon, place the guns in the loopholes, and, with a lighted fuse in his hand, await the coming of the enemy.

The enemy, for him, was whosoever should want to enter the citadel.

Now this was the very thing his comrades, who were returning with the sacks of provisions, desired to do.

Francœur called to them with an imperious voice, "Keep off."

"There!" said the soldiers, "it is Francœur at his tricks again. What a queer fellow he is!"

And they continued their march towards the citadel.

At that moment a cannon-ball whistled over their heads.

They continued to advance, but a shower of bullets followed.

It was Francœur, who, after a cannon-shot, was giving them a fusillade.

The whistling of the bullets, like that of the cannon-ball, indicated that if Francœur was joking, his joke could have unpleasant consequences.

It was decided, since he was acting in a military style towards others, to act similarly towards him.

A soldier with a handkerchief on the end of a stick went forward to make terms, but Francœur called out that he could not treat with a mere soldier, that he was King of Ratonneau, and that it was his intention to reside in his kingdom alone and without any subjects.

And he drove home this pretension to solitude and royalty by a gunshot which, fortunately, took effect only on the handkerchief.

This done, he fired off his guns, each in its turn, a performance which was an easy one, seeing that they were already pointed and loaded.

The squad began to seek shelter from this hailstorm in the clefts of the rocks; then, as the fire continued, it gained the beach, embarked in a boat, and returned to Marseilles, where the sergeant, being in command, related the strange pretension of Francœur and the fashion in which he had laid stress on it.

The next day another squad was sent to ascertain whether the report was true, and to retake the place, if it were so.

But during the interval Francœur lusted for conquest, so he spent the night loading his cannon, and at daybreak began to fire on the Château d'If.

The Governor of the Château d'If was awakened by the unexpected noise of the bombardment of his prison. From a post of observation he saw that the fire came from Ratonneau. For a fortnight he had had no communication with Marseilles. He believed that during that time war must have been declared between France and some power that had taken possession of the island. He also had cannon, so he ordered them to be loaded, and he fired in his turn. Marseilles was puzzled what to think of this early morning cannonade.

Since the previous night, the military authorities of Marseilles knew of Francœur's usurpation. A boat was despatched to the Governor of the Château d'If to inform him of what had occurred the previous day. Happily, the two forts, in reinforcing their arguments with cannon balls, had made more noise than holes in the walls.

It is true that a soldier of the garrison of the Château d'If was wounded; but as regards Francœur, he was as merry as Old King Cole. He had no doubt that it was his superior gunnery which had silenced that of his adversary, and he became more proud and arrogant than before.

As will be remembered, however, he had not allowed his comrades to return to the citadel with the provisions, and his supply of victuals was beginning to get low.

It was just then that a Dutch vessel sailed bravely into the port of Ratonneau. Francœur began by sending a ball into the main-sail and fore-sail, after which, seeing the terror that this unexpected aggression caused on board, he called to the Captain—

"Heave to at once, and send to the King of Ratonneau a boat-load of biscuit and salt beef."

The Captain, who did not understand the tongue in which the King of Ratonneau spoke, had his harangue translated by a French sailor of the Protestant persuasion, whose parents had reached Amsterdam after the revocation of the Edict of Nantes. The sailor was in doubt who the King of Ratonneau was, but as only kings have the right to fire off cannon, he told the Captain it seemed that Ratonneau had a king, and that this king demanded biscuit and salt beef.

The Captain then proceeded to deposit on the beach the supplies demanded by the King of Ratonneau, and directly his boat returned he tacked about, promising himself never again to approach that inhospitable spot.

In the meantime the King of France found himself unable to tolerate such an usurpation of a part of his kingdom, insignificant though the part was, and M. le Duc de Villars, his representative, resolved to end it.

Only, as it was clear that Francœur was mad, and that it would have been deplorable to make men who were of sound mind and understanding victims of this madness, it was decided to use strategy in laying hands on Francœur.

Francœur, as the sole inhabitant of his kingdom, enjoyed many advantages, but they were attended by certain drawbacks—he had to do everything himself, including his cooking and his looking-out.

As regards the cooking—it existed only in our imagination, since he had biscuit and salt beef.

But his looking-out was another thing altogether.

It was noticed that Francœur, like Tiberius at Capri, like Denis at

Syracuse, and like Louis XI at Plessis les Tours, spent very restless nights; at night-time he got out of his bed and made his rounds to assure himself that no one menaced the tranquillity of his kingdom, or conspired against his absolute authority.

So as to see the more clearly into the devious entanglements of conspiracies, Francœur made his rounds carrying a lantern. This lantern had its uses in showing him where to tread, but it betrayed where he was.

One evening de Villars landed some men near the centre of the rocks of Ratonneau; these men were guided by a fisherman named Ganay le Trapu of the district of St. Jean. He was a smart fellow, who had never met his equal in feats of strength—who had never been thrown in a wrestling match.

He knew everything about Francœur. He lay in wait for him, and as he came along seized him under the arms from behind, and told him he was his prisoner.

Francœur made but little resistance. He recognised that the King of France was more powerful than the King of Ratonneau, and Ganay stronger than Francœur.

He asked to know the terms of capitulation.

They were dictated forthwith.

Francœur I, King of Ratonneau, was to restore to Louis XV, King of France, the citadel, the arms, and the other munitions of war that it contained—the restoration of the citadel naturally including the restoration of the island itself.

As regards Francœur, he was to leave Ratonneau with all the honours of war—that is to say, with his haversack and his pipe.

The next morning he was embarked for Marseilles.

He found the quays thronged by a crowd in expectation of seeing his fallen majesty. At that time fallen majesties were rarer than they are in ours, and people even put aside other engagements to see them pass by; and so it was that Francœur came in for some attention, which is much more than now falls to the lot of monarchs in Francœur's situation.

Free to do as he pleased, though under the eye of the police, who wanted to ascertain definitely whether he were mad or not, Francœur for some days promenaded the streets of Marseilles, relating to all who cared to hear, the events, few in number but dramatic in quality, of his reign.

Unfortunately this relation, too often repeated, ended in brain fever and a dangerous state of madness.

Francœur was taken to the asylum.

Contrary to all expectations, he was cured, but he never recovered his sanity. De Villars, who could not help taking an interest in his fallen majesty, obtained for the ex-King of Ratonneau admission to the *Invalides*, where for several years he entertained the veterans of Fontenoy and the conquerors of Mahon with the recital of his transient reign.

Such is the story of the King of Ratonneau, which you may consider as good as another.

In fact, it is time that it finished, for the Captain is tacking, Berteaut being the cause of the manœuvre. With might and main he insists on being cast into the sea—the sharks are to eat him, or he the sharks —it matters little, but he will not remain on board a second longer.

Regnier, as haggard and as desperate as Berteaut, makes the same demand.

Cape Croisette is only a half-knot off, a hundred fathoms from the Ile de Maira, where Monte-Cristo landed. We will put them ashore, and they will return to Marseilles on foot.

Regnier is able to fall into the boat, but Berteaut has to be carried into it, without giving any sign of life.

At the very first opportunity I will use the telegraph to obtain news of him.

The yacht continues on her course, and a quarter of an hour later Marseilles, the Château d'If, and Ratonneau are hidden by[1]

When shall we see them again?[2]

[1] The manuscript has a blank here.
[2] The changes wrought in the French Riviera since 1860 may be ascertained from "The Coast of Pleasure," by Grant Richards. (London, 1928.)

CHAPTER IX

THE CHÂTEAU OF M. CHAPON AND THAT OF QUEEN JEANNE

LOOKING on deck again, I saw that all were much in Regnier's and Berteaut's condition. The "Admiral," as befitted his rank, had set the example and gone down to his room. Paul Parfait had followed suit. The doctor, whose back was turned, had attached himself to the rigging, where the convulsed movements of his shoulders betrayed the agony he was suffering. Legray, who in his life-time allowed Valdin to take all manner of liberties with him, was dead, or nearly so. He lay stretched out on his stomach on deck, and Valdin, taking advantage of his immobility, treated him like a milestone with no inscription on it. Lockroy sat grave and motionless in the *youyou* hanging from the yacht's stern, making pretence to sketch the landscape: anyone who looked over his shoulder would have seen that he was only crunching *pastilles de menthe*.

The sailors apart, Théodore and I were the only two who kept on our legs.

None of us had thought of asking how it fared with the cook: we heard about him when dinner-time came. He was lying near his fire, which he had not had the courage to light, and to all questions, answered in a dying voice, "The chimney does not draw."

Even if the dinner had been cooked, there would have been no one to serve it. Vasili and the cabin-boy were without one sign of life about the two of them.

Brémont cooked us some eggs and grilled some cutlets for the Captain, Podimatas, Théodore and myself.

As dusk fell, Legray was borne down to his room, just as Berteaut had been carried to his boat; but one must do him this justice, being accustomed in his voyages to sea-sickness, he only complained of the improprieties committed by Valdin.

The next day things were better, and, owing to my having dinner served on deck, two persons only failed to answer the summons. The following day, Legray was alone in insisting on remaining in a horizontal position, and Valdin in molesting him.

On the fourth day, as we passed off the islands of Hyères, and I heard parched lips speaking with longing of orange groves and palm trees rivalling those of Nice, I had not the courage to refuse a surcease to my poor convalescents. Before I had well signified my intentions, cries of gratitude burst out from all sides. The Captain directed our course straight for the little port of Hyères, which is about a league distant from the town. The wind changed and helped us to make for the port. We passed between Porquerolles and Point d'Estrel, and three-quarters of an hour later we anchored about half-a-mile from the shore.

The French fleet was there, engaged in manœuvres; we passed right under the bowsprit of the *Bretagne*, a magnificent ship with 160 guns and Admiral Barbier de Tinan on board. He had glanced down on the humble and graceful seagull which glided by his prow, skimming the waters. He had recognised my yacht from the description he had read in the Marseilles journals, and the same moment as she reached the jetty his small boat did the like, bearing an *aide-de-camp* who came to say that the Admiral wished to be of any service to me. He took back with him my thanks and my respects, and I asked him to tell the Admiral that if in a year's time I should meet him at the other end of the Mediterranean, he would be in great danger of my accepting his offer.

There were two or three omnibuses on the sea-front which would have taken us in half-an-hour, for twenty sous each, to Hyères, but the mere idea of carriage exercise too much suggested the motion of the sea for us to become their fares. We unanimously declined the offers of the conductor, which, I must state, were most attractively presented. And as we should have filled the entire omnibus, the conductor's loss was a deplorable one.

We stepped out for Hyères. At the end of a hundred yards Lockroy left us. The landscape pleased him, he opened his umbrella, settled himself down apart from us, and began a sketch in colour.

We went on our way, exposed to a temperature approaching 90 degrees and dust worthy of Sahara. But as we left the sea further behind, the road grew green and the landscape gradually became delightful. Soon we were in groves of olive and mulberry trees, which, planted alternately, grew on both sides of the road. Slopes strewn with Easter daisies and buttercups, and, in places, topped by hedges of hawthorn and pomegranate in flower, caught the eye everywhere. Nearing a stream which crossed our path, we found ourselves under an arcade, composed of a double row of interlaced trees. Two nightingales, about a hundred paces apart, were answering each other as methodically as Virgil's shepherds, and letting fall, for the mere pleasure of doing it, the endless rosary of their song— the only one which is an eternal improvisation.

I had dropped behind. I seated myself on the parapet of the bridge, and let the shade bathe me, the harmony steal within me. I had left Paris still in winter, and here, after a journey of 200 leagues, taking a fortnight, I found myself in full summer. All the delights of Nature were in this little spot: water, shade, and verdure, the murmur of the brook, the song of two nightingales, hot sunshine, which one saw but did not feel. And not a house to be seen!

Here we were, only half a league from a town which was blistering in the sun, and no one had had the idea, I will not say to build a château, but to put up a tent in this Eden. It is truly said that ever since man was turned out of paradise, it is he who does not want to re-enter it.

If I had not been afraid that my companions would wait my arrival for dinner and would not wish to dine without me, I certainly would not have gone further than this little bridge. How was it that they had passed over it without stopping? and how was it that I had stopped and felt unable to proceed? The answer is that they were five or six, and that I was alone.

To be alone! It is perhaps the only ambition that I have not realised. Certain positions exclude solitude: I have gone 20,000 leagues in my life to find it, and I have never found it—everywhere there has been someone who knows me, who has known me, or who wants to know me. Alas! this someone is almost always an importunate person, a curiosity-monger, or a fool. To be alone is to gather up all the mental threads, scattered, disordered, broken by the distraction of society; to enter into possession of one's own mind, which is at the mercy of the first comer's indiscretion; to think anew of the dear departed, of loved friends; to get together again bits of one's own heart that one has scattered on the road, since one possessed a heart and since one started on the road of life. Oh! think of me, all of you, of whom I think when I have the happiness to be alone.

I have mentioned why I could not remain. I said farewell to my brook, to my verdure, to my shade, to the murmur of the water, and the song of my two nightingales; and I set out again on the hot and dusty road.

What I had foreseen had occurred; they did not know what had become of me. I came on my young friends stationed in the town: one waited for me at the beginning of the street, another at the door of the Hôtel de l'Europe. Should you ever dine at that hotel, order what dinner you please, but have it served on the terrace. You will have there, on a 12th May—the day we were there—in first perspective, palms, lilacs, oranges, honeysuckles; in second perspective, mulberries and evergreen oaks, with peeps of red-roofed houses; and beyond these, grey rocks, blue waves, shores with capes and promontories, and island scenery in the distance, all of which keep you in such ecstasy that you dream and dream while your dinner cools. When you have seen it all, you will have seen the most ravishing scenery, I will not say in Hyères, I will not say in the province, I will say in the whole world.

We returned in the cool of the evening; everyone was rested, refreshed, merry, ready to brave the sea, chaffing his companion, and eager for the yacht.

In a moment we were on board; we saluted the French Admiral by dipping our flag, and we set sail again. But the wind had freshened. The Captain shook his head and showed me the fort of Brigançon, which, rising up at the end of the peninsula, looks as if it were isolated in the middle of the sea. "There," said he—"look! In all probability it is there that we shall spend the night—it is an excellent anchorage when the east wind blows, and even the south-east." And, indeed, we found that we could not pass between the island of Levant and the mainland.

Two hours later, we had cast anchor in the shelter of Fort Brigançon. This hill, with the fortress on its top, was in days of yore surmounted by a château. This château has memories of love, and of terror also. I speak of a *tour de Nesle*, of a queen homicidal like Marguerite de Bourgogne, dissolute as the daughter of the Comte Robert, and who died not less tragically than the wife of Louis le Hutin.

"What are you plaiting that beautiful silken-golden cord for?" asked André de Hongrie of his wife.

"To strangle you with, Monseigneur," replied the beautiful queen, showing her dazzling white teeth in a smile.

And, in fact, it was with this elegant silken cord that André de Hongrie was strangled.

Jeanne married the assassin, Louis de Tarente. But another Louis—Louis de Hongrie—André's brother, resolved to avenge his death. Louis de Hongrie marched on Naples, and Jeanne, abandoned by her people, fled into the land of Provence, to which the hill, where to-day stands Fort Brigançon, belongs. What the hill was then called is not known.

It was there that she stayed for some time with her several new lovers; there she had all that she thought to have lost in leaving Naples—in the morning delightful sunshine; during the day breezes; the perfume of the orange groves of Hyères—another Sorrento—in the evening.

There were islands which she could call Tetsia, Procida and Capri, caressed by waves as blue as those which break in murmurs in the Gulf of Baia; but two things were lacking: Boccaccio, her favourite teller of tales—those crowned courtesans, called Jeanne de Naples and Lucrèce Borgia, had drained all voluptuous pleasures, even those of the mind—and the revenues of her good city of Naples.

She could not forget that it was for his mistress, the natural daughter of King Robert, whom he called Fiametta, that the Florentine poet had written his "Decameron." The world did not contain two Boccaccios—Provence had a hundred troubadors, but no poet. Perforce, she had to be resigned.

As regards the second thing that was wanting—that is to say, the revenues of her good city of Naples—she replaced them by selling Avignon at the price of 80,000 florins to Pope Clement VI, the same who, finding himself so happy at Avignon, declined to return to Rome. The price of 80,000 florins was a bargain one. It is true that the deed of sale contained a secret clause : it was that the Pope should give Jeanne absolution for her crime of murder; no, we mistake— that the Pope would declare Jeanne innocent of the murder of her husband; and this he did with great pomp. Like his predecessor Clement V, he was a man who kept his word, was this Pope Clement VI. Only, Clement V declared the Templars guilty, and they were innocent; while Clement VI declared Jeanne innocent, and she was guilty.

These are the little traditions which put the philosophers and historians in doubt respecting the infallibility of the popes.

This sale of Avignon by Queen Jeanne to Clement VI had its effect for four and a half centuries—that is to say, from 1348 to 1791. While governed by her popes, she extended hospitality to Petrarch and Giotto; while governed by their vice-legates, she gave birth to Crillon, Folard, and Joseph Vernet.

As for Jeanne, she being innocent according to the solemn decree of Pope Clement VI, nothing prevented her return to Naples, since it was a parricide queen who had been dismissed.

During her exile her lover was Don Jayme, Magorgue's son. Her husband, Louis de Tarente, having died, she married Don Jayme; but having no child, she adopted her cousin Charles de Duras, known as Charles de la Paix.

Kings and queens alike commit mistakes in going on living after making such adoptions. The heir naturally becomes impatient, and one fine day, poignard or poison in hand, claims his inheritance.

This was what occurred to Queen Jeanne, who, having reached the age of sixty-seven, obstinately went on living.

One day, two Hungarian barons appeared in her oratory while she was praying, and bade her follow them. The queen followed them. They led her into the side chamber in which André de Hongrie had been strangled. There she found her adopted son, Charles de la Paix. His brow was clouded, and his look menacing. But it was not these that struck her—it was a silken cord plaited with gold, which he held between his hands. Charles de la Paix handed the cord to the barons, and withdrew. Jeanne understood that her last hour had struck. She knelt, prayed, and gave herself up to her executioners.

Now be advised, O queens! when you strangle your husbands take away the cord.

We passed the night behind Fort Brigançon with a man on the deck keeping the look-out, as the Captain had said; so—apart from a nightmare on the part of Paul Parfait, who got saved in his shirt— with Vasili on deck, nothing could have been more peaceful. Paul dreamt that he was being assassinated, and Vasili declared that he dreamt he was rescuing him.

In spite of this affirmation of Vasili's, his courage, on the night of 12th to 13th of May, is questioned by unbelievers.

The next morning, as we were weighing anchor, we saw a little fishing-boat coming with the speed of a race-horse; and, like one, making the foam fly. It came on in such a direct line that one would have supposed it meant to pass between our two masts. At twenty paces distance, it clewed up its sail and stopped.

"M. Dumas," called out the man who appeared to be the master of the three or four who formed the crew, "would you like, you and your friends, to come to that château in front of you for a *bouill-abaisse* made of the fish we caught last night?"

"Certainly that would please me," I replied, without knowing who gave the invitation—"the offer is made too gracefully to be declined."

"Good," the man answered. "In an hour I will come for you."

The little skiff hoisted its sail, rounded our bowsprit, and made for the land as fast as it had come.

Ten minutes later, it had landed everyone on the shore, and an empty craft was dancing gracefully on the water at the end of its chain.

The château where we had been so courteously invited to partake of a *bouillabaisse* was a mediæval-looking structure with a tower at each end, whose only drawback from the point of view of the archæo-logist and the landscape painter was that it made a huge white blot on the countryside, instead of harmonising therewith.

While we—that is, my companions—were gazing at it through telescopes and field-glasses, and I with my eyes—which see poorly near at hand but which outvie for distant objects all the collection of glasses to be had at Chevalier's, we saw the tricolour flag run up on the lightning conductor. By way of reply to this courtesy, we decked the *Emma* with flags.

So great had been our curiosity that our toilette was still in the making when the boat returned, and one of our host's friends, who represented him, informed us that our invitation came from M. Chapon, formerly a banker at Marseilles, and now landowner, hunter, and, above all, fisherman, at Brigançon. He had known me when I first went to Italy, and had then been my banker. The journals had informed him, like Admiral Barbier de Tinan, of our departure from Marseilles, and seeing on board of us, besides the sailors, five or six idlers in red blouses looking on at the hauling of the anchor, he had supposed that it could be no one else.

On nearing us, he had recognised that his supposition had become a certainty.

We got into the boat, Captain Beaugrand leading the way, and soon landed.

A large carriage, used on hunting excursions, with some twelve seats, and drawn by a pair of horses, awaited us on the shore. We bowled along through a delightful forest of pines, then through a plantation of mulberries, then across a heath—to my mind more picturesque than any plantation—and thus reached the château.

All the marvels that could be performed in two hours to provide the most lavish hospitality had been performed by our host, his wife, and his daughter. The *bouillabaisse*, made as tradition dictates—not by the cook, but by the head of the house—served as the pretext for a splendid luncheon. M. Chapon had travelled much, and he had brought something back from each of his voyages—Madeira from Teneriffe, Marsala from Mount Erix, *Chypre de la Commanderie, Xeres des Chevaliers:* we had to taste all, and in such a way as to satisfy our host that we appreciated all. Anything save an acceptance to taste again, he met with Meyerbeer's theory: "To understand my music it is necessary to hear it six or seven times." The illustrious *maestro* has been so fortunate as to make people put his theory into practice; and this, while assisting the music, does no harm to the composer's interests.

Some day I shall compose dramas which will only be understood at the sixth or seventh performance; if they reach the eighth, they will reach the fifth hundred.

Monsieur Chapon's wines were as successful as Meyerbeer's musical scores.

We returned to the yacht at five o'clock only. The wind, for once, was favourable; since our departure from Marseilles it had not shown us a similar favour.

If our passengers returned from the dinner of Hyères brave men, they returned from M. Chapon's luncheon-party boasting of deeds of prowess to be performed.

At the moment of doubling the point of Brigançon and that of Porquerolles, everyone was performing his duty, or nearly so.

The Admiral, faithful to his tradition of the eighteenth century, was busy with embroidery-work. Legray was only sitting instead of lying down. Théodore, who had climbed into the shrouds, was marooned there by the sailors, who held him up to ransom. Brémont was giving a lesson in boxing to Paul, and a lesson in single-stick to Lockroy. As for me—I was dreaming.

What makes me so passionately fond of the sea that I can say with Byron: "O sea, the only love to which I have been faithful"? Is it that I can not only dream as I like, but that I dream in spite of myself?

The need to work which, on land, unceasingly goads me, which pursues me at my meal-times, even when with a loved friend or with a pretty woman whom I admire, not only entirely ceases, but becomes almost distasteful. I, who, whether in Paris or in the country, reproach myself for spending an hour away from my dear writing-paper, from my own good table, from my ink which flows so easily from the nib of my pen, at first I remain idle on board not for an hour, but for hours, not for a day, but for days. And without a second of lassitude, of weariness, or *ennui*. As soon as my sight is lost in immensity, my thought gives place to a dream; I dream of what? God only knows—of the infinite, of the worlds rolling above me, of the sea sparkling below me. Then there falls on my senses a delightful twilight, different from but as sweet as the dawn of day or the evening light, something that smokers of opium and eaters of hashish can alone understand—that voluptuous absence of the will. Whatever the nature of the occurrence which distracts me from this waking repose, I receive it with a smile, for shall I not find my ecstasy again where I left it? And let me say that the *Emma* seems made expressly for dreams. No sooner is she on the sea than she glides on it without a tremor. All is easy to this dreambird, this swan from Liverpool. Even when sailing near the wind, which, next to a calm, is the most trying thing asked of her, her pitching can scarcely be felt. She cuts the waves like a fish, without an effort, without fatigue or suffering, not a creak to be heard in the frame; in heavy weather one is quite easy, there are none of the shocks which are so trying on steam-boats. How I should work, if the sea did not give me horror of work!

It is true that no sooner am I on land than the desire captures me again; and the proof is this long chapter which I dare not read, so great is my fear of finding it worthless. Others, in all probability, will be full of descriptions of events: a happy chapter this one, then, to be only full of my dreams.

ALEXANDRE DUMAS' STUDY

CHAPTER X

ROSES AND NIGHTINGALES

15th May, Evening

YESTERDAY, the 14th May, favoured by a good breeze, we arrived before Nice. I was calculating that within an hour or an hour and a half we should be in the roadstead, when I saw our mate Brémont, who listened to my calculations with his hand on the helm, shaking his head significantly.

"What is it, Brémont?" I asked him; "don't you agree with me?"

"Oh," said Brémont, "had I the wind for sale, I would give it for nothing."

"And you think that the wind will not be as generous as yourself?"

"I will not answer for what it will do, but I think that within a short time it will close its shop."

"You hear that, Captain?"

"I do."

"And your opinion is the same as his?"

"I am always of Brémont's opinion."

"Then we have another reason for making the most of the breeze."

"We *are* making the most of it."

"There is nothing to be said, Captain. We must await the event."

Indeed, not the slightest reproach could be made to the *Emma*. With a scarcely perceptible breeze, she had sailed three miles an hour; with a good one she had sailed nine, with the appearance of being able to sail ten or even eleven. She had passed in easy fashion all vessels going her way. She had distanced a cutter and come up with a felucca—the two kinds of craft which sail the fastest. But to this nothing more in praise can be added; as Brémont philosophically observed, she could not make a breeze when there was none. And, following Brémont's prediction, an hour later we had no breeze— or so little as not to be worth the mention. As we were more than three miles from Nice, it was sheer ill-luck.

I was vexed. I had been planning a surprise visit to Alphonse Karr;[1] and it was clear that, if we could not get in that evening, the next day, before we landed, all Nice would know of our arrival. On seeing this, the Captain ordered the lowering of two little boats to tow the yacht. It was humiliating for the yacht, but, as Brémont had expressed it, when there was no wind she could not make any.

---

[1] The famous novelist, publicist, and horticulturist had then been living at Nice for some four years.

Noticing our trouble, a pilot boat left the harbour and came to us.

As it was doing so, a craft—like unto the dragon-flies which, in the spring, flit over the water-lilies expanded on the surface of lakes—a little craft flitted about us.

She was rowed by two charming little fellows of about nine or ten; a man, whom I took to be their father, held the rudder. He was decorated with the Legion of Honour, and was a naval officer, I fancied.

Recognising in him a fellow-countryman, I thought I might speak to him.

"Monsieur," I asked him, "can you tell me whether I shall find Alphonse Karr at home?"

The officer rose.

"If he is not there now, it is since this morning," he replied, "for I spent last evening with him."

Then speaking to his boys—

"Salute M. Dumas," said he.

His boys, while still rowing, rose and saluted.

"You have a pair of charming oarsmen there," said I.

"I am bringing them up for the sea."

In the meantime the Captain, addressing himself to the pilot, asked him when the port closed.

"Usually at eight o'clock," replied the pilot, "but for M. Alexandre Dumas a little exception will be made."

It was truly fortunate that I had no reason for travelling *incognito*.

Reassured about our getting into port, I was able to resume my conversation with the officer and his boys, and, still conversing, we entered the harbour together.

It was a quarter-past eight. Fifteen minutes ago it should have closed, but, warned of our arrival by the pilot, the port was open.

During the formalities of landing, the officer and his two young oarsmen vanished.

No sooner was my foot on land than I asked where Alphonse Karr's house was.

"Is it to his shop or to his farm that you wish to go?"

I was perplexed—in a breath two things were told me of which I was ignorant. So Alphonse Karr had a shop and a farm.

"Where is the shop?" I asked.

"The shop is in the town," came the reply.

"And the farm?"

"Oh, the farm! That is different. It is outside the town." I thought that the best plan was to go to the nearest; besides, it was only half-past eight, and supposing the walk to take a quarter of an hour—

it was giving a margin for a town like Nice—we should be there at a quarter to nine, so perhaps I should find the shop open.

I was mistaken: the shop was shut.

We inquired the way to the farm, and were directed.

We found ourselves in a long lane closed in on both sides by high walls, on the tops of which glistened pieces of broken glass set in cement.

What was curious, seeing the precautions adopted against people climbing the walls, was the fact that the doors were open to all comers.

This contradiction—real or apparent—was explained to me next day by Alphonse Karr.

In Nice, unlike all other places, house owners, with a few exceptions, spend the summer in the town and the winter in the country. The reason is that in the summer no one visits Nice, while from the end of the autumn strangers abound there. The house owners leave their town domiciles towards October, and prepare them for letting (*pour les familles*). Then, as, generally speaking, the gardens are large ones, and the houses are at the farther end of the gardens, and consequently far from the doors, they are left open so as to save the trouble of going to open them. The families who come to spend the winter at Nice are informed of this custom, and so they take advantage of the doors being open to enter and view the gardens. If a garden pleases them, they knock at the house door. In this way, the landlords are not troubled except by callers with an object in view. (The custom of not closing the doors in the daytime is the cause of their being left open at night.)

We knew nothing about this custom; we were careful not to push one of these half-open doors, nor to pass inside one of the open ones.

No; on the contrary, we rang at a door which we found shut. I considered it too bad to disturb a good *Nicard*, or an honest *Nicarde*, merely to ask the direction; so I held myself aloof along with the most timid of the party. Two of my companions, however, braved the storm which I considered would fall on them.

The bell had rung once without result. It rang a second time still louder: we heard steps; we saw a light; the door opened.

I got farther into the angle of the wall, but all at once, after a "What do you want?" brusquely articulated by an individual with a lantern, I heard Legray utter a cry of surprise, and saw him leap into the man's arms.

Legray had recognised, in the man with the lantern, not merely a *confrère*, but a friend.

This *confrère* was Crette, the Legray of Nice.

Without knowing who the unknown man was, but reassured by his friendly demonstrations, I approached them. Soon the situation was clear. We thanked our stars that it had come about, and we ended by begging the gentleman to take us to Alphonse Karr, if he did not live too far off. He lived two hundred steps from M. Crette. It was doubly a matter of chance. The two hundred steps made, our guide stopped before a half-open door, pushed against it, and entered without hesitation.

It was a wondrous moonlight night.

In the moonlight we struck bravely into a path hedged on each side with roses, at the foot of which ran two streams in stone troughs.

The air was scented with the perfume of roses and oranges. Fire-flies, those flying sparks which glow in the air in the early days of a fine spring, glistened in the branches of the trees.

We went thus for perhaps two hundred steps, when all at once, on our right, we saw shining, on the other side of a sort of grove of rose-trees and a palisade of jessamine, the light of two windows of the house trying to pierce the shades of night.

Suddenly a strong and resonant voice asked, "Is that you, Dumas?"

I recognised the voice of Alphonse Karr, but I confess that the introduction of my name into his question astonished me.

"Yes, it is I," I answered, crossly enough at not having caused a greater surprise, "but how did you know?"

"I have been expecting you for two days," said Karr, coming out from the gigantic grove of roses, through the flowers and leaves of which filtered rays of light from the two windows.

We threw ourselves into each other's arms, exactly as Crette and Legray had done.

How is it that if two friends living in Paris—that is, in the same city, each having his own work to do, and, as a consequence, not seeing each other for a year, two years, three years, do meet by chance, they shake hands as calmly as if they had been together on the previous evening? If, on the contrary, one of these two friends goes abroad, leaving the other in Paris, and then the latter goes abroad also, and they chance to meet, it is a joy, a transport, an outpouring from the heart, such as to make one believe that, being united once again, they will be unable to separate. In France we are fellow-countrymen; in a foreign land we are brothers.

The embrace over, I looked at the grove from which Karr had appeared.

It was a veritable virgin forest of rose-trees, with roses of every colour as large as a baby's head, of leaves interlaced like bindweed, of jessamine with petals as big as periwinkles. Above this perfumed grove rose the house, draped in greenery, just like a woman of Arabia draped in her veil, having but the two holes for the eyes.

Two ladies were taking the air in this delightful arbour. They were introduced to me as members of my host's family. Then, in my turn, I introduced my companions.

"You know that everyone meets here for *déjeuner* to-morrow," said Alphonse Karr to our group.

Then, taking a candle, he said to me—

"Come and embrace someone who knows you and who loves you without having seen you."

I followed him up to the first floor. He led me into a little room all hung with white curtains, and in a bed, as white as the rest of the room, he showed me a charming little girl of seven or eight.

She was sweetly asleep. Over her closed eyelids I saw long black lashes, where, under the arch of beautifully pencilled brows, large and fine black eyes were ready to open. Her forehead seemed to me to invite the touch of the lips of the angels who watch over sleeping children.

It was not an angel who, sighing, bent over her, but a man with all a man's weaknesses and infirmities, a little less bad, perhaps, than most of his kind, but that is all.

"She murmured before going to sleep, 'If Dumas comes you will wake me, won't you, father?'" Karr said to me; "but, as you see, she is sleeping so soundly that it would be a sin to wake her."

"All the more so," I laughingly replied, "as she probably sees something in her dream which is better than anything she would see when she wakes."

"*Diable*," said Karr. "She would see a father who loves her, and a man who loves her father. Is that something which is seen every day, or even every night?"

Each took the hand of the other without saying anything, there, beside the bed of the sleeping child. Twenty years before her birth we had, for the first time, grasped hands, not so tenderly, but just as loyally. It is something to hold during a space of thirty years all that has been, and still is, great and good in France—the hands of Lamartine, of Hugo, of Méry, of Michelet, of Karr, of Delacroix, of Boulanger. It is only—and I say this with pride—it is only the hands of mediocre men, of envious men, of bad men that are strangers to mine.

We went downstairs. The mother waited for us smiling. She knew that the first words I should say would be—

"The sweet child!"

We seated ourselves in the wonderful arbour and chatted. There was but one discord in this harmony of fresh breezes, of clear sky, and of perfumes—it was the metallic and insistent croakings of frogs of the *reine verte* species which bellow like bulls.

"Wait," said Karr to me, looking at his watch, "I have not ordered the musicians until eleven o'clock; at present we have only the tuners."

A moment later eleven o'clock struck.

At that very moment, and as if by enchantment, the croaking of the frogs stopped, and from the grove next to ours burst forth the pure liquid notes of the king of songsters.

"Ah!" said I to Karr, "I understand why the rose lovers have come to live with you."

"Listen," said he. "He is ahead of Jeanne; she knew that you *were coming*, he knows that you *have come*. And he has two or three new airs that Amat[1] makes believe to have composed for him, and for which Banville[2] is going to write the words."

"What! Amat and Banville are here!"

"You will take *déjeuner* with them to-morrow. And, in the meanwhile, listen."

And, indeed, it was impossible to hear a more lovely symphony. Even the frogs seemed to be silent only to listen to it.

"Ah!" said I, at the nightingale's first pause, "what a happy idea of yours that was to leave France."

"It is because of it," he answered, laughing, "that France has come to find me."

"And now I think of it, what does Nice say of its reunion to France?"

"I will tell you later—it is so astonished that it has not had time to rejoice."

The conversation then took a more serious turn.

"And what about Garibaldi?" I asked him: Garibaldi's name came to be mentioned naturally enough, by reason of the reunion.

I had arranged with Garibaldi to meet him to finish his "Mémoires," begun with him at Turin.

In like measure as my departure for Marseilles approached with the leisureliness which naturally accompanies the preparations for a voyage to take a year or eighteen months—in like measure, I say, has my uneasiness increased. I had heard of Garibaldi's resignation as a general of the Sardinian service.

This resignation was given in these terms—

"Sire, I beg your Majesty to accept my resignation. I do not see why

[1] Paul Léopold Amat, the musical composer and singer.
[2] Théodore de Banville, the distinguished poet.

I should keep the title of general, and the pay which is mine in consequence, when there is no more fighting. Besides, I wish to be free, seeing that next spring I shall probably be making war on my own account."

And the King of Sardinia, in compliance with this singular request, had given Garibaldi his liberty.

Then the month of April went by. The month of April is the best month for making a campaign in Italy.

The spirit of adventure, in the pursuit of which I was engaged, should have found something better to do than to make me wait. Already, in fact, in Paris I had seen in a journal that Garibaldi had left Genoa for Sicily. That was very like Garibaldi; and a campaign in Sicily seemed to me truly one of those that a man like him makes on his own account. Consequently I had, that very moment, written to Vecchi, author of a fine history of the last Italian campaign, and he had replied, without giving me any explanation—

"Garibaldi is with me at the Villa Spinola, where we are thinking of you. Only, come quickly."

Two days after receiving this letter I left for Marseilles. There I found the same rumours about Garibaldi's departure.

I sent a telegram to Dr. Bertani—the Bertani who had followed Garibaldi in his campaign of '49 and in that of '59, the Bertani who had received the last sighs of Manara at Rome and of Bronzetti at Treponti—and the next day I received the following telegram from him—

"Garibaldi is still with Vecchi at the Villa Spinola, but come quickly."

Unfortunately I could not come quickly, however much I might have desired to do so, and I was obliged to remain a few days longer at Marseilles. Only I was convinced that one day or other, if he had not left already, Garibaldi would leave for Sicily. So when the Neapolitan Consul—following the laudable custom of Neapolitan Consuls—had refused a *visa* for Palermo and Messina, not only for my passport, but also for those of my companions, I contented myself by answering—

"Very well, I will have it signed by Garibaldi."

And he remained in a state of amazement, just as M. de Ludoff, twenty-five years before, was amazed when, after his refusal to give me a *visa* for Naples, I asked him whether he had no commissions for that city.

At last I read the news that Garibaldi had left for Sicily on the night of 5th to 6th May.

I had left on the 9th. I could not then have news of the illustrious *condottiere*—as he is called in France—when I reached Hyères, or Nice.

"But," said Karr to me, "if the *Patrie* is to be believed, it may be that he has been hanged as a pirate?"

"What? Hanged!"

"Just look at this." Karr handed me the *Messager de Nice*. "Read this official despatch from Naples—'Naples, 13th, in the evening.' "

I read—

"A despatch received by the Neapolitan Government announces that near Marsala two Neapolitan frigates fired on and killed some buccaneers. The steamer *Lombardo* has been sent to the bottom. The *Piemonte* has been damaged. The Royalist troops attacked the men that landed."

"Good," said I to him; "official despatch!"

"Well, what do you want better?"

"My dear friend, I greatly distrust official news ever since I read in the *Moniteur de Trieste*: 'Yesterday, at Magenta, we surprised the French, and in a bloody combat have completely beaten them. To-day, not a Frenchman remains on the soil of Lombardy.' The day after that on which 'not a Frenchman remains on the soil of Lombardy' we entered Milan, my dear Karr."

"Then you are not yet uneasy about Garibaldi?"

"No; and that is why I would like you now to read in the *Patrie* how it is that he should have been hanged by this time. Yesterday, to my face, the Brazilian Consul said of Garibaldi: 'He is a man who should be hanged!' 'Then why did you not hang him when he was in Brazil?' I asked."

CHAPTER XI

A PHILOSOPHER, A POET, AND A GARDENER

WE were in no danger of forgetting Alphonse Karr's invitation, and the next day at eleven o'clock were all with him. There, under the roses, we found the table already spread, and at the entrance to the arbour containing it were Banville, Leopold Amat and Bazancourt[1]—that is to say, Paris, represented by a poet, a composer, and a historian. How many of us sat down? I cannot say, but the table was as long as the arbour, and the arbour was a sort of long arcade. Before us lay the garden, of which, the previous evening, we had got a glimpse, only guessing at the flowers through our noses. And it is a wonder. Karr has really merited the title of gardener which I accused him of having usurped. Indeed, Alphonse Karr has had the honour, in his quality of gardener, of being visited by an Empress—an honour which she certainly would not have done him as a poet.

The story is really funny enough to deserve being related to you. You recollect what I told you about the high walls which protect the gardens of the house-owners who let their domiciles, and of the ever-open doors which allow the families to walk into those gardens.

You must know, then, that last year her Majesty the Dowager Empress of all the Russias was at Nice, towards the end of February, and, just then, Karr had splendid ripe strawberries. This was not all. He had fowls which gave him a constant supply of eggs.

Having become a gardener and a property owner, Karr made certain reflections respecting his strawberries and his eggs. As a *gourmet*, he asked himself why, with such wonderful sunshine and the miraculous fertility of the soil of Nice, one could only have wild strawberries which are found all over Italy—and none but those. I know very well that there are people who do not care to pay more than two sous for a plateful of strawberries and who say that those little ones are better than the cultivated types such as *Duchesse d'Orléans* and *Comte de Paris*, a plateful of which costs twenty-five or thirty sous. But Karr thought that as the people who come to Nice for the winter and spring are neither miserly nor needy, it would perhaps be a good speculation on his part to introduce into Sardinia (Nice was then a part of Sardinia) those fine large strawberries, full of sweet aromatic juice, produced originally a long time

[1] Baron Le Cat Bazancourt (1810–1865) was the author of a history of Sicily under the Normans and of many other works.

ago by Gabriel Pelvilain, the celebrated gardener of Meudon. Of these strawberries, Harpagon, as Karr said, could have offered a slice to each of his guests—supposing, that is, that Harpagon could ever have had guests. Now these plants, which in France do not fruit until June, give Karr—thanks to the pains he takes with them, pains seconded by the soil and the sun—berries at the end of February.

As regards eggs, this is what Karr thought—

"At Nice in winter eggs are not so scarce as at St. Petersburg, London, Vienna, or Paris, but, nevertheless, they are scarce. At Nice, moreover, the foreigners, who are mostly in search of health, and in such search collected in one spot, consume more fresh eggs than are boiled and eaten in any other given spot of equal size in the whole world. So, in the summer, new-laid eggs are laid up for keeping by artificial means, as is done everywhere. The scarcer new-laid eggs are, the dearer they are; and the dearer they are, the more delightful it is to sell eggs as new-laid when they are not new-laid. Now among a number of preserved eggs, even well-preserved ones—they are never as fresh as newly laid ones"—Karr had gone on with his cogitations—"there are some that are not preserved at all, from which it follows that they are so nearly being chickens that it would be more logical to roast them than to put them into boiling water. And so"—Karr was nearing the end of his reflections at this point—"and so, it seems to me that it would be good business to have, during the months of December, January and February (the period when eggs are at their dearest and worst), eggs respecting which the most malevolent of critics could not dispute the perfect freshness."

Consequently, in September, Karr had obtained fowls with the reputation of being the best layers in the county. He had placed them in the most splendid poultry-run that existed in that part of the world; he had put them on grass, as long as there was any; he had lavishly fed them on lettuce when the grass gave out. And the grateful hens had, even at the worst, given him from fifty to sixty eggs a day.

In this way, Karr had a fine lot of customers who were either devourers of strawberries or swallowers of eggs, or both. And among these customers of his was her Majesty the Dowager Empress of Russia, the widow of Nicholas I.

Let us add now that express orders had been given by Karr to his men on the farm to sell eggs and strawberries to the servants of the Empress at exactly the same price as to everyone else. The Empress found them so good that she longed to see, not the author of

"Les Guêpes," "Sous les Tilleuls," "Une Heure trop tard," "Gene-viève," "Clotilda," "Fa dièze," "La Pénélope Normande" and of twenty other stories, but the gardener who grew such fine straw-berries and who conjured from the fowls such large new-laid eggs.

Meanwhile, Karr had made the acquaintance of a Russian gentle-man who was intent on two things which had some analogy to the things on which Karr was intent when he was not engaged with literature, in the form of microscopical researches into the love affairs of plants and methods of teaching little children how to learn to read without wearying them.

On two occasions this Russian gentleman had casually said: "I think that some day or other the Empress will be coming to see your garden." Karr is well used to people coming to see himself in the first place, and his garden in the second. So that they should not come to see his garden as they came to see those of the people who let their houses to families, he had even taken certain precautions. Such precautions consisted in having had engraved on a small copper *plaque:* "*Monsieur Karr.*" This *plaque* he had placed on his garden door. To him, it seemed that the door-plate would, by the passers-by, by the visitors, and by the simply inquisitive people, be understood to say:

"Gentlemen, or ladies, pass on, I beg. If your concern is with my books, go to my publishers; if your concern is with my strawberries, my *petit pois* and my *haricots verts*, or my eggs, go to my shop. Here resides not Alphonse Karr, but M. Karr, a gentleman, a *bourgeois*, a peasant if you prefer, a man who cultivates his garden and covers paper with ink, but who, when not at work, knows how to do nothing as well as you do; a man who, by virtue of his rights as a citizen, has and claims the right to shut his door against everyone who is not a creditor—supposing him to have a creditor—to remain at peace by his fireside, and to see no one enter but friends and acquaintances. Not that he is regardless of occasions which induce certain people—unknown friends—to desire his acquaintance; but in such cases he wishes to be consulted and to be protected by the ordinary usages of polite society and good breeding."

So, when the Russian gentleman first observed to him: "I think that her Majesty will some day come to see your garden," our philosopher, who all his life has been very little changed by con-tact with the Great, contented himself with replying, "To say the truth, my dear friend, I should prefer her Majesty not to come. Nevertheless, if it be her intention to do me this honour, I will receive her with all the respects that are her due, but I repeat, my dear friend, that I should prefer it to be otherwise."

But when Prince —— had repeated with the same careless air: "I believe that her Majesty the Empress will some day come to see your garden," he saw that he had something to grasp which, as a Frenchman, prodigiously astonished him—it was that her Majesty the Empress believed that, because she bought strawberries at his shop and eggs at his farm, she had the right to walk into his garden as if she were walking into the Jardin des Plantes or the Brussels Zoological Garden.

Then Karr tried to make his prince understand that, in France, a French prince, or even a king, would not allow himself to walk into the house of the most humble peasant without having asked, or having had asked for him, that peasant's permission. Now there was nothing in the words "I think that her Majesty will some day come to see your garden" that was like asking permission.

At last he laughingly added: "Her Majesty the Empress is too well bred to come here without letting me know beforehand of the honour she deigns doing me." Then, as Prince —— said nothing further, Karr thought no more about it.

Now one fine day, as our philosopher was working in his garden with his men, one of them, who happened to be looking towards the great central walk, said to him:

"M. Karr, a number of people have come in."

"This is insupportable!" said Karr. "Are they women or men?"

"Most of them are women," was the man's reply.

Had they been men, Karr, who was not, perhaps, in the best of humours that morning, would have had something not very pleasant to say to them. But they were women, and, in his quality of Chevalier, Karr contented himself with stamping his foot, murmuring, "It is insupportable." And then he went indoors and shut himself up in his study, not so much to work as to devise a means of preventing similar invasions. He took up a book and lit a cigar.

This is what was happening in the garden, and especially under the arbour of roses of which I have spoken to you as an oasis come straight from paradise.

In the arbour were sitting three persons—one a lady of Karr's family, the Comtesse ——, her friend, and the Russian prince who had twice spoken of the intention of the Dowager Empress of all the Russias to visit Karr's garden.

Suddenly there appeared at one end of the arbour an old lady with a mild, aristocratic, melancholy expression. Karr's relative rose, made two steps towards her unknown visitor, and bowed. The lady passed by, stiffly erect, without taking any notice of her, and, having reached the other end of the arbour, left it, still in the same rigid silence. After her came a young man, and, like her, he passed by without bowing. After him came two ladies. They seemed to glance round as they went by, just as did the old lady, without bowing. After them came two more, then four more, and, in like manner, a regular *cortège*.

Observing the old lady's behaviour and that of her suite in copying it, Karr's relative sat down again by the Comtesse ——, who was as astonished as she was. Both turned simultaneously to question Prince —— about this procession of mutes; but, without saying anything, he had risen, and he, too, passed before them without speaking, and without bowing.

The two ladies were dumbfounded—the thing seemed like a pre-concerted game, with something at stake.

By and by, the last person in the *cortège* passed—it was a man; whether he was more polite than the others, or whether he was sure of being unseen by the Empress, I do not know, but he thought that he could allow himself to be polite, and he bowed. One bow, when there should have been eighteen, was not too much, as you see. One of the two seated ladies could not restrain herself from recognising this courteous act by saying: "This last gentleman appears to be better bred than the others."

At that moment one of the women who worked for Alphonse Karr appeared in the arbour in a great flutter, crying out:

"Mesdames, Mesdames, it is the Empress." The ladies were very surprised : neither knew her Majesty.

While all this was happening, Prince —— had disappeared round the first bush, after having made sure that the Empress had noticed him, and rushed into Karr's study, calling out:

"The Empress, the Empress, in the garden. Go down quickly—I say, quickly—to receive her."

"Has her Majesty asked leave—sent anyone to inform me of the honour that she deigns to do me?"

"She has done better, my dear Karr, she has come."

"Allow me to say to you she has, on the contrary, done worse, for she has exposed herself to something disagreeable for herself and for me—she has found me absent."

"How, absent?"

"Yes, absent, so that as I am not here I cannot receive her Majesty."

"My dear friend, I do not joke. Quick, quick! go down."

"As I am not here, I cannot do so. If her Majesty had let me know that she wished to visit my garden, it would have been very different. I would have stayed at home, not altogether because she is an empress, but because she is a woman. We Frenchmen are so polite to women that it is difficult for us to be more so to empresses."

"But—but, why do you not wish to go down when I come to tell you that the Empress is there?"

"Do you come on her behalf?"

"No."

"Then, I repeat, I am not going down, and if you do not understand why I stay in my study, I will tell you that it is because I give no one the right to walk in my garden without my permission."

Prince —— retired, astonished that a gardener, that a peasant, less than that, a poet, did not rush down his stairs when told that an empress had done him the honour to come within his gates, for whatever reason. I need hardly say that he took his place again in the *cortège*.

The next day Karr's woman went as usual with her basket of eggs and strawberries to the Empress's palace, when, to her exceeding surprise, she was told: "The strawberries and the eggs of Monsieur Alphonse Karr are too dear; indeed, her Majesty is not rich enough to afford them." The woman returned in tears; she was afraid that the refusal would be considered to be due to her fault. Alphonse Karr consoled her by saying that the fault was his own. But, as from that moment, he forbade anything more, "whether a pea or a bean," to be sold to the servants of her Majesty the Empress.

During the first day all went well; only the Empress ate little strawberries instead of big ones, and preserved eggs instead of new-laid ones.

Early the next morning a big fat woman rang lustily at Karr's door. On its being opened to her, she piteously stated that she came to ask an immense favour of M. Alphonse Karr. On hearing this, he ran downstairs four steps at a time. To moderate his speed, he was told that the woman was a common woman, but that only hastened him.

He saw the fat woman. She had red eyes, which she rubbed with a cotton handkerchief, a proceeding which made them redder.

"What is it, my good woman, and why do you rub your eyes so much?" he asked her.

"I rub my eyes, Monsieur Alphonse Karr, because my daughter is *enceinte*."

"It is a misfortune; above all, if your daughter is unmarried."

"Oh, my daughter is married, Monsieur."

"Well, then, all is right, if she is strong and well and nothing is going wrong with her. In any case, it is necessary to call, not on a gardener, but on an *accoucheur*."

"That is all right, sir, she is made like me, and I have had seventeen children."

"Then I don't follow as to what use I can be to you."

"Oh, a very great one, Monsieur Alphonse Karr, only I do not know how to explain it."

"Tell me, my good woman."

"Well, then, Monsieur, the poor dear has all sorts of fancies."

"That is often the way with women when they are not *enceinte;* so it is only reasonable it should always be so when they are."

"And mine has one which I am greatly afraid I cannot satisfy."

"What she wants is then beyond your means to supply, or is altogether an impossibility for you?"

"Ah, Monsieur, it is like this; the poor dear has seen the strawberries that are each morning carried from you to the Empress, and she longs for them. She longs for your strawberries—do you follow me?"

"*Diable!*"

"And, as you know, it is a terrible thing when a woman in her condition longs for something and cannot satisfy her longing: the baby is marked."

"I do not entirely share in that belief," said Karr.

"Ah, Monsieur, in our family that never fails to happen. My grandmother longed for grapes in a January, and she was marked with bunches of grapes from her neck down to her shoulder. My mother longed for a peach in a February, and she was marked with peaches from her waist to her hip. I, myself, Monsieur, longed for an apricot in a March, and I am marked with an apricot that——"[1]

Karr interrupted her.

"My dear woman," said he, "I believe in the longings, from having heard them so much talked about, but I have to criticise what you say about the way babies are marked."

"Monsieur Karr, would you like to see my apricot?"

"No, thank you, my good woman; I only wished to say to you that women in your daughter's condition have not only hankerings for grapes, peaches, apricots and strawberries, they also have hankerings for opera boxes, Cashmir shawls, either blue or green, and pairs of dapple-grey carriage horses, and I have never heard tell that a woman had on her skin a ticket of admission for a box, a Cashmir shawl of any colour whatsoever, or a pair of horses, whether dapple grey or dapple anything. There is, of course, the case of Pasiphaë, who had a child with a bull's head, but I believe that this misfortune happened to her not because she could not satisfy her longing, but, on the contrary, because she had done so."

[1] Why the *mothers* were "marked," the translator does not understand!

"Monsieur, my daughter's child will have strawberries all over her face; it is I who tell you so."

"I do not wish to be the cause of such a misfortune, my good woman," said Karr.

Then, to one of his own women:

"Give this lady a basket of strawberries exactly the same as for the Empress," said he.

"Ah! Monsieur Alphonse Karr, you save my life; for you know that grandmothers love their grandchildren more than mothers love their children. How much do I owe you, Monsieur Alphonse Karr?"

"Nothing at all, my good woman; I have given, not sold."

The "good woman" curtsied, and hastily retired, turning round now and again to bestow benedictions on Karr.

And she went at her best speed to sell the strawberries to the steward of the Empress—only, having paid so dearly for them (so she said), she made him pay double the usual price.

There was not a single word of truth in what she had so glibly told Karr. She was not married, but she was a retailer of vegetables. She had no daughter in a delicate condition, but she had promised the steward strawberries as fine as Karr's. Perhaps she had the apricot of which she had spoken, but it was strawberries and not an apricot for which the Empress wished.

Early the next morning, the steward arrived at Karr's. He wore a dress-coat and knee breeches, though it was only five o'clock.

He was in fault, in very great fault, for having refused Karr's eggs and strawberries. Yesterday, thanks to the stratagem of the good woman, he had procured strawberries, but he had not procured eggs, so that something had been wanting to the Empress for a whole twelve hours. He came now to apologise. When he had said that the eggs and strawberries were too dear, he had lied; and he was now ready to pay twice as much as before. When he had said that her Majesty was not rich enough to eat the strawberries and eggs of M. Alphonse Karr, he had permitted himself to joke in a manner unworthy of a steward of a banker, and therefore even more so of the steward of an Empress. He placed himself in M. Karr's hands—he would pay anything asked, but he must have them for the *déjeuner* of her Majesty the Empress.

This long speech was delivered, as will be understood, not to Karr, but to his work-people. Karr had given orders that under no pretext whatsoever was he to be troubled by any of the Empress's servants. Moreover, he had forbidden, as we know, anything being sold to them.

The steward retreated, tearing out his hair as he went. Great was his astonishment, therefore, when with a bowed head, handkerchief in hand and a watering eye, he dared to approach the Empress to tell her of the necessity on her part to put eggs and strawberries out of her imperial mind, and saw two eggs on her plate and a splendid basket of strawberries on her side table. *Alphonse Karr*, in his character of dealer in eggs and strawberries, had refused to sell them to the Empress, but *M. Karr* had been happy in the opportunity of giving her Majesty free, gratis and for nothing, strawberries, which were lacking in her garden, and eggs, which were wanting in her poultry-yard. He had gone further; Alphonse Karr, the poet, had joined in the gift, and the Empress had found these four verses amongst her eggs and strawberries:

> *"Nice de son climat, peut-être, un peu trop fière,*
> *Idoltâre, au soleil rend un culte fervent,*
> *Aujourd'hui, convertie, elle adore le vent*
> *Qui sur ses bords fleuris vous retient prisonnière."*

And during all the time that the Empress remained at Nice, she had, by the courtesy of Alphonse Karr, the eggs and strawberries which she could not do without. Moreover, on the day of her departure, she received a double-sized basket, so that she could eat one half at her *déjeuner* and enjoy the remainder on board her ship.

I have forgotten to ask Karr if the Empress paid a second visit to his garden and thanked him verbally.

Poor princes! They are so badly brought up that it is necessary for gardeners, peasants, poets—that is to say, persons who pass as being the most sadly brought up in all the world—to give them lessons in politeness.

I need not say that we had at *déjeuner* some of these famous eggs and famous strawberries—but as *hors d'œuvres*. I question whether the steward of the Empress of all the Russias, in spite of his dress-coat and knee breeches, often gives to his illustrious sovereign, under the gilt ceilings of her Winter Palace or in her châlet de Selagin, dinners equal to those given by Karr under his roses.

An unexpected event doubled, and in its sequel tripled, the number of guests.

Nice has two *théâtres français*. The *artistes* of both theatres, knowing of my arrival, and knowing of the *déjeuner* which Karr was giving me under the roses, asked his permission to pay me their compliments at his place. Karr, I need hardly say, threw his double doors open. The two *troupes* arrived, each with its director at its head. And so it was that we were sixty in number for a brief time under the roses, each holding his brimming glass of champagne and clinking it with a "bon voyage."

8

But wait, this is the most curious part of the story. I was sitting next the Comtesse Apraxin. After having clinked her glass against mine, she had the idea—I was going to say the fantasy—of taking her diamond ring from her finger and of asking me to engrave my initials on her glass, requesting Karr's permission to take it away with her. The permission was given, be it understood, and I engraved the two letters in my best manner. But the fantasy of the Comtesse Apraxin was contagious, so that each one, having caught it, asked Karr for his permission to take his glass away, and begged me to engrave an A and D. The result was that Karr supplied not only five-and-twenty bottles of champagne consumed in the glasses, but also the glasses from which it had been drunk.

But here comes the best part of the story. A farmer, a gardener, a poet can have in his cellar, without reckoning other wines, twenty-five, fifty, a hundred, two hundred bottles of champagne, but he has not sixty champagne glasses among his glass ware. The consequence was that, as the wishers of "bon voyage" agglomerated, Karr sent to borrow glasses, at first from his neighbour on his left, then from his neighbour on his right, then from his neighbour opposite him.

So that it was not only Karr's glasses that I had to engrave and that were carried off, but also those of his neighbours. How he got out of the situation caused by this annexation of property, God alone knows.[1]

To-morrow we take our *déjeuner* at Monaco ; half of us go by carriage, half on the yacht. I have invited my two little oarsmen of yesterday— the charming halcyons who guided me into the port of Nice—to join us, as also their father, Captain R . . ., in the maritime part of the expedition. I ask your permission not to speak to you about Monaco on this occasion, presuming that for you and also for me I have said enough about it in my book entitled "De Marseille à Florence."

Léopold Amat leaves expressly this evening to order the *déjeuner*. We shall therefore fare well, which is the principal thing.

I was forgetting to tell you that Crette and Legray together have made two or three delightful photographs of the arbour of roses and the guests sheltered by it, also of our host and of charming little Jeanne, whose forehead, as she slept, I kissed last evening.

As soon as I awoke I was, I admit, much flattered to hear her answer to her surname of *Mohican*, which her father had given her in honour of my book called " Les Mohicans de Paris."[2]

[1] In his "La Mer de Nice" (Paris, 1861), Théodore de Banville gives a delightfully written account of this *déjeuner* and of his subsequent visit to the *Emma*, which he found a miracle of perfection in every detail.

[2] One of Dumas' great romances, then recently published. He himself figures in it as one of the characters, that of Jean Robert.

ALEXANDRE DUMAS

Geoffroy   *Pinx. et Sc.*

CHAPTER XII[1]

THE VILLA SPINOLA

On the 16th of May at four o'clock in the afternoon, the wind being favourable, we took leave of Alphonse Karr and Amat—that is to say, of France; we returned to the yacht and sailed for Genoa, where we arrived on the morning of the 18th.

About Genoa I have nothing to tell you, having visited it perhaps some thirty or forty times already. I know it as I do the rue de Saint-Denis, and am known in it as I am known on the boulevard Saint-Martin. But, at Genoa, I wanted to ascertain what had become of Garibaldi. On this subject there were various rumours. The town talked of nothing but the expedition; each person, in the absence of reliable news, gave that which most flattered either his imagination or his desire. What stood out clearly in all this was that Garibaldi had landed at Marsala in the midst of some cannon shots fired by two Neapolitan vessels, the *Stromboli* and the *Capri*, and had immediately taken the road to Palermo. Beyond this nothing was certain.

Primarily, I had come to Genoa for the purpose of writing the conclusion of the "Mémoires de Garibaldi"[2]—I should perhaps say, of the first part; for, at my hero's rate of progress, his exploits promise to provide material for a long series of volumes.

Garibaldi had left on the night of the 5th to 6th of May; but before his departure he left notes for me with Vecchi,[3] and begged Bertani, Sacchi, and Medici to give me the remaining details for the "Mémoires," as he had not had time to write them himself. As a result, I am now installed at the "Hôtel de France," where I am working sixteen hours a day—a proceeding which does no violence to my daily habits.

The only other authentic communications at my disposal were a letter written by Garibaldi to Bertani—a copy of which I am going to give you, and two others written to Colonels Sacchi and Medici respectively.

The letter to Sacchi was merely to tell the Colonel how much he

[1] This and the succeeding chapters contain details of great interest to students. Dumas' information, derived, as it was, from Vecchi, must, in general, be accepted as correct.
[2] 2 vols., Paris, 1860.
[3] Augusto Vecchi, the veteran soldier, one of Garibaldi's dearest friends. Dr. A. Bertani, Garibaldi's agent in Genoa. Colonel Gaetano Sacchi who had followed Garibaldi in every campaign since 1842. General G. Medici, one of Garibaldi's best advisers, and a fine soldier.

regretted his inability to accept the offer of his services. Sacchi wished to send in his resignation of his commission in the Sardinian army, in order that he might follow Garibaldi, whose standard-bearer he had been in Monte Video; but the General has already told us that he is waging war on his own account; and that, in order not to compromise King Victor Emmanuel by this expedition, which might end in a failure, he has refused to take with him any Sardinian officer or soldier.

So you see the letter alleged to have been written to King Victor Emmanuel by Garibaldi, just before his departure for Sicily, is entirely apocryphal. Neither directly nor indirectly has the King been made aware of the projects or departure of the General.

I have read both the letter to Sacchi and the letter to Medici. The latter was simply intended to console the recipient for being left behind at Genoa; "but at Genoa," added Garibaldi, "you can be more useful to the expedition than in Sicily."

And, as a matter of fact, it is Medici who is preparing two expeditions at Genoa: the first is a steam-boat, which left yesterday, with 150 men and 1000 muskets on board; and the second will consist of two other steam-boats, which are to leave in a few days carrying 2500 volunteers, with arms and ammunition.

The two vessels have been bought at a cost of 700,000 francs. Medici, who will command both, is enrolling volunteers daily. The funds are supplied by subscriptions raised in all the principal towns of Italy, and at the present moment exceed 1,000,000 francs.

I have already spoken of the letter sent to Dr. Bertani, to whom, along with La Farina, Garibaldi has entrusted the management of these funds; here it is:

Genoa, 5th of May, 1860.

"DEAR BERTANI,[1]

"Called once again to the scene of events of national importance, I leave to you the following mission: to get together all available means of assisting us in our enterprise, and to make Italians understand that it is only by mutual aid and devotion that Italy will become a nation, and this in but a short time and at little cost. Make them realise that they will not have done their duty if they limit their efforts to a subscription—which is sterile unless backed by action; that Italy, now nearly free, ought to have, not 100,000 soldiers, but 500,000, a number certainly not disproportionate to its population, and one which would only equal the army of neighbouring states which have no need to fight for their independence. Let Italians realise that with such an army they will not need foreign patrons who, little by little, eat up the resources of our country under a pretence of helping it; and that wheresoever Italians are fighting against their oppressors, the brave must be encouraged, and everything provided to help them on their way to join us, for the Sicilian insurrection ought to be aided not only on the spot, but wherever there are any enemies to fight. I never advised the insurrec-

---

[1] This letter is not quoted by Mr. Trevelyan in his "Garibaldi and the Thousand." In connection with this and similar foot-notes the reader will bear in mind Mr. Trevelyan's limitations of space.

tion in Sicily, but I considered it my duty to help my fellow-countrymen as soon as hostilities began. Let our battle-cry be, 'ITALY AND VICTOR EMMANUEL'; and I hope that once more the Italian banner will not suffer shame.

"Yours affectionately,
"G. GARIBALDI."

I saw it would be necessary to go to the fountain head for the details of Garibaldi's stay in Genoa, so I set off for the Villa Spinola, Vecchi's country house, situate two leagues from Genoa, where Garibaldi had spent the month that preceded his embarkation, and from just below which he had sailed. I felt that I should there find some forgotten biped, who would tell me more than the general run of Genoese news-mongers could.

What I did find was the master of the house himself, my old friend Vecchi, who had been left at Genoa with Medici and Bertani, the chief organiser of this sublime affray which was going once again to decide the great question of popular right *versus* right divine. Vecchi did not know anything more than did the others about the results obtained, but what he knew better than they, was what had happened at his house from the time of Garibaldi's arrival until that of his leaving. The recital seemed to me so curious, not only from the picturesque view-point, but also from the historical one, that I resolved to spend two or three days in his house—more even, if necessary—the better to gather all the anterior details of the expedition.

As regards the expedition, my fixed intention was to join it as soon as possible, so that I could see all with my own eyes, and thus mingle my recital with action.

Here, then, is the story of the events which preceded this heroic enterprise, written on the very spots where they occurred, and dictated by one of the principal actors in the great political drama—a recital which we put under the eyes of our readers, so that they may see it all unroll, whatever be its changing fortunes, whatever the *dénouement*, from the beginning to the end.

Having reached Genoa on the evening of the 14th April, 1860, Garibaldi, the next morning, went to the Villa Spinola, where he knew he would find Vecchi, his old comrade in the war of 1849, of which he is the faithful and polished historian.

Vecchi's coachman recognised the unexpected visitor afar off, and ran up the stairs, four steps at a time, to his master's room, calling out:

"The General! The General!"

In Italy, when anybody shouts, "The General!" it means General *Garibaldi*, as if there could not be in Italy any but one general. Vecchi, therefore, had no need for any explanation as to who was his guest. He came down in all haste, and appeared at the door of the Villa at the moment that Garibaldi reached the door of the courtyard.

"Now that Nice belongs to Italy no longer, my dear Vecchi," said the General, "I am like Jesus Christ; I have no longer a stone on which to lay my head. You are the richest of my apostles, that is why I come to ask for your hospitality."

"The house and its master are yours, General; do what you will with both."

"Good," said Garibaldi, "but Jesus Christ is not alone. He has with him his military establishment."

"The house of his apostle is large enough to receive his eleven associates."

"Happily, for the moment, they are reduced to five," said Garibaldi.

"Their names?"

"Fruscianti,[1] Elia,[1] Stagnetti, Gusmaroli[1] and Menotti."

Menotti is Garibaldi's son.

"There is room for all," said Vecchi.

"Show me," said the General.

And only then crossing the courtyard, he embraced his host and entered the house with him.

They went up to the first floor, where the inspection began, the ground floor being devoted to the kitchen and vestibule.[2] The first floor consists of an ante-room, a dining-room, a small *salon*, a large bedroom, a dressing-room, and a small bedroom. The large bedroom was to be the General's, the small one his son's. The others went up to the second storey. It consisted of five rooms. One was already occupied by Vecchi, the four others were allotted to the four disciples, who, thereupon, took possession.

Vecchi, who had left the General in his room, now went down and found him enjoying a wash—the first thing he does when he calls a halt. While undressing, he had put his purse on the table. Vecchi took it up and tossed it in the air. He found it very light, and productive of little jingle.

"*Diable!* General," said he, "you are a rich man, it appears."

"I agree," replied Garibaldi, "for I have enough to live on for a week."

Vecchi believed that the coins in the purse were of gold. He

---

[1] Dumas spells these names Fruscinanti, Elias, Guzmaroli. Mr. Trevelyan in his "Garibaldi and the Thousand" does not mention the presence of these men at the Villa.

[2] Mr. Trevelyan states that only the first floor was occupied.

opened it and emptied it into his hand. It contained four francs thirty centimes. It was on this sum that Garibaldi considered he could live for a week.

They went down for a meal, and when this was over, went to play at bowls. One of the General's weaknesses is to believe that he is excellent at the game!

At dinner, as if the amphitryon had desired to prophesy the place of landing, Vecchi had put a bottle of Marsala before the General—a useless extravagance, as he drinks water only. But he had on his left and right two neighbours who did not detest Marsala; one was Vecchi, the other was Cattina.

Let us tell you briefly about Cattina. Cattina is a red, blue, green, and yellow parrot, a native of Rio de Janeiro, the scene of the General's first exploits. Vecchi bought her for thirty francs from a sailor of Nervi, and when he and his housekeeper were asked her name, the parrot said twice:

"Cattina! Cattina!"

"Cattina, let it be," said Vecchi.

The General and Cattina understood each other perfectly from the very first. Before the General touched anything on his plate, she had her share. At three o'clock in the afternoon the General has some fruit, alone in his bedroom. Immediately Cattina saw Fruscianti coming with it, she used to climb down from her perch, then making her presence known by her cry of "Cattina," crossed the sitting-room, and, at the heels of Fruscianti, entered the bedroom.

On the first day, the General threw the quarter of an apple on the floor, but, as if she was offended by such lack of manners, she would not look at it. She then began to climb up the General's leg, and, on reaching his knee, uttered the little cry habitual with her when pleased. Garibaldi picked up the piece of apple and offered it ceremoniously to Cattina, who swallowed it whole. From that day complete harmony reigned between Cattina and the General.

Cattina arrogated to herself a right which was not even Fruscianti's —that of interrupting the General in his most profound meditations.

Of what was the General thinking, when his gaze became fixed, when his brow became clouded, when his hat was lowered over his eyes? We shall see presently.

On the 6th of April the insurrection of the 4th at Palermo was known by means of a telegram. Later, I shall tell you all about the hero of this rising, whose name was Riso.[1] Crispi was at the moment at Genoa.

[1] Francesco Riso, a plumber, who was inspired by Baron Riso.

I have written the name Crispi[1] and, in doing so, I have recorded that of one of the most intelligent men in the Two Sicilies—an exile since 1849, who, after having lived successively in France, England, and Piedmont, had returned to Genoa at the conclusion of a second journey made in Sicily for the purpose of feeling the pulse of public opinion and preparing the revolution. During these two journeys, at the risk of being shot, or, what is much worse, hanged, he had, with false passports, traversed Sicily in every direction—the first time under the name of Emmanuele Pareda, and the second under that of Glivais. In the course of these journeys he had fanned whatever living sparks remained of the conflagrations of 1848 and 1849. Like everyone else, he learnt the news: he hastened to Bertani, with whom was Bixio[2]—those two other apostles of Garibaldi. Two months before, Crispi and Rosolino Pilo[3]—the latter is more than an apostle, he is a martyr—had obtained from Garibaldi the promise that immediately the Sicilian revolution should break out the General would put himself at the head. After an hour's conversation with Bertani, Crispi and Rosolino Pilo left for Turin, where they knew the General to be. On the 6th April at eight o'clock in the evening the two friends reached the Hôtel Grande Bretagne; but the General had left it, and was living at 57 rue Sainte Thérèse, so they went on there. Contrary to his custom, the General, who usually goes to bed very early, had gone out. Fruscianti was in the house alone. Bixio stayed with him, while Crispi went to find Garibaldi. Two hours later, Crispi returned and found the General in bed, taking his supper, consisting of a biscuit steeped in coffee. He listened with evident joy to what they told him of the revolution at Palermo; then, after he had finished his biscuit and his coffee, he sent them away, giving them an appointment for the next day at noon.

That day the General went to the English minister, Sir James Hudson,[4] who confirmed the news, and gave him an assurance of the sympathy of England for the cause of Sicilian revolution.

At noon the meeting took place as arranged. The General ordered Crispi to go to Milan to inquire for muskets that were stored there, and for money which had been contributed with a view to military operations. Meanwhile, Bixio was to return to Genoa and procure a steamboat with which to make the embarkation; and Garibaldi,

---

[1] Francesco Crispi (1819–1901), the celebrated statesman. He is usually considered to have planned the Sicilian revolt of 1859–60.

[2] Nino Bixio, Dumas' old friend, with whom he had fought in the streets of Paris in 1830. Bixio's character may well have been in Dumas' mind when he wrote "The Three Musketeers."

[3] Pilo was Mazzini's agent.

[4] Dumas calls the Minister "Sir Hudson."

having made an interpellation in the Chamber[1] as arranged, would then go to Genoa also.

Crispi returned there three days later. He had obtained from Besana, who had the rifles, the promise to send them to Genoa at an opportune moment with the money. Finzi,[2] Besana's partner in the great work of the collection of subscriptions for the Million Rifle Fund, was away.

Crispi no sooner had arrived in Turin than he went to rue Sainte Thérèse, although it was ten o'clock at night. He found the General in bed studying the Sardinian constitution, to see whether he could find a means of attacking Cavour. The General renewed his promise to rejoin Crispi at Genoa as soon as his interpellation was made.

On the 10th, Crispi left Turin, and, on reaching Genoa, found Bixio, who had arranged with Fauché[3] to surprise at a given moment two boats of the Rubattino Company.

Five or six days went by, without any news coming from Milan either of the money or the rifles. Meanwhile, Garibaldi, faithful to his promise, came to stay with Vecchi, but seeing that nothing came, he ordered Crispi to return to Milan. There, Crispi learnt that the rifles were ready, but that an order had been given to Arnolfo, colonel of the Carabineers, not to let them leave the city. Crispi returned to Turin to beg M. Cavour to remove the difficulty; but he was with King Victor Emmanuel in central Italy. Finzi then went to M. Farini with the same request, but he replied that he could not take such a decision on himself, and that it was a matter for arrangement between Cavour and Garibaldi personally. Now, the General knew Cavour to be absolutely opposed to the expedition to Sicily, which, to him, was a mere dream.

Such, then, were the divers pieces of news which caused Garibaldi's meditations; and at such times Cattina[4] alone had the right of audience.

---

[1] At Turin.   [2] Dumas spells the names Fensi and Bisana.
[3] Fauché was the paid agent of the Rubattino Company.
[4] Cattina certainly deserved to be immortalised by Dumas, whose fondness for birds induced him to keep a vulture! *Vide* his charming book: "Histoire de mes Bêtes."

CHAPTER XIII

THE ANNIVERSARY OF THE 30TH APRIL

NEVERTHELESS, Vecchi one day violated his instructions; and on that day he found the General sad.

"What is amiss, General?" he asked.

"You must recognise," said Garibaldi, replying to his own thought rather than to the question, "that King Victor Emmanuel has not our education."

"*Our education!*" repeated Vecchi, laughing; "his father, nevertheless, was richer than were our fathers, and was able to give his son an education at least as good as ours."

"You do not understand me," said the General, shaking his head. "I am saying that he has not received the education of sorrow; he has not suffered as we have done; he has not been in exile as we have; he has not, like us, spent whole days fruitlessly trying to find a bit of bread." Then, with a sigh, he added: "And that is what he lacks; if he had it, it would be too much happiness for us, too splendid for Italy." He paused, and then went on with an accent of deep melancholy: "Nevertheless, I said to him 'Sire, if you wish, in six weeks, you and I can remake Italy; rid yourself of this diplomat who ties your hands, and then we will go forward.' "

"And what did he reply?" Vecchi asked.

"He did not reply, and that is what maddens me." Then the General continued, as if speaking to himself: "Nevertheless, if he does not any longer hear, I still hear the cry of sorrow which comes at once from the east and from the south, from Venice and from Palermo."

And he let his head fall on his breast again.

Vecchi remained for a moment before him, but seeing that he kept silence, went away. He knew what gigantic projects sometimes resulted from these reveries. It should be added, however, that few of those about Garibaldi were in favour of the expedition to Palermo, and Vecchi, perhaps, less than anyone. Crispi and Bixio, its great promoters, were looked on as mad. Bixio, unable to endure this state of uncertainty, felt that the longer the delay the more likely was the matter of the boats to get abroad; and, pressed on by a natural impatience of character which almost amounts to impetuosity, Bixio broke the ice.[1]

One day he went to the General's room and said to him:

[1] Bixio's friends would have smiled on reading this. His "impetuosity" approached delirium.

"Now, General, we are here with the object of doing something; what are we doing?"

"And what means have you of doing anything?" the General asked.

"Have we not subscriptions for the Million Rifle Fund?"

"Yes: look here," said the General, "here is where the subscriptions are."

And he showed him Crispi's letter reporting Finzi's reply, and his unsuccessful visit to Farini.

"Well, let us leave the rifles and the money at Milan. Just say a word, and all purses and hearts will be opened."

Garibaldi shook his head. He was in a mood of discouragement.

"Well," said Bixio, desiring to wound the General's feelings so as to remove his apathy, "give leave to Crispi and myself to do what you do not wish to do, and we will start at once. If the thing turns out well, you will join us; if we are shot, you will say, 'They died for Italy, like so many others,' and our funeral oration will have been delivered."

"Wait until Friday," said Garibaldi.

It was on Fridays that the boat used to arrive from Palermo, and the General impatiently awaited Fridays for news.

Crispi's impatience for their arrival was no less, but their news did not suffice: he made his own news.[1] According to him, the insurrection was of gigantic proportions, extending from Palermo to Messina, from Girgenti to Milazzo. The telegrams, thus corrected, revised, and augmented, were sent to Turin, and, strangely enough, were reproduced even by the journals of M. Cavour, which were antipathetic to the insurrection.

Fridays apart, the days succeeded each other monotonously. Each morning the General rose a little before daybreak. Fruscianti, once a monk, as Gusmaroli was once a curé; Fruscianti, who unites the duties of a valet with those of telling him unpleasant truths; Fruscianti, one of the bravest of *aides-de-camp* on the battlefield, and one of the most devoted servants in the house, brought him his cup of coffee. The General loves good coffee; while drinking it he experiences a moment of sensual enjoyment that no other drink gives him; this moment of well-being belongs entirely to Fruscianti; it is his recompense. It is only men like Garibaldi who have such devotion offered to them.

After he had drunk his coffee, the General dressed, and, followed by Fruscianti and Gusmaroli—who appeared on the horizon as

---

[1] As Dumas' information came from Vecchi this statement is very interesting. Mr. Trevelyan says that it is "not proved" that Crispi forged the telegrams.

regularly as the morning star—used to ascend Mount Fasce, after walking through the little village of l'Apparition. This morning walk was taken with the object of combating rheumatism contracted in the pampas, which, if left unconquered, he feared would then take sides against Italy. Two hours later, he would return in a sweat and change everything he had on.

On one day only did he fail to take his morning walk:[1] it was the anniversary of the 30th of April—the day of General Oudinot's attack on Rome.

That day, Vecchi, who is as late as the General is early, and has all the habits of the sybarite, rose at three o'clock in the morning and went into the General's room at the moment he was stretching his leg out of bed.

"Hallo! what is it?" he asked, astonished by this apparition. "Is the house on fire?"

"No, General, but to-day is the anniversary of the 30th April."

The memory of this combat, in which Garibaldi held in check the French—that is to say, the first soldiers in the world, as he himself calls them—is most agreeable to the General. He has won the victories of San Antonio, of Varese, of Treponti, of Calatafimi, of Milazzo, of Como, of Volturno; but, as he says himself: "On those days I had only to fight the Americans, the Austrians, the Neapolitans, the Croats, but on the 30th of April I had to fight the French, and I am prouder of having resisted them than of having conquered the others."

History herself will not have a more real admiration for the soldiers of France than has Garibaldi. So, on this day, it was decided to have a celebration; and, to begin it, they were to go to Nervi by the old road of the Genoese republic, which—we speak of the road— is the most execrable of any in the world; but at the turning into the royal road from Nervi to Quinto, the General, fearing recognition by the sailors or captains who had navigated with him, or had seen him in America, turned homewards. Nothing is more distasteful to Garibaldi than the ovations which are the ambition and the joy of the vulgar.

On retracing his steps, he met five or six little children who were on the way to school with their satchels slung across their shoulders. Two of them looked pale and sickly. They passed the little group, but after having gone four or five steps, the General, who has never met a sufferer without trying to help him—by his consolations,

---

[1] Mr. Trevelyan states, on the contrary, that Garibaldi seldom went outside the wall of the enclosure, "for all around lurked spies and busybodies."—"Garibaldi and the Thousand," p. 181.

when he had nothing else to give—the General turned, and looking at the two sick children,

"Poor things!" he murmured, with a gesture of pity.

Then, going to them, he took up the sickliest looking of the two, and lifting him up to the level of his own face said: "Grow up to be a support for Italy; seek to be its glory. You have a great country, be yourselves as great as she, and may God give you the happiness of turning out the vermin which devour it." Then he gave them two *mezze mute* (a small Piedmontese coin worth twenty centimes), which, with the alms already bestowed, represented the balance of the four francs thirty centimes which he had when he arrived at Vecchi's.

A little further on, they sniffed the aroma of coffee. It came from a ground-floor apartment open to the street, in which a sailor's wife was roasting some coffee in an iron cylinder.

Garibaldi, attracted by the perfume, went in.

"Madame, are you selling your coffee?"

"No, I am preparing it for my family."

The General inhaled the aroma.

"General," said Vecchi, "may I make you known? In two minutes your cup will be ready."

"No, no, no," cried Garibaldi, hastening out.

On entering the Villa they found Ripari, to-day doctor-in-chief of the Southern Army, who, with Nino Bixio, was waiting for the General.

They sat down to *déjeuner*, and each at every turn introduced the 30th of April into his conversation. At dessert, while Vecchi, who was fond of sweet things, was not looking, the General filled his cup of coffee with sugar.

Vecchi, on tasting it, complained that he had made syrup of it.

"Bah," said Ripari, "it is the 30th of April."

This joke produced more effect than Ripari had intended. Vecchi choked, and got a bit of sugar across his wind-pipe. He sprang up, rushed out of the room, and fell on the threshold of the General's bedroom.

Bixio heard him fall, and rose; but the General was first, and on reaching Vecchi, whose face was scarlet, he emptied a bottle of water over his head.

Vecchi then swallowed the sugar. He was saved.

With his ordinary gravity, the General felicitated his friend on the happy issue of the event. "Nevertheless," said he, "you see, gentlemen, on what a man's life depends. I forbid you to speak again, to-day, of the 30th April." The order was obeyed.

During the afternoon Garibaldi took the apostles with him for a walk, and it was then, in all probability, that he chose the place of the embarkation.

At dinner all Garibaldi's friends were present—Bixio excepted. He came in during the meal, looking greatly cast down. Everyone realised that something grave had occurred.

"What is it?" all the guests asked.

"Bad news," said Bixio, and taking a paper from his pocket, he read it aloud. It was a telegram from the captain of the *Governolo*, the Marquis d'Aste, which announced from Palermo that all was over in Sicily, and that the Bourbon troops were the masters of the situation.

Garibaldi, in the midst of a dead silence, rose, slowly raised his glass above his head, and then uttered these words of mourning:

"To our dead friends, and to those who have caused their death!"

Then, by common consent, each left the table, and silently retired.

The servants extinguished the lights, and at ten o'clock that night the Villa Spinola was silent as the tomb.

BUT Crispi watched.

The next day a special despatch arrived which announced that if the revolution was repressed in the city, it had taken refuge and lived in the mountains. Then something occurred which re-animated the General's courage: it was the sight of the arrival of volunteers from all sides. In truth, the Villa Spinola became, little by little, the *rendezvous* of all the patriots. Besides Medici and Bixio, who lived at Genoa, Sirtori,[1] Simonetta and Besana had come from Milan; Manin[2] from France, Crispi, at the beginning, from London, and Cairoli from Pavia.

A word about this family, which seemed transported from antiquity into our time. During the war of 1859 Madame Cairoli brought her four sons to Garibaldi, who was then at Corsi, where he was organising the Alpine Bersaglieri. They were named Ernesto, Enrico, Luigi and Benedetto. They went through that campaign, in which Ernesto fell gloriously at Varese, struck by an Austrian ball. The three survivors returned to their mother after the Peace of Villafranca. When the eldest, Benedetto,[3] learnt that Garibaldi was at the Villa Spinola, he suspected that his stay there was the prelude of some great patriotic enterprise, and, without saying anything to his mother, left Pavia and came to put himself at the General's disposal. The General received him as his own son. After *déjeuner*, the new arrival left for Genoa with Menotti. He just missed seeing his mother on the road. This noble woman had guessed where he had gone. She at once took the train for Genoa, and from there drove to the Villa Spinola. Garibaldi, seeing her enter suddenly, went to her and embraced her.

"You have seen my son, have you not? The naughty boy has not had faith in his mother. Well, to confound him, I have come to offer you my second son. Only, do not forget that I am a mother, leave me the youngest one."

The General took her hands; tears were in his eyes.

She looked round.

---

[1] One of Garibaldi's best advisers and soldiers.
[2] The creator and defender of the Venetian Republic of 1848.
[3] "Benedetto, who alone of his brothers survived the heroic era, though not for lack of exposing himself in the forefront of Garibaldi's wars, became Prime Minister of the country ransomed by their blood."—"Garibaldi and the Thousand," p. 95.

"You are looking for him?"

"Yes; where is he? so that I may scold him."

The General gave her the address of her son. He had gone to one of the poorest hotels in Genoa, the Hotel Roseghino, where she found him sitting at table with Menotti and Elia, eating a dish of *ravioli*.

Ever since, the General has called Madame Cairoli, "Cornelia, the Mother of the Gracchi."

Of her two children, the one who fled from home was wounded in his leg at Calatafimi. This was Benedetto, the eldest of this glorious family, which has deserved so well of the country. He was captain of the seventh Company, which, on the battlefield, Garibaldi baptised with the name of "The Company of Honour."

Enrico, whom she had brought with her, was wounded in the head on the day of the 27th at the entry into Palermo; and, by decree of the *pro-dictator* Mordini, he was made major, and was given leave to go to Pavia, where his mother lived, to convalesce.

Luigi, the third, whom she had kept at home, looked on this as being shameful, and, in his turn, he escaped; he was as the General's Benjamin. The poor lad, worn out when he reached Naples, contracted typhoid fever, from which he died on 17th September.

"*Fortes nascuntur fortibus et bonis.*"

Every day new volunteers presented themselves. Two peasants arrived one day from Pondebba, a village of 1400 inhabitants, built on the bank of the river which is the boundary at Frioul and Carinthia. On one side of the river Venetian was spoken, on the other side German: since Austria has occupied a part of Italy, not a single instance of friendship or of trade has been recorded. On one bank of the river you have Italy, on the other Germany; on the one side the South, on the other the North.

These two peasants came without a sou in their pockets from remotest Frioul, to offer their services to the General. Both could read and write—a rare thing in Italy. To amuse themselves on the journey, they had read a little book for children, answering to our fairy tales, entitled "Bertoldo, Bertoldino, and Cacasenno." The eldest of the two was twenty-four years old. They asked for Major Vecchi. He came down, and found the two peasants in the courtyard. When he heard that they came from Pondebba, and saw their manly, distinguished appearance, he thought that they were two gentlemen in disguise. They told him their story, and this cleared his mind of erroneous suppositions. Vecchi then presented them to the General, who was astonished at the journey they had made.

"What!" said he to them, "you have crossed Bologna, you have crossed Florence, you have left behind you 80,000 Venetian emigrants, of whom 20,000 are under the standards of General Fanti; and, instead of getting arrested, you have reached me!"

"Oh, yes," answered the younger brother, while he devoured the General with his eyes, "you see, you are the Beloved General."

I need not say that they were enrolled. The General asked Vecchi to give ten francs to each of them. This done, he gave them the address of an hotel-keeper, but they preferred to bivouac in the garden.

That same day the General was the happiest man in the world, for he had received a magnificent saddle from Buenos Aires. A child with a new dress could not have been prouder of it.

Here is the history of this saddle. In the life of such a man as Garibaldi, everything is important because everything has its significance. Of six horses that he had at Como he could only ride one; the others were sore from the European saddles. In consequence, he wrote to his friend, Giambatista Cuneo, living in Buenos Aires, to send him a saddle similar to the one he had at Monte Video. When Cuneo received the letter he was at the Stock Exchange. Now a letter from Garibaldi was an event; so he got on the table and read it aloud. Immediately a subscription for the saddle was opened, and within two hours it amounted to 32,000 francs.

Then Antonini, one of the leading bankers, a comrade of the General's, and godfather of his daughter Theresita, ordered one with silver mounting, but of a simple design.

Such was the saddle which arrived on the 4th of May—that is to say, just before the departure for Marsala. It is the arm-chair-saddle, the pillow-saddle, the sofa-saddle, the writing-desk-saddle—in short, it takes the place of all articles of furniture regarded by the General as useless. But another friend, wishing to make a present rivalling Antonini's, ordered from a gaucho with a great reputation another saddle costing 6000 francs.

Garibaldi asked Vecchi for one of his horses, so that he might try Antonini's saddle. An American saddle is quite different from ours, and consists of three or four separate pieces of ornamented leather, each with its own covering. But unfortunately there was no horse in the stable: the coachman had taken them to Genoa to be shod. The General, impatient as a child, asked continually: "Have they come back?" As they had not, he fitted the saddle on the back of two chairs.

While he was thus engaged, Türr [1] and brave Colonel Tüköry

[1] Colonel Türr, the gallant Hungarian, Garibaldi's diplomatist and a fine soldier. He was an old friend of Dumas.

9

(who has since died from the wound he received at Palermo)
arrived.

"How did you come?" the General asked.

"On Vecchi's horses, which we found at Genoa," replied Türr.

"Then they are in the stable?"

"I should think so," replied Vecchi.

The General caught up his saddle and rushed into the courtyard.
Then he took out one of the horses and put the saddle on it, so as
to show its advantages to the two Hungarians, whose nation produces Europe's most famous horsemen. The horse was mounted
successively by Menotti, Türr, and Vecchi, and the saddle gave the
General infinite satisfaction. When the trial was over, Garibaldi
went for his usual walk, which always ended at a *belvedere* on one
of the rocks which rises above the road, and from which he could
see all the sea-shore from Bocca d'Asino to the watchman's little
house. On this rock the General was accustomed to sit absorbed in
his thoughts. What were they? Was he simply admiring the sea—
the scene of his earliest exploits; or was he selecting the most suitable spot to embark on an expedition which would bring freedom
to people afar off?

Good tidings were now arriving; Crispi came each day to see the
General, and twice a week translated the telegrams in cypher which
arrived from Malta, and which he alone could read. These despatches,
explained by Crispi and commentated by him, had for their theme
the great revolution which was going on in Sicily, the victorious
fights engaged in by the insurgents, the formidable losses suffered
by the Royalists, whose columns, attacked on all sides, could no
longer keep the field.

It goes without saying that the greater part of these telegrams were
due to Crispi's lively imagination. The General, ostensibly at least,
reposed faith in the great Sicilian movement, and positively promised
to lend it the aid of his arm and his name. At the moment he made
this promise it was all the more meritorious, as the expedition was
to be composed of 150 or 160 men at the most.

It was then that Giovanni Acerbi came to offer his services as
organiser.

We have on many occasions spoken of Bixio, of Crispi, Bertani,
Medici, Türr, and Vecchi, so there is no need to say more about
them; but for the first time we write the name of Acerbi. Let us
say briefly who he was, and from whence came this young patriot,
whose courage, activity, and integrity are so admired in the army.

Acerbi, born in the province of Mantua, was the nephew of the
Cavaliere Acerbi, whose name is known in Italian literature.

Although he was scarcely thirty-four, he had had some fifteen years' experience of political life and persecution. On the third day of the struggle in Milan—the 20th March—he found himself a prisoner in the dungeons of the city. Released from his captivity by the people who bore him in triumph, he escaped from them, caught up a gun and ran to rejoin, in face of the Austrian bullets, the Manara, the Dandolo, the Cataneo and the Cernuschi. We know how the armistice of Salarco overthrew the work of the barricades. Acerbi, having nothing to do in Lombardy or Piedmont, hastened to where the revolution still survived—Venice. Seeing artillery to be the most active agent in the defence of a siege, he entered it; Marghera, that glorious name in Italian annals, saw him, as a sergeant, encouraging his young companions when surprised by the enemy's terrible fire; General Ulloa mentions him in his narratives; and subsequently coming under the notice of the brave and unfortunate Rosalcot, he became his friend, and later was one of his avengers.

When Venice fell, Acerbi was one of those men in whose soul patriotic fire continued to burn, who never ceased to carry on, in spite of scaffolds and the Austrian bludgeon, the great work of restoring Italy. General Garibaldi's enterprise, therefore, naturally attracted him; he joined in at the moment when Bixio and Crispi, the one with his military daring, the other with his civil courage, were pushing and pressing on the expedition to Sicily.

Under Acerbi's organisation, the 150 men reached more than 1000. This little army, thanks to his activity, was ready to start on the appointed day.

At last, on the 4th April, the General announced that the embarkation would take place the next day.

Some days previously, Vecchi had learnt at Genoa, through Mignona—the same man who, later, was President of the Provisional Government of Potenza—that M. La Farina had arrived from Turin with the offer from M. Cavour of money and arms. This news greatly astonished the General, for, three days before, the Gazette of Turin had contained the following:—

"It would be useless to conceal the gravity of the latest news from Sicily. We have dealt conscientiously and sincerely with the events of this heroic struggle. We have dared to hope, when we heard of those courageous efforts; but, at present, with an equal sincerity, we submit ourselves to the sad office which duty imposes on us.

"Once again, brute force has overcome justice and reason."

Yet, at this very moment, M. Cavour untied his purse strings, and held the gate of the arsenal ajar. Vecchi was afraid that the General, in his more than just resentment against the minister, would refuse both arms and money. But, on the contrary, he answered:

"When arms are given me, I accept them from whomsoever they may come."

Vecchi, on going out, ran against M. La Farina in the dining-room. The General received M. Cavour's messenger very graciously: he had come to offer 3000 muskets and 8000 francs. But, instead of 3000 muskets M. Magenta, the Governor of Genoa, never wished to send more than 1000: as a matter of fact, he sent 1019. As regards the 8000[1] francs, they all arrived; and the General at once handed them to Vecchi to be changed into gold.

That same evening, Bixio came with twenty friends, who spent the night tying the muskets in threes, in order to facilitate putting them on board.

The Volunteers were all to meet either at the Villa Spinola or at La Foce on the evening of the 5th of May. The previous day, Madame Crispi asked her husband to let her accompany him, but he told her quite bluntly that Garibaldi was against any woman being in the expedition.

She went to the General, and begged him so insistently that he held out his hand, laughing:

"Come then; but I warn you that it is at your own risk and peril that you do so."

Madame Crispi not only accompanied the expedition, but gained the Medal of the Thousand.

At seven o'clock in the evening, each soldier on leaving the Villa carried three muskets with him, and made his way to the gate. From there to the sea is but a step; it beats against the rocks beside the road.

At half-past nine, the General himself left the Villa. He was in high spirits. His decision once reached, any doubt of success disappeared, or seemed to disappear. He and Türr marched in front; Tüköry and Vecchi followed them. The General carried his *puncho*, made of thick Sardinian cloth, in bandolier fashion; otherwise his costume was his usual grey trousers, and red shirt and scarf. He wore his sabre, his knife in his belt, his revolver slung on his back, and his Colt's repeater carbine on his shoulder. He was accompanied by a number of his officers. La Farina, the historian, was at his side, but Medici was absent. When I asked the latter recently why he did not see Garibaldi off, he replied: "If I had been there, I should never have had the courage to let him go without me."

The General personally directed the embarkation of all, placed Türr in the boat, embraced Vecchi, gave him brief written directions about the formation of committees having the duty of

---

[1] Dumas says, "Huit cents" (eight hundred); but this is an error.

collecting money, arms, and soldiers, and then, giving him a packet of letters for the post, embarked the last.

Among the letters, was one addressed to the King. Here it is:—

"SIRE,
"The cry of distress from Sicily, which has reached my ears, has profoundly moved my heart, and those of some hundreds of my old companions in arms. I did not advise the insurrection of our Sicilian brothers, but from the moment when they rose in the name of Italian unity, of which Your Majesty is the personification, I dared not hesitate to put myself at their head against the most infamous tyranny of our times. I know that I am embarking on a dangerous enterprise, but I put my confidence in God, as also in the courage and devotion of my companions. Our war cry will be always:—

'*Long live Italian unity! Long live Victor Emmanuel, her first and bravest soldier!*'

"If we fail, I hope that Italy and liberal Europe will not forget that this enterprise has been decided by motives free from all egotism, and purely patriotic. If we succeed, I shall be proud to decorate Your Majesty's crown with this new jewel.

"I have not communicated my project to Your Majesty, for the sole reason that I feared that, in consequence of my devotion to Your Majesty's person, you would succeed in persuading me to abandon it.

"Your Majesty's most devoted subject,
"G. GARIBALDI." [1]

We wish that we could here inscribe, for posterity, the names of all the brave men who, in following the General, took part in this gigantic struggle; but it has been impossible to collect anything more than the names of their provinces, and the numbers the provinces had furnished.

Here is the record: 150 Brescians, sixty Genoese, 190 Bergamasques, 170 young men and students of the university of Pavia, 150 Milanese, thirty Bolognians, fifty Tuscans, sixty Parmesans and Placentins, twenty-seven Modenese, 110 Sicilian and Neapolitan emigrants, eighty-eight Venetian emigrants. Total, 1,085 men. [2]

Of them, how many remain to-day? And what is their reward?

[1] Mr. Trevelyan does not give this important letter.
[2] Mr. Trevelyan says that the exact number was 1089. Dumas leaves out four Hungarians. On the other hand, he gives the numbers for eleven groups to Mr. Trevelyan's five.

CHAPTER XV

IN SEARCH OF GARIBALDI

As regards the progress of the expedition, there was scarcely more news at Genoa than the despatch from Palermo: "Garibaldi has landed at Marsala." After that, nothing more was known.

Unfortunately, I was condemned to endure, for three or four days, the same anxiety as everybody else. I had received from the hand of Vecchi and Sacchi the continuation of the "Mémoires," of which, on my way to Turin, four months previously, Garibaldi had given me the first part. It seemed to me that, judging by the way that events were now shaping, the second part of the "Mémoires" should be at least as interesting as the first. Anyway, it was clear I should not be able to leave Genoa before the 24th of May at the very earliest.

During the first four days that I was at Genoa, the most contradictory news reached us. There was nothing certain beyond a letter from Bixio announcing that the expedition was in sight of Marsala and that it was about to land there.

As for the news that we have received in Genoa of events since the 9th of May, it is of the most contradictory character.

You may judge for yourself.

Official news transmitted by the Neapolitan Government, Evening 13th May.

Two Neapolitan frigates opened fire before Marsala, and killed several buccaneers. Their vessel, the *Lombardo*, was sent to the bottom.

Naples, 17th May, at Night.

The latest news to hand informs us that a column of the royal troops valiantly attacked the revolutionists, and put them to flight. One of their leaders, Rosolino Pilo, was left dead on the field. They were compelled to abandon their position at San-Martino.

Our men, after unceasing pursuit of the enemy, were able to engage them again in a second glorious battle at Partanico, since when they have given them no rest.

News transmitted from private sources. Turin, 14th May.

The news of Garibaldi's disembarkation has been officially confirmed. The landing met with opposition, and four men were killed.

Morning of 17th May.

Garibaldi has attacked and completely defeated the royal troops at Catalafimi, near to Monreale. The battle was fought along the whole line; the royalists were utterly routed, with the loss of many standards, guns, and prisoners.

Naples, 17th May, at Night.

The royalists were beaten in the two engagements of the 15th and 16th. The position at Monreale, which commands the road to Palermo, is blocked by Garibaldi's troops. He is marching on Palermo.

Naples, 19th May.

The results of the engagement at Catalafimi were not altogether decisive. The Neapolitan troops have retired to Palermo, whence two columns, of 3000 men each, have been sent forward in pursuit of the enemy.

20th May.

No fresh news. The royal troops are in close pursuit of Garibaldi.

Palermo, 18th May.

The royalists have evacuated the environs of Trapani and Palermo; they have retreated in utter disorder upon the latter town.

20th May, at Night.

Garibaldi has attacked Palermo with 9000 men and twelve guns. A squadron of Neapolitan cavalry has laid down its arms. Garibaldi has entered Palermo amid general rejoicings.

They were crying this last despatch about the streets of Genoa on the fifth day after my arrival. The whole town was illuminated; groups everywhere were discussing the news, and flags displaying the colours of United Italy floated from every window.

I rushed off to Bertani's, as I could not believe the bulletin to be authentic. Bertani did not believe it either, for he thought it impossible that this march could have been executed with such rapidity and success.

I wanted to set out on the very next day for Palermo, but he advised me to wait for a while.

As a matter of fact, the next evening the last news was contradicted; but this much seemed certain, that Garibaldi was master of Monreale, and was preparing to march on Palermo.

As one passes through the streets of Genoa, maps of Sicily nailed on the walls may be seen everywhere, and upon them the victorious march of Garibaldi indicated by little tricolour flags; the white flags are confined to Palermo and its environs.

Subscriptions and benefit performances in aid of the revolutionary cause add more and more to our funds.

At five o'clock this evening (28th May) I received the following message from Bertani:

"Read this printed despatch which is now being posted on all walls in Genoa. It seems to be authentic, since the Piedmontese Government has permitted it to be made public. This is the source of the information:

"The English consul at Palermo sent it to his colleague at Naples, who, in turn, telegraphed it to London.

"In transmission, it was copied at Genoa and sent to the Government; and they made it public at three o'clock this afternoon.

"A. BERTANI."

The poster ran as follows:

"A telegram from Naples, dated half-past nine this morning, announces that Garibaldi, at the head of his army, entered Palermo on the 27th, and set up his headquarters in the centre of the town.

"The bombardment lasted several hours.

"The attacking force was very small, but led by their valiant chief, they gained, so it is said, a decisive victory.

"A great many were killed."

I intend to spend the night in finishing the second volume of the "Mémoires de Garibaldi"; and whether this news be true or not, I shall certainly leave for Palermo to-morrow.

But the news is true, of that I am certain. There are some men who can achieve anything, and Garibaldi is one of those men. If he were to say to me: "I am setting out to-morrow on an expedition to capture the moon," I should doubtless reply, "Very well, go; only write and let me know as soon as you have taken it, and add a little postscript saying what steps I must take to come and join you."

Now, it is not quite so difficult a task to seize Sicily as to capture the moon.

Moreover, I have a certain personal pride mingled with the pleasure I feel in seeing Sicily captured by Garibaldi. Just as Hernani was at war with Charles V, so I, for a long time, have been at war with the King of Naples, and I might say in the words of the banished Spaniard :—

"La meurtre est, entre nous, affaire de famille !"

I have never killed any member of the royal family of Naples; but my father, on his way home from Egypt, after having been taken prisoner at Taranto, was confined in the dungeons of Brindisi, together with General Manscourt, and the *savant* Dolomieu.

All three prisoners were poisoned by order of the grandfather of the king now on the throne. Dolomieu died, and Manscourt went mad; but my father resisted the effects of the poison more successfully for the time, and it was not till six years later that he died, at the early age of forty, from cancer of the stomach, due to this attempt to kill him.

In 1835, I visited Sicily in defiance of the father of the present king. I entered into relations with the Carbonari of Palermo, but more especially with Amari, the learned historian, who became Prime Minister in 1848.

At that time the Sicilian patriots placed in my hands complete plans for an insurrection, with particulars of the forces which Sicily had at its disposal, and a calculation of the sum to which their revenue would amount. I was entrusted with the mission of delivering these documents to the Count of Syracuse, the King's brother, who, having, for a short time, acted as governor for his brother, had become very popular in the island.

I took the plan with me to Naples, stitched in the lining of my hat. I arranged a meeting with the Count of Syracuse, on the very night of my arrival, on the promenade of Chiaïa by the sea, without, however, informing him beforehand of the reasons why I wished to see him.

When we met, on the one hand, I placed before him the plans of the Sicilian patriots, and, on the other, I pointed out to him my vessel, a *speronare*, only fifty yards off, ready to take him to Sicily.

I must do him the justice of saying that he did not hesitate for a moment; for whilst he fully recognised the wrongs he had suffered at the hands of his brother, and admitted that he went in constant fear of his own safety, and even went so far as to beg me to ask the Duc d'Orléans if he would permit him, at any given moment, to take refuge at the Court of France, yet he clearly and decisively refused to enter into any conspiracy against his brother.

And thus it was that the plan for the revolt in Sicily which I had just handed him, and which he did not so much as read, was, at his entreaty, torn up by me into minute fragments which the wind carried away, to disappear in the Gulf of Naples. So ended the hopes of Sicily that centred round a soul that was more loyal than ambitious, and with them, much of the sympathy that was felt for him.

To-day, I can tell what I could not utter during the lifetime of the former King of Naples. This man, however, had every reason to be grateful for the conduct of his brother.

It is this same Count of Syracuse, who, not long ago, wrote a letter to his nephew, filled with liberal sentiments and good advice, which, however, he did not follow.

"*Quos Jupiter vult perdere prius dementat.*"

At the present moment, 28th May, 1860, we may say of the royal House of Naples what Napoleon said of the House of Braganza: "From this day onward, the House of Braganza has ceased to reign."

As for myself, I desire but one thing, and that is to reach Palermo in time to see it wrested from the hands of the King of Naples— Palermo, the most beautiful jewel in his crown. So I shall hasten with all possible speed to the *rendezvous* that Garibaldi gave me. His telegram says: "Ralliez-vous au canon" (Rally to the sound of my guns). I shall leave to-morrow.

31st May, 3 o'clock p.m.

We are just leaving Genoa harbour in execrable weather. There is a heavy swell on the sea, and the wind is blowing hard. The

Captain has requested me to give him a certificate stating that he is sailing by my orders, and not upon his own responsibility.

The yacht has twice failed to get out of the harbour, so I have requested the harbour-master to lend two tugs; these will tow her out into the open sea. Once there, the *Emma* will have to sail, one way or another.

The Captain has just tried a final protest; but my only answer is to order a streamer to be run up, on which is inscribed this device:

> *Au vent la flamme!*
> *Au Seigneur l'âme!*

We are now three miles out at sea, the yacht close hauled.

Farewell, Genoa! Palermo, I come to greet you!

ITALY, at time of Garibaldi's Campaign of 1860

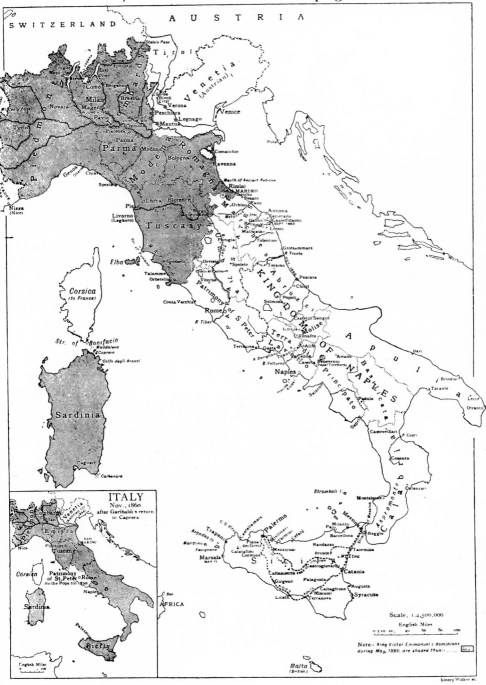

Reproduced by permission of Messrs. Longmans, Green & Co.

CHAPTER XVI

ON THE WAY TO SARDINIA

Port d'Azancourt, Sardinia, 4 June, 11 p.m.

GET out the map of the Mediterranean, and, having found the Strait of Bonifacio, follow what is called *la petite passe* with the eye; then direct it to the right, and the first little indentation represents the bay of Azancourt.

It is there that our yacht lies at anchor, and that we are camped near a little nameless stream which loses itself in the sand ten paces short of the sea.

We have taken four days, as you perceive, to get as far as this. The reason is that since leaving Genoa, having continual head winds, we let ourselves be carried to the west, so as not to get tired of tacking about. A little before yesterday morning the wind changed from south-east to south-west, so that we had it behind us, but it was only a weak and fitful breeze. The sky also was overcast and sad; the barometer, moreover, changeable.

Towards noon we began to see a big blot of mist, which was really Corsica; but much more distinct were the French mountains, which we had neared in our diagonal course, induced by the wind.

Little by little the French mountains began to disappear, and those of Corsica to stand out distinctly in the mist. Soon, through this dark veil, we saw white patches—they indicated the summit, streaked here and there with snow, of Mount Calvi. But it needed a sailor's eye to make certain about the patches, which really looked more like bits of semi-transparent haze.

An hour later there could be no doubt; then the lace-edged coast of Corsica distinctly appeared.

My intention had been to stop at Ajaccio. I had wanted to see the few remains of the house in which Napoleon was born. Of the room in which he came into the world on the 15th August, 1769, nothing remains except the four walls, but these walls witnessed his birth.

Whilst there, I should have liked to write a letter to the one member of the Bonaparte family with whom I am still friendly—Princesse Mathilde. I knew her when she was an exiled child, and spent such happy days with her at the Villa Quarto; and living, as she now does, once more in France, wealthy, powerful, and happy, I hope she remembers those days also.

Yes, I should have liked to anchor at Ajaccio, but so slow was our progress that it seemed probable we should not be there until the evening of the next day. On heaving the log, we found that in spite of our yacht's finesse, in spite of her readiness to profit by a cat's-paw of breeze, she was making only three knots an hour. By-and-by the little breeze that we had, dropped. We got into a dead calm, and the yacht ceased to answer her helm.

The motionless *penaud* failed to indicate any air current.

What is a *penaud?* We had better explain. The day succeeding that of our departure from Marseilles I noticed Brémont intent on carving a piece of wood. This carving represented a fish about as big as a sardine. Having made it, Brémont cut a slit in the tail and inserted a little streamer. Then with a gimlet he bored a hole right through his fish, down from the back. He next drove a headless nail into a broom-handle, and fitted the nail into the hole in such a way that the fish could turn like a weather-cock. Next he inserted the other end of the broom-stick into the rail of the yacht, so when there was a breeze the head of the fish turned towards it, and the yellow streamer fluttered out in the direction towards which the wind was blowing—westwards.

What is the etymology of the word *penaud?* Perhaps it is from *pennon* (flag); or perhaps it is really *penaud* (sheepish, abashed), because it looks foolish when the absence of wind makes the streamer hang listlessly down the stick; or it may be from *penna* (feather), as my learned friend, Charles Nodier, was of opinion, I believe.

A *penaud* is essential on board a sailing vessel. Placed, as it is, in the stern, the helmsman keeps his eye on it as much as on his compass. At the least change of the wind, which otherwise would not be ascertainable, he notifies the Captain. As soon, therefore, as a vessel leaves port, a *penaud* is made. But almost anything serves the desired purpose—a few feathers from the first fowl that is killed on board, or from the first gull that is shot, tied to the end of a string and looking like the tail of a kite, answer well enough. But as our yacht is a yacht *de luxe*, Brémont had made a *penaud de luxe*.

Having finished it, Brémont, who is mad about fishing, began to make something more, and I confess that I watched him at work with some curiosity.

Round the shank of a hook, some twelve or fifteen centimetres long, he wound, as tightly as possible, a strip of linen of graduated width. In fifteen minutes he succeeded in making it look like a fish. Two white feathers attached to the end served for a tail, and hid the hook. Then the whole was attached to the end of fifty fathoms' length of line.

Asked what was the object of this piece of work, he said it was to catch lots of dorados and bonitos.

I do not, on all points, share the ideas of learned persons and sailors respecting the stupidity of fish. Without considering them to have as much instinct as the dog, or cunning as the fox, I still believe that they are much less deficient in sense than is usually considered to be the case. I have seen salmon, carp, and mullet manage to escape both from hooks and nets cleverly enough, although the brains behind the actions were those of fishes.

Following my ideas respecting the inhabitants of the watery element, as M. Lebrun and M. Viennet term it, I maintained, when conversing with Brémont, that he could easily have a fisherman at one end of his line, but he would seldom have a fish at the other.

Brémont laughed at my incredulity, and launched his handiwork into the sea.

All this occurred on the 11th May. To-day is the 4th June, and during the twenty-four days of interval the result of the fishing has justified my opinion.

Brémont has not even caught a *rascasse*.[1] It is true that he is fertile in giving reasons for the want of success of his enterprise—sometimes there has been too much wind, at others too little,—but I am not deceived; I am sure that, really, Brémont is furious.

Whenever there has been a complete calm it has been the turn of Podimatas—as great a fisher of fish before God as was Nimrod a great hunter among men. Podimatas seats himself on the rail and fishes *à la palangrotte*—that is to say, he throws his line vertically over the water. Brémont's plan has the advantage that the motion of the yacht does his fishing for him, while Podimatas' arm is at work all the time; this he finds fatiguing after an hour or two, especially when, at the end of that time, he has caught nothing.

It is a competition between Brémont and Podimatas. In any event, their lines are alike guiltless of taking anything.

Just now, as there is a calm, it is Podimatas who is the busy man. While he was thus innocently engaged, I noticed Louis Passeret in the rigging. I was curious to know what he was doing there, and I asked the question.

"I am on the look-out," he replied.

"For what, Louis?"

"Turtle."

So each of them has his ambition. I can say that up to the present Passeret has not taken more turtle than Podimatas *rascasses*, or Brémont bonitos, but I will bet that it will be Louis who will be the first to succeed.

[1] A fish of the sea-devil type.

Five or six hours passed, during which the yacht remained perfectly still. Towards seven o'clock some breaths of wind reached us, and just moved our *penaud*.

Suddenly we heard a deep, noisily drawn breath at some fifty paces from the yacht. We all turned in the direction from which it came. It was neither a bonito, nor a dorado, nor a *rascasse*, nor a horned beast; it was a whale.

It came on majestically and noisily towards our stern, at thirty paces from which it seemed to be passing by, without appearing to mind us.

"The big gun! the big gun!" Paul and Edouard called out together, disappearing down the stern stairs.

The "big gun" is a sort of little double-barrelled cannon, which was made for me by Zaoué of Marseilles. Unfortunately I had no ball cartridge, but only buck-shot. These latter cartridges are charged with 180 grains of powder and thirty-five or forty buck-shot. I had a carbine for explosive balls, but I had no cartridges ready.

I had, therefore, to content myself with my Lefaucheux No. 4.

It was handed to me already loaded, so I had only to put it to my shoulder, and await the monster's reappearance.

The water opened at thirty paces from me, and the whale offered me its left side at full length. At the same moment I fired. The noise made by the buck-shot striking it was just as if they had struck a roof. For a moment the animal stayed motionless with astonishment and pain, then it rolled over so as to show all its belly. I thought that I had killed it.

The Captain thought so too, and called out—

"Lower a boat."

But, almost at once, the whale breathed noisily, and disappeared. The water, for a moment, remained disturbed at that place, but the disturbance quickly subsided, and the surface of the sea again became as calm and as brilliant as a mirror.

Perhaps the whale was mortally wounded, but in this case it had gone to the bottom to die.

I went down to my cabin with my gun, and had been for a few moments lying on the divan, when, all at once, I heard a great trampling overhead and the noise of some manœuvres on the part of the sailors.

I went up a few steps to see what was going on. Everyone was bustling about. A strong breeze from the south-west had sprung up right in our course, just as if my gun-shot has given the signal for it.

The yacht flew along the water on which she had so long remained becalmed.

The Captain heaved the log. We were now making eight and a half knots an hour.

He came to me, and I said—

"If we get along like this, and you think that the wind will hold, let us steer straight ahead, for I want to reach Palermo with all speed; if, on the contrary, the wind drops, enter the roadstead and let go the anchor. We will then reach Ajaccio to-morrow morning, and leave with the first favourable breeze."

"Now point south-south-east," said the Captain to the helmsman.

Then, turning to Brémont: "Brémont," said he, "take the watch at eight bells. At midnight call me. I will take the watch from twelve to four."

And he went to his cabin. Certainly, since we left Marseilles, the Captain has not had four hours' sleep out of twenty-four.

At eleven o'clock, I, in my turn, went down and threw myself on my divan. I did not wish, when the time came, to influence the Captain's judgment, for I had just as much desire to stop at Ajaccio as to sail on for Palermo. I left the responsibility to the Captain.

I awoke at half-past two. We were rolling badly, a thing which we never did except in a calm. I went on deck. The breeze had completely failed. At a distance of seven or eight miles in the rear I saw the light of the lighthouse at Ajaccio twinkling like a star. We had been making seven knots as we passed it, and the Captain had not thought fit to stop. After seven or eight miles, the yacht had stopped of her own accord.

The aspect of the sky was now livid, a dirty yellow with black marblings like the belly of an enormous turtle. A great black cloud rose above the horizon, as if trying to extinguish the little light shed by the moon. The atmosphere was warm and clammy.

I believed that we were in for a bad time.

" Captain, I am thinking that at the first breath of wind you will do well to get farther from land."

"That is just my intention," said he, "but I do not think that we shall get any wind before to-morrow."

"Very well then, till to-morrow."

Like a waverer, I bring the play to an end with this tag: I should have done better if I had espoused Célimène.[1]

I returned to my cabin saying, "I think that we should have done better to stop at Ajaccio."

I awoke at seven o'clock, and at once went on deck.

The weather looked just the same. The sun seemed to be struggling

---

[1] The "Célimène" of Molière's "Misanthrope," to whom Dumas likens the fickle winds.

in masses of mist, which it tinged but failed to get through. The sea was the colour of ashes. Land was hardly visible. We had got farther, without losing sight of it, but it was so hidden in mist that we guessed at rather than saw it.

At last the sun, after a two hours' struggle, managed to pierce its surrounding veil, but could not dissipate it. Its rays, as it were, slipped through openings, but, in between, the mist still held dominion.

"Good," said the Captain, "we shall have some wind before evening. Here is the sun *qui s'affourche.*"

As a sailor, he meant to say: "The sun is anchored fore and aft." A craft which *s'affourche* is taking its precaution against the wind.

And, in fact, towards noon the clouds were rent into great pieces, and went rolling, like a sea above a sea, towards the south-south-east.

At that moment the *penaud* gave signs of life, and almost as soon as the *penaud* the *Emma* shivered, her sails filled, she inclined to her right side, bent to the waves, and seemed to be telling us that she wanted nothing better than to pursue her course.

Our drinking water was not very good, and we were without fresh meat.

"Where shall we stop?" asked the Captain.

"I can choose? "

"Certainly, you can go where you wish; provided that it is only thirty or forty miles off, and we do not try to baffle the wind, I will get you there to-day."

"Very well, then, to Maddalena."

Maddalena is a little island which you will find on the map immediately in front of the Gulf of Azancourt, the position of which I have indicated to you already.

The words "to Maddalena" were hardly out of my mouth when, as if she had heard and understood them, the *Emma* leapt forward.

"How far is Maddalena?" I asked the Captain.

"Thirty-five miles; in five hours, if this breeze holds, we shall be there."

The breeze promised well.

We were just at the entrance to the strait, towards which two steam-boats were directing their course; to our left was Bonifacio perched on a height; to our right the arid coast of Sardinia, fantastically fretted, with some grey houses hardly visible against the rock, with its lighthouse like a little clock-tower, and its Genoese or Saracen tower which had been recently restored; and right in front of us the two channels bristling with reefs, upon one of which the *Sémillante* was lost.

We flew along at a speed of nine knots an hour, skimming the surface of the water, leaning to larboard without our feeling any rolling or pitching.

In less than an hour we were in the narrower of the two channels.

The Captain came to me. "Have you a special liking," he asked, "for Maddalena rather than for any other spot in the isle of Sardinia?"

"I have no preference except for a good anchorage, fresh water, fowls, and eggs."

"Then I would offer you the bay of Azancourt, where we can hunt and fish, while I send the boat to Maddalena for provisions."

I saw Brémont's eyes glisten with pleasure at the idea of fishing. Let me tell you that I had bought at Genoa a seine-net, which, like Brémont's drag and Podimatas' *palangrotte*, was guiltless of the death of a single fish, so far. Brémont had suggested this purchase, on the plea that he could do nothing either with Vasili's *épervier* or with an English net which we had on board. With the seine-net he promised to do wonders.

"Forward for the bay of Azancourt," I replied to the Captain, and, above all, to Brémont.

In the meanwhile, as rapid as an arrow, we had shot through the strait. The Captain's order was to let her go, until we had the wind behind us. We rounded the Cape. We closely hugged the eastern side of Sardinia, and in half an hour we saw the bay of Azancourt open on our right, while on our left the village of Maddalena became visible.

The Captain had been correct. There was no comparison between the two anchorages. The isle of Maddalena was but a bare and arid rock. The Sardinian coast, on the contrary, was green, covered with mastics, arbutuses, and tamarisks. One could discern, by reason of a more vigorous growth of vegetation, the windings of a small river. Moreover, there were two beaches which seemed as if expressly made for our fishing operations, one facing the east, the other the north.

An hour later we were anchored 200 fathoms from the land. Both the Captain and the wind had kept faith with us; in four hours and a quarter we had done our thirty-five miles.

CHAPTER XVII

HUNTING AND FISHING

WE had two hours left of daylight.

The idea of hunting and fishing had turned everyone's head. Podimatas and his two fellow-countrymen tucked up their trousers to the knees and began to explore the rocks, which were covered with a kind of barnacle. Brémont, Louis, Calvi, and the cook laid hold of a boat, and threw the seine-net into it. The Captain, the doctor, Legray, Paul, Edouard, and Théodore each took a gun, and getting into the yawl, took the shortest way to the shore.

I stayed behind to take care of the yacht. I am beginning to be of an age in which my greatest pleasure is to see others enjoying themselves.

Scarcely had the sportsmen landed when the sound of gunshots resounded from all sides, the while Brémont, without losing any time, had thrown out his seine-net.

I felt entirely easy as regards Brémont, but not at all so about the sportsmen, three of whom—Edouard, Paul, and Théodore—did not know what a gun was. Happily, I saw them disperse themselves on the hill at a great enough distance between them to enable me to be at least sure of this—that they would not shoot each other.[1]

Podimatas was the first to return, leaving the two friends to continue their fishing; the sound of the gunshots had made his mouth water; he wanted to take a gun.

I handed him one of my Lefaucheux and cartridges No. 6, and he left to find the quarry.

Meanwhile, from where I was, I saw Brémont fishing like St. Peter; the fish drawn to land glittered like pieces of silver. With my pair of glasses I could almost see what kind they were.

Suddenly, in the most thickly wooded part of the coast, on the green banks of the little river, just by a grove of evergreen oaks, I saw smoke mounting, and heard burst out five or six gunshots.

Then the smoke and the shots were succeeded by loud halloos and shouts of encouragement.

It was clear that our sportsmen had raised game of some kind, but the place was too thickly wooded to enable me to make out either the hunted or the huntsmen.

---

[1] Dumas, himself, was an excellent shot and a good all-round sportsman. Bred up at the edge of the large forests then surrounding Villers-Cotterêts, he had been in at the death of many a wild boar.

I stayed, therefore, in a state of uncertainty; only I saw those who were on the heights dashing down to the valley, and directing themselves towards the point where the gunshots had been fired and the shouts raised.

They were guided by the smoke which, sheltered from the wind by the semicircle of hills, dispersed slowly.

Night fell. The Greeks returned to the yacht with a fine lot of shell-fish.

Brémont, Calvi, and Jean then rejoined us, in their turn, with a basketful of fish.

It was only the huntsmen who were absent. I could not understand the reason. For quite half-an-hour the best-sighted of them could not have seen the end of his gun-barrel.

Then, in a flash, I understood the cause of their delay. Edouard's halloos sounded from different places. In all probability he had lost himself, and the others did not want to return without him.

The halloos were followed by gunshots. It was a sight worth seeing —those lightning-like flashes of gunfire in the darkness, each followed by the noise of the explosions. It was as if the whole hill were the abode of huge glow-worms.

All this continued for more than an hour. I began to be seriously uneasy, and was preparing to go in search of the lost man, when a gunshot, fired from the top of the highest hill, replied to the musket-shots that had blazed for a period which perhaps had seemed to me to be longer than it actually was.

Presently, in the midst of the darkness, I heard two boats full of confused voices approaching. Such a return from the chase, when each relates all he has done, all he has seen, when all speak at once, and no one listens to anybody—such a return, I say, is always delightful.

I first inquired as to what had happened to Edouard Lockroy. He had found the scenery so much to his liking that he had walked on and on, as long as the light lasted, so that, when night had fallen, he had found himself, if not lost, at all events at a great distance from the others.

As to them, this is what had happened : in getting through a thicket, the doctor, Legray, and Podimatas had stumbled on a band of wild boars, consisting of some thirteen or fourteen red ones, with a father and mother. Not being used to being disturbed, as this side of Sardinia is but little visited, the boars did not budge until my friends were actually stepping on their bodies. On sighting the grunting band, the doctor and Legray had fired into the middle of it four times, the charge being rabbit shot. As to Podimatas, instead of firing he had thrown his gun down and fallen bodily on the animal nearest to him, seizing on the tail with one hand and on a foot with the other, calling out—

"I've got one—help! help!"

The animal, frightened out of its senses by this rude treatment, which boded so ill to the posterior portion of its anatomy, fled with terrific grunts. Podimatas held on, letting himself be dragged along, and repeating his cry of "I've got one, help!" But his fellow-huntsmen, instead of going to his assistance, were bent on following the rest of the band. Podimatas found it difficult to relate what next occurred to him. He felt himself being dragged during a minute or more through a thicket which tore his hands and face; then it seemed to him that he had passed through reeds, and next he had suddenly felt water over his head. It was only then that he let go of the beast.

He was in the stream when the doctor and Legray, in hot pursuit, rushed past him, calling for his help in their attack on the enemies' stronghold.

Podimatas let them go on, and went to find his gun.

This twofold adventure was rewarded with different results. Podimatas retrieved his gun, but the doctor and Legray did not retrieve their boars.

To the assistance of the three men who were calling for help came Paul Parfait and the Captain. But, in spite of this reinforcement, the boars were not to be found anywhere.

Meanwhile, Théodore, who had been pursuing blackbirds, which he had taken for partridges of an unknown kind, came up.

As to the Captain, he had explored the banks of the little river, which he had found very fishable, and made up his mind that, while shooting on the bank next morning, he would get Brémont to throw the net.

Night had already fallen, and it was only then that they found Edouard missing.

Thus had begun the hallooing and the gunshots as signals.

In the middle of all these different recitals, or rather when they had ended, I asked permission to speak. It was given to me.

"What most strikes me in all this," said I to the sportsmen (who as the result of their prowess had brought in five or six larks, two or three speckled magpies, and as many finches), "is that the band of wild boars excites general enthusiasm."

"I shall be there to-morrow morning at daybreak."

"I, before break of day."

"I, at three o'clock."

"What a misfortune to have no bullets!"

"I shall fix my hunting-knife at the end of my gun."

Such were some of the answers I received. Then, I again asked permission to speak.

"Is the general opinion," I inquired, "that the boars should be attacked to-morrow at daybreak?"

"Yes, yes, yes," resounded from all sides.

"Well, then, this is what I propose. Take six carbines with their bayonets, two or three tents, iron bedsteads, and mattresses. Place your tents on the bank nearest to the lair of the boars, and sleep ashore; then, to-morrow, at break of day, with bayonets fixed at the end of the guns, loaded with bullets No. 3, attack your boars."

Never had an orator such a success, never was there a proposition received with like enthusiasm.

The bedsteads and the mattresses were declined as superfluities, for the banks of the stream were covered with beautiful sand; but the tents were unpacked, shouldered, and laid in the canoe. All bade me good-night, assuring me that they would spend a better one, and each then dropped into the canoe. The moon had risen; I followed with my eyes the silver streak left by the canoe on the sea; I saw the landing on the beach.

A little later a big fire, kindled at the margin of the sea, lit up with its reflection the two white tents, before which I saw shadows passing and repassing.

Tranquillised about my companions, sure of their pleasures on the morrow, confident in God as regards accidents, I went down to my cabin to write all this.

The wind is just what I needed, and I rather regret not having gone on my way to Palermo; but my poor children are going to have such a good time.

Moreover, the Captain, who, for his part, has enjoyed himself like a child, has not yet obtained his provisions, and to-morrow, while these gentlemen halloo in pursuit of wild boars, he will himself go to Maddalena. He will bring us fowls, eggs, salad, and news.

CHAPTER XVIII

ON LAND; ON SEA; IN HARBOUR

5th June, 7 *a.m.*

THE Captain, who has returned with the provisions, saw the French Consul, who told him that the news of the taking of Palermo, as announced by the last telegram, is denied. According to the Consul, Garibaldi, although at the gates of the city, had not, as yet, entered it.

However this may be, whether Palermo has been taken or has not been taken, I will sail to-day; I will land either at Trapani, Alcamo, or anywhere else that is in the hands of the insurgents.

I shall therefore write in bits and scraps from day to day, and even from hour to hour. I will begin on land, I will continue on sea, and, in all probability, I will finish this chapter in harbour.

At the present moment this is what is happening on the northern side of Sardinia.

Since four o'clock this morning I have heard a certain number of gunshots, but at such distances from each other that it seems more than probable that the boars have not been found again.

These shots were fired by a number of red spots, which looked exceedingly effective against the iron-grey of the rocks and the sombre green of the myrtles and lentisks.

Of course, the red spots represented our sportsmen's blouses.

Seeing that the fusillade has lasted for three hours, I think that I may fairly recall two or three sportsmen; so I send the yawl to the shore for Legray or the doctor—that is to say, the pick of the bunch— hoping that one or the other will tell me exactly how things have gone.

With my pair of glasses I follow the course of the yawl, and presently I see Legray get into it. I look carefully, but I fail to see the body of any animal beside him.

Yes, I was right. The wild boars decamped in the night, not, I am sure, because of the marksmanship of Legray and the doctor, but because of the unbecoming behaviour of Podimatas with regard to one of them.

On the other hand, as, to be on the safe side, the sportsmen had taken not only carbines but fowling-pieces, the bag contains a good many little birds, including one fellow with splendid blue-green and orange plumage, which I fancy is of the shrike tribe.

This is the decision I have come to:

Some of our provisions and a part of the result of Brémont's fishing

expedition will be taken on shore. Jean will row over with his cooking utensils, and *déjeuner* will be enjoyed under the lentisks and
myrtles. After *déjeuner*, there will be fishing in the river and hunting
in the valley, and at three o'clock all will meet on the *Emma*, to sail
at four. And, having started, we will stop nowheresoever except at
Palermo, or, at all events, in Sicily somewhere.

Well, these gentlemen (Lockroy, the enthusiast among them, not
excepted) have not exaggerated anything. I find the scenery enchant-
ing. It comprises volcanic heights with bare summits, their sides
covered with pink heather and yellow and white flowers like eglan-
tine, but growing on bushes without thorns. The lowlands are covered
with almost impenetrable thickets of myrtles, lentisks, arbutuses.

The stream winds through all this, its banks covered with tamarisks,
its waters dimpled with the gliding motion of fish, due to our presence,
and showing glances of silver.

One of them is so imprudent as to rise to the surface, and a shot
from Legray severs it in two. Unfortunately, like my whale, it goes
to the bottom.

Valdin and Touche, though held on the leash by me, are wild with
delight. The poor things have not been on *terra firma* since we left
Monaco, but in the circles they describe they only put up some blackbirds and a dozen of the blue-green and orange birds.

A larger bird takes wing from behind the tamarisks; I fire, and it
falls on the other side of the stream in the midst of a thicket, but the
Captain, who is near, calls to me not to trouble myself about it.

Meanwhile, Brémont fishes at the mouth of the stream. When I
say the mouth, I am leading the geographers astray, for the stream
has no mouth, losing itself, as it does, in the sand ten paces from the
sea, and reaching it underground.

For the distance of a kilometre inland, the water is brackish and
undrinkable. Vasili, who has drunk of it, declares that, as the result,
he is incapable of serving the *déjeuner*. He is so much engaged attend-
ing to his own needs that he cannot look after those of others.

We give him permission to retire to a distance.

Brémont has captured a certain number of fish—almost all are
mullet; but after three casts of the seine-net, he declares that river
fish are more cunning than sea fish. It seems that some burrow their
noses in the sand, so that the net passes over them; others jump over
it. The result is that the meshes contain only small fry whose education is incomplete.

Vasili had brought his *épervier* with the idea of rivalling Brémont,
but the river water has put him entirely *hors de combat*.

This is certain : *Déjeuner* served on the grass is enjoyed only by young people of from fifteen to five-and-twenty. Exposed to the great heat of the sun, we have had a *déjeuner*, a good third part of which has consisted of sea-sand.

The Captain has returned, not with a dead bird but with a live one. He has captured an injured, parti-coloured crow about three weeks old. The bird I shot was probably its father or mother. I will adopt the orphan. It will form part of the menagerie on board, under the name of "Half-Mourning" (*Demi-deuil*).

The Captain and I are the first to return on board—he to prepare for the voyage, I to write these lines. A flag—white, with a cross of St. André azure—has been chosen for the recall of our friends to-day, and from henceforward.

At four o'clock everyone is on board. The breeze holds good. The anchor is weighed, and we are off.

The Captain reckoned on a supply of water from the stream, and so brought none from Maddalena. Vasili calls out, "You cannot drink that water; I did so, look at me." So we cannot risk it. Each one of us will have a litre of water a day, and salt water to wash with—that is to say, we shall not wash.

For the last three days we have had no bread, and have munched biscuit. We have asked Jean to make bread, but he has absolutely refused to do so. The Captain has threatened him, but Jean has answered—

"The worst you can do to me is to shoot me, is it not so? Very well, then, I prefer to be shot rather than make bread."

No answer to such a declaration being possible, we have not made one; and so we shall eat biscuit. Fortunately, we all have good teeth.

Half-an-hour later, we were passing through the strait of the "Bear," so called from one of its rocks, which, in its fantastic shape, seems to represent a bear in the act of walking with its muffled and cautious step. Reefs just beneath the surface of the water make this strait very dangerous. To our left lay the island of Caprera, the property of Garibaldi.

When outlawed and virtually a prisoner on the island of Maddalena, Garibaldi saw lying before him the desolate and rocky island of Caprera. This man, who had spent twenty years of his existence in fighting for the liberty of two worlds, whose life had been one long devotion and never-ending self-sacrifice, smiled sadly when he reflected that he had not so much as a stone upon which he could lay his head. Then he said to himself:

"The man who possesses that island, who can live there alone, far away from men whose main thoughts are persecution and banishment, that man surely should be happy!"

Ten years later, Garibaldi, who had never dreamt that he would be the happy mortal, inherited 40,000 francs by the death of his brother.

He at once bought this island, the object of his ambition, for 13,000 francs; next he bought a little vessel for 15,000 more; and with the rest, assisted by his son and his friend Orrigoni, he set about building that little white house which one sees from the sea—the only building, indeed, upon the island.

Should he be lucky enough to escape death from the Austrian and Neapolitan bullets, it is here that he will return to die. This man, who will have bestowed provinces, and—who knows?—maybe even a kingdom upon a sovereign, deems himself rich in the possession of his rocky island, and will accept nothing from that king, no, not so much as six feet of ground for his last resting-place.

In him, may we institute a parallel to Cincinnatus, who, on laying down his sword, returned to his plough? Well, Cincinnatus must, at least, have possessed a field, since he had a plough; so he was an aristocrat and a millionaire when compared with Garibaldi.

Caprera has three ports: two small ones, unnamed, and the third, which is much larger, is called Porto Palma.

I supposed that, when Garibaldi was away, the island was completely uninhabited; and I had a strong desire to anchor in one of the three ports and make a pilgrimage to the house. I noticed, however, by the aid of my glasses, that one of the windows opened and that the head of a woman was looking out, so I came to the conclusion that my pilgrimage would be an intrusion, and gave up the idea of anchoring there. Besides, we were fortunate enough to have a favourable wind just then: we were making eight knots an hour. We soon doubled the isle of Pacco, and got well out to sea.

We now felt as if we were entering into possession of our kingdom; but, an hour later, the wind declined somewhat and our speed slackened.

Were we going to enter one of those terrible Mediterranean calms which last a fortnight, three weeks, or a month?

The wind lasted all the evening and through the night, but so feeble was it that we were only going at the rate of two miles, and, subsequently, one mile, an hour.

6th June.

During the night we were visited by two or three whales. We heard their noisy breathing; we saw, thrown up in silvery jets, the twofold columns of water from their blow-holes, but not one of them approached us near enough to let me repeat on him the attempt I had made on one of his species when we were between Calvi and Ajaccio.

This morning we saw two sharks. They were on an excursion. We summoned the cook and made him cut a bit of meat; we fixed it on a swivel-hook, and threw the whole into the sea. But their lordships had, no doubt, already dined and were replete; they did not deign to turn their noses in our direction, and passed by, a hundred paces from us.

One knows of the neighbourhood of a shark by the dorsal fin which is visible above the water, while its owner is hidden beneath it. This fin, which only sharks have, always gives them away to the observer.

Towards nine o'clock the sea became entirely calm.

We were about to take our *déjeuner* on deck, according to our custom, when Lockroy suddenly called out—

"There, what is that?"

All eyes turned in the direction to which he pointed, and there was a general cry of—

"A turtle! A turtle!"

"Launch the yawl!" cried the Captain.

And in a moment the yawl had left the deck and was in the sea. Podimatas and Louis Passeret let themselves fall into it. I have mentioned that Louis' speciality, as a fisherman, was turtle-fishing.

I need not say that our *déjeuner* was instantly forgotten, and the turtle was all that we wanted.

The creature was swimming quietly along, its carapace making a rotund blob on the mirror of the sea, its head and, from time to time, two feet appearing out of the water.

The oarsmen had made their boat manœuvre in a big circle, so that, presently, they were navigating behind the turtle, which continued on its way in voluptuous enjoyment of the water, without seeming even to suspect the presence of danger. Nevertheless, danger approached it nearer and nearer. As it did so, Podimatas rowed ever more gently, while Louis, lying in the prow, had nearly half of his body outside the boat.

The turtle still went happily along, as though feeling absolutely sure of its safety. The two fishermen were now within two boats' lengths of it.

Podimatas made one stroke with his oar and then stayed motionless. The boat glided on, rapidly and silently. Louis held out his arms at full stretch and seized the turtle by its two hind feet. There was then a moment's struggle, during which, one did not know whether it would be the turtle that would drag the man into the water, or the man who would drag the turtle into the boat. At

ALEXANDRE DUMAS

The Reproduction of a Portrait belonging to
Madame Alexandre Dumas *fils*

last, success, as is almost always the case, was with injustice and cunning. We saw the yellow belly of the turtle shine in the sun : an instant, and it was in the boat.

Loud cries of felicitation broke out on the *Emma* and were borne over the surface of the sea to repay the conquerors, who, at the same moment, began to row towards us : they were about a mile off.

The turtle, which at the spot where we had seen it captured had looked as big as a medium-sized plate, now turned out to be three and a half feet in diameter and to weigh fifty-two pounds.

On placing it on deck Louis put it on its back, telling every one to keep away from its jaws. The bite of a turtle is a terrible one. Like the bulldog, it takes hold and never lets go.

There was joy on board. Traditionally, rather than actually, sailors love turtle. For myself, I have never eaten it but as soup, once at Greenwich, and again at Phillipe's, where, let me say in parenthesis, it is excellently served.

In my capacity of chief cook, the second cook, maître Jean, came to ask me how I wished the portion reserved for me to be treated.

Like Jean, I, too, was ignorant in the matter of cooking turtle, so I asked them to bring me the cookery books from the shelf. First I consulted Durand's "Cuisine du Midi," but the result was a blank. Next I appealed to Mademoiselle Catherine's book. No mention of turtle. I saw that I should have to go to the foremost authority : "Dictionnaire de Cuisine" by Courchamps. This book will be only the second authority on cooking, when I have published my own work; but as this is not yet out,[1] Courchamps is still the first.

As you, dear reader, may some day be in my situation—that is, on board a ship from which a turtle has been caught—I have thought it well to set down the name of an authority who gives you full directions for killing and dressing turtle. But now let me tell you that, for my part—excepting turtle soup, which is excellent—I find turtle, prepared in any other form whatever, an execrable dish. I merely mention the Courchamps cookery book for the relief of my conscience.

The capture of the turtle has been the sole incident of the day.

Towards five o'clock the wind shifted to north-north-east which gave us a pretty good night as far as progress was concerned, only by an error of the compass we were steering too much to the right. We thought we were sailing towards Ustica, but in reality we were making for Trapani.

---

[1] Dumas, who was a cook of great merit, did not live to see his own "Grand Dictionnaire de Cuisine" published. Lemerre issued it in 1873, and a very handsome volume it is.

On the third day after our departure, near ten in the morning, Henri, our Greek sailor, signalled "land ahead."

All telescopes were at once pointed in its direction, but it was soon found that what had been taken for land was only a low bank of clouds.

Henri maintained that though it might be, and even was, a bank of clouds, nevertheless, behind the clouds there lay the land.

The Captain, in answer to the sailor, said that Ustica, towards which they were steering, had a low coast, and was one which would not stop the clouds in their course.

About two o'clock the same sailor approached the Captain respectfully, and pointed out to him the summit of a mountain which was clearly visible and rose above the clouds like a giant tooth.

A second and a third peak soon appeared on the same line. This time, there was no use denying it; it really was land; only, where were we?

The Captain had recourse to his chronometer, and soon found out that, for the second time since our departure from Genoa, the compass had been playing tricks with us: instead of making for Ustica we were now near Trapani!

To our right we had the islands of Maritimo, Favignana, and Pianezza, and facing us, the bay of Alcamo. Reaching Ustica was now out of the question, for we had deviated almost thirty-five miles from our course.

We held a consultation to discuss what course we should now adopt. Should we make inquiries at Marsala, at Trapani, or at Alcamo, as to how things were going? Or should we make straight for Palermo, happen what might? As the last mentioned was my proposal, it was the one adopted. Only, in order to steer the true course, we found we had a head wind to contend with; but this did not matter very much, for the *Emma* displays her best qualities when she sails close-hauled.

So, this is what we do.

9th June.

This morning we passed a frigate to our larboard side. This was probably a Neapolitan vessel cruising on the route to Genoa for the purpose of intercepting the supplies of men, arms, and money which Medici was to send, and which Garibaldi was awaiting; but as we sail very quickly, we soon lost sight of the frigate.

Next we saw a brig ahead of us; it issued from behind Cape St. Vito, and is now going through a rather singular manœuvre, tacking about, two or three miles from shore. Suddenly it alters its course, and is heading straight for us.

This was rather disquieting; but the Captain, with the aid of his telescope, discovers that it is a sailing vessel. From that moment we knew we had nothing to fear, for our yacht is a match for any sailing vessel whatever.

We let the brig approach, having made ready to put about, if she should display any hostile intentions.

Nothing of the kind, however: her intentions are entirely peaceful, and she passes us at a distance of half-a-mile. It turned out to be a merchant vessel.

Land is now clearly visible: we can make out Cape St. Vito. Careful observation with a good telescope reveals to us that we have, to larboard, the isle of Ustica, just emerging from the water at a distance of about six miles.

Night came on gradually. We saw the two capes of the Gulf of Castellammare, but as yet we could not see its further extremity. We have right facing us Capo di Gallo, behind which Palermo lies. If we had had a good voyage, we should have been there by five o'clock; but it is now six, and we are still twenty-five miles off.

With the wind which we now have, we might cover these twenty-five miles in three hours; but it would be foolish to risk anchoring in the bay at night. If Palermo is not in Garibaldi's hands, we shall fall into the clutches of the Neapolitans. So, we shall continue our journey till we are off Palermo, and then we shall lie-to until daybreak.

At nine o'clock in the evening we hear the firing of cannon seven times. What is the meaning of this? Is the bombardment still in progress? Or does this firing, which is only faintly audible to us, indicate the close of the day's fighting, which will be resumed on the morrow?

Nothing is more likely.

Night has closed in completely. Towards ten o'clock we are able to see the lighthouse of Palermo, by the water's edge.

Our business is not to get past the point fixed upon, and the Captain gives the order to bring-to. I go down into my cabin, hoping that I shall be able to sleep undisturbed. But this is impossible; for the wind is blowing in violent gusts, and at every gust the sails make a fearful noise, just as though they were going to be ripped in twain, the whole way down. The masts quiver and creak as if about to break across. The entire rigging grinds harshly in its fixings, and every joint seems ready to give way.

So I write; but what I am writing is scarcely legible. The rolling of the vessel causes my pen to describe fantastic figures.

My companions are no more able to sleep than I am. I hear them going from the deck to their cabins, and then back again. Although there is no danger, still all this noise, all this disturbance, all this creaking and groaning set one's nerves on edge.

Finally, overcome by fatigue, I fall asleep for two or three hours.

10th June.

On waking, I go up on deck, and notice that we are still in the same place. The beacon of the lighthouse still sends forth its rays, five or six miles away, and the ship still groans and trembles with every fitful gust. The coast is not visible; all that you can see is a sombre mass of clouds in which the moon is about to disappear from view.

Two steamers leave the harbour and pass us, one on our right, no doubt going to Genoa, the other, on our left, no doubt bound for Naples.

A sailing vessel now bears straight down upon us. As a precaution, the Captain has ordered the ship's lanterns to be extinguished; and we are now obliged to warn the stranger by raising and lowering a signal-light and by vigorously clanging our bell. She turns aside and passes us on the larboard, but almost grazes our side. We hail the stranger:

"What news from Palermo?"

The reply is: "I don't know. I come from Messina. I believe they are fighting."

The vessel moves along and is soon lost in the darkness.

At half-past three in the morning a band of reddish hue lights up the eastern sky, and announces the break of day. At half-past four the sun makes its appearance, rising from the sea, it crosses a small space of clear sky, shines for a moment, and then disappears behind a sea of dark clouds.

Mount Pellegrino is silhouetted on our right, the cape stretches out on our left, and the white houses of Palermo become visible.

As far as one is able to judge, the harbour is full of warships, but they are too numerous for all to be Neapolitan. The Captain believes that he can recognise British and French vessels amongst them.

If there are English and French vessels in Palermo harbour, there is no reason whatever why we should not be there also; so the Captain gives the order to get the breeze behind us, and we advance towards Palermo at the rate of three miles an hour. As we get closer in, we can see that one of the ships bears the French flag, three the English flag, and two the American. The others have the Neapolitan standard. Though it is only five o'clock in the morning, all have their flags flying, notwithstanding that the usual practice is to lower them at eight in the evening and run them up again at eight in the morning.

Something extraordinary must be happening.

With our telescopes we see the Quattro Venti barracks full of Neapolitan soldiers, who are swarming in front of the doors like ants. The Sardinian standard is floating over the town, with the exception of the forts of Castellammare and Castellucio-del-Molo, over which the Neapolitan flag still waves; so we are going to anchor between the fort of Castellucio-del-Molo and a Neapolitan frigate. We thus have the guns of the fort on our starboard side, and the sixty fiery mouths of the frigate to larboard.

The greatest commotion seems to prevail on the quay and in the streets which open on to it. What is happening?—and what is the meaning of these Piedmontese flags flying over the town, and the Neapolitan one over the fort, and the frigates in the harbour?

A boat laden with fruit accosts us, without troubling to inquire whether we have complied with the usual formalities. The three men on it are wearing the Piedmontese cockade. We question them about the strange spectacle which lies before our eyes, and they inform us that at present there is a truce, but that this expires in a couple of days, when hostilities will begin again.

"And what about Garibaldi?"

"He is master of the city."

"Since when?"

"Since Whitsunday."

"Where is he?"

"At the palace."

"Can you take me to him?"

"We know of nothing to prevent it."

"Then let us start."

I jump into their boat, and we row for the quay.

Two of my friends, Edouard Lockroy and Paul Parfait, the youngest and most high-spirited of the crew, have one of the boats of the yacht lowered, and follow me at some distance.

Ma foi! we seem to have arrived just at the right moment.

CHAPTER XIX

GARIBALDI

Palermo, 11th June

I AM writing this from the Royal Palace, where Garibaldi has found quarters for all of us in the apartments usually occupied by Court dignitaries.

If anyone had told the King of Naples that I should some day occupy one of the principal rooms in the ancient palace of the Norman kings, he would have been astonished to no small extent; but if someone had gone further, and told his Majesty that in this same palace I should write a description of the taking of Palermo by Garibaldi, he would have been still more astounded. And yet, this is just what has come to pass.

It is in the room of Governor Castelcicala, and on his very desk that I am now going to write of the almost fabulous events which have just come to pass.

First of all, and by your leave, let me resume the story where I left off. In the previous chapter I was telling you about being rowed to the quay in a fruit-seller's boat.

Well, on landing, I felt, like Brutus, ready to kiss the soil which I never expected to see again, and which now welcomes me, because it has become free.

O Liberty! thou great and sublime goddess, the only queen that can never be dethroned, even though she be banished for a while! All these armed men are thy children. A week ago, their heads were bowed and they were full of sadness, but now their heads are erect and they are full of joy.

They are free!

And who are those in red blouses who are rushing about on horseback or on foot, who are being embraced, whose hands are being clasped, upon whom everybody smiles? Ah, those are their deliverers: they are heroes, all.

O Palermo! Palermo! of a truth, to-day, you may be called *"Palermo the fortunate!"*

And yet, at first sight, how wretched and devastated you seem, poor Palermo!

Your answer is: "Barricades close my streets, my houses are crumbling to dust, my public buildings are in flames, but I am free! Stranger, whoever you are, you are welcome: look where you will, but attentively, and then tell the world all you have seen."

Barricades have been erected at intervals, fifty feet apart. They are wonderfully made, and you can see that the constructors are the same as those who made the ramparts of the people in Milan and Rome. The enormous half-metre paving-cubes which the streets of Palermo furnish, being admirably adapted for the purpose, were used for building the barricades, which look like cyclopean structures. Some of them have a narrow opening in the centre, through which protrudes the mouth of a cannon.

But here is a notice posted. Let me read it to you.

ITALY AND VICTOR EMMANUEL!

"I, Giuseppe Garibaldi, Commander-in-Chief of the National Forces in Sicily, at the invitation of the leading citizens, after due deliberation on part of the free communes of the island, considering it to be necessary that in time of war all functions, civil and military, should be vested in one man—

"Do hereby decree, that, in the name of King Victor Emmanuel, I assume the office of Dictator of Sicily.

"GIUSEPPE GARIBALDI."

"*Salemi*,[1] 14*th May*, 1860."

Well and good; here we have something which is simple, plain, and free from ambiguity. If there should be a reaction some day, people will know against whom they have got to rise.

Let us proceed on our way. The sight of the barricades has made me feel thirty years younger. This revolution, in every respect, I find identical with that of 1830. Nothing is wanting to make the resemblance complete: it is only another Bourbon who is being driven out; and Palermo, like Paris, has its Lafayette—one who had previously fought for liberty in America. I took my part in that first revolution, though I fear I have arrived too late to take part in this one.

Ah, yes, I remember this spot. It is "la Piazza delle Quattro Cantoni." Twenty-five years ago, I lodged in that hotel opposite, going under the name of François Guichard. So I am indeed grateful to him who has made it possible for me to take up my abode here, in my own name, to-day.

Now, turn to the left, and we reach the palace. The door is guarded by men in the red blouse. They are the same men—or, anyway, some of them—who fought, one against eight, at Salto San-Antonio, and more recently at Palermo, were fighting, one against twenty.

When I was at Milan, five months ago, I said to Garibaldi—

"Heaven knows when I shall see you again. Give me, therefore,

---

[1] Girolamo and other authorities tell us that the Dictatorship was offered, and accepted, at Marsala. Probably, it was offered there only.

11

some scrap of writing which will enable me to come in touch with you, wherever you may be."

He took a sheet of paper, and wrote the following in Italian:

"*4th January*, '60.

"I recommend my illustrious friend, Alexandre Dumas, to all my other friends.
"GARIBALDI."

I had this pass in my hand, but I had no need for it now. The door-keeper let me go in, without asking me where I was going.

The outer aspect of the Palace of the Senate is absolutely the same as that of the Hôtel de Ville at Paris in 1830. I went up to the first floor, and addressing a young man in a red blouse, who had been wounded in the hand, I said:

"Where is General Garibaldi?"

"He has just gone out to pay a visit to the Convent of La Gancia, which has been burnt and pillaged by the Neapolitans."

"Can I speak to his son, then?"

"I am his son."

"Then embrace me, my dear Menotti! I knew you a long while ago."

The young man embraced me with perfect confidence; then, as I wished him to know who it was that he had so frankly greeted, I presented him the letter of recommendation from his father.

"Ah!" he exclaimed, "you are welcome! My father has been expecting you."

"Well, I should like to see him as soon as possible. I am bringing him news from Genoa in the shape of letters from Medici and Bertani."

"Let us go in search of him, then."

We went downstairs, and made our way along the Strada di Toledo.

Paul and Edouard had joined me again; they would not have left me to gain an empire. They were going to see Garibaldi!

We had to walk between barricades, or to clamber over them and various mounds of rubbish. Twenty-five or thirty houses destroyed by shell are still smoking; almost momentarily more bodies are being removed from the ruins.

We soon reached the magnificent cathedral, built by Roger. One of the statues that stood on the wall which encloses the edifice had had its head carried away by a cannon-ball; several others had been shattered by shell.

Opposite the cathedral stands the house of the Neapolitan consul in London. This was burnt by some Neapolitans who took refuge there in order to defend themselves. When they quitted it, they set fire to it. It is now a smoking ruin.

Perhaps you think that I am inventing these stories for the sake of slandering the Royalists. You can rest assured that I am not, for I could show you a score of photographs by Legray which will prove to you that I am far from telling the whole truth.

"Oh! just look; there is my father," exclaimed Menotti.

You know that, when Garibaldi's son was born, the father wanted to give him the name of one of the martyrs, and not that of one of the saints.

Just as I turned my eyes towards the General, he caught sight of me, and uttered a cry of joy which went right to my heart.

"My dear Dumas! how I have longed for your coming!"

"And, as you see, I was anxiously looking for you. My congratulations, General."

"It is not to me that they are due, it is to those men over there. They are veritable giants, my friend."

This he said, indicating men who were not far from him, and wishing, as ever, to ascribe the glory of his exploits to his companions in arms.

"And where is Türr?"

"You are going to see him. He is the bravest of the brave! You would scarcely believe what he has accomplished. What splendid fellows these Hungarians are!"

"He is not wounded this time, I hope."

"Bullets everywhere, except in him."

"And Nino Bixio? You know that he is reported killed."

"No, it is really nothing: hit by a spent-ball in the chest. He is a dare-devil that nobody can keep back."

"And Manin?"

"He was twice wounded. Poor fellow, he does not get the best of luck. As soon as he shows himself, he is sure to get hit. You are coming back with me to the Palace of the Senate, are you not?"

"Certainly."

He threw his arm round my neck to embrace me and we then set off together.

This Dictator, who has just given 2,000,000 men to his King, truly looks a wonderful being, in his felt hat, damaged by a stray shot, in his red shirt and the traditional grey trousers, with his silk handkerchief, in a loose knot around his neck and forming a hood behind.

I noticed a significant rent in his trousers, just above the instep.

"What is that?" I inquired.

"Oh," said he, "some awkward fellow, talking to me, let his

revolver drop, and it went off. This burnt my trousers and carried away a bit of my boot. It is nothing."[1]

"Really, you bear a charmed life," I replied.

"I am beginning to believe so myself," he said, laughing. "But come, let us get forward."

We soon reached the Palace of the Senate again. The square upon which the front looks, has a very imposing appearance, with its fountain adorned with sculptured heads of animals. Armed men are in groups around the basin, and a battery of four guns taken by Türr at Orbetello stands there.

Garibaldi saw me looking at these cannon.

"Ah," said he, "those are not of much use; but they serve to give confidence to those that use them, and inspire fear in those against whom they are used."

In the General's room we found Türr, who had already heard of my arrival, and was waiting to see me.

We were all in high spirits. The only one missing was poor Téléki.

Edouard Lockroy and Paul Parfait came back with me. They could not help gazing at Garibaldi, amazed to find a man who was at one and the same time so sublimely great, and yet so simple.

I presented them to the General, who then suggested that it was time we went into *déjeuner*. We agreed. As a matter of fact, they were engaged in laying the table when we entered.

The *déjeuner* consisted of a piece of roast veal with a dish of sauerkraut. Twelve of us sat down to table, and the charge for the whole of the General's staff and for us three guests was only six francs.

Garibaldi will not be accused of ruining the finances of Sicily.

But now that he is Dictator, he has considered his position more important: he has allowed himself food, lodging, and ten francs a day—there is a buccaneer for you!

"Where are you lodging?" he inquired of me at dessert.

"At present, on board my yacht."

"But you are not thinking of stopping there, surely. Circumstances might arise which would make your residence there very undesirable."

"Then show me a spot where I can pitch three or four tents, and we shall camp there."

"Wait a moment, I can do something better than that for you. Cenni!"

Cenni is his chief of the staff.

"General?" said the latter, coming forward.

---

[1] According to some accounts, the "awkward fellow" was his son, Menotti.

"Are there any vacant lodgings in the palace?"

"There is nobody there, as yet, General."

"Give the best to Dumas."

"He shall have the Governor's room, if you like, General."

"What do you mean by *if you like?* I mean it, of course. Here is a man who brings me letters announcing reinforcements of 2500 men, 10,000 rifles, and two steam-boats. The Governor's room for Dumas; and keep the next room for myself."

"It shall be done, General."

"Make yourself as comfortable as possible there, and stop as long as you can. The King of Naples will be delighted, when he knows that you are a tenant of his. By the way, what about those rifles?"

"They are on board."

When at Turin, I had promised Garibaldi a dozen rifles whenever he should make war on his own account. He was, therefore, justly entitled to claim them now.

"Very well," said he, "I will send for them."

"At your convenience."

"Meanwhile, you are free to come and go, as may please you, for you are at home."

"With your permission, General, I will now go and inspect the Governor's apartment."

"Pray do."

Just at that moment, three or four priests entered.

"Good gracious! what is this?"

"Not so fast," exclaimed Garibaldi. "They have done splendidly. Each of them has marched, cross in hand, at the head of his flock; and some did not hesitate to handle a rifle."

"Oh, perhaps you have been converted?"

"Yes; and I now have a chaplain—Brother John. I will ask him to pay you a visit, my dear fellow: he is another Peter the Hermit! He had a horse killed under him, and his crucifix broken in his hand. He is just the sort of man I should recommend to you."

"Do send him: I will have his portrait taken."

"Have you a photographer with you?"

"The finest photographer in Paris––Legray."

"Well, then, let him photograph our ruins. It is only right that Europe should know what is going on here: 2800 shells rained on us in a single day!"

"And, possibly, not one of them has touched the palace where you reside."

"Oh, the intention was there, right enough; only, they were lacking somewhat in skill."

Garibaldi showed me two houses, close to the palace, which had been unroofed, and the windows of which had been destroyed.

"We shall take all this, and you, too, in the midst."

"Me? Why do you want to take me?"

"Well, I have only seen you as a General; and, really, you do not look yourself in that guise. I would prefer you in your own costume."

"Be it so, do what you like with me. As soon as I saw you, I knew for certain that I should be one of your victims, in one way or another."

"Now, I am going to leave you with your priests. Adieu."

After taking leave of Garibaldi, I followed Major Cenni to the palace, accompanied by Türr.

I found the rest of my companions in the square in front of the palace. I had arranged to meet them "near to the fountain," although at the time I had not the slightest idea that the spot was close to my future abode.

Subsequent to 1835, the fountain had been replaced by a statue of Philip IV; but my friends guessed that this must be the place I meant.

When I came up, I found them in anything but an amiable mood. I had told them that I should be there at nine o'clock, and it was now eleven. They were dying of hunger; but when they heard that in order to get any *déjeuner* they would have to go right across the town—no small distance—there was a regular chorus of imprecations.

Just then some sort of a scullion-lad passed by, carrying on his head a long basket containing a decanter of wine, another of water, a piece of veal, a dish of sauerkraut, some over-ripe strawberries and some half-ripe apricots. This was going to the house of the Chief of the Staff, and was precisely similar to that which the General had just had. It seemed as if they followed the example of the Spartans: the same broth for everybody.

Türr laid a hand on the youth's shoulder, and said:

"Pardon me, my young friend, you will have to leave this *déjeuner* here, and go and fetch another one."

"But, sir," exclaimed the startled youth, "what am I to say to my master?"

"Simply tell him that Colonel Türr has taken it; besides, I am going to give you a receipt for it."

Türr then tore a leaf from his note-book, and gave a receipt to the cook's messenger for the *déjeuner*, which was immediately laid out on the steps of the Philip IV statue.

The famished men sat down on the lowest step and at once set to work on the veal and sauerkraut.

I then left them busy and went to rejoin Major Cenni, who had not the slightest suspicion of the cause that detained my companions.

"Allow me," he said, "to put you in charge of the inspector; he will take you everywhere. You can choose the rooms you like best. Will you excuse me now, for I want to go and get *déjeuner?* I am dying of hunger."

The Major little thought that his *déjeuner* had fallen into the hands of highwaymen, just when he was looking forward to enjoying it.

The inspector showed me over all the rooms in the palace. I chose the drawing-room, the dining-room, and the bedroom of the late Governor. The drawing-room was vast—in fact, big enough to be used for a dormitory. The windows look upon the square. Hearing a dispute going on below, I opened one and went on the balcony. I found that Colonel Türr was giving a second receipt to the cook's boy, who was bringing the Major's *déjeuner* for the second time. It seems that the first one had not been sufficient for Türr's company.

CHAPTER XX

THE THOUSAND AT SEA

BEFORE following further the fortunes of Garibaldi in the campaign in Sicily, let me give my readers the story of the General's voyage, from the embarkation at Genoa to the landing at Marsala.

We have said that Garibaldi got into the last boat to leave. There were thirty of these boats waiting to embark the volunteers, and, as soon as each was filled, it put to sea to join the steamers. The sea was perfectly calm, and a splendid moon lit up the azure waters.

The steamers were to have come at eleven o'clock. The boats were awaiting them, but at half-past eleven there was still no sign of these vessels. Let me tell you, firstly, how they were acquired, for this will explain the delay. At nine o'clock, Nino Bixio, Orlando, Castilla, and Campo, together with thirty men, embarked in two boats at La Marina in the port of Genoa, and rowed towards two steamers, the *Piemonte* and the *Lombardo*. These they promptly boarded, and then confined in the fore-cabins the officers, engineers, and crew. Up till then, everything had gone well; but when they wanted to get up steam and weigh anchor, grave difficulties began to present themselves to the captors. On board the two vessels, there was nobody amongst them who was an engineer, or a stoker, or a sailor. Progress was impossible.

Garibaldi, seeing no sign of the vessels, began to get impatient; and putting Türr into another boat, he set out, accompanied by six oarsmen only, for the port of Genoa, which was nearly three miles distant.

There he found the captured steamers, but those in possession puzzled to know how to set them in motion; with his arrival these difficulties were surmounted; steam was got up, the anchors were weighed, and the vessels soon ready to put to sea.[1]

In the meanwhile, a boat rowed by a single man entered the harbour of Genoa.

This man was no other than Türr, who, in his turn getting impatient, wanted to find out what had become of the General, just as the General had wanted to find out what had become of the steamers.

Türr got on board the *Piemonte*, which was to be under the chief command of Garibaldi.

---

[1] Garibaldi, according to other accounts, did not reach the vessels, which were able to get under steam without his assistance. Dumas probably got his information from Türr.

Nino Bixio, who was the next best sailor to the General, was in command of the *Lombardo*.

The steamers now put off, and came up with the boats at about half-past three in the morning.

Most of the men, after being tossed about on the waves for five hours, were suffering from sea-sickness and were lying prone at the bottom of the boats. A few, who had not suffered, were standing up and a few more had gone to sleep. All were now transferred from the boats to the steamers; but in the confusion which is inseparable from such an operation one of the boats got astray. Nobody noticed its disappearance; but it was the one that carried the powder, the bullets, and the revolvers.

The vessels now directed their course for Talamone, with the intention of landing at that spot sixty men charged with a very dangerous and very thankless, but, nevertheless, very important mission: this was to make an incursion into the Roman States, for the purpose of raising the cry, "Long live Victor Emmanuel! Long live Garibaldi!"

The news would spread rapidly that a *coup de main* had been attempted in the Papal States; and this would reassure the King of Naples when Garibaldi's departure became known, for he would think that the General's objective was the Papal dominions, and would apprehend no danger to Sicily. Meanwhile, Garibaldi would push on and land his men on the island coast.

This was the reason for a landing on the Papal States, which would have been an act of madness, if seriously intended, but which was, in reality, a very clever *ruse de guerre*.[1]

The sea remained calm until eleven o'clock in the morning, but at that hour the wind rose and the sea began to swell. The *Piemonte* took the lead, and the *Lombardo* followed at three or four miles distance.

Garibaldi really commanded both ships—his own by word of mouth, and the other by means of signals, for on board there was neither map, nor sextant, nor chronometer.

The sea continued to swell, and three-fourths of the volunteers lay helpless on the decks of the two ships, with the sirocco blowing over them. Whilst in this condition, they were suddenly aroused, towards evening, by a cry of "A man overboard!"

In a moment, everybody who could keep his feet rushed over to the side whence this cry had come. Garibaldi, who saw to everything, jumped upon the paddle-box of his vessel, and gave orders to lower a boat; then, getting down, he ran to the engines and stopped the vessel. Four men and an officer jumped into the boat.

[1] In truth, the landing was seriously intended.

The boat flew through the waters in the direction of the spot where the man had disappeared. All followed its course with anxiety, till they saw one of the rowers quickly drop his oar, plunge his arm and the upper portion of his body into the water, and bring out a man by his hair.

There was but one cry from all aboard. Five hundred voices exclaimed: "Alive!"

"Alive!" was the response of those on the boat.

"Bravo!" exclaimed Garibaldi; "it would have been a bad omen if that man had been drowned."

The man, who had lost consciousness, was placed on the ship again; and then all on board found out that he had not fallen into the sea, but had deliberately thrown himself in. He was more or less crazy, and had already thrown himself into the water from off one of the boats; so this was the second time that they had fished him out.

Soon after the accident Garibaldi signalled to the *Lombardo* to draw near his vessel, and when within earshot, the General asked—

"How many muskets have you on board?"

"One thousand," replied Bixio.

"And how many revolvers?"

"Not one."

"How much ammunition?"

"None."

It was then that it was discovered that the boat [1] laden with ammunition and revolvers had not put its cargo on board the steamships.

This answer caused a cloud to pass over the usually calm countenance of our chief. He seemed troubled for a while; then, hailing Bixio, he cried:

"Bring your vessel alongside of mine."

This was all that he said. The General remained thoughtful, but soon recovered his usual serenity. He, however, was evidently thinking out a plan for recovering his lost ammunition.

He now went to the helmsman and ordered him to steer in a certain direction, which he indicated to him, simply saying: "Now, mind, keep to that."

It would have been useless to say to this man, "East, south, or south-east;" for the helmsman, though a very good soldier, was no sailor, and would not have understood any order in technical language.

[1] It is usually stated that there were two such boats, both of which went astray— probably through the fault of the guides appointed by Bixio.

Garibaldi now summoned his officers to his cabin and addressed them thus—

"Gentlemen, I suppose you have heard that there is neither ammunition nor revolvers on board. Revolvers are not of much consequence just now, but what can you do with muskets if you have no ammunition? We must therefore get some."

"But how?" inquired the officers.

"I believe that there is only one way. When we reach Talamone, we shall only be twelve miles from Orbetello. One of us must then go to Orbetello, see the Governor of the fortress, and try to persuade him to let us have what we want."

The officers looked at one another in amazement.

"But suppose the Governor has the messenger arrested," interposed one of them.

"Well, of course, there is that to be feared," was Garibaldi's response.

The officers again maintained silence.

"Never mind," said the General, "I have someone who will go."

"But we will all go!" exclaimed the officers. "The interest we have in the cause must prompt us to say so."

"That I quite understand," said the General; "but do not trouble yourselves about it. I have one who will go. Where is Türr?"

"Türr is asleep on the deck."

"Very well," replied the General.

"General," said one of the officers, "it is no use relying on Türr whilst we are at sea; for when I passed him just now, he said, in a mournful voice: 'Do you know why that poor devil threw himself into the sea?' 'No,' said I. 'But I do; he was sea-sick. If I should throw myself into the sea, be good enough to ask the General not to have me pulled out. It is my last wish; and the request of a dying man is sacred.' With these words he fell back motionless."

Garibaldi began to laugh, left his cabin, and went in search of Türr among the more or less unconscious forms stretched out on the deck. He soon recognised him by his Hungarian dress.

"Türr," said he, "I have something to say to you when we reach land."

Türr half-opened his eyes and murmured:

"When shall we reach land?"

"This evening," answered the General.

Türr heaved a sigh and closed his eyes again. He had done all he could, just at that moment, to further the Sicilian cause.

As soon as Türr reached Talamone on the morning of the 7th, he regained his usual spirits, and went to interview the General.

"Come now, are you ready to be shot?" inquired Garibaldi.

"I should certainly prefer that to going back to sea," replied Türr.

"Well then, take a *calessino*, summon to your aid all the diplomatic eloquence of which you are capable, and induce the Governor of Orbetello to give you all the ammunition we require. We want it badly, for we haven't a single cartridge."

Türr began to laugh.

"Do you think that the Governor of Orbetello will give me as much as a percussion-cap?"

"Who knows?" replied Garibaldi. "At any rate, have a try."

"Give me an order upon him, then."

"And in what capacity am I to give you an order upon the Governor of a Tuscan fortress?"

"Well, at least give me a letter of recommendation to him."

"Oh, as to that, very willingly."

Garibaldi took a piece of paper and wrote:

"Believe everything that my aide-de-camp, Türr, tells you, and assist us with all at your disposal in the expedition which I am undertaking for the glory of Piedmont and the greatness of Italy.
"Long live Victor Emmanuel! Long live Italy!

"G. GARIBALDI."[1]

"With that," said Türr, "I would be ready to go and claim Proserpine from Pluto. Hand it to me."

A quarter of an hour later, Türr was flying along in a *calessino* towards the fortress.

Türr was as eloquent as Cicero, and persuasive as Talleyrand, but still the poor Governor hesitated. So Türr said—

"I expected a refusal, and consequently am prepared for it. Give me a reliable man who will take this despatch to the Marquis di Trecchi, confidential *aide-de-camp* to the King. The sole question is to get his Majesty to bestow on us a second time what he has already done once, but which we have been stupid enough to lose. Only, consider the consequences of this delay: it would take three days to go to Turin, two more to get the ammunition sent to Genoa, or to send an order to that place for it to be handed out, and two more before the material can reach us. Seven days lost! And then you must bear in mind that in the passage of these orders from one person to another we might compromise the King, who must not appear to have anything to do with these matters. I will not speak to you of the unfortunate Sicilians who await our coming as that of a saviour. Finally, let me beg you to reflect on what I have said. Here is the letter for the Marquis di Trecchi, the King's *aide-de-camp*."

The Governor took the letter and read what follows:

[1] Mr. Trevelyan refers to this letter, but does not quote it. The Governor's name was Colonel Giorgini.

"My dear Marquis,

"When embarking, we lost, by some inexplicable accident, the boat containing our arms and ammunition. Will you, therefore, be good enough to ask his Majesty's permission for us to be supplied with 150,000 cartridges, and, if possible, a thousand muskets and bayonets to fit?

"Colonel Türr." [1]

The way in which Türr addressed the chief *aide-de-camp* to the King left no further doubt in the Governor's mind.

"Take all that you require," said he to Türr; "I know that, from the military point of view, I am committing a fault, but I consider my action justifiable because I am persuaded that it will be to the advantage of my sovereign and for the welfare of Italy."

Türr, for a moment, was on the point of admitting that King Victor Emmanuel knew nothing whatever about the expedition; but, reflecting on the consequences of such a confession, he thought that it would be better for one man to be reprimanded, or even punished, than to leave the Sicilian people without succour. So he thanked the Governor in the name of Garibaldi, and took away with him 100,000 cartridges, 300 cannon charges, and four pieces of artillery.[2]

The Governor ended by being as enthusiastic for the cause of Sicily as Türr himself. He now wanted to go to Talamone, and personally hand over to Garibaldi the arms and ammunition. This he actually did, wishing the General every success.

Next day, the 9th of May, Garibaldi set sail again, leaving the Governor of Orbetello quite destitute of ammunition.

Garibaldi, when on board, wore, as was usual with him, no insignia of military rank; but when he learnt of the arrival of the Governor, he retired to his cabin, and shortly after emerged dressed in the uniform of a lieutenant-general of the Piedmontese army.

Before reaching Talamone, and whilst still at sea, the General issued his first "order of the day." When it was drawn up, he sent for Colonel Carini,[3] and requested him to read it out in a loud voice. Carini mounted the platform of the room which served as an office for the General, and read as follows—

"*The 7th May,* 1860. *On board the* '*Piemonte,*'
"*Corps of the Alpine Bersaglieri.*

"The mission of this corps will be—as it ever has been—based on the most complete self-abnegation, and will aim at the regeneration of our native land.

---

[1] This letter is much more precise in its terms than the version given by Mr. Trevelyan.

[2] These details are not given by Mr. Trevelyan.

[3] This was Giacinto Carini to whom Dumas addressed his "war-letters," published in *La Presse.* He was the son of the Sicilian Director of Finances, and took part in the Sicilian Revolution of 1848, when yet very young. He arrived at the Villa Spinola, as a volunteer, about the 24th of April, together with La Masa and Orsini.

Our brave *Cacciatori* have served, and will continue to serve, their country with the devotion and discipline of the best military corps, without other hope or claim than that of a clear conscience.

"Neither rank, nor honour, nor reward has ever been the attraction for these brave men. When dangers had passed away, they returned to the obscurity of private life; but now that the trumpet sounds a new call to battle, Italy sees them, once again, in the van, full of joy and good-will, and ready to shed their blood for her. The battle-cry of the *Cacciatori delle Alpi* is the same as that which resounded, but a year ago, on the banks of the Ticino, when they were fighting against the French army:

"Italia e Vittorio Emmanuele!"

"Issuing from our lips, this cry will everywhere strike terror into our enemies.

(Here follow details of the organisation of the corps.)

"Observation:—This organisation is identical with that of the Italian army, to which we belong; and the various ranks—the award of merit rather than of position—are those which have already been won on the battlefield elsewhere.

"G. GARIBALDI." [1]

The organisation of the corps is as follows— [2]

Commandant-General: Garibaldi.
Chief of the Staff: Colonel Sirtori.
Staff-Captains: Manin and Calvino.
Officers: Majocchi, Borchetta, Grigiatti, Bruzzesi.
Principal *aide-de-camp* to the General: Colonel Türr.
Attached to the staff of the General: Tüköry, Cenni, Menotti, Montanari, Bandi, and Stagnetti.
Private Secretary: Giovanni Basso.
Attached to the expedition with the title of Civil Commissioner: Francesco Crispi.

The whole regiment was divided into seven companies, the commanders of which were as follows: Bixio, Orsini, Stocco, Carini, La Masa, Anfossi, Cairoli.

Chief Engineer: Minutilli.
Commissary-General: Acerbi.
Surgeons: Ripari, Boldrini, Julini.

The expedition was properly enrolled later on, and resumed its voyage at half-past three on the morning of the 9th of May. At five o'clock the vessels reached San Stefano. Here registers for the roll were bought, and coal was taken aboard. About three in the afternoon they put to sea again, steering a course between Sardinia and Sicily.

The morning of the 10th was spent in distributing arms to the seven companies on the two vessels. As to the four cannon smuggled aboard at Talamone, Colonel Orsini was named artillery commander, and Major Forni was made company officer. After the distribution

---

[1] This "order of the day" is not quoted by Mr. Trevelyan.
[2] In Mr. Trevelyan's book, "Garibaldi and the Thousand," some particulars will be found of most of these men.

of arms, a small number of red shirts, and such articles of equipment as they had been able to procure at Genoa, were given out.

We have already said that Garibaldi was on board the *Piemonte*, which was under the command of Castiglia, and it was this vessel that led the way. Bixio, as we have also said, commanded the *Lombardo* by virtue of his knowledge of seamanship. Carini was in command of the soldiers on board.

It had been agreed that the two vessels should proceed on their way, apart from one another, but without losing touch, if possible. Lights, however, were not to be lit at night, so as to avoid the risk of making their presence known to Neapolitan cruisers. The sea was calm, but there was a thick fog: a circumstance that favoured them.

On the 10th at a quarter-past noon, the man with the suicidal mania who had already thrown himself into the sea from the *Piemonte*, and had been transferred to the *Lombardo*, threw himself into the sea again. Bixio, who was continuously on deck, immediately ordered the vessel to stop, and a boat manned by four volunteers to be put out. After superhuman efforts, they succeeded, as before, in fishing this maniac up, more dead than alive.

After having received from the doctors—please note that this man was a doctor—the treatment that his condition needed, he was bound and handed over to two sentries, with instructions not to let him out of their sight.

This accident, however, turned out to be providential, as we shall see later on.

As a result of the *Lombardo* having to stop in order to rescue one of those on board, she lost two hours, and consequently got very much in the rear of the *Piemonte*—which was, in addition, the swifter vessel. Towards the middle of the night period of the 10th to 11th, Garibaldi, having come to the conclusion that the *Lombardo* must have fallen very much into the rear from lack of speed, decided to heave-to, and wait for her.

Now, either because the agreement about the absence of lights had been forgotten, or in order to make it easier for the *Lombardo* to rally to the sister ship, not only were the latter's lanterns hoisted to the masts, but the cabins also were illuminated as they would be under ordinary circumstances.

The *Piemonte* presented herself to the astonished view of the *Lombardo* right athwart her track, and as if intending to bar her passage. Consequently, it is not difficult to understand that the *Piemonte* was taken for an enemy vessel, because of being fully illuminated. Nino Bixio, who was in his cabin, was called by the men on the look-out. A consultation was held with certain other sea-captains who happened to be aboard as volunteers and with Carini, in case of any signal for action which would necessitate serving out ammunition, and it was decided to treat her as an enemy vessel and board her. This seemed to be the only course open.

On the other hand, the *Piemonte* seeing a steamer approaching, and not being sure that it was the one she was waiting for, began to manœuvre to the larboard of the doubtful vessel. Then, finding herself within earshot, she began to hail the other, in order to set matters at rest:

"Hallo! men of the *Lombardo!*"

The chief officers, sailors, and others were on deck and heard the call. Carini was going to answer, when Bixio put his hand over the other's mouth, saying:

"Hold your tongue! It's a Neapolitan warship, which knows us and wants to take us by surprise."

Silence reigned.

Then, in the midst of this silence, the sonorous voice of Garibaldi was heard shouting twice:

"Captain Bixio! Captain Bixio!"

There was no further need for doubt. The supposed enemy vessel was the *Piemonte*.

"The devil take you!" shouted Bixio; "we had agreed to keep lights out, and you are bright as day."

The two vessels were now side by side, and Bixio, with the aid of a megaphone, explained the cause of the delay.[1] They then resumed the journey, and when day was dawning, Garibaldi ordered Bixio to follow him at a distance.

On the morning of the 11th, at half-past three, they thought they espied land; but they found that they had been gazing at distant clouds, for the rising sun soon convinced them of their error. At half-past six o'clock, the Ægades group of islands was clearly discernible, and by ten in the morning they were quite close to Favignana. Then the *Piemonte*, always well in the van, suddenly changed her course to her right.

"There you are!" said Bixio with another oath, "he is changing his mind once again."

And he ordered the helmsman to follow in the wake of the *Piemonte*.

The reason for the change of direction was that Garibaldi had seen an English merchantman leaving Marsala harbour; so the General bore down upon her, and as soon as he could make himself heard, asked in English from the captain whether the Neapolitan fleet was in the harbour.

The Englishman answered that it had left barely an hour previously, proceeding in a southerly direction.

"For what port are you sailing?" asked Garibaldi.

---

[1] Dumas' account differs in some important details from that adopted by Mr. Trevelyan.

"For Genoa," was the answer.

"Ah, well," said Garibaldi, "tell them at Genoa that Garibaldi's expedition has successfully landed at Marsala."

The *Piemonte* changed her helm to the left, and the *Lombardo* followed suit.

Passing very close to the English vessel, Bixio threw on to her deck a loaf of bread containing a letter for delivery in Genoa.

When quite close to Marsala, some fishing-boats were encountered, and one of them was hailed. This boat belonged to a big, good-natured fellow named Strazzera.[1] At first, he was obviously frightened, but plucked up courage when he saw the smiling faces of the volunteers and heard everybody offering him something, and consented to come on board the *Piemonte*. Garibaldi kept his attention fixed upon him; and first of all got a confirmation of what the Englishman had said—not, however, without some slight variation.

The two enemy vessels stationed in the harbour were now indeed some distance away, but whereas the *Capri* had left on the previous evening, the *Stromboli* had taken its departure only an hour previously. The latter vessel was commanded by Carracciolo, grand-nephew of the admiral who was hanged in 1799 by order of Nelson, and the former was under Acton, grandson of the Minister who contributed in no small degree to that hanging.

So it amounts to this, that if the volunteer with the suicidal mania had not thrown himself into the water again, and if the *Lombardo* had not lost two hours in fishing him out of the sea, the two Garibaldian vessels would have run straight up to the *Stromboli*, and the first gun-shots would have recalled the *Capri* and the sailing frigate *Parthenope*.

It is, then, with good reason that we have said that what happened on the *Lombardo* was providential.

Strazzera informed the General that Royalist troops had come to Marsala with the intention of disarming the population, but had left again. The Neapolitan army, therefore, would not be found there.

The dispositions for the landing had been settled soon after passing Favignana. Türr, with twenty-five of the Guides, in the first three boats leaving the ship, was to seize the gate of the city, and then make a dash on the barracks. Captain Bassi with the 8th Company was to follow, and to support Türr's attack.

So the Garibaldian vessels continued on their way to the harbour of Marsala, in which they could now recognise two English war-vessels lying at anchor.[2]

---

[1] Dumas gives this name as Strazzesi, but, as in other instances where proper names are concerned, it has been thought best to follow Mr. Trevelyan.

[2] H.M.S. *Argus* and H.M.S. *Intrepid*. Captain Marryat, the novelist, commanded the latter, and Captain Winnington-Ingram the former.

CHAPTER XXI

THE LANDING AT MARSALA

MASTER STRAZZERA was retained on board to act as pilot of the *Piemonte*. This vessel, under the direction of the General and Captain Castiglia, was now negotiating the difficult entrance to the harbour, and the *Lombardo* was following close behind. Carini and Bixio were on deck. Bixio was giving orders to the helmsman, some were making preparations for the landing, and others not troubling about anything, as they considered there was nothing to be done, except to follow in the wake of the first vessel. But instead of following the track of the other vessel, Bixio now seemed to be resorting to a special manœuvre. He was entering the harbour, apparently without the least attention to the hidden rocks on both sides of him.

"Take care," said Carini, "or you will soon find yourself on the rocks."

Bixio turned his keen eyes on him, and, with an air of derision, pointed out two vessels coming towards them at full steam.

"Do you see those ships?" said he.

"Ah! ah! Yes, indeed."

"Well, they are the *Stromboli* and the *Capri*."

"What then?"

"What then? Surely you understand that it will be better if they get the *Lombardo* with a hole in its side than if they capture her sound and seaworthy."[1]

As Bixio spoke, a shock went through his vessel, and a dull noise was heard. The *Lombardo* had struck a rock; but by that time the *Piemonte* had started landing her men. Large as the hole was, and rapidly as she was filling, there was still plenty of time to disembark those on board. They set to work. As soon as the commanders of the companies were able to leave the vessel in the ship's boats, they, with the assistance of some armed men who accompanied them, seized all the boats in the harbour, with anyone on board. Some boats belonging to good patriots in Marsala also came along to help in the task.

A crowd began to collect upon the quays, anxious to know what all this meant. Some of these onlookers then began to shout: "Italy for ever! Long live Garibaldi!"

Two-thirds of the men were now already landed, and were forming

---

[1] Mr. Trevelyan says nothing about this conversation, merely observing that the *Lombardo* "grounded on the shallows."

up ready for action. Amongst these were two companies called the Sicilian Companies, as they were entirely composed of Sicilians. Their commanders were Carini and La Masa.

The Neapolitan vessels, by this time, had reached the entrance to the harbour. The *Stromboli* was in the van, and the *Capri*, with the sailing frigate in tow, steaming at some little distance from her, arrived a quarter of an hour later. As soon as the *Stromboli* arrived, she opened the attack, but the first gun missed fire. Seeing what was taking place, the captain[1] of an English warship which was on the spot went on board the *Stromboli* and informed the commander of that vessel that some English officers and part of his crew were ashore, and that he would hold the Neapolitan commander responsible if anything happened to them.

At first, Carracciolo[2] answered to the effect that he could not enter into matters of that sort. Before everything else, he had to do his duty. And as a proof that he was prepared to do that duty, whatever it involved, he ordered his men to fire again.

A second round was fired; but the result was the same as in the first case. The cap exploded, but failed to fire the charge. Carracciolo, seeing a sort of providential interposition in this double miss-fire, decided to await the arrival of the *Capri*, and further orders from the *Parthenope*.

Garibaldi had now landed most of his men, and when the *Capri* and *Parthenope* lined up to open fire, the column of volunteers was already drawn up in battle formation on the jetty which commands the entry to the harbour of Marsala. So, they might either have taken cover, or have marched into the town immediately; but as Garibaldi was still on board the *Piemonte* supervising the disembarkation of the munitions and stores, they absolutely declined to leave till all was finished.

Meanwhile, the fire from the vessels continued, but it was so badly directed that nobody was hit. The only casualty was the death of a poor dog, who had joined the expedition. When all the artillery and munitions had been landed, Garibaldi left the ship preceded by Türr. When they were on the mole, a shell burst about ten paces from them. Neither was hurt, although they were covered with earth as a consequence.

The General now gave the order to march on the town; and this they did, to the great astonishment of the townspeople, who cheered lustily. Assembled in the streets, or at their doors and windows, they could not believe their own eyes.

[1] Mr. Trevelyan says the captains of both warships went.
[2] Mr. Trevelyan says that the commander was Acton.

The Neapolitan vessels then turned their guns on the town [1] and fired lots of shells. Whilst this was in progress, Garibaldi, who was expecting, or rather, ought to have expected a landing from these vessels, took steps to have all posts on the sea front occupied, and the following proclamations posted on the walls of the town.

The first, addressed to the Sicilian people, was as follows:

"Sicilians! [2]
"I have brought you a handful of brave men, survivors from the battles of Lombardy, who have responded to Sicily's cry. We are in your very streets now. We seek nothing but the liberation of Italy. If we are all united, the task will be both easy and brief. To arms! Those who do not respond to the call are not merely cowards, but traitors to their country.

"Do not make a pretext of saying: 'We have no arms.' We shall have the guns; but at the present moment any weapon serves its purpose in the hands of a brave man. The municipalities will take care of the old men, the women, and the children who are left behind.

"To arms then! Sicily will once again show the world how a country gets rid of its oppressors, with the assistance of a friendly people.
"G. GARIBALDI."

The second proclamation, addressed to the Neapolitan army, was couched in the following terms—

"It is not discord between Italians, it is foreign arrogance which has got the upper hand in Italy. But on the day when the sons of the Samnites, united with their brothers in Sicily, will join hands with the Italians of the North, on that day will our people, of whom you are the fairer part, take their place again among the foremost nations of Europe, as they did in the past.

"Soldiers of Italy! I have but one ambition, that of seeing you ranged alongside of the soldiers of Varese and of San Martino in one common fight against the enemies of our country.
"G. GARIBALDI."

Meanwhile the municipality of the town of Marsala had met, and approved an address to General Garibaldi, begging him to assume the dictatorship.

On entering the town, the General gave orders to Türr to seize the telegraph station, and to cut the communications.

Türr entrusted the execution of the order to a lieutenant. The telegraphist took to flight when he saw the lieutenant and his men approaching. These entered the office, where they found the draft of a message to this effect—

"Two steamships, flying the Sardinian flag, have just entered the harbour and are landing men."

The despatch was addressed to the officer commanding at Trapani.

Whilst reading this message, the lieutenant noticed that the

---

[1] This statement seems to need some correction. Some badly directed shots may have fallen into the town.

[2] This and the following proclamation are not quoted by Mr. Trevelyan.

machine wished to communicate an answer. One of the volunteers, who had been a telegraphist at Genoa, translated this reply—

"How many men are landing, and what are their intentions?"

The officer replied—

"Please pardon my mistake. I find I was wrong. The two steamships are merchantmen from Girgenti, laden with sulphur."

The machine is in motion again, and spells out this response—

"You are an idiot!"

The officer, thinking that this dialogue has gone far enough, then cuts the wires, and returns to give an account of his mission to Türr.

It has been said that Garibaldi was received at Marsala with only moderate enthusiasm. There is a certain amount of truth in this. As a historian, I have two duties to fulfil: that of stating facts, and that of giving explanations of those facts.

Now, we admit that the reception given by Marsala was much colder than was expected; but this was due to two causes: firstly, to the bombardment which still thundered over the town, and thus infused a feeling of hesitation into most minds; and then to the insurrection which had broken out a fortnight previously and had been put down. This suppression had either led to prison, or had put to flight all the young people of the town.

With this explanation we end our account of Garibaldi's voyage.

CHAPTER XXII

THE FIRST MARTYR

Palermo, 15th of June

WE have just spoken of an insurrection which had broken out a fortnight previous to Garibaldi's arrival at Marsala.[1] This rising was at Palermo, and it is the story of this that I am going to narrate; but, so that the reader may get a better grasp of the situation, we will first give a brief survey of what had previously transpired in Sicily.

Even from the beginning of the war in Italy in 1859, it was easy to see that an ardent spirit of agitation was penetrating to the very heart of the island, and was uniting in a common bond of sympathy three distinct sections of society—the nobles, the middle classes, and the masses.

At that time the head of the police was Salvator Maniscalco, who has since become so painfully notorious. He was in his early days in the *gendarmerie*, and, there, became the favourite of Del Caretto, who made him his own personal officer. Then, coming to Sicily with Prince de Satriano, son of the celebrated Filangieri, he first filled the post of Provost-Marshal in the army, and soon afterwards was appointed head of the police of his city. But promotion did not end there; a little later on, he was nominated Director-General of Police for all Sicily.

In virtue of his position, it was his duty to suppress any revolutionary movement that threatened to break out in the island.

The early career of Maniscalco at Palermo had been greatly to his own advantage. Clever, courteous, very deferential to the aristocracy, he soon gained admittance to the most exclusive society; but the moment came when he had to choose between social success and the orders he alleged he had received from the Government. He chose the latter alternative.

Everybody was conspiring at Palermo, if not actively, then, at least, most sympathetically; but the most conspicuous conspirators were the nobles.

Maniscalco determined to break with them. At the moment when symptoms of agitation, inspired by the victories of Montebello and Magenta, showed that there was great excitement amongst the aristocracy, he took a score of *sbirri* with him, and, under the pretext of dispersing a seditious assembly, made an irruption into

---

[1] The day of the rising was the 4th of April.

182

the Casino, broke the mirrors, put out the lights, and, having cleared everybody out, locked the doors. This happened just about the time when French generals were receiving the rank of marshal, and sometimes also titles associated with the names of victories they had won. So, in honour of his victory, the Director of Police was nick-named: "Il Conte di Smuccia-Candele," otherwise, "Count Candle-snuffer."

This brutal aggression of Maniscalco bore its fruits. Either through the influence of the nobles, or by mere force of circumstances, an armed rising broke out at Santa Flavia, a little village eleven miles from Palermo. The police got the upper hand, suppressed the rising, and made a certain number of arrests.

Then a twofold sentiment began to develop amongst the Sicilian people : the desire for political amelioration in the state of the country, and a personal hatred of the police and their head. Needless to add that over all this there brooded an ever-increasing antagonism between Sicilians and Neapolitans.

We are now going to see how these two sentiments developed, and to note their influence on the progress of events.

One day, as Maniscalco was about to enter the cathedral by a side door, a man, whose face was not clearly recognisable because of a broad-brimmed hat and a red beard, walked straight up to him, and simply saying the two words, "Die, wretch!" stabbed him with a knife.

Maniscalco, uttering a scream, fell back. It was thought that, like Rossi,[1] he had been killed; he was, however, only severely wounded.

His assailant disappeared; and in spite of all efforts to track him down, the police were never able to put their hands upon him. Twenty arrests were made, and five or six people tortured, but all exertions to discover the man were in vain.

The King of Naples compensated Maniscalco for his wound with an annuity of two hundred ounces of gold, although he was very rich already.

Then began a period of Royalist terrorism, during which Maniscalco ceased to be regarded as a political enemy, and now became an object of personal detestation to the people, like Narcissus under Nero, or Olivier le Daim under Louis XI.

He first made additions to his police force by enrolling men recruited amongst malefactors; and then let loose this band of thieves and assassins upon Palermo and its suburbs.

The *sbirri* were ordered by him to arrest the proprietor of the tavern

[1] Count Pellegrino-Rossi, a French diplomatist of Italian birth, assassinated in a rising at Rome in 1848.

del Fiano-Catolica. They found only his wife and daughter at home —the latter had gone to bed. They would not believe what the woman said about the absence of her husband.

"Who then is in that bed?" said they.

"My daughter," was the reply.

"Hold the mother," said one of the *sbirri*, laughing, "while I go and find out the sex of the person in bed."

The mother was held down, and the daughter outraged before her eyes.

A countryman, named Licata, having escaped from the clutches of Maniscalco, was punished by having his wife, who was about to be a mother again, thrown into a dungeon along with all his children, until he should give himself up to procure their release.

Then a triumvirate was formed, composed of Captain Chinicce, Commissary Malato, and Colonel Simone of the *gendarmerie*. These men racked their brains to invent new punishments.

The most horrible were called "the Angelic Instrument" and "the Cap of Silence."

"The Cap of Silence" was a kind of gag of diabolical perfection; and "the Angelic Instrument" is an iron mask which encloses the head, and when put into operation by means of a screw, slowly compresses it till it is entirely crushed.

I was shown a pair of handcuffs which cannot be closed without piercing the flesh to the bone, however thin the wrist may be upon which they are put.

They have also renewed that form of torture used in 1809 by the Spaniards against our soldiers: hanging by the waist.

These cruelties were principally employed by Maniscalco against the aristocracy, whom he considered to be those who instigated revolution. He was, however, mistaken in his supposition. The aristocracy did not content themselves with rousing up the people; they themselves conspired against a Government which, in the words of an Englishman, was "the negation of God."[1]

All this while, Sicily beheld Lombardy, the Duchies, Tuscany, and the Legations entering on an era of peace and prosperity, in becoming united to Piedmont, whilst she herself was still chained to Naples under a regime that ruined property, dishonoured individuals, and engendered misery and degradation.

Flesh and blood would not stand it: a revolution was surely at hand.

[1] "I have seen and heard strong and too true expressions used: 'This is the negation of God erected into a system of government.'" [W. E. Gladstone, in a letter to Lord Aberdeen, 1851.]

It should, however, be noted that this famous epigram was of Italian origin, and was quoted by Gladstone, as the context shows.

Maniscalco, however, made no attempt to pacify the people's minds, he only sought to disarm their hands. Searches were, therefore, made in all houses for the purpose of seizing all guns, swords, or bayonets that were to be found.

In the midst of these persecutions, a Sicilian committee was formed under the title of "The Committee of Public Welfare," and included the leading nobility and citizens, as well as representatives of the masses.

On all sides subscriptions were opened for the purchase of arms and ammunition. Preparations were now made for the rising, which was anxiously awaited.

The police, who guessed that trouble was brewing, were on the alert. They could hardly fail to be aware of what was going on, for the spirit of revolution was not in this spot, or in that: it was everywhere; in fact, it was in the air.

Then came the news of the union between Piedmont, Tuscany, the Duchies, and the Legations. The influence of Victor Emmanuel, a progressive prince amongst reactionary kings, and his devotion to Italian unity, moved Sicily deeply. By the common consent of nobles, citizens, and people, the union between Sicily and Piedmont was decided on.

One point alone gave rise to discussion: should there be a rising at once, or should they wait for a while?

The representatives of the nobility and the citizens were in favour of waiting, whilst those of the people wanted immediate action.

Amongst those who favoured an immediate revolt was a master-plumber, named Riso, who had amassed a tolerable amount of money by his industry. (Yesterday, his house, a meeting-place for all Sicilian patriots, was pointed out to me.) He declared that the nobles and citizens might do as they liked, but he was not waiting any longer. He could count upon the support of at least two hundred friends.

"Very well, then," said the nobles and the citizens, "begin when you like; and we will join you, if your movement shapes well."

Riso then appointed a meeting with his friends at the Monastery of La Gancia on the night of April the 3rd. Riso's own house stood close by the monastery.

All the patriots were informed that a rising would begin at dawn on April the 4th. Maniscalco gave himself up to despair, for he was fully persuaded that something was going to happen, but something which he could by no means prevent. He accordingly assembled all the police chiefs on the night of the 2nd of April, and informed them that he could not prevent a revolution breaking out; so he would have to content himself with putting it down, when it did break out.

Meanwhile the whole city was nervous and anxious: In the day-time on the 3rd of April, everybody got in provisions in case they should be compelled to remain at home for several days, and in the evening, families and relatives assembled together and doors were locked. Some knew what was going to happen, others guessed that something unusual was about to take place.

Unluckily, at about eight o'clock in the evening, Maniscalco received information from a monk—the traitor's name is unknown —of what was to occur that very night.[1]

He rushed off in great haste to see General Salsano, commandant of the city, and got the monastery surrounded. Riso was already there with twenty-seven of his confederates: the others had not yet joined him, but would, doubtless, arrive during the night. Riso knew his men to be reliable, and that they would be there by the hour agreed upon.

At daybreak, Riso partially opens a window, and sees the street closed by soldiers and artillery.

His companions are of opinion that the best thing to do is to abandon the whole enterprise, and to let each one of them try and save himself as best he can.

"One thing is still lacking to this country," exclaimed Riso,— "martyrs! Let us give to Sicily that of which she stands in need."

And from the half-opened casement he opens fire upon the Neapolitans.

Now the deadly combat has begun. Cannons are placed in position before the monastery gate. Two balls shatter it to splinters and then bury themselves in the tower which faces the courtyard.

The Neapolitans now enter with fixed bayonets. The Superior of the convent advances to meet them, and is immediately pierced by their weapons.

The twenty-seven brave men commanded by Riso perform pro-digies of valour. They fight for two hours, contesting their position from corridor to corridor and from cell to cell.

Riso now gathers his men together for the purpose of making a sortie by the gate which had been broken open by the cannon. The Neapolitans fall back, but still maintain their firing. Riso falls, struck by a bullet which breaks his leg above the knee. His comrades force an opening, leaving ten or a dozen of their number prisoners.

Riso endeavours to rise; two soldiers advance, and, holding their rifles close to him, discharge them into his abdomen. He falls a

[1] Mr. Trevelyan disputes the truth of this allegation.

second time, but is still alive. He is then placed in a cart and paraded round the town, as a bloody trophy from the encounter. The procession stops at all cross-roads and public places, whilst the *sbirri*, the *gendarmes*, and the police mount on the wheels of the cart in order to spit in the face of the dying man.

Whilst this was in progress, another monk was killed, and four more were wounded. A "Bambino Gesù," much loved by the people, was also put to death by being impaled on bayonets, and then carried through the streets.

The silver vessels in the church were stolen. One soldier mistook for pure gold the heavy cyphers over the door, which are made of iron, gilt on the surface, so he wrenched these off and put them in his knapsack.

An order arrived from Maniscalco for Riso to be conveyed to the hospital, and every care taken of him.

The surgeons dress the wounds, which, in any case, are mortal. Still, he may survive two or three days, they think.

That was all that Maniscalco wanted. He arrested Riso's father, who had taken no part in the rebellion, but who, on account of his anxiety for his son, had been seen in his dressing-gown standing at a window overlooking the convent.

He and the thirteen other prisoners were tried and found guilty. All the fourteen were shot on the 5th of April.

The same evening, Maniscalco came to Riso's bedside.

"Here," said he, "is the order for the execution of your father. Tell us all you know; give the names of the nobles who incited you to this rebellion, and your father's life will be spared."

Riso hesitated for a moment, but in the end took the whole responsibility upon himself, and declared he had no accomplices.

Maniscalco inquires of the surgeons, who inform him that the wounded man may live twenty-four hours yet.

"Very well," says he, returning to Riso, "I'll come and see you to-morrow, so that you may be able to sleep over the matter."

The patriots, however, got news of the infamous trick that had been tried upon him, and succeeded in letting him know that his father had been shot that very morning, and that the life he was to save by his revelations was extinct six hours before the offer had been made.

Riso died in the night; some say from the shock caused by hearing of his father's execution, whilst others declare that death was due to tearing the bandages from off his wounds.

Now that Riso was dead, and his father and accomplices were shot, Maniscalco thought he had got the upper hand of the revolutionary movement. Now the golden age for spies began. Money and rewards were showered on all who had anything to do with the police.

But this sense of security did not last long. Prompt as had been the suppression of the insurrection at Palermo, it nevertheless broke out again in the country districts. The *Picciotti*[1] met, and endeavoured to stir up the revolution again by offering all insurrectionists an inviolable refuge in the mountains.

The tocsin from La Gancia was answered by every other belfry in Sicily.

At La Bagheria two companies of soldiers in garrison were attacked; the garrison of Misilmeri was driven out of the town, as far as the Ammiraglio bridge; Altavilla and Castellanza sent their contingents of armed peasants; and Carini, making ready for the expected summons from Palermo, had already hoisted the flag of United Italy on the 3rd of April—that is to say, on the eve of the outbreak at La Gancia. This was the signal for other flags to be unfurled, and to cries of "Long live Victor Emmanuel!" they were forthwith hoisted.

Unfortunately, want of arms, ammunition, and organisation prevented the insurrection becoming general. Just then, one saw nothing but meteors and flashes of lightning—the tempest had not yet broken loose.

Palermo still kept on hoping that the country would come to her assistance. Terrified by the executions, groaning under the iron hand of Maniscalco, she remained utterly crushed by this first failure, yet firm and constant in her hatred of her oppressors, turning to every point of the horizon to beg of God and man that aid which would lift her up again from out of her fallen state.

In the meantime a sort of general headquarters had been established at Gibilrossa. Guerilla attacks were made on the troops for the purpose of drawing them out on to the heights and thus breaking, first in one place and then in another, the iron circle drawn round the city.

Maniscalco now resolved to extend into the country the system of terror which, till then, had been confined to the city. Sorties of troops, headed by artillery, were then made; country-houses were pillaged; villages were destroyed; and if there were no armed men that opposed them, they contented themselves with firing on women and children.

About this time the names of certain insurrectionary leaders began to be talked about. Amongst them, we may mention Cavaliere

---

[1] The name *picciotto* is given to all young countrymen—especially from fifteen to twenty-one years of age.   (Author's note.)

Stefano Santa-Anna, the Marquis Fimatore Corteggiani, Pietro Pediscalre, Marinuzzo, and Ludovico de la Porta, who after ten years of exile and persecution was still unwearied in fighting and conspiring for his country.

Skirmishes took place at Gibilrossa and at Villabole; then Carini was chosen as a point of concentration for a march on Palermo.

It would be impossible to describe the state of rage and exasperation to which its citizens had been driven. Daily there were isolated encounters between Maniscalco's myrmidons and respectable citizens who were quietly going about their business in the public streets, or crossing the squares. These encounters were purposely arranged, so as to furnish a pretext for police interference. The citizens, of course, were always supposed to be transgressing in some way; and, without the opportunity of discussion or explanation, they were promptly handcuffed and taken to prison. After a while, shops began to close, business to stagnate, and the streets to become deserted.

Just then, a ray of hope dawned, and the drooping spirits of the citizens were unexpectedly raised. A Sardinian paper, smuggled into Palermo in spite of the police, announced the formation of a committee at Genoa, having for its object the bringing of aid to the Sicilians, by all means possible. The journal added that an expeditionary corps was then being organised in northern Italy to come to the rescue of the Sicilian patriots. At this news all hearts beat faster.

One man came forward and declared he would spread the good news throughout Sicily. This man was Rosolino Pilo, who landed at Messina on the 10th of April. After ten years of exile, he was returning to his native land, bringing the good news that not merely was an expeditionary corps being formed, but that Garibaldi himself was to command it.

Rosolino Pilo went through Sicily in all directions working indefatigably. Everywhere one found the writing on the walls—

"*Garibaldi is coming! Long live Garibaldi! Long live Victor Emmanuel!*"

In every village, therefore, every peasant who could read, or who could get someone to read the words to him, knew that succour was near at hand.

Another patriot, Giovanni Correo, did the same; and soon, through the length and breadth of the island, there echoed the one cry: "*Long live Garibaldi! Long live Victor Emmanuel!*" All pledged themselves to annexation.

Then Maniscalco sought to drown these cries of liberty by a thunder-clap. Prince Pignatelli, Prince Niscemi, Prince Giardinelli,

Cavaliere San Giovanni, Father Ottavio Lanza, Baron Riso, and the eldest son of the Duke of Legiaro were arrested and thrown into prison, like common felons.

But the name of Garibaldi sustained the people and consoled them amid all their sufferings.

Children when passing the *sbirri* chanted in varying tones—

"*Long live Garibaldi! Garibaldi is coming.*"

The wife deprived of her husband, the mother who had lost her son, the sister bereft of her brother, instead of shedding tears, cried to the *sbirri* in threatening tones—

"*Garibaldi is coming!*"

The *sbirri* felt shudders pass through them, when they heard this name which was so terrible to tyrants.

A new star had risen upon Sicily—the star of Hope.

In Garibaldi the people were going to see the bearer of a name famous all over Italy, a captain of genius, and one from whom action radiated wherever he went.

As the news of his coming was more and more confirmed, there was but one question put everywhere—

"And Garibaldi?"

"He is coming! he is coming!" was the invariable response.

It was now desired to ascertain if a spirit of solidarity existed amongst the people. It was accordingly made known that between such and such hours everybody was expected to join in a promenade in the Strada di Macqueda. The street was crowded. Everybody was on foot, even the most fashionable women: carriages would have impeded circulation, so nobody came in one.

Maniscalco was furious. What could he do to these harmless people who were walking about, unarmed and not causing any disturbance.

The devil came to his aid and inspired him with an idea. It was this: since these people are not crying "Long live Garibaldi! Long live Victor Emmanuel!" why not make them cry—

"*Long live the King of Naples!*"

A group of soldiers and *sbirri* then came along shouting—

"*Long live Francis II!*"

There was no response from the people.

The soldiers and *sbirri* then surrounded a group of them, saying: "Shout, 'Long live Francis II!'"

Profound silence reigned.

Then suddenly the silence was broken. A man threw his hat in the air, shouting—

"*Long live Victor Emmanuel.*"

He fell dead instantly, pierced by bayonets.

Then musket, bayonet, and dagger got to work. Two more were killed, and thirty, including women and children, were wounded.

The whole population then went home, without any response to these murders and this shedding of innocent blood other than the exclamation:

"Garibaldi is coming! Garibaldi is coming!"

Next day, the details of these horrible deeds were the theme everywhere: fathers whilst walking with their children had been wounded —often both father and child. Men and women who had taken refuge in some café had been pursued thither, and attacked by mounted *gendarmes*.

Next day, indeed, Palermo had an alarming aspect. Like the warning to Balthazar, the walls everywhere bore a similar terrible *"Mene, Mene, Tekel, Upharsin"* in the inscription—

"Garibaldi is coming! Garibaldi is coming!"

During the whole day the streets were deserted, and the windows shuttered; but when evening came shutters opened again, and through the night all eyes were turned to that amphitheatre of hills which surround Palermo, in the hope of seeing the beacons which were to announce the long-expected assistance from the country to the city.

One morning—it was the 13th of May—a cry rang through the city— "Garibaldi has landed at Marsala!"

The Avenger had come!

CHAPTER XXIII

FROM MARSALA TO SALEMI

THIS coldness on the part of Marsala, the news given by skipper Strazzera, the statement that the revolt had been crushed—all these had caused a certain feeling of discouragement in the national army, but none the less they resolutely set out on the march to Salemi on the 12th of May at four in the morning, along paths of such difficulty that it was a miracle they were able to bring the artillery along with them.

Some citizens of Marsala had joined the column as volunteers.

As night came on whilst the troops were still some little distance from Salemi, the General ordered them to halt and bivouac. Just then attention fell on a very picturesque spot on the left side of the road. It was *"la fattoria di Rebingano,"* belonging to Baron Mistretta of Salemi. The column, which was dying of hunger, directed itself to this point, reached the summit of the hill, and came to a halt round the buildings.

The men were entirely without provisions, but Providence came to the rescue. Baron Mistretta, having heard of the landing of Garibaldi at Marsala, and thinking that the column might pass near to his factory, might even halt there, had sent his nephew to place at the disposal of the General everything on his farm: sheep, fowls, cheese, bread, milk, flour, wine, etc.

Just when the men were enjoying this improvised repast, they descried a small body of armed men approaching the bivouac. When they reached us, we found ourselves face to face with the two brothers Santa Anna, whose names have been mentioned in the dispatches, and who took part in the first conflicts with the Royalists. They were accompanied by Baron di Mocarda, brother-in-law to the Marquis di Torre-Alta, of Trapani, and fifty armed men, round whom had gathered all those from Marsala who had fled far from the scene of the outbreak of which we have spoken.

Baron Mocarda himself was a fugitive and was concealing himself in the mountains. Reaching Marsala in disguise, he had chartered a small vessel and had already left for Malta, when he saw the *Piemonte* and the *Lombardo* coming into port. He guessed that this must be the long-expected Garibaldi expedition, so he turned back to Marsala.

In addition to those already mentioned, there were M. Marcedo and M. Coppola. It was from these gentlemen that we got the first reliable details of the progress of the insurrectionary movement in the towns. The whole may be summed up as follows: some armed bands who had escaped from the affair at Palermo and the skirmishes which had taken place in the two towns of Monreale and Carini still kept the field, without anyone knowing precisely where they were. The only thing known was that Corrao and Rosolino Pilo were with them, and that Sicily was prepared for a general rising as soon as Garibaldi's arrival in the island became known.

The bands had for their leaders Luigi La Porta, Marinuzzi and the brothers Bruno, all of Palermo. Let us add to these names that of Paolo Cucuzza, a celebrated bandit of the Sicilian mountains, whither he frequently escaped—and with greater luck than Fra Diavolo—from the *gendarmes* and *sbirri* of the Neapolitan Government. Let us hasten to add that eleven years as a settler in America followed, and his exemplary conduct redeemed him from the stigma of his wild, and rather more than picturesque exploits in the mountains.

Yet another recruit, having no resemblance whatever to the one we have just previously enrolled, was also made on this day.

A short distance from Salemi, just when the General was watering his horse at a spring, a monk belonging to the reformed Franciscan order, with an intelligent face, a keen eye, and close-cropped, frizzled hair, approached him.[1] This monk belonged to the convent of Santa Maria degli Angeli di Salemi, and gave lessons in philosophy. He expressed his great joy at seeing the General, but was astonished to find so simple a man. Suddenly he fell on his knees, and cried: "I thank Thee, O God, for allowing me to live in the days of the coming of the Messiah of Liberty. From this moment forward, I swear that I am ready to die, if necessary, for his cause and that of Sicily."

Türr instantly saw how many adherents might be gained amongst so superstitious a population as the Sicilians, by the exhortation of a young, eloquent, and patriotic priest. So he said to the young monk: "Will you come with us?"

"That is my sole desire," was his reply.

"Then, come along," said Garibaldi with a sigh; "you shall be our Ugo Bassi." So saying, he put into the monk's hands a copy of a proclamation which he had previously got printed:

"TO ALL GOOD PRIESTS"[2]

"The clergy at the present time are making common cause with our enemies. They are hiring foreign soldiers to fight against Italians. Whatever happens,

---

[1] This "monk," whom Dumas calls "Brother John," was a friar, named Father Pantaleo. He became famous from his devotion to Garibaldi and his bravery in battle.

[2] This proclamation is not given by Mr. Trevelyan.

13

whatever be the fate of Italy in the future, her clergy will be detested by all generations!

"We, however, have one consolation, one that leads us to believe that the true religion of Christ is not yet dead, and that is, to see priests in Sicily marching at the head of the people against their oppressors.

"Men like Ugo Bassi, Verità, Gusmaroli, Bianchi are not all dead yet; and on the day on which the example of these martyrs, these champions of the national cause, shall be followed, the foreigner will have ceased to trample on our soil, and to be master of our sons, our wives, our property, and ourselves.

"G. GARIBALDI."

"This proclamation is not for me," said the monk after he had read it; "for I have already been converted. I, however, will give it to those whose faith needs sustaining."

At dinner, which was had at the house of the Marquis di Torre Alta, where the staff had its headquarters, the General placed Brother John—for that was his name—on his right.

All Garibaldi's officers were not exactly of an unimpeachable orthodoxy, and Brother John was the butt of a good deal of jesting. One officer said:

"Now, Brother John, since you have become our chaplain you must put off the hood of the monk and carry a musket."

But Brother John, shaking his head, answered: "I have no need of one. I shall fight with the Word, and with the Cross. He who bears Christ on his breast has no need of a musket on his shoulder."

Garibaldi saw that he had to deal with a man of spirit and intelligence, and indicated by a gesture that he wished this banter to cease.

After dinner, Brother John left for Castel Veterano, his native town. He returned, next morning, with 150 peasants, all armed with guns. These men, as has already been mentioned, were called *Picciotti.*

Let me revert to the halt at the farm, in front of which the expeditionary corps was at the time of the arrival of Brother John.

After a delightful night spent under a star-spangled sky, and in a sweet and pure atmosphere such as only a Sicilian spring gives to its elect, and amid which the Garibaldian hymn resounded on all sides, they resumed their march towards Salemi, on the morning of the 13th. The only precaution taken was to separate the column into two parts: the volunteers took the direct road to Salemi, whilst the artillery was obliged to follow a longer but, for them, a more practicable route.

Garibaldi conceived the idea of this disposition of his forces, after hearing that 4000[1] Royalist troops, commanded by General Landi, had arrived at Calatafimi, and were threatening to occupy Salemi. It was, therefore, important to arrive at Salemi before the Royalists.

---

[1] About 3000 would be nearer the mark.

Salemi was the first town in Sicily in which General Garibaldi and his companions in arms received a truly enthusiastic welcome. Men came from all parts to place themselves at his service; lodgings were immediately found for the volunteers; cartridges were made from the powder which had been procured on the march or which had come from Trapani; and lastly the two engineer-mechanics from the *Piemonte* and *Lombardo*, Achille Campo and Giuseppe Orlando, were entrusted with the task of making some gun-carriages and waggons.

The day was spent in resting at Salemi, and preparing all necessary dispositions in regard to the organisation of the forces. All money in the public exchequer at the time was requisitioned, and was used principally in buying horses for the commanders. A provisional government was set up, and Baron Mistretta was placed at the head of it. Everybody submitted to it with the utmost goodwill. The priests, especially, were notable in their patriotism and devotion. On seeing how well disposed the clergy were in Sicily, the General addressed to them the manifesto that he had already read to Brother John.

News and messages were arriving hourly at Salemi from the country round about. In every direction the populace declared their readiness to join the movement. Garibaldi then complied with Colonel La Masa's request, and authorised him to bring together these new volunteers, form them into platoons, and assemble them at a central spot.

Meanwhile the principal citizens of Salemi and of some other communes begged the General to assume the dictatorship. We have already seen that he acceded to the general request, as the proclamation posted on the walls of Palermo has shown.

A second order of the day was signed on the same date at Salemi. Its purpose was to constitute a national army by the conscription of all men fit for service, between the ages of seventeen and fifty, graded as follows:

From seventeen to thirty, for active service in battalions of the line; from thirty to forty, for active service in their respective districts; and from forty to fifty, for service in their own communes, or on works of public necessity.

On the morning of the 15th the General was notified that a Royalist column was operating in front of Calatafimi. He immediately gave orders to the expeditionary corps and also to the companies commanded by Santa Anna and Coppola to take the road to Calatafimi. The expeditionary corps had been reorganised. The seven companies had been increased to nine, and the command of these two new ones had been entrusted to Captains Bassini and Grigiotti respectively. Then the nine companies, and likewise the Piedmontese Carabineers, had been divided into two battalions, the first being commanded by Colonel Bixio, and the second by Colonel Carini.

This is how the forces were disposed for the attack on the enemy by Colonel Sirtori, the Chief of the Staff, acting for the General. The left wing was thrown forward.

Coppola's and Santa Anna's companies were to scout on the flanks of the column; the 9th company, under Grigiotti, was the advanced guard; a hundred paces to the rear followed the 8th under Barrini, the 7th next under Cairoli, the 6th under Ciaccio (in place of Carini, promoted), the 5th under Anfossi. These five companies had Carini as battalion commander.

Now followed the artillery and engineers under Orsini and Minutelli, and in addition a company of volunteers, formed from the crews of the steam-boats, under Castilla. Immediately after the artillery came Nino Bixio with his four companies; and the Genoese Carabineers under Morto, who had enlisted them at Genoa.

Marching in this order, the column went through the village of Vita—so well known for its brigandage. The wounded from Calatafimi were sent here some hours later.

The General, accompanied by Türr and Sirtori, and followed by his staff, had gone on in front of the column, and by ascending the hill had been able to study the enemy's position. The artillery commander then brought orders that the volunteers were to quit the road and to proceed along the elevated positions on the right, leaving the artillery and a supporting company to keep the road.

Whilst the national army was making these changes in its disposition, it was noticed that some companies of the 9th battalion of the Royalist light infantry were descending into the valley to come and attack. For the first time, Patriots and Royalists were face to face.

CHAPTER XXIV

THE BATTLE OF CALATAFIMI

On the morning of the 15th, as I have said, a courier arrived with the news that the Neapolitans were at Calatafimi, and apparently intended marching on Salemi. Bixio and his company were sent forward in the van; the General and his staff followed immediately after, and the rest of the expedition brought up the rear.

At Salemi they had a triumphal reception, and spent the day there. It was at Salemi that Garibaldi proclaimed himself Dictator in the name of King Victor Emmanuel. We have already given the text of this proclamation.[1]

Türr had profited by the day of rest to draw up regulations for the organisation of the army, and the decree was signed by Garibaldi.

Early in the morning of the 15th, the march on Calatafimi was resumed. On arriving at Vita, which is situated three miles before you reach Calatafimi, you find, on emerging from a defile, some admirable positions facing you. It was at once assumed that, owing to the excellence of the ground, the Neapolitan army must be camped in the neighbourhood. Garibaldi therefore ordered his troops to halt. On the previous day he had taken with him Türr and Major Tüköry and Captain Missori, and then ascended a mountain lying to the right of the road, for the purpose of making observations. On reaching the summit, he had seen that his suppositions were well grounded; they were, in fact, facing the Neapolitan army.

The main body of their forces is at Calatafimi itself, which is on the mountain slope, whilst their advanced posts are placed about a mile in advance of the town.

No sooner do the Neapolitans recognise that the Legionaries are at Vita, no sooner do they see a group of officers reconnoitring on the top of the mountain which faces them than they leave the town and descend into the valley, in order to occupy three mamelons on the left, and one on the right, by means of which they can command the road.

The General comes down from the mountain and issues orders as to the disposition of the troops. Türr is to take the Genoese Carabineers, all excellent shots and armed with Swiss rifles. (In their ranks several very wealthy young men have enlisted as volunteers.) Behind Türr, the 7th Company will march on the right, and the 8th on the left. The 6th and 9th Companies will follow in support,

[1] See Chap. XIX, p. 161. Also see note at foot of page.

together with the *Picciotti* under Santa Anna, and those under Coppola who joined the volunteers at Salemi—about 450 men. On the left the only two serviceable pieces of cannon will be placed in position, the other two have no carriages.

In this formation they await the advent of the enemy, who now begin to advance in skirmishing order, shouting and making much noise. None of their officers spoke; each yelled his commands at the top of his voice.

The General, seeing this, and reckoning that ten minutes must elapse before they can be within range, orders his men to sit down in their ranks. "Let us take a little rest now, we shall have plenty of time in which to tire ourselves later," he remarks. By way of example, he seats himself between the Genoese Carabineers in front, and the two supporting companies behind.

As soon as the enemy are within the double of the range, the General orders the buglers to sound his favourite call. At the first trumpet note, the Neapolitan skirmishers halt, and some of them fall three or four paces to the rear. Just then, on the top of a hillock, to the right of our troops, or on the left of theirs, a strong column of Neapolitans appears, and places two guns in position. The Royalists resume their advance to the attack, which had been momentarily interrupted by the trumpet call, and as soon as they are within range, they open fire.

The volunteers received the first volleys without stirring from their sitting position. Some of the *Picciotti*, however, disappeared at the first shot. About 150 of these men remained firm, under the exhortation of their commanders Santa Anna and Coppola, and of the two Franciscan monks who, armed with rifles, are fighting in their ranks.

Then Garibaldi thought it was time to begin; so he rose and called out:

"Up, boys, and go for them with the bayonet!"

No sooner were the words uttered than Türr rushes to the front and leads the first line. Nino Bixio with two companies follows suit. A moment later the General takes Türr's place, and sends him to give orders for a general attack. The order, however, was unnecessary, for the battle had already become general.

The Neapolitans recoiled before the advancing bayonets of their foes; but they immediately afterwards rallied on reaching a better position than the one they had just abandoned. In the midst of the general fighting, some splendid charges are made by separate groups. Every officer who can place himself at the head of a hundred men, or of sixty, or even of fifty that he has rallied round him, charges with the utmost vigour. Most of the charges are led by Garibaldi, Türr, Bixio, and Schiaffino.

At each of these charges the Neapolitans hold their ground: fire, reload, and fire again; until they see the bayonets of the Legionaries glittering at a distance of ten yards from them—and all the more terrible from being fixed on muzzles that are silent. They then retire, but form up again, always in a better position, and supported by their cannon, which vomit forth grape-shot and shells.

The General, in the midst of the heavy firing, gave his orders with his usual composure. His son, Menotti—the boy who was born at Rio Grande, and whom his father carried, during a retreat that lasted a week, in a handkerchief tied round his neck, in order that his breath might keep the infant warm—this Menotti was now receiving his baptism of fire. He had seized a tricolour standard, ornamented with ribbons, and inscribed with the word "Liberty," and had dashed to the head of the *Bersaglieri*, with a revolver in one hand and the flag in the other.

When within twenty yards of the enemy, he was hit by a bullet in the hand that was carrying the flag. The flag falls. Schiaffino picks it up, and dashes forward with it, but he is shot dead, when about ten yards from the enemy. Two other Legionaries take the flag in turn, but both are killed. The Neapolitans now get possession of it. One of our Guides—Damiani—dashes into the midst of them, seizes the flag and ribbons, and carries it off, leaving nothing but the bare pole in the hands of the enemy.

During this time, the Legionary artillery has silenced one of the enemy's guns. Three students from Pavia and one of the Guides then make a dash for the remaining gun, kill the gunners on the spot, and take possession of it.

An order was now given to our artillery to advance and fire whenever the position did not put our own men in danger. The battle had lasted for about two hours, and the weather was fearfully hot. The men who had been in the thick of the fighting all the time were utterly exhausted, and seemed unable to continue. In the midst of a charge upon one of the higher mamelons, they stopped and lay down quite exhausted.

"Well," said the General, "what are we doing now?"

"Don't be uneasy, General; we are just taking breath," said the Legionaries. "We shall start again presently, and things will go better than ever."

Garibaldi alone remained standing amongst the men lying on the ground. The Neapolitans, no doubt, recognised him, for all their fire was soon concentrated on him. Some of our volunteers, seeing this, jump up and want to make a rampart with their bodies in order to protect the General.

"Oh, no," said the General, bidding them disperse again; "I shall never find a better day on which to die, nor amid worthier company."

After a brief rest, all spring up and charge the foe with renewed fury. Sirtori has a horse shot under him, and receives a slight wound in the leg, but he continues to advance with his men. The Royalists are finally dislodged from this mamelon, as they have been from others; but two still remain to be taken.

"Follow me, students of Pavia!" cries Türr.

Fifty young men instantly respond to his appeal.

"But, Colonel, you are always telling us that this is the last one," they protest to their colonel, when quite exhausted. But they continue to follow him, however worn out they may be.

The Neapolitans, driven from their positions at the point of the bayonet, finally abandon the field of battle, and retire on Calatafimi. Every soldier of the Legionary army drops where he stands, and goes to sleep. You would almost imagine that the Garibaldian army had been entirely destroyed; but it was only reposing after its victory. A heavy price had to be paid for that victory, as indeed is stated in the following "order of the day," issued by Garibaldi, and read the same evening on the battlefield.

"SOLDIERS OF ITALIAN LIBERTY![1]

"With such comrades as you, I would venture on anything. This, indeed, I have proved to you by placing you in front of an enemy four times as numerous as yourselves, and masters of a position, impregnable to any save you. I placed my faith in your bayonets, and I see that I did not do so in vain.

"Whilst deploring the bitter necessity of fighting against Italian soldiers, let us confess that they have put up a resistance worthy of a better cause. And let us rejoice in this, for it is a proof of what we shall be able to accomplish, when we are all united under one glorious flag of a redeemed country.

"To-morrow, the whole Italian continent will celebrate your victory—a victory won by its own free sons and the valiant sons of Sicily.

"Your mothers and your sweethearts are already proud of you; but to-morrow they will glorify you, and go on their way, with head erect and radiant of countenance.

"The fight has cost the life of many a dear brother of ours who fell in the van. The names of these martyrs to the cause of Italian freedom will be gathered together and inscribed on the brazen tablets of history.

"These names, I say, are worthy of national gratitude; and likewise those of the brave men who led our young and inexperienced soldiers into the fray, and who will lead them afresh, to-morrow, to still more glorious fields—the men who will finally destroy the last links in the chain of bondage which keeps in subjection our well-beloved Italy.

"G. GARIBALDI."

In reality, the Neapolitans had fought so well that when defending that mamelon where the attackers had to pause half-way, they

[1] This address is not given by Mr. Trevelyan.

found they had spent all their ammunition. They then resorted to hurling stones at their enemies. Garibaldi was struck by one of these, and nearly had his shoulder dislocated.

Now that this battle was won, the position was such that, by a final effort, it would be possible to cut off the Neapolitan retreat. But Garibaldi's men could not go a step further. The army had been severely tested. For example, let us mention the Guides, under the command of Missori, who received a wound in the eye from a grape-shot: out of eighteen men, one was killed and five were wounded. Our total losses were 110 men killed or wounded, including sixteen officers.

During the night, the Royalists quitted Calatafimi, and the Nationalists entered it at daybreak.

The following letter subsequently came to light. It was written by General Landi to the Prince of Castelcicala, whose apartments in the royal palace I am at present occupying.

"Very urgent.

"*Calatafimi,* 15*th May,* 1860.

"MOST EXCELLENT PRINCE,[1]
    "Help, immediate help, must be sent! The armed band which set out from Salemi this morning has enveloped all the hills from south to south-east of Calatafimi. Half of my advanced column was sent forward to skirmish, and attacked the rebels. Their fire was well sustained; but the masses of rebels, united to the Sicilian troops, constituted a large force.
    "Our men have killed the Commander-in-Chief of the Italians and have captured their flag, which is in our hands now. Unfortunately, one of our guns, which had fallen from off a mule's back, was seized by the enemy—a loss that grieves me much.
    "Our column has been obliged to retreat somewhat, and to occupy a new position at Calatafimi, where I shall remain on the defensive for the time being. As the rebels, who are present in considerable numbers, apparently intend to attack us, I beg your Excellency to send me, without delay, considerable reinforcements of infantry, or half a battery, at the very least. I repeat, the mass of rebels is enormous, and they are in a very aggressive mood.
    "I fear they will attack me in the positions I now occupy. In such a case, I shall defend myself there as long as possible; but unless prompt reinforcements arrive, I cannot foresee what will happen. Our artillery ammunition is almost exhausted, and that for our infantry is considerably diminished; so, it will be seen that our position is very critical, and needs the provision of all means of defence. Want of such means of defence fills me with the utmost consternation.
    "I have sixty-two wounded. I cannot give you an exact list of the dead, for I am writing this to you immediately after our retreat. In a subsequent despatch I shall give your Excellency fuller details.
    "In conclusion, I must notify your Excellency that if circumstances compel me to do so, I shall retire to a more elevated position, so as not to jeopardise the safety of my columns.
    "I hasten to submit all the above to your Excellency, so that you may know that my column is surrounded by considerable hostile forces, who have seized the mills and all the flour prepared for the use of our troops.

---

[1] This deeply interesting letter, which is not quoted by Mr. Trevelyan, was doubtless obtained from Türr.

"I trust that your Excellency will not entertain any doubt as to the way in which our piece of artillery was lost. I repeat that the gun had been placed upon the back of a mule that was killed during the retreat. It was, therefore, impossible to save it. I can only end by assuring you that all our troops fought, under very heavy fire, from ten o'clock in the morning till five in the afternoon, at which hour our retreat began.

"LANDI, COMMANDANT-GENERAL.

"*To His Excellency*
The Prince of Castelcicala."

At the foot of this letter, Türr, into whose hands it had fallen, wrote as follows:

"REMARKS BY ADJUTANT-GENERAL STEFANO TÜRR

"The cannon was captured whilst it was still in action, and on its wheels; and as a proof that the mule was not killed, I may add that, on the contrary, both mules attached to this piece of artillery fell into our hands also.

"Fortunately for Italy, our Commander-in-Chief was not killed. As for the captured flag, it was not the regimental standard; it was simply a fancy banneret which the brave Schiaffino had brought with him and was carrying in the ranks of the column in which he met his death, pierced by two bullets.

"I would ask if General Landi can show me a similar flagstaff in the records of war?

"It is only necessary to read his despatch to know, from his own admission, how he was defeated by men clad in the garb of simple peasants, but who, nevertheless, can fight with all their heart and soul to give freedom to their country."

CHAPTER XXV

BLESSING THE EXCOMMUNICATED

Palermo, 16th of June

AT Calatafimi one day's rest was granted to the men, and another day was devoted to working at urgently necessary matters.

On the previous evening, Brother John rejoined the troops with his 150 volunteers. On the morrow, the army arrived at Alcamo. When nearing that town, Brother John, who was riding beside Garibaldi, leant over and whispered: "Do not forget, General, that you are excommunicated."

"I do not forget it, Brother," answered the General, "but what am I to do?"

"This is what you should do, General: We are living amongst a religious people—more than religious; indeed I would say, superstitious; I therefore wish that when you pass the church of Alcamo you would enter it, for the purpose of receiving the benediction."

Garibaldi hesitated a moment; then, with a sign of acquiescence, he said: "Very well, I will do as you wish."

Delighted with this concession to a proposal which he had thought would be met with objections, Brother John galloped in advance to the church, alighted and entered. He then placed a cushion in position for the General to kneel upon, put on vestments, and waited the arrival of Garibaldi.

But the General either forgot his promise or wished to avoid its performance, and rode past the church. Brother John was grieved. Every monk, from the Bishop of Rheims when baptising Clovis, down to Brother John blessing Garibaldi, seeks to put, not God, but the priest above the general, the chief, or the king. So he rushed out of the church in his vestments, and went after Garibaldi. On coming up with him, he seized him by the arm and exclaimed:

"What is the meaning of this? Is this the way you keep your promises?"

With a smile Garibaldi said: "Brother John, you are right and I am wrong. I am prepared to make the *amende honorable*."

"Come with me, then."

"Yes, I will, Brother John."

And this terrible man (who, according to Neapolitan journals, has received power from the Devil to send out fire from his eyes and mouth) not only let himself be led, like a child, by the priest, but also, moved by that sentiment of religion which can never be entirely suppressed, he knelt down on the outer steps of the church before the eyes of the populace, the peasantry, and the army.

This was, indeed, more than he had promised to Brother John. So the monk, seeing much nobility in this gesture of Garibaldi, rushed into the church with that Italian vivacity which even the wearing of ecclesiastical garments cannot suppress, and quickly returned, bearing the holy sacrament. Addressing all present, he said:

"Let all behold: the victor humbles himself before Him who alone giveth victory."

Proud of this new triumph of religion over arms, he then proceeded to bless Garibaldi in the name of God, of Italy, and of Liberty.

A halt was made at Alcamo, at which place these Legionaries—one of whom, it will be remembered, was shot during the Roman campaign for having stolen thirty sous from a woman—heard of the cruelties which had been committed by the Neapolitans during their retreat. At Partinico they had ransacked the whole town, set fire to half of it, killed women, and trampled children to death.

All this brigandage had produced an effect altogether contrary to that which its perpetrators had anticipated. Instead of intimidating, it had only exasperated the people. Men who up till now had taken no active part in these events eagerly sprang to arms.

Pursued on all sides by the peasantry, shot at from behind hedges, trees, and rocks, the Royalists had strewn the roads with their dead and abandoned both baggage and prisoners at all points.

When the liberating army arrived at Partinico, it was received, we will not say with joy or enthusiasm, but with a feeling that amounted to delirium. Another halt was made at Partinico to give the men a brief rest. Whilst the men were reposing, their commander, who never seemed to know what fatigue meant, set to work to reconnoitre. (This same "Commander-in-Chief of the Italians" had been recently killed, according to a bulletin issued by General Landi.) Taking Türr with him and no other escort than two of his staff officers, he pushed forward, and forming the groups of *Picciotti*, whom he met on the way, into a sort of advanced guard, he made a very satisfactory survey of the enemy's position.

With this advanced guard the General arrived at Renda where he pitched his camp to right and left of the high road, extending his outposts as far as Pioppo, from which place you may catch sight of Monreale and part of Palermo.

This was on the 18th of May. On the 19th a halt was made at Pioppo; on the 20th the outposts were advanced to within a mile of Monreale; and San Martino and its mountains were occupied by the *Picciotti*. In the evening of the 20th the column advanced on

Misero-Cannone. On the following morning, when the General and his staff were at the foremost outposts held by the *Picciotti*, the Royalists took the offensive; and this necessitated a retreat on the part of the *Picciotti*, who fell back on Misero-Cannone. Garibaldi then took up his position with the Genoese Carabineers and a battalion of *Cacciatori*.

The Royalists advanced till within a range and a half of their opponents. Whilst still at that distance, they opened fire, but the Carabineers and *Cacciatori* made no reply. Thereupon the Neapolitans retired, as though they had triumphed.

Their bulletin then announces that the Neapolitan army has encountered the rebels, who did not dare to join battle!

The General, having ordered his favourite call to be sounded, advanced and retook possession of his advanced posts, without opposition.

In the afternoon Garibaldi advanced along the road to Monreale in company with Colonel Türr and two or three officers, and, after surveying, found that if he persisted in trying to reach Palermo by this road, it would involve the loss of 200 to 300 men. He then figured out in his mind a plan for reaching Palermo by the road to Parco, instead of the road to Monreale. Such a proposition would have been deemed insane, if contemplated by any other general.

To carry out this plan the army would, owing to the absence of any road, be obliged to climb and pass over summits where neither hunter nor mountaineer had yet set foot; both men and guns would have to be taken into the region of the goats and clouds; in fact they would have to do something more difficult than the passage of the Great St. Bernard—for this, at least, has a road.

When night fell, the troops set out for Parco. The men attached themselves to the guns, marching in single file, and sometimes going on all-fours. The night was dark and rainy, and the journey fraught with danger, as there were precipices on either side of them. If the victory of Calatafimi was a marvel, the arrival at Parco would be a miracle.

In order to deceive the Neapolitans, the bivouac fires had been left burning, and the *Picciotti* had been entrusted with the task of keeping these fires going. In this way our army had made a march of eight hours' duration, and had crossed the summit of three mountains, whilst the Neapolitans thought it was still in its old bivouac.

The crossing was carried out without the loss of a single man, or gun, or cartridge. Towards daybreak the advanced guard reached Parco. At three in the morning, the whole army was assembled there. Garibaldi's first thought was for his men. He busied himself in seeing that they were able to warm themselves and get a meal; and not till then did he think of himself. The mayor of Parco lent him a pair of trousers, and another to Türr; after which the General and his lieutenant remounted their horses and set out to explore the neighbouring country.

The march was resumed on the road from Parco to Piana, which takes a zigzag form, and passes high above the village. When a roadside Calvary was reached, it was transformed into a position for cannon, and two other mamelons were made available as points of defence. All this work was executed during the day by men who had been marching all night. Then they bivouacked, some round the work they had just finished, others in the surrounding villages. These events took place during the day and the night of the 22nd.

The next morning, at daybreak, the General and Türr climbed to the top of Mount Pizzo del Fico—a very fatiguing task. On arriving, suddenly one of the *Picciotti* appeared and challenged them with: "Who goes there?" This man was one of the peasants of the neighbourhood, appointed to guard this position. He had never seen the General, and was overjoyed when Garibaldi and Türr made themselves known.

From the summit of this mountain the General and Türr could see all Palermo, and distinguish the troops encamped on the plains round about, and in the castle square. The practised eye of Garibaldi enabled him to estimate the number of these troops to be 15,000 or more.

And he had 750 men upon whom he could rely!

Moreover, on turning his eyes in the direction of Monreale, he could see a body of 3000 to 4000 who were on the move towards that place. Two companies of them were taking the path that leads to Castellucio; and a battalion with two pieces of cannon and some cavalry were following the route to Misero-Cannone.

After marching about two miles, the Neapolitans halted.

In the evening there was a skirmish between the Neapolitans and the *Picciotti*, in which the latter defended their positions fairly creditably. Desultory firing between them went on during the night.

Next morning, at daybreak, the General directed his march towards the mamelon round which the road from Piana to Parco winds. Making further observation of the Neapolitans, he saw that their troops, which had left Monreale on the previous day, were advancing and threatening to envelop his left wing. At the same time, he noticed troops moving from Palermo on Parco. The General instantly guessed their intentions, so he ordered Türr to move the artillery from its positions, to send the Genoese Carabineers to the left wing, to make the *Picciotti* their support, and then to get together all the rest of the corps. Then, without loss of time, and whilst Türr was executing his commands, he himself, with some of the Guides and his *aides-de-camp*, set out on the road to Piana.

Presently sounds of musketry were heard coming from the other side of the mountain where the Carabineers were. These troops, when attacked by a force three times their own number, defended themselves heroically; but abandoned by the *Picciotti*, who could be seen in full flight along the road, the Carabineers were forced to retire to the summit of the mountain.

When Türr sees this, without waiting for orders from the General, he sends the 8th and 9th Companies to join the Carabineers; but as he cannot send the artillery by the same route, he leaves two companies to defend it and to place it in position on the road. By this disposition, the artillery and the two companies form the right wing of a new position.

At two o'clock in the afternoon, the General arrived at Piana, after keeping to the mountain peaks during the entire journey. He then gave his men a rest. In the evening he summoned, for the first time, a council of war to which came Colonels Türr, Sirtori, and Orsini, as well as Secretary of State, Crispi.

Addressing them the General said: "You see that our little army is compelled to march along impossible roads, with its flanks continually menaced by an enemy ten times as numerous as we are. It is therefore indispensable that we should keep at a distance the largest possible number of the Neapolitans. If, now, we send our cannon to Corleone, the enemy, misled by this movement, will divide their forces, and thus render the march on Palermo more easy of accomplishment."

This proposal of the General's was adopted. Orsini was sent with the artillery, the baggage, and fifty men for an escort, on the road to Corleone.

For a distance of half-a-mile, the whole of the little army had to follow the same route as the artillery, before it could reach the road that the General wished to take. On reaching this path, which strikes into the road to Marineo on the left, the main body separated from the artillery, which continued on its way to Corleone.

The night was fine, the moon was shining, and the heavens sparkled as with diamonds. Türr, as usual, went along beside the General, when the latter, raising his hat and disclosing a rather more smiling face than usual, remarked to his companion:

"My dear friend, everyone has his own particular whim, and I confess I am no more exempt from this than any other man. I heard it said, in my young days, that everyone was born under a certain star; so I sought for mine, and fancied that I recognised the one that presided over my destiny. 'Look: now can you see the Great Bear?' Yes? Well, a little to the left of the Great Bear there are three stars, and of those three stars, the most brilliant is mine. It is called 'Arcturus' in the chart of the heavens."

He remained lost in thought, with his eyes fixed on it.

Türr looked and found the star. It was magnificent. So he remarked:

"Well, General, if that is your star, it is certainly smiling on us. We are going to enter Palermo."

Yet there was nothing in the position of that little army which would lead one to suppose that Türr's prediction would be realised. A numerous body of Neapolitans had just started its march to Piana dei Greci, whilst 18,000 men and forty guns were left at Palermo to defend it.

Towards midnight, the troops entered a forest, where they bivouacked. At twenty-five minutes past four in the morning, the march towards Marineo was resumed, and they arrived there at seven o'clock. The whole day was spent there till the evening, when they continued the journey to Misilmeri, which they reached by ten o'clock. Türr and Colonel Carini had gone on in advance to get accommodation provided for the men.

The night passed without any incident worth noting.

At Misilmeri they met some members of the Committee of Sicilian Liberty of Palermo, and also La Masa, with 2000 to 3000 *Picciotti*. The General informed the Committee that it was his intention to attack the town on the morning of the 27th, quite early, at the gate of Termini. Türr, knowing that his compatriot, Colonel Eber, correspondent of *The Times*, was at Palermo, begged these gentlemen to let him know of their approach, so that he might join them at Misilmeri and might take part in the triumphal entry into Palermo. Moreover, this would enable him to send a very complete account of the taking of Palermo to *The Times*.[1]

Not an eye was closed during the night.

In the morning, at four o'clock, the General mounted his horse and, followed by Türr, Bixio, Missori, and some *aides-de-camp*, paid a visit to the camp of La Masa at Gibilrossa. There the General passed in review the *Picciotti*, and afterwards ascended the mountain to have another look at Palermo. On the same day the army camped between Gibilrossa and Misilmeri.

---

[1] *The Times* was strongly pro-Italian. This detail about Türr communicating with Eber is not mentioned by Mr. Trevelyan.

Towards evening the troops formed up on the plateau of Gibilrossa in the following order:

The Guides, led by Captain Missori, together with three men from the Alpine *Cacciatori*, thirty-three men altogether, under the command of that brave Hungarian, Colonel Tüköry, formed the advance-guard. Behind them came the *Picciotti;* then Bixio's battalion; then the General with his staff, followed by Carini's battalion; and finally a second corps of *Picciotti* and the baggage closed the line of march.

In all, there were 750 Legionaries and 2000 to 3000 *Picciotti* to oppose 18,000 Neapolitans.

14

CHAPTER XXVI

PALERMO THE FORTUNATE

Palermo, 17th June

THERE was no road suitable for a march on Palermo, so a descent by means of a ravine was made into the valley that opens out on to the high road to the city. It was eleven o'clock at night.

As soon as the advanced guard reached this high road, they halted and retraced their steps, for the *Picciotti* who were to support it had all vanished. The halt was necessary for rallying the column. A false alarm from the heights had been sufficient to make the *Picciotti* take to flight. It was now necessary to spend nearly two hours in re-forming the column which was thus reduced to 1400, or even 1300 men.

At half-past one in the morning the troops were three miles from the town. They continued the march, in close formation, till they were near the Neapolitan outposts. At half-past three they came into collision with these. The enemy fired three shots and then retired to a house near by, which was full of their comrades. These three musket-shots, however, were quite sufficient to disperse two-thirds of the *Picciotti* that remained.

The advance-guard of thirty-two men then pushed on as far as the Ammiraglio bridge, which spans a dried-up torrent. This was found to be defended by 300 or 400 men. A vigorous attack was delivered from under cover on both sides of the bridge, and from behind the trees which line the road. A hand-to-hand combat ensued; so close was it that a Legionary captain, named Piva, armed only with his six-chambered revolver, killed four Neapolitans. At this juncture, Missori requested Bixio to come to his assistance.

Bixio arrived at the double with the first battalion; and Türr rushed the second battalion forward when he saw the *Picciotti* take to flight. The position at the bridge of the Ammiraglio was then carried at the point of the bayonet. The Neapolitans, thereupon, fled in utter disorder to the right; but just then we were attacked by a strong column on the left, so Türr detailed thirty men to check the advance of this column, and the rest of the Legionaries continued their advance at the charge with fixed bayonets. The Neapolitans then fell back on the road to San-Antonio. This road, which is lined with houses, cuts across the road to Termini along which the Legionaries were proceeding, so the Royalists placed two cannon in position and swept it with grape-shot. At this juncture the General came up, together with Colonels Türr and Eber; but at the very same moment Colonel Tüköry was hit by a bullet and fell mortally wounded. The column now halted for a few moments, about ten yards from the cross-roads.

The guide, Nullo, was the first to dash across. He was carrying the flag of Italian Independence; and was immediately followed by Damiani, Bozzi, Manci, Tranquillini, and Zazio. By degrees, the whole column got across, under the supervision of the General, who was all the more exposed to the enemy's fire, as he remained mounted, and never ceased urging his men on.

The first few who dashed up the street, now joined by 200 of the Legionaries, scattered themselves along the streets leading to the Termini gate. Nullo, Damiani, Manci, Bozzi, Tranquillini, and Zazio penetrated as far as the Fiera Vecchia—that is to say, to within 300 yards of the gate.

During their progress the Legionaries found nothing but closed houses and deserted streets; but at the Fiera Vecchia, when the General arrived in the midst of the firing, he came across eight or ten members of the Committee of Palermo. And so it was that this handful of men, scarcely 200 in number, scattered over a space of about half-a-mile, had, by their amazing intrepidity, driven all before them, and repulsed, perhaps, 3000 or 4000 men.

On reaching the Fiera Vecchia, the General ordered barricades to be constructed. By dint of shouting, the inhabitants were attracted to the windows. They were asked to throw their mattresses out. Instantly a shower of mattresses came from all the neighbouring windows; and these were piled up to form barricades at the points most exposed to artillery fire.

Shortly after this, some of the inhabitants began to show themselves in the streets, and were urged to get the people of the town to rise. The invariable response to this request was:

"We have no arms."

With the General at their head, and preceded by this handful of leaders, the rest of the legion had succeeded in entering Palermo. An immediate attack was launched against the Strada di Toledo and the Strada di Macqueda; and the Neapolitans, who thought they were being opposed by a force three times as large as it really was, fell back on the Royal Palace and the Macqueda Gate. Fresh barricades were instantly constructed from the vehicles in the streets.

The General established himself on the Piazza Bologni; but just then the war vessels in front of the town and the guns of the Castle opened fire. The 8th Company and the Genoese Carabineers now made an attack on the square of the Royal Palace by way of the

Strada di Toledo and the lanes leading into it, or by firing from the houses looking on to the square. Superior numbers of their opponents, however, compelled them to retire, and Garibaldi moved his headquarters to the Palazzo Pretorio.

A Neapolitan column made an advance along the Strada di Toledo, and had penetrated nearly as far as the Piazza Bologni, when some *Picciotti*, in conjunction with twenty Legionaries, who were in ambush behind one of the barricades, held them up, and twenty more men, bearing down on them from the right, attacked them on the flank and in the rear. The Neapolitans soon took to flight.

Minor combats took place during the entire day. The keenest of them were at the Albergheria. Captain Cairoli, of the 7th Company, which was composed of students, was seriously wounded; and by the evening there were also several other losses to deplore.

On the second day, Missori and Captain Dezza at the Albergheria made use of a bomb, which exploded right in the midst of the Neapolitan barricades; and this made them cease fire for some minutes.

It was at this point that twenty-five men of the 7th Company held the Neapolitans in check for twenty-four hours.

This second day was a repetition of the marvels of the first one. We reached the Macqueda Gate and were thus able to cut the enemy's communications between the sea and the Castle. In the course of these two days, Sirtori, in particular, performed prodigies of valour, and exhibited at the same time marvellous self-possession.

On the morning of the third day, the Neapolitans tried to regain lost ground; but the town was now bristling with barricades made of stones, and they were repulsed at all points. The same morning, news was brought to the General that the *Picciotti* had carried off a cannon at Montalto. Garibaldi, who had his doubts about the prowess of the *Picciotti*, ordered Missori to go and make inquiries; and if it was so, to utilise the gun for a position. He was told to send for assistance, if the forces at his disposal were insufficient. Missori, accompanied by a few Legionaries, set out for the Convent of the Annunziata, and on arriving found the *Picciotti* fighting with the Neapolitans. They had not captured any cannon, but all the same they were fighting resolutely, encouraged as they were by the exhortation and example of Brother John, who was standing in the midst of them with his crucifix in his hand. Missori then took command of the operations and got possession of the convent, which dominates Montalto. The Neapolitans received considerable reinforcements, but were again driven back; and the Legionaries and *Picciotti* finally quitted the convent to go and entrench themselves in the bastion of Montalto.

Missori wrote to the General to tell him that no gun had been taken, but at the same time was able to announce that the bastion had been captured, and requested him to send reinforcements.

Brother John now thought it advisable to come within twenty yards of the Neapolitans and start preaching to them a sermon on fraternity. One of their captains, by way of reply, snatched a musket from the hands of a soldier near by, and fired on the monk. Brother John's cross was broken to pieces by the bullet which struck it within six inches of his head; but a *Picciotto* fired back on the captain, and stretched him dead with a bullet in his forehead.

A move forward was then made. The *Picciotto* who had killed the captain took possession of his sword, while Brother John, having claimed his sword-belt, fastened it round his body, and fixing the remains of the cross in it, exclaimed: "The sword has given place to the cross."

About this time, two companies of Neapolitans set out from the Royal Palace and launched an attack on Montalto. The *Picciotti* fled precipitately. Missori was compelled to abandon the bastion and return to the convent. Luckily, Sirtori arrived at this juncture with the reinforcements from the General. He formed up his thirty-five men and checked the forward movement of the Neapolitans. The fight became more furious, and the convent was bombarded by cannon; but in the end the Neapolitans were forced to retire and we regained possession of the Montalto bastion.

Colonel Sirtori, understanding the great importance of a position which commanded the Royal Palace, sent for a dozen Carabineers and twenty Legionaries, and placed them behind a house, from which place their fire would effectually prevent the Neapolitans renewing their attack on the bastion. But the enemy, having obtained fresh forces, launches a third attack, brings up two pieces of artillery, and continues bombing. Finally, after about an hour's fighting, the fire of the Genoese Carabineers silences the two guns; and the Neapolitans, finding themselves beaten, have to abandon the position. Missori then left the convent to go and communicate to the General the results of the day's operations in the region of the Royal Palace. In this affair those who particularly distinguished themselves were Colonel Sirtori, Captains Dezza, Mosto, and Missori; and Major Acerbi, above all, must be singled out for the way in which he constructed barricades under the most galling fire.

Just as the General was going to sit down to dine, after inviting the officers present to join him, news was brought to him that the Neapolitans had driven out Santa Anna from the position that he occupied near the cathedral, and that they were advancing without there being any opposition offered to their progress. The General rose from table, saying: "Come along, gentlemen, it is we who must stop them." Then, on foot, followed by Türr and Gusmaroli—the inseparables—and by his officers and a dozen Guides, and bidding all Legionaries he met on the way to join him, he hastened to the scene of the combat. There he found the Neapolitans masters of the situation, as regards three barricades, and the *Picciotti* routed.

They immediately set to work to construct a new barricade under continuous fire from the Neapolitans. Whilst this was in progress, a man who was standing beside the General was struck in the head by a bullet and fell. The General tried to support him, but he was dead. A vigorous attack was now launched against the Neapolitans, who soon had to abandon the first barricade, and this was immediately occupied by the Legionaries. Whilst retiring, the enemy set fire to two houses, but a handful of *Picciotti*, directed by the General in person, took them on the flank and completed their defeat.

By the end of the third day, the Garibaldians were masters of almost the entire town. During these three days and four nights, they had scarcely had a moment's rest, for alarms had been continual. They had scarcely had time to eat; sleep was out of the question; and fighting was incessant.

On the fourth day, the Neapolitan General, Letizia, made overtures for an armistice, through the medium of the English admiral.[1] Towards one o'clock Garibaldi, Menotti, his son, and Captain Missori went down to the shore, orders having been given to cease fire everywhere. Nevertheless, as they passed near to Castellaccio, two shots were fired, and the bullets whizzed past the head of the General. On the shore, they awaited the arrival of General Letizia, who, as an additional safeguard, got Major Cenni, *aide-de-camp* to Garibaldi, to accompany him.[2]

A ship's boat, sent by the English admiral, took on board the two generals and the officers who accompanied them. The interview took place in the Admiral's state cabin and in his presence, together with the French admiral, and the American[3] and Neapolitan naval commanders. The outcome of this conference was a truce of twenty-four hours, during which the Neapolitans were to be allowed to transport their sick and wounded on board their ships, and to supply provisions to the Royal Palace.

[1] Admiral Mundy on board H.M.S. *Hannibal,* his flag-ship.

[2] Dumas omits to mention that the Garibaldians were then without ammunition and, but for the armistice, would have been destroyed. Nor does he mention Von Mechel and his four battalions which had returned from Corleone a day too late to fight against Garibaldi. It is obvious that these important facts were forgotten in the enthusiasm caused by the victory.

[3] Captain Palmer.

At the end of this period hostilities were to be resumed; but next day, at eleven o'clock in the morning, the Neapolitans requested an extension of the truce for four days, so that General Letizia could go to Naples and confer with the King.

On General Letizia's return, the armistice was renewed for an indefinite period; and he left again for Naples. When he returned from his second visit, definitive conditions for the surrender of Palermo were signed.

On the morning of the day on which the evacuation was to begin, the Neapolitans requested an escort to accompany them from the Royal Palace and from the Fiera Vecchia to the sea. At the Fiera Vecchia three of the Guides and a staff-captain—four men in all—carried out this duty. Those escorted numbered 4000 or 5000. At the Royal Palace four Guides and Major Cenni escorted 14,000 men. On the admission of Neapolitan officers of high rank, there was an army of 24,000 men in Palermo.

It was all over now. The Neapolitans had been driven out of Palermo, and Sicily was lost to the King of Naples. But we should add that they retired—to use the conventional phrase about capitulations—*with all the honours of war.*

Let us consider for a moment how they had deserved these honours. On the 24th May, when they knew that Garibaldi was approaching Palermo, bills were stuck on the walls of the city, stating that citizens had nothing to fear provided that they remained indoors. That is why, on arriving at the Fiera Vecchia, Garibaldi found all doors and windows closed. We have already mentioned the hour at which the bombardment began. It lasted three days; and in a single day no less than 2600 shells were fired upon the city. The firing was more particularly directed upon public monuments, charitable institutions, and convents. From my window I can count thirty-one breaches in the lovely steeple of Palermo's cathedral. Ten or a dozen palaces have been razed to the ground; out of these one may specially mention that of Prince Carini, our ambassador in London, and that of Prince di Goto. Fifteen hundred houses have been shattered from roof to cellars; and, when we arrived, most of them were still burning.[1] The entire quarter situated near the Castro Gate had been pillaged, and all the inhabitants robbed, murdered, or crushed to death in the ruins. All the young women were carried off, and sent to the Royal Palace, where they were forced to remain ten days and nights with the 14,000 troops quartered there.

So much by way of a general survey; let us now mention a few details.

[1] On the 6th of June.

A Neapolitan captain named Scandurra, seeing a Garibaldian Legionary fall, wounded in the shoulder, burst in the door of a café, got a bottle of spirits of wine, emptied it upon the body of the wounded man, and then set fire to the alcohol. The soldier would have been burnt alive, if the captain had not received a shot in the head which stretched him out dead.

At the Albergheria (whose inhabitants can count some 800 dead out of their number) some Neapolitan soldiers, on the morning of the 27th, burst into a house, and finding there a family composed of father, mother, and daughter, they proceeded to kill the father and mother, whilst the corporal seized the daughter, a young woman named Giovannina Splendore, and claimed her as part of his booty. Captain Prado, however, met these ruffians, and seeing the girl covered with blood and in tears, took her and sent her to the house of the Marquis di Milo. Her terror of what she had undergone had left her dumb.

In the same district some soldiers burst open the door of a house, and found there a man, his wife and two children, one four years and the other eight months old—the child of four was lying at his mother's feet and the infant at her bosom. They killed the father, tore the infant from its mother's bosom and sent it to join the father, set fire to the house, and threw the other child into the flames. The poor mother, mad with grief, rushed at the soldiers, but was instantly killed by their bayonets.

In another house the Neapolitans found a mother and her three children. They made the poor woman give them what little she possessed, then went out, fastened the door, and set fire to the house. In the establishment kept by Diugari, soldiers entered, outraged all the women, then, on leaving, locked the doors and set the place on fire. Not one of these women escaped.

The Neapolitans set fire to three nunneries, at Santa-Catarina, at Badoïa-Nova, and that of The Seven Angels, and the nuns were forced to save themselves as best they could from the flames. Along with Garibaldi, I have visited the ruins of these convents. All the sacred vessels have been stolen. At Badoïa-Nova the soldiers had cut off the head of a statue of the Virgin in order that they might carry off a coral necklace, and had broken off a finger in order to steal a diamond ring. All the small possessions of the poor nuns were scattered about the floors; their prayer-books alone were in their places in the choir of the church.

Behind the hospital, eight men were found drowned in a ditch: their heads had been held under water till they were suffocated.

Major Pollizi directed the setting on fire of the houses of Colli and

San-Lorenzo, and the sacking of the house of the Marquis Spina, where he had dined a short time previously, and had then praised the magnificence of the silver plate.

The Royalists wanted to compel Antonia Ferraza to reveal to them the place of refuge of her son who sided with the *Picciotti*. She refused to comply, so they held her, head downwards, and burnt her with vitriol.

The French also came in for their share of insult, robbery, and murder. At L'Agua-Santa, Barthélemy Barge thought he would protect his house by hoisting the tricolour flag; but this flag was obnoxious to the officer commanding the Neapolitans at the Lazaretto, and he ordered Barthélemy Barge to take it down. As the order was not obeyed at once, a trumpeter rushed forward, tore down the flag, and trampled it underfoot. A servant sought to defend his national colours, but was knocked senseless with blows from the butt-end of a musket.

M. Fuirand, a professor of the French language, made the same mistake as Barge—that is to say, he thought his national flag would be a protection, so he hung it from his window. The Neapolitans rushed into his house, tore down the flag, trod it underfoot, and killed M. Fuirand with their bayonets. There are now six fatherless children. All this took place under the very eyes of our consul, M. Fleury.

CHAPTER XXVII

WHAT WE OURSELVES SAW

Palermo, 18th June

It is really very curious to see 20,000 Neapolitans, equipped with forty pieces of artillery, confined within their forts, or their barracks, or war-vessels, and guarded by 800 Garibaldians who bring them their daily rations. Every day steamers arrive from Naples, and take away 2000 or 3000 of these men, who go on board with manifest signs of joy. During the first two or three days of my stay at Palermo, I went to bed each night with the idea that we should be aroused by the noise of musketry. It seemed to me to be absurd that this 20,000 men, confined behind a mere wooden railing, and not ignorant of the small number of their adversaries, should not entertain the idea of a bloody revenge. But nothing of the sort happened. To-day there are scarcely 3000 or 4000 Neapolitans left here; and they will leave just as quietly as their predecessors in the great exodus. When the last of the Neapolitans has left, the Sicilian prisoners, in confinement at Fort Castellaccio, will be set at liberty.

In proportion as the Neapolitans depart, so do the barricades decrease in height and thickness; and they are only guarded by boys of twelve to fifteen, armed with lances. A corps of these is now being formed, the number of which will be some 2000. During the Roman campaign, Garibaldi had under him a company called "The Boys' Company": the oldest of its soldiers was only fifteen. They did marvellously well at Velletri under the command of Daverio.

The *Picciotti* simply swarm in Palermo. One incessantly hears the beating of some damaged drum. It is this which announces the arrival of fresh companies of *Picciotti* from all four points of the compass, and their entrance into the town, headed by their drum, their flag, and a monk—Capucin or Franciscan—shouldering a musket. You might almost fancy yourself back again in the times of the League.[1]

Every now and then you hear the discharge of firearms. It is a musket going off in the inexperienced hands of one of these *Picciotti;* and the bullet perhaps smashes a pane of glass or makes a hole in a wall already sufficiently battered.

On the third day after our arrival, Garibaldi left the Palace of the Senate to come and take up his residence at the Royal Palace, in the

[1] Of which Dumas had written so happily and well in his romances, "La Dame de Monsoreau" and "Les Quarante-Cinq."

ALEXANDRE DUMAS

Photo. Goupil et Cie.   *Cliché Carjat*

room next to mine. On arriving there, however, he found the room
was too large, so he went to take up his quarters in a little pavilion
at the end of a terrace, leaving the whole of the first storey to my
companions and myself. Thus we had eighteen rooms on the same
floor for our own use.

Since Garibaldi has been at the Palace we have had a band to play
to us twice daily. As there are two bands, one of the National
Guard, and the other of the Legionaries, the one that comes first takes
up its position under Garibaldi's windows, and the other and later
one under mine. Then, as soon as the Garibaldi band has played
its programme, it comes and plays beneath my windows, whilst my
band goes away to play under Garibaldi's.[1]

At daybreak the square in front of the Royal Palace is filled with
volunteers who are being drilled. It is quite impossible to sleep in
the midst of this hubbub. Next to, or even perhaps more than, the
Neapolitans, the Sicilians are the noisiest people on earth. Their
loquacity fairly bewilders an English colonel [2] who has taken service
in the Garibaldian army, and has been entrusted with the task of
drilling 200 or 300 recruits. The poor instructor takes the Sicilians
much too seriously. The day before yesterday he actually wanted to
have one of them, in charge of a post, shot, because he had changed
guard at all sentry points, at the barracks and forts, without giving
the password. You must bear in mind that this man was one of the
Picciotti. Türr found it difficult to make the gallant English colonel
understand that you cannot maintain the same strictness with these
makeshift soldiers as with regularly-trained troops.

As the red shirt is the distinguishing feature of the uniform of the
Garibaldi soldier, this red has become a fashionable colour, and all
red materials have doubled their prices. A simple red cotton shirt
now costs as much as fifteen francs, and the result is that all the
streets and public places of Palermo give one the impression of being
in a vast field of poppies.

In the evening, every window hangs out its two lanterns, by the
side of the national colours—green, red, and white—and this gives
a curious appearance to the town when viewed from the Piazza
delle Quattro Cantoni—that is to say, from the spot where the Strada
di Toledo and the Strada di Macqueda intersect. It looks like four
rivers of flame coming from one fountain-head.

At the Palace, Garibaldi is waited on by the servants of the former
viceroy. They wished to carry on in the old style, and keep up the

[1] Poor Dumas! Like Charles X, he was "not afraid of music"; but that is all
that can be said.
[2] Probably Colonel Dunne.

traditions of the princely table; but he informed them that all he
desired for dinner was some soup and a plate of meat with vegetables.
It was not without considerable difficulty that he succeeded in
getting them to fall in with such an austere rule of life. There is
another thing which has exasperated Garibaldi: this is that the
Sicilians, in spite of all his protests, will persist in calling him
"Your Excellency," and in trying, almost by force, to kiss his hand.

The day before yesterday, whilst the band of the National Guard
was playing under my window, I saw a passage cleared through the
crowd by the application of a powerful pair of shoulders. These
belonged to Durand-Brager.[1] He had arrived that very morning on
board the *Donavert*, which was under the command of Admiral
Jehenne, who has come, under the instructions of the French Government, to report on what is happening at Palermo. Durand-Brager
has accepted my offer of one of my eighteen rooms as a place of
residence. To-morrow he is going to pay a visit to the battlefields
of Parthenico and Calatafimi.

Everything is frightfully dear here. One might almost be in San
Francisco in the palmy days of California: an egg costs four sous, a
pound of bread six sous, and a pound of meat thirty sous. You must
remember, too, that a pound, at Palermo, means twelve ounces.
Yesterday, whilst we were walking about amongst the ruins of the
town, two poor women showed us the bread they had just bought,
complaining of the miserable quantity for the expenditure of a *tari*.
Every morning, however, a distribution of bread and money is made
at the Palace gate to the poor by Garibaldi's *aides-de-camp*, who take
turns in performing these duties. The superstitious population cannot
grasp the meaning of this at all: they were being nearly starved under
a Catholic viceroy, and were now being fed by an excommunicated
general. Brother John, however, does his best to explain the situation
in his own way, by telling them that Pius IX is the Antichrist and
that Garibaldi is the Messiah!

We are assured that the Neapolitans abandoned Catania yesterday.
If this be the case, then they have only two footholds in Sicily—one
at Syracuse, and the other at Messina.

Garibaldi is at present preparing an expedition into the interior,
which will be commanded by Colonel Türr. Medici is expected
daily, with the 2500 volunteers already mentioned. These troops are
to guard Palermo with the General, whilst Türr is away on his
expedition; but if they do not arrive speedily, Türr will set out at
once, and Garibaldi will guard Palermo with 300 or 400 men. No
doubt he alone would be adequate protection for the town, for I am

---

[1] The author of "Quatre mois de l'expédition de Garibaldi" (1861).

sure that his name would be quite sufficient to keep the Neapolitans at a respectful distance.

Legray spends his days in making magnificent photographs of the ruins of Palermo. I shall send a collection of them to Paris for the purposes of exhibition; and I shall include splendid portraits of Garibaldi, Türr, and Brother John.

Unfortunately the opportunity of doing so does not present itself at the moment, for the only vessel which used to come to Palermo was a Neapolitan one, and, naturally, it comes no longer now. The *Messageries Impériales* should order one of their vessels to put in at Palermo, when passing. People from all countries, and especially the English, would like to see Palermo as it is just now. They would see Palmyra in reality, once again.

In the midst of all that is going on, private vengeance is also at work. Every now and then, you may hear a cry of "Sorice! sorice!" (Mouse! mouse!). This is the nickname given by the populace to the *sbirri*. When this is heard, everybody rushes out. A cry of agony is heard; a man falls. It is a *sbirro*, or perhaps it is not; but, anyway, you will see a dead man.

The day after we arrived, one of Maniscalco's myrmidons was recognised in the street by a man whom he had previously arrested, and who had been tortured under his superintendence. The police agent was killed by being held against a wall, and everyone who went by gave him a stab, till the dead body was nothing but one ghastly mass of wounds.

During the first few days after Garibaldi's arrival, they used to bring the *sbirri* before him, in order that he might mete out justice to them; but, like all great victorious generals, Garibaldi is, above all things, a merciful man. Not only did he release these unfortunate wretches, but he even gave them a sort of passport. When the inhabitants of Palermo saw this, they took the law into their own hands.

If, however, one compares the few *sbirri* assassinated with the thousand or twelve hundred Palermitans either killed, burnt, or tortured by the Neapolitans, one will find that popular vengeance was restrained within very modest bounds. So far as I am concerned, I am only trying to give you the pros and the cons of the matter, so as to put you in touch with the exact truth. There are always so many conflicting interests. Everyone is given to exaggerating the wickedness of his enemy. Keen as my sympathies are, I, nevertheless, entertain no feelings of hatred; so I am in a position to give you the simple story of what is taking place under my own eyes.

To-day (18th of June) news has reached us, through the French

Consulate, of an engagement between the Calabrians and the Neapolitans, near to Reggio. Two hundred wounded Neapolitans have been brought into the citadel of Messina.

I think I have told you nearly all there is to be told about Palermo just now. In subsequent communications I shall be able to tell you what is taking place further inland, and something about the real feeling of Sicily; for I and my companions have resolved to accompany Colonel Türr on his expedition. My yacht will proceed through the Straits of Messina and will await us at Girgenti.

When I travelled through Sicily in 1835, I did so in company of a brigand chief to whom I had given ten *piastres* to protect me. This time I am going with an escort of 10,000 men, for the purpose of delivering it from its two greatest scourges—thieves and the Bourbons. Of course, there has been progress made since 1835; and this makes me pin my faith more and more in the policy of Providence, which, fortunately for us, is antagonistic to mundane diplomacy.

19th June at 8 o'clock in the morning.

Colonel Türr has just paid me a visit in order to communicate to me two pieces of news which will keep us here till to-morrow evening. The first is the arrival of Medici with his 2500 men. He is now at Partanico, and will be at Palermo to-morrow. He is bringing 10,000 muskets with him. Garibaldi has gone in his carriage to meet him. The second event is the departure, to-morrow, of the last of the Neapolitans, and the setting at liberty of six prisoners: Prince Pignatelli, Baron Riso, Prince Niscemi, Prince Giardinelli, Father Ottavio Lanza, and the Marquis of San Giovanni. Some of these wish to accompany us on our expedition.

Garibaldi told us yesterday that these six men cost Sicily six million francs. If the Neapolitans had not had them in their hands, we should have been able to impose much harsher terms in the matter of the surrender than those which were actually laid down.

Thanks to the arrival of Medici, our expeditionary corps now numbers 4000 men instead of 2000.

Lest they might be able to say in the Chamber of Deputies in 1860 that I was compromising the French tricolour, just as they said in 1847 that I had hauled it down,[1] you must understand that this time my tent will be surmounted by my personal flag only. So, if I compromise anybody, it will only be myself.

Durand-Brager has gone to ask Admiral Jehenne's permission to

---

[1] Dumas was accused of having requisitioned a war-vessel, the *Véloce*, for his own purposes.

take part in our expedition. If the Admiral refuses consent, then he will sail on my yacht, to see what is going on at Messina.

Colonels Türr, Sirtori, and Orsini have just been promoted to the rank of general.

I have just returned from visiting Carini, one of our heroes in the expedition to Sicily. After performing prodigies of valour, in the battle of Calatafimi, and in the three days' struggle for the taking of Palermo, Garibaldi sent him to recover possession of one of the barricades which had been captured by the Neapolitans from the *Picciotti*. The enemy were soon driven out, but, whilst on the barricade, Carini's arm was broken by a ball which chanced to hit him. Not only am I delighted to find that his arm has been saved, but also that there is every hope that he will be able to use it again. Carini, whom I met at the houses of Hugo and Girardin, established a Paris paper called *Le Journal Franco-Italien*.

19th June, 7 o'clock in the evening.

Whilst at dinner we heard a great uproar outside, so we all ran to the balcony. An immense crowd surging out of the Strada di Toledo came rushing towards the Palace, shouting, screaming, and whistling. At first it was impossible to distinguish anything except four Garibaldians who were trying to defend one man from the crowd. We knew they were Garibaldians from their red shirts. But as they drew nearer, we were able to recognise that the man whom they surrounded had a chain round his neck. They were evidently bringing him to the Palace, so we went downstairs and met him, just as he was being brought in by being put through the window of a sort of porter's lodge. The man was a *sbirro* named Molino, who, on the night of the 4th of April, had denounced Riso, and the two monks, Brother Ignazio and Brother Michele. The populace had recognised him, and were going to tear him to pieces, when, luckily for him, four Garibaldians came across him and brought him safely to the Palace.

Garibaldi returns to-morrow, and will then pass judgment on the case. It will be difficult to show any reason why he should not be shot.

The two leaders of the *sbirri* bore the names of Sorrentino and Duche: at the time of the capitulation they left the town, disguised as Neapolitan soldiers, and are now at Castellaccio, but are about to depart with the Neapolitan forces. They hope that Francis II will give them both pensions and titles.

A Frenchman living at Palermo, whose name I dare not give, in case of any reaction, has brought me an unfortunate fellow who has undergone torture. The mildest of the punishments to which he has been subjected was that of being tied up into a ball, and then made to roll down from top to bottom of the staircases of the Palace, the steps of which had previously been studded with nails placed point uppermost and knife-blades with the sharp edge upwards.

At the time of the Neapolitan retreat, this man's sister was outraged by their soldiers, who subsequently cut off her head, and then left the severed head and her body, which had been stripped naked, in the streets. The head and body were found by the Genoese Carabineers, and reverently buried by them.

When the Royalists had to march against the Genoese Carabineers —clever men, who killed their enemy at every shot—these Neapolitans rushed into the houses, dragged out the women and girls, and putting their bayonets behind them, made them march in front of them. But the Carabineers, marking their men, from time to time fired over the heads of the women, a few of whom were wounded by the Neapolitan bayonets, but not one by the Genoese shots. And the Neapolitans were put to flight too, in spite of trying to protect themselves with this living wall.

The Marchioness of San-Martino yesterday told me a story which is, at one and the same time, sad, bombastic, and comic.

General Letizia—the man who had requested the first truce from Garibaldi, and who had also pledged his word to a gentleman of Palermo that Garibaldi should never enter that town—came one day to the house of the Duchess of Villa-Rosa, and with the gravity of a man about to make his will laid at her feet a valise, saying—

"Duchess, I am about to set out on a very dangerous expedition. If I come back, you will return me the valise; but if I do not, you will dispose of the contents as may seem best to you."

The "dangerous expedition" of which the General spoke was nothing else than robbing the country house of the Marquis Pasqualino.

Perhaps you will be surprised that I give the full name of the heroes of these anecdotes instead of just designating them by their initials; but I have always been of opinion that, with some men, it is not sufficient to take the mask off, you must tear it off.

19th June, midnight.

Whilst I was writing just now, a sharp cannonade suddenly broke out. The reports followed one another at irregular intervals, and sounded like firing under separate controls. I left my desk and went to the balcony, where I found all my companions assembled. They had just jumped out of bed, and were variously attired: two were in the stage costume of *La Juive*, three others were garbed as Britannicus, Nero, and Narcissus. As I still had my trousers on, I was the most clothed of them all.

Not only did we hear the noise of the firing, but we could see the flashes of fire. Two of our party take out their watches, and by observing the time which elapses between the flash and the report, come to the conclusion that the combat is going on fifteen to eighteen miles off, out at sea.

The whole town is soon awake and all agog. All along the girdle of sentry-posts one hears the challenge being given. Those who have no great faith in the honour of Neapolitans—and their number is not small—believe that they are taking advantage of the truce and of the demolition of the barricades to attempt a *coup de main* in Palermo. Others are of opinion that some Sardinian ship, bringing reinforcements of men and guns, has fallen in with some Neapolitan frigate, which was cruising about, and is now being pursued by it.

Everybody deplores the absence of Garibaldi;[1] but one thing seems quite certain, and that is that a truce agreed upon in the presence of the English, French, and American naval commanders cannot be broken without exposing the Neapolitans to the risk of a collision with the landing forces of those nations. Besides, it is not likely that men who, when twenty-two to one, fell back before Garibaldi's advance were going to ask for trouble with three great nations, simply in order to try to retake a town which they had so meekly surrendered.

I ran over to see Major Cenni, who jumped up, exclaiming: "Let no one stir." I found the Duke of La Verdura, the prætor of the town, at his house, or rather I should say at his door, looking much alarmed. Whilst Cenni was dressing, I took the prætor on to the balcony, from whence the firing might be seen.

In the midst of all these conflicting views, one of those present lifted up his voice and said—

"Gentlemen, I was breakfasting this morning with Admiral Jehenne, when a messenger arrived to inform him that the English corvette was about to weigh anchor for the purposes of firing practice out at sea."

Everybody began to laugh at the idea that an English corvette would think of carrying out firing exercises at one o'clock in the morning, before a town which had been recently bombarded, which had lost 1000 or 1500 of its inhabitants in that bombardment, which is in a state of unrest all day, and in an agony of suspense all night.

And now detachments of troops were to be seen in motion in the

---

[1] He had gone to greet Medici with his reinforcements.

15

obscurity of the castle square, a vast open space, about a kilometre square, lighted by eight oil-lamps. I then proposed to go up to the observatory in the highest point of the Palace, whence one can get a clear view of the sea; but after about fifty more detonations, the firing ceased.

Just then, a horseman comes galloping across the square at full speed, and stops at the door of the Royal Palace. Everybody guesses that he is bringing news, and all rush forward to meet him. The intelligence he brings is this—

"The English Admiral trusts that the inhabitants of Palermo have not been alarmed: the disturbance is merely due to gunnery practice by his corvette."

"Didn't I tell you so?" was the remark of the man who had previously suggested that this was the true solution of the matter.

"Well, what of that, my dear fellow?" I answered. "I always knew the English were very eccentric, but I never suspected that they were quite so idiotic."[1]

Everybody went back to bed, and I went back to work.

20th of June.

At ten o'clock Garibaldi arrived. The first thing he did was to set the *sbirro* at liberty, and to give him his card of security. Woe be to the next of his comrades who happens to get caught!

At eleven o'clock, La Porta, the hero of the people, the illustrious guerilla chief, who has been actively at work since the 4th of April, who was the first to join Garibaldi, and whose men alone kept their ground at Calatafimi, came to ask me to be present at the liberation of the prisoners. We got into a carriage and drove to the harbour pier. There was not a window in the Strada di Toledo but it was adorned with the colours of the Independence, not a door that did not bear the following poster:

VOGLIAMO L'ANNESSIONE
AL GOVERNO NAZIONALE DEL RE
VITTORIO-EMMANUELE.

This scarcely needs translating.

The balconies were crowded with the ladies and children "belonging to the gentlemen," as they say in this part of the world. As for the steps, thresholds, and porches, they were filled with the masses, to whom these places belonged as by right. In a continuous line from Palace to pier there stretched a hedge of Garibaldians, *Picciotti*, and

---

[1] Dumas forgot that all the English are not admirals!

guerillas, armed with guns of every conceivable pattern, from those on stands, for use on ramparts, to a weapon made from a pistol-barrel attached to a branch of a tree, and fired by applying a match.

The proper way would have been along the Strada di Toledo; but opposite to the cathedral the street was blocked by the ruins of the Carini Palace, and at two other points similar ruins obstructed progress. So it was necessary to make a roundabout journey. When we were about a hundred yards from the mole, we heard loud shouts; then, suddenly, we saw an immense crowd of people moving forward in front of us, dancing, waving handkerchiefs, and crying—"Viva l'Italia!"

We stopped our carriage.

What seems to me so extraordinary in these popular fêtes is that horsemen and horses, pedestrians, men both armed and unarmed, women, children, old men, all are packed together, jostle and obstruct each other, and yet no accident happens, although no precautions have been taken, and notwithstanding there are no gendarmes, police, or *sbirri* present.

We soon found ourselves in the middle of a crowd of 2000 or 3000 people, and these were only the advanced guard, so to speak. The band played the Sicilian national air, as it marched along. In front of it, behind it, and around it, men and women danced. In front of all there was a priest who impersonated King David before the Ark; and then came five carriages containing the liberated prisoners and their families. They were literally buried beneath the masses of flowers showered upon them from all sides. Then followed a long file of carriages, and behind these we took our places.

No sooner had the prisoners entered the town than the shouts, and applause, and "vivas" burst forth. When the climax was reached, the enthusiasm was almost terrifying. Flowers were thrown, bouquets were thrown, and they ended by throwing out the flags and adornments of the windows.

As every carriage had one or more flags, I stretched out my arm to get one, when La Porta said:

"Wait a moment, I will give you mine."

And calling one of his *guerrilleros*, he said:

"Tell my standard-bearer to bring me my flag."

The standard-bearer came up quickly. La Porta placed in my hands his flag pierced in thirty-eight places by balls; and so it came about that the honours of the day fell to me, because of this flag. To every group crowded on a doorstep, I was obliged to lower the flag; and the women seized it with both hands and kissed it with that ardour which Sicilians put into everything that they do. On the way we passed a nunnery; and the poor recluses, crowding round their barred windows, frantically cried, "Viva l'Italia!", clapped their hands vigorously, and exhibited every sign of great joy.

The march lasted more than an hour, and was marked by a delirious enthusiasm in its later stages. At last we reached the great square in front of the castle, which was roomy enough for this big crowd. Garibaldi awaited them on the gallery of his pavilion, seeming to soar above all this noise, as if he had already reached a more serene plane of existence.

The carriages now disappeared beneath the gloomy arch of the Palace, and when we got out, I left the prisoners to go and thank their liberator, whilst I returned to my apartment. But no sooner had I appeared on the balcony, accompanied by La Porta's standard-bearer, than the cheering broke out again. This people with their boundless enthusiasm filled the poet's rôle in this solemn celebration, so charged with poetic rapture.

Oh, my thirty years of struggle and toil, how blessed ye are! If France has nothing for its poets than a crown of misery and the staff of exile, foreign lands keep for them the crown of bays and the triumphal car. Oh, my dear Victor Hugo, my dear Lamartine, had you been here with me on this balcony, you two who are nearest to my heart, it is to you that the triumph would have belonged! Share it with me; nay, take it all; may the gentle breezes of Palermo waft it to you, with the smiles of its women and the perfume of its flowers! You are the two heroes of our century, the two giants of our epoch. As for me, I am like this poor *guerrillero* of La Porta, only the standard-bearer of the legion.

But no matter; two years ago I left traces of my footsteps in the north, and now I am leaving them in the south. The applause bestowed on me—from Mount Elbruz to Mount Etna—is really for you. Be ungrateful, oh, France!—you can be so; the rest of the world is not ungrateful!

A day such as this, in which I have had a share, is not one out of the days of a year, nor out of the days of a century, but out of the life of a people!

20th June, 5 o'clock, evening.

As soon as the liberated prisoners had left Garibaldi, they came to pay me a visit, together with their mothers and wives and sisters. The wife of one of them, the Baroness Riso, is the daughter of my old and worthy friend Du Halley, the referee in all affairs of honour.

10 o'clock.

Well, after all, there is such a thing as retributive justice!

A great crowd is just now coming out of the Strada di Toledo. Fifty men, in the midst of this crowd, hold lighted torches in their hands, and all seem to be kicking along some shapeless mass, which they are howling at, reviling, and hissing. Then, when under my windows, they begin to dance round this object, bestowing kicks on it from time to time.

Paul Parfait, Edouard Lockroy, Legray, the doctor and Théodore go down to find out what this object was, whilst I remain on the balcony with Durand-Brager.

Do you know what was this object, which the populace was dragging, I will not say through the mud, but through the dust of the streets of Palermo, which it was spitting on and pelting with offal? It was the head broken off from the statue of the man who poisoned my father: the head of Ferdinand II!

I wonder if he, in his royal tomb, has any sense of what is passing just now—the man who presided at the massacre of '98; who witnessed the hanging of Carracciolo, Pagano, Cirillo, Eleonora Pimentele, and the decapitation of Hector Carafa; who was obliged to give an annual salary to the executioner, because the payment of twenty-five ducats for each execution threatened to ruin the royal treasury?[1]

Not a single Neapolitan is now left in Palermo. We now have the exact number of the royal army which has left its shores during the last eight days. It amounted to *twenty-seven thousand* men.

Lest it might be said that we have been guilty of exaggeration in our accounts of the cruelties committed by the Neapolitans, we quote here an official report furnished by the Swiss Consul, M. Hirzel. We reproduce it word for word: the original is still in our hands.

It is a report to Marshal Lanza, the second in authority in Palermo, and is therefore couched in those niceties of expression which representatives of nations usually employ when addressing one another.

"To His Excellency, Marshal Lanza, invested with plenary powers by His Majesty the King of Sicily.

"*Palermo, 2nd June*, 1860.

"YOUR EXCELLENCY.—

"Upon information received from various persons that Alberto Tich Holzer, a native of Switzerland, husband of Donna Rosa Bevilacqua, living at No. 778 in the Grande Piazzeta, and shop No. 22 in the street leading from the Piazza Ballero to the Porta Castro, had had the misfortune to have his house rifled

---

[1] Dumas wrote later his marvellous romance "La San Félice," dealing therein with this dark episode of history.

and burnt, that his shop and warehouse had both been plundered, that his son, age twelve years, on trying to escape from the flames, was shot by a soldier with his rifle, that nobody could tell me what had become of the rest of the family; I thought it my duty to make a personal investigation into the matter, and inquired of his neighbours, but none of them could furnish any information. Some, indeed, supposed that they must have been arrested by the royal troops, but that was as much as they could say. They could only imagine that this numerous family must have been taken to the convent of the White Benedictines, imprisoned in the refectory there, and probably had met their death by being burnt alive when the soldiers set fire to the convent before retreating to the Royal Palace.

"As I was unable to believe the truth of such a report, I went personally to the above-mentioned Benedictine Convent.

"Whilst on my way, going through a part of the town which has been entirely ruined, among burnt-down houses, from which issued a pestilential odour, I asked everyone I met, who was the author of all these horrors, and from each of the few survivors of this wretched quarter I received the same answer, and it was this: that the troops in their flight towards the Palace, and when expelled from their position of defence at the Porta Montalto, killed everybody they encountered on their way.

"When I arrived at the convent of the White Benedictines, I was shown a large space which, I was told, was the spot where the refectory had stood. There I saw men bearing away charred corpses, which, so I was informed, were the bodies of people who had lived in that part of the town. The survivors declared that these people had been arrested and shut up in this hall by the royal troops, who then proceeded to sack the convent, and finished up by setting fire to it when they left.

"I then asked the grave-diggers how many bodies they had already removed; and they said, 'Forty.' I next asked them how many they thought still remained, and the reply was, 'Twenty.' So there were sixty people done to death in this convent alone.

"I therefore turn with feelings of deep anxiety to your Excellency to obtain some information concerning the fate of my countryman: to know whether he is a prisoner at the present moment, together with the rest of his family, or if you can throw any other light upon the present position of these unfortunate people.

"I present my demand to your Excellency in the name of humanity and justice. If they are prisoners, I claim from your Excellency an order for their immediate release, reserving the question of any damages which my countryman may claim at a more suitable time and place.

"(*Signed*) G. C. Hirzel,
"Agent of the Swiss Confederation."

This memorial of the Agent for the Swiss Confederation may be considered by some as being a little too prosaic; but I presume that nobody will say it is not in accordance with facts.

21st June, 7 a.m.

The first battalion of the Piedmontese volunteers, Medici's division, has just arrived, headed by a band. They are all admirably armed and equipped, and look like old campaigners with ten years' service.

As we were only awaiting their arrival, we shall, in all probability, start to-night, or at latest, to-morrow.

CHAPTER XXVIII

ON THE ROAD

Villafrati, 22nd June.

AFTER leaving Palermo, our first halt was at Misilmeri. In marching away from the capital of Sicily, we were following the same route as Garibaldi had taken in order to enter it.

When we reached the bridge of the Ammiraglio, we came across the bodies of three *sbirri* half-eaten by dogs, although they had evidently been killed only the night before. It was at this bridge that the Royalists and Garibaldians first met in deadly conflict. It was here that thirty-two men under Tükőry and Missori attacked 400 Neapolitans, and completely defeated them, although they had no further support than Nino Bixio, and a company of Piedmontese. (All volunteers, no matter what nation they belong to, are given this name here.)

On the eve of my departure from Palermo, I received this certificate, in pursuance of a recommendation given by myself:

"To-day, the 20th of June, 1860, the following were enrolled in the light cavalry regiment of which I am colonel:

"Prince Conrad Niscemi.
"Baron Giovanni Colobria Riso.
"Prince Francesco Giardinelli.
"Cavaliere Nosarbartholo San Giovanni.

"(*Signed*) COLONEL GIULIO SANTO STEFANO, Marquis de la Cerda."

An hour before starting, I went to say good-bye to the General. As I had asked him what were the precise terms in which his resignation had been presented to the King of Piedmont, he had been to the trouble of looking it up in a file of papers, and now handed me a duplicate copy, written and signed by himself.

The document is in Italian, and the following is a translation:

"*Genoa, 26th November, 1859.*[1]

"I am deeply grateful to your Majesty for the high honour you have done me in naming me a lieutenant-general; but I should like to point out to your Majesty that, with its acceptance, I should lose that freedom of action which might enable me to render services to Central Italy. I therefore beg your Majesty to be so good as to consider carefully the justice of my plea, and to suspend, even if only for the time being, the above-mentioned appointment.
"I am, with the highest respect,
"Your Majesty's most devoted servant,
"GARIBALDI."

---

[1] Mr. Trevelyan does not cite the text of this important document.

231

What a difference there is between this letter and the exclamation which came from the depths of the heart of one of our Marshals of France: "They will never deprive me of my emoluments unless they deprive me of my life!"

Before leaving Palermo, we took a photographic group of the six principal prisoners, and two magnificent portraits, one of Türr, and the other of the General. When I offered the General the copy intended for him, he begged me to write a few words on it, as a souvenir of our friendship.

So I took up a pen, and wrote the following:

"MY DEAR GENERAL,[1]

"Avoid Neapolitan daggers; become the head of a republic; die as poor as you have lived; and you will be greater even than Washington or Cincinnatus.

"ALEX. DUMAS."

"*Palermo, 20th June,* 1860.

Our camp includes our three Greeks, Podimatas, Risos and Henri, armed to the teeth, and in charge of the transport of our two baggage waggons, tents, kitchen equipment, and cook.

Our cook is no longer Jean. Jean was not cut out for a sailor, and as soon as we reached Palermo, he begged us to send him home again as quickly as possible. Now, our consul at Palermo, M. Fleury, is full of sympathy for his countrymen out here, and takes four francs from each for placing him on board the *Vauban* under the protection of the French flag; but unfortunately, for what reason I do not know, he declines to repatriate M. Jean. So we have to send him to Malta first, and from there arrange for his return to his native country.

M. Fleury has also made us pay him harbour-dues for the entry and exit of a pleasure yacht.

M. Fleury is decidedly a man with ideas!

Our cook is now Antoine. He was given to us by M. di Salvi, Captain of the *Protis*, temporarily in the service of his Majesty the King of Naples, to which kingdom he had been busy returning a portion of the Palermo garrison. Antoine is a young fellow, eighteen years old, who learnt the culinary art under the famous Parroul at Marseilles.

After our three Greeks and the cook—or before, if you prefer to say so—comes our fighting corps, composed of the doctor, Legray, Paul Parfait, Edouard Lockroy, the "Admiral," myself, Vasili, and the cabin-boy.

All except the cabin-boy were armed with a double-barrelled rifle and a revolver.[2] We also had two light-travelling carriages.

[1] This letter brought Dumas into considerable disfavour with the French Government, being considered as a slight to Napoleon III!

[2] The "Admiral" must have presented a formidable appearance!

Count Tasca, one of the richest landed proprietors of Palermo, was desirous of doing us the honours of Sicily; so, for a distance of a score of leagues, we shall have the opportunity of staying at his castles, his farms, and his houses, or those of his friends. He is taking two carriages, one for himself, and another for his valet. The only thing that one has to fear, when on the road to Girgenti or Syracuse, is an encounter with robbers.

When the Neapolitans were fleeing before Garibaldi's victorious army, they abandoned the city prisons and the custody of their inmates—mostly robbers or assassins, either paying the penalty of their crimes or awaiting judgment. These malefactors then escaped, and, not considering the city to be a very safe place of residence, fled to the mountains. Once there, they formed bands of ten, fifteen, or even twenty, and took up their old line of business once again— that of holding up and robbing all who came their way. As we are not going to follow very closely the line of march of the column, in all probability we shall have a bone or two to pick with them. As an example of the difference in our respective plans, I would mention that we made our first start at three o'clock in the morning, whilst the column left at five o'clock in the previous afternoon.

We arrived at Misilmeri at six o'clock in the morning. Türr was there, but we found him ill and in bed. He had been seized with a bad attack of vomiting of blood. Our doctor arrived just in time to prevent the doctor in attendance on him proceeding to bleed him —a course of treatment which might have had very grave consequences for the patient, seeing how weak he was from a wound not yet healed, and from what he had undergone at Calatafimi. In consequence of Türr's illness the Legionary soldiers will not resume their march till the evening; but as for ourselves, we leave at half-past three in the afternoon, so as to get our lodgings ready at Villafrati.

Misilmeri has one thing to boast of: it was the first place in Sicily to revolt after the 4th of April. There were at that time in the town four Neapolitan soldiers, eight mounted gendarmes, and eight *sbirri*. The people began by driving these men out from amongst them; they then hoisted the Italian banner, and so the tocsin was sounded. A committee was formed, the President being Don Vicenzo Rasmolo. The Vice-President was our host, Signor Giuseppe Fiduccia; and two priests, named Pizza and Andolina, formed the rest of this insurrectionary tribunal. When these priests were introduced to me, I recognised in Andolina the one who danced so energetically before the carriage of the liberated prisoners on their withdrawal from Castellaccio.

On the 11th April these insurgents advanced to the attack on a body of Neapolitans, a little in advance of the Ammiraglio bridge; but the noise of the combat drew to the spot a column which was far too strong for them to think of opposing. The insurgents, to the number of about 2000, therefore, withdrew to the mountains.

On the 16th Rosolino Pilo, the forerunner of Garibaldi, arrived in their camp and roused the patriotic ardour of all when he told them that the General was on the point of embarking. He had some English gold, and our host changed part of it into Sicilian money.

Just then La Masa arrived with 300 to 400 men. He called the committee together again, and it was then decided that Misilmeri should be the headquarters of the revolt, and, further, that it should be the base for communications with all other parts of the island.

This taking the initiative on the part of a man placed so much higher than his associates, marked him out for the post of commandant of the guerrillas; and it was with this rank that he rejoined Garibaldi at Salemi, bringing with him 600 to 800 men. The *Picciotti* were present at the battle of Calatafimi: how they behaved there, I have already told you.

Opinions differ greatly about La Masa: some say he has done great things, others say he has done nothing at all. Needless to say that there is considerable exaggeration on both sides. My own opinion is that amongst men so brave and simple-minded as Garibaldi, Türr, Nino Bixio, Sirtori, and Carini, La Masa is making a blunder in using the word "I" so frequently and so emphatically. He is at present in this neighbourhood, and I shall see him, in all probability, before my departure from Villafrati.

We left Misilmeri at three o'clock in the afternoon, the thermometer registering about 130 degrees in the sun. The Garibaldians were to follow at eight o'clock at night, to halt on the road from midnight till three o'clock, and then resume their march so as to arrive at Villafrati at six o'clock in the morning.

Villafrati can be discerned from a distance by a little Norman castle, still in a fair state of preservation, situated on the summit of a rock, and called the "Castle of Diana" by the country-people. Down below in the valley, screened from view by a peasant's house, are the ancient Arabian sulphur baths. The building bears an Arabian inscription, half, or perhaps I should say three-parts, erased by the hand of time; nevertheless, a learned man of Palermo has deciphered it. It is really wonderful what these blessed "learned men" can decipher! The vaulted roof of these baths is just as it was left by the

Arabian architect, and has holes pierced in it to allow the sulphur-
ous fumes to escape.

Villafrati, or the Town of the Priests, is built on a rather steep slope
of a hill. Our coachman took it into his head to make his horses
gallop for three-parts of the ascent. The horses responded to the call
nobly; but suddenly, and without the slightest warning to their
driver of their wicked intention (which they possibly whispered to
each other), all three, with one accord, threw themselves down on
their sides. Luckily the hind wheel of our carriage was wedged by a
big stone, which stopped us short, otherwise we might have found
ourselves in the same plight as Hippolytus on the road to Mycenæ.
Thank God, however, nothing happened; but it was not the fault
of the horses that they did not succeed in their intention to break our
necks. As we were then not more than a hundred yards from the
house of the Marquis of San Marco, which stands highest, and is
evidently the noble residence of the town, we decided to finish our
journey on foot. Thanks to Salvator, Count Tasca's valet, we found
the stoves lit when we arrived, the dinner nearly ready, and the beds
made in all the sleeping-rooms.

Our Greeks, Vasili and Antoine, have set up two tents upon a
terrace which runs along the eastern side of the house, and have
pitched their camp there. As for the rest of us, we have prosaically
accepted the accommodation of the house which was offered us with
such cordiality.

Villafrati is situated in a delightful country, amid mountain scenery,
diversified by golden fields of corn, with stalks gracefully undulating
to the breeze, and groves of the loveliest green. Just opposite to our
windows rises the ancient Castle of Diana. A raised terrace stretching along the façade, and surmounted by busts of the Roman
emperors and empresses, made at Faenza, overlooks the whole
village and commands a view of that road which our coachman so
unluckily proposed we should ascend at full gallop. This terrace is
paved with faïence tiles, and is adorned with wild hollyhocks in
abundance. It is a delightful place from five till nine o'clock in the
morning, and after five in the evening.

Accordingly, the morning after our arrival, following a night of
constant torment by gnats and fleas, the two chief scourges of Italy
—for, to my thinking, the Bourbons and Austrians only rank third—
at five o'clock I found my way to this terrace, and there caught sight
of the advance-guard of our column, as it came into view at the bend
of the road. A quarter of an hour later, it reached the entrance to the
village. Five minutes afterwards, a horseman entered the courtyard
at full speed. The rider was none other than Brother John, his head

adorned with a broad-brimmed hat ornamented with silk tassels. If the tassels had been of gold thread instead of silk, and the colour had been red, you would have had the hat of a cardinal. Brother John! Brother John! can such an ambitious idea have entered the heart that beats beneath the sober garb of a reformed Franciscan?

My first care in addressing him was to ask news of Türr. He told me that Türr had had a recurrence of the vomiting, and was now coming along in a carriage drawn by three white horses, which he pointed out to me, as it followed after the column. It was quite clear that Türr could not ascend to the elevated position of the Marquis' residence, where quarters had been prepared for him; so I and Brother John set off in search of others. We found such at a house about three-quarters of the distance up the rise—in fact just at the spot where our horses had tried to rid themselves of us. Half-an-hour later our sick friend was in bed. The column is to halt here for three days.

I have just written to Garibaldi to inform him of the serious illness of Türr, whom he loves as his own son. It is probable, therefore, that to-morrow, or the day after, Türr will receive orders to return to Palermo.

June 24th, at mid-day.

Yesterday, at four o'clock, Count Tasca came to inform me that an officer, whose name he did not mention, desired to make my acquaintance, and, in consequence, begged my permission to invite him to dinner. As the officer was in the adjoining room, I went straight to it, so as to press the invitation, if such should seem necessary. In five minutes time I found out who this officer was: it was La Masa. He was just the sort of man I had expected to find: a Gascon—using this word in the favourable sense. More of the Arabian than of the Norman element has remained in Sicilian blood.

La Masa, born at La Trebbia, is probably thirty-five years old; is of fair complexion, with blue eyes, and has a well-proportioned figure. He wears the Garibaldian uniform—that is to say, the red blouse, and grey trousers with silver stripes. Garibaldi simplifies this costume very much in his own case. Instead of a blouse, he simply wears a red shirt, and his well-worn grey trousers have no silver stripe.

La Masa stayed with us till nine o'clock in the evening. He spent the time in talking about himself and his men, and of the services which they had rendered to Sicily. His style of conversation is agreeable, easy, and even elegant.

On leaving, he gave me a collection of his proclamations and orders of the day. Here is a specimen:

"*The Heights of Roccamena, 17th May,* 1860.

"BROTHERS,[1]

"The sacred love of country, and the divine favour have drawn me to you, my old associates in enterprise and victory, to fight along with you, for the last time, against the armies of the tyrant.

"The valiant general, Giuseppe Garibaldi, *aide-de-camp* of His Majesty, Victor-Emmanuel II, *has joined us*—Sicilian emigrants of the continent—with a corps of invincible patriots, to aid us in breaking the Bourbon yoke, and in bringing to fruition our plans of insurrection, which aim at annexation to the government of Victor-Emmanuel II, and the creation, as quickly as possible, of a united, free, and powerful Italy.

"All the insurgents will proclaim this great Italian general, Dictator.

"To arms, my valiant brothers!

"Our expeditionary corps, with the brave General Garibaldi at its head, has, in one epic day of battle, defeated and put to flight, at Calatafimi, the royal armies, who had under their dominion the whole land of Sicily from Marsala to Alcamo.

"It now remains for you, brothers, to arm yourselves in any way open to you, to organise, to unite with those valiant ones who fought against the Bourbon troops in the mountains round Palermo and its environs. Sicily in arms, from Marsala to Partinico, has rushed, crowding eagerly, to swell the ranks of the Italian troops. That you may become strong and mighty, strive to emulate the deeds of the patriotic *guerrilleros* who fought at Parco, at Piana dei Greci, and in the suburbs of the capital.

"At the invitation of some of our brothers, I hastened to these mountains to examine your position, to put you into intimate contact with the army of our valiant General, and to secure that unity of action which is indispensable to a successful issue in our struggle for freedom.

"Brothers, the eyes of all Italy are upon you! You, I know, will be true to yourselves, and to your brothers of the continent who have come with wondrous generosity to shed their blood in Sicily in aid of our common cause!

"Viva l'Italia! Viva Vittorio Emmanuele!

"G. LA MASA."

There is a big difference between this prolix effusion of La Masa and the simplicity and precision of style which you find in all proclamations made by Garibaldi since he left Talamone—and he must have issued something like twenty of them. In the whole of these proclamations Garibaldi has not referred to himself so much as La Masa has called attention to himself in this single one.

I might mention that, as Türr has arrived, La Masa has disappeared altogether.

Yesterday evening, after the departure of La Masa, the Count, whilst conversing with me on the terrace, informed me that we were close to the spot which was the scene of the exploits of the famous Fra Diavolo; that the mountains facing us were his habitual retreat, and a little olive grove, three miles off, belonging to the Marquis di San Marco, was the scene of his last fight. Being desirous, whilst on the spot, of gathering more detailed information about a man whom the words of Scribe and the music of Auber have made so familiar

[1] Note the italics: *has joined us.* "There was a strange rumour," says Mr. Trevelyan, "that Garibaldi had not landed at all, but was being personated by a Pole." Mr. Trevelyan does not cite this proclamation.

to the French public, the Count sent for one of the *campieri* of the Marquis di San Marco, a man of about fifty-five or sixty, who had personally known Fra Diavolo. This is what he told us about him:

Fra Diavolo, whose real name was Antonio Borzetta, was born at Carini, towards the end of last century or the beginning of this one. His father was a landed proprietor, and he also had a younger brother named Ambrozio. Having suffered too severely at the hands of justice for certain youthful escapades, he betook himself to the mountains and became a bandit. In six months time he had acquired such fame that he became known by no other name than "Fra Diavolo." Owing to the great courage and skill he displayed, all attempts to capture him failed. Daily, one heard people talking of some fresh robbery or killing carried out with matchless audacity.

Now, the Viceroy, the Marquis Don Pietro Coppola, caused a big reward to be offered to anyone who would put Fra Diavolo into his hands; and a bandit imprisoned at Palermo had a message sent to the Viceroy to the effect that if, in place of the promised reward, he would set him at liberty, he would undertake to hand over to the Government Fra Diavolo, alive or dead.

In putting faith in the word of a bandit, they were running the risk that he would break his pledge; but in declining to trust him they were running a much bigger risk still; and this was, that Fra Diavolo would continue to be at large, whilst each day would be marked by the commission of some new outrage. So they released the convict from prison. His name was Mario Granata and his home was Misilmeri. The Viceroy asked him what he needed in the way of money, and his answer was that all he required was ten ounces—about £5— to buy powder and bullets. This was given to him. He then requested that, in place of being released, he should be allowed to escape from prison. This proposition was also assented to, and he escaped. Mario Granata now bought his powder and bullets, and set out to rejoin his old crony, Fra Diavolo.

From the very first his return gave rise to suspicions in the mind of Ambrosio, Fra Diavolo's brother. The two brothers held a consultation as to what was the best way of putting Granata to the test; and it was decided that the best was to entrust Granata with a fairly large sum to buy provisions and other necessaries for the band. If he returned with the goods, they thought they might safely trust him, for he must know quite well that he would not incur any punishment if he decamped with the money.

Mario Granata set out to execute his commissions and came back. From that moment he was welcomed as a member of the band.

The fair of Castro Giovanni was drawing near, and that of Lentini was to take place shortly before. It was to this fair that all the big graziers who supply Palermo with meat generally go; and, as is the case in all countries, these dealers who come to buy or sell have a great deal of money on them. Granata's advice, then, was that they should all go and lie in ambush in the mountains of Villafrati. His proposal was adopted; and the band, which consisted of six men, Fra Diavolo, his brother Ambrosio, Mario Granata, Giuseppe and Benedetto Davi di Torretta, and Vitali di Cinesi, then set out for the appointed place.

Shortly before they reached Misilmeri, Granata asked Fra Diavolo for twelve hours leave of absence that he might pay a visit to his wife. Fra Diavolo, not distrusting him in the least, readily gave permission, it being understood that Granata was to rejoin his companions before daybreak in the mountains of Villafrati. The bandits continued their journey.

Morning came, but there was no sign of Granata. They were now on the mountain of Chiara Stella; so Fra Diavolo halted, and sent one of their number, Vitali, to make inquiries at Villafrati. Vitali took the road leading down into the town, and as the day happened to be the Feast of the Annunciation, the first thing he did on his arrival was to attend Mass, and hear the sermon of the Capuchin, Father Innocenzio di Bisacquino. On coming out of church, he set to work to gather what information he could.

Whilst he was inside at Mass, the *gendarmerie* from Merzoïero had come into the town. This unusual movement of armed police gave him all the information he wanted. They were evidently on the track of Fra Diavolo. He therefore turned his steps back to the mountains; but on arriving, found himself confronted by a cordon of troops, consisting of two companies, posted by the Viceroy in accordance with the information furnished by Mario Granata. These troops were commanded by Captain Antonio Orlando, the Lercaza Fredde, and Antonio Pessione, of Palermo. They at once asked Vitali what he was doing in the mountains, and he replied that he had come in search of simples for herbalists and druggists. Whilst the military were discussing the advisability of arresting him, he sent the officers sprawling by a dextrous use of his elbows, made a dash for the mountains, and disappeared.

Within a quarter of an hour's time, he had rejoined Fra Diavolo and told him everything. Then the brigands tried to escape by every pass, but they found all guarded by troops. The soldiers had been gradually closing in. Towards eleven o'clock in the morning the first sounds of firing were heard at Villafrati. Fighting all the time, Fra Diavolo beat a retreat towards the Marquis di San Marco's olive grove. Towards two o'clock firing ceased. At four o'clock the dead body of Fra Diavolo was brought into Villafrati. He had shot himself with a double-barrelled pistol on the right side of the head, to prevent his falling into the hands of the soldiers alive. It was clearly a case of suicide. The two bullets had made a single orifice on entering the right temple, but had caused two wounds in passing out on the other side.

In the course of the fight, two or three soldiers were killed, and a *sbirro* and Giuseppe Davi were wounded. Antonio Schifari's uncle, who was chaplain of the church, took the viaticum up into the mountains to the two dying men.

Two of the brigands were killed, and the others were made prisoners. Ambrozio and Vitali had, indeed, made good their escape, but preferred to share the fate of their companions, and were shot at Carini. Both died with a smile on their lips. As all the townspeople were following them on the way to execution, Ambrozio addressed them thus:

"My mother has lost nothing in not making me a priest; for, whatever reputation for holiness of life I might have gained, I certainly should never have found myself at the head of so numerous a procession as the one which is following me to-day."

Benedetto Davi was condemned to eighteen years in irons. In the case of Fra Diavolo, the body was decapitated, and the head, after being plunged into boiling vinegar, was forwarded to the Viceroy at Palermo. He, in turn, sent it on to Carini, where it was placed in an iron cage and exposed to public view, just as was the head of his no less celebrated comrade, Pascal Bruno, the story of whose exploits I related to you—it must be some twenty years ago.

CHAPTER XXIX

S A N T O   M E L I

Villafrati, 23rd June

JUST as the *campiero* was finishing his narrative, copies of the official newspaper for the 22nd and 23rd were brought to Count Tasca. He kept the one of the later date, and handed me the other. I opened it mechanically—"official" journals have little attraction for me—and was perusing it still more mechanically, when my eyes were arrested by seeing my own name. Had I been in France, I should have felt pretty sure I was going to read something uncomplimentary, and should have cast the journal aside; but in Sicily I read on. It was a paragraph on current events, and read as follows—

"At a meeting of our Civic Council, it was moved that the celebrated romancer Alexandre Dumas be elected a councillor. The resolution was carried unanimously that this honour be accorded to a man who, by his works, has certainly added to the glory of France, and who is now in Sicily to get acquainted with what is taking place in our war against the Bourbons, in furtherance of the great cause of United Italy."

The motion had been made and passed the day after my departure. This action of the Council may be regarded as a delicate act of courtesy, added to a favour. I wrote to the Municipality of Palermo, tendering my sincere thanks for the honour done me.

After this item of news, personal to myself, I came across the following—

"The Duke of Verdura, our prætor, states, in continuation of the details given by him concerning the dead bodies found in the ruins, that on the 18th two more bodies, and on the 19th eight more bodies were discovered. Although the most strenuous efforts are being made to restore to the town its former splendour, the horrible scenes revealed to the eyes of the people incense them more and more against the Bourbons."

And this is sent to us from Messina, dated the 12th of June—

"The royal garrisons of Trapani, Termini, Agosta, Girgenti, Catania, and a part of that of Palermo, have now arrived at Messina, where, in addition to these, there are great numbers of sick and wounded, of *sbirri*, police agents, and civil employés: these now number at least 15,000 men.

"Monteleone, Cosenza, Cantanzaro, and all the towns of the interior in Calabria are in a state of insurrection. It is stated that a body of volunteers has disembarked at Pizzo.

"Five French war-vessels have entered our port, but we are unable to say with what intention."

And this proclamation has been distributed amongst the Royalist troops, in the name of the people of Messina—

"NEAPOLITANS! You are the children of Italy; Italy! a land stretching from Mount Cenis to the waters of Sicily, which is now red with blood.

16   241

"Rise in the name of Italy and of liberty!

"The valiant men of Varese and Como are with you, and yet you fight against them!

"God said to Cain: 'What hast thou done to thy brother? Now art thou cursed from the earth.'

"And Italy says to you: 'Ye accursed! what have ye done to your brothers?'

"Every drop of blood spilt in Sicily is a curse upon your own heads, and upon the heads of your sons, and of your sons' sons!

"Neapolitans! Italy pardons you the past; but rise now against all who bear ill-will to Italy!"

25th June.

We learnt this morning that the diligence was stopped by twenty armed men, two miles from here, and that the four passengers in it were robbed of everything upon them.

25th June, eleven p.m.

For the first time in my life, at this hour of the night when one ponders over the events of the day, I have a feeling akin to that of remorse. I will now tell you a story, which will probably have a tragic termination.

This morning I was by Türr's bedside. The window was open, so as to admit the rays of the sun which are always so welcome to the sick, whilst the door was ajar so as to allow of the free passage of air. Suddenly my attention was arrested by hearing the steps of several horses. I went to the window, and saw a party of seven horsemen armed with rifles and pistols, the last two of them, however, being mounted on the same horse. At the head of the troop was a man who seemed to be the chief. His head-dress was a Neapolitan *Kepi*, with the four braidings which indicate the rank of captain; and suspended from his waist was a dragoon's sword adorned with a silver knot. Now there was nothing remarkable about this; but I must confess that my attention was riveted upon one of the cavaliers, who had half-a-dozen chickens sticking out from his saddle-bow. Turning to Türr, I said:

"*Diable!* one of those beggars is not likely to die of hunger!"

Türr rose, took a glance at the men who brought up the rear, and then threw himself on his bed again, without saying a word. The rapid slope of the road quickly shut them off from distinct view.

"What are these men?" said I.

"Some of La Masa's *guerillas*, I should think," was his reply.

Then, addressing me a moment later, he said:

"Have a look and see where they are going."

I rose again and went to the window.

"It looks as if they intend going through the village and taking the road to Palermo," I observed.

Just then Major Spangaro came in.

"Major," said Türr, "do go and see who those men are who have just gone by."

"Oh!" said I, "they are now a long way off. You can just see them on the far side of the village."

"General," said one of the young officers who were taking care of Türr, "shall I jump on my horse, and bring back their captain?"

"Take four men with you and bring back the lot of them. Do you hear, Carbone?"[1]

"Oh! that is quite superfluous," said the young officer. "Why trouble four men for a trifle of this sort. I shall go by myself."

He went downstairs, and, leaping on a horse without a saddle, galloped off in pursuit of the seven men.

Türr then started a conversation with the major, whilst I went to the balcony and watched the progress of the young officer in pursuit. In less than ten minutes he caught up the little troop, which was continuing its journey very leisurely. Their captain had already looked round several times; but, as he only saw one man coming along, he concluded there was no need to disturb himself on that score. From where I was, I could see everything that took place; and although I could not hear a word that was said, I could guess from their gestures all that was passing.

"Well," exclaimed Türr, "can you see them?"

"Perfectly."

"What are they doing?"

"Nothing, at present, except chatting in a friendly way. But stay— the Captain leaps to the ground and is moving his hand towards his gun. Carbone now draws his revolver, and is holding it against the other's breast."

"Quickly," shouted Türr, "send four men to Carbone's assistance."

"Needless! The captain of the troop has remounted his horse and submits to Carbone, who, revolver in hand, now has the whole seven making a return journey in front of him."

"He is bringing them back?"

"Yes."

As a matter of fact, in five minutes' time the head of the little column had reached the end of the street, and was wending its way to the General's house. Not long after, it pulled up at the door.

"Tell Carbone to come up and see me alone," said Türr, "after he has handed over these fellows to the care of his comrades."

I accordingly requested Carbone to come up alone; but as to telling the Garibaldians to look after the seven men, that was super-

[1] Francesco Carbone who distinguished himself at the taking of Palermo by sitting on a chair in the middle of a road swept by Neapolitan fire.

fluous, for they had already formed an impenetrable ring round them.

"Well," said Türr to Carbone, who came up in obedience to orders, "so it seems they began to offer resistance."

"Yes, General; but, as you see, everything has turned out better than I expected."

"How is that?" said Türr. "Tell me all about it, and omit no details. Before seeing their leader, I want to know what sort of a man he is."

"General, I caught them up about fifteen hundred yards from here, and only then did I realise that I was tackling a much more difficult job than I had previously thought. Consequently, I addressed their captain very politely."

"Quite right," said Türr, laughing, "always be polite, Carbone. And what was it that you told them so politely?"

Carbone continued: "'Noble captain,' said I, 'the General has sent me to inquire whither you are going.'

"'I am going to Palermo,' was the response.

"'That is very fortunate, for the General has despatches and a sum of money to send to Palermo, and he wishes you to take charge of them.'

"'What, I?'

"'Yes, you; and he wants you to come and see him, so that he may hand you the letters and money.'

"'I am very sorry,' replied the chief, ' but I am in a hurry.'

"'Oh, if that is the case, then it becomes quite another thing The General does not ask you, he orders you.'

"'By what right?'

"'By the right of being your superior officer. If you are the officer which your *Kepi* and sabre indicate, you must obey him; but if you are not an officer, I must arrest you for wearing that *Kepi* and sabre without authority.'

"Then," said Carbone in conclusion, "he tried to dismount and make use of his gun, but I promptly drew my revolver and, holding it against his breast, said: 'If you do not follow me instantly, I shall kill you.' That settled the matter, and here he is."

"Very good indeed," said Türr. "Send him up."

I was about to leave the room, when Türr, calling me, said: "Stop here; he is probably some sort of bandit, so there will be no harm in your seeing what takes place. Moreover, you are entitled to be here, for it is you who caused him to be arrested."

"Oh, come now, I must deny that."

"Anyhow, you will stop?" said Türr.

"Yes."

The door opened and the man came in. He was from twenty-five to twenty-eight years old, of fair complexion, with blue eyes, well built, and of medium height. He entered with an air of most complete assurance, but when he caught sight of Türr lying on the sofa, he stopped short and turned pale.

Türr, on the other hand, fixed his steady, honest eyes upon him, but showed not the slightest sign of astonishment, save perhaps a slight movement of his moustache.

"So, it's you, is it?" said Türr.

"Excuse me, General, but I don't know you," replied the prisoner.

"But I know you. Just try and walk across the room without limping."

"I cannot, General, for I have been wounded in the leg."

"Yes, by a ball just above the knee; but it was not facing the foe that you got that wound."

"Why, General . . ."

"It was when you were trying to rob the treasury of Santa Margarita. Come now, I know you: you are Santo Meli. I had you on my hands at Renda, and you would have been shot then if we had not been obliged to march on Parco without loss of a moment. I then handed you over to Santa Anna, who does not seem to have guarded you very closely; but I will not hand you over to the first comer, this time. You will be better looked after, I can promise you!"

Then, turning to Major Spangaro, he said:

"Major, to-morrow you will hold a court-martial, of which you will be President, for the trial of this man. Now disarm him, some of you, and take him to prison."

An officer advanced and took away the prisoner's sabre; and two soldiers, taking their places on either side of him, marched him out of the room on the way to prison.

"*Diable!* you are getting on finely, old fellow," said I to Türr.

"In these times that is the only way to deal with thieves, murderers, and incendiaries."

"But, after all, are you quite sure that this man answers this description, in all respects?"

"Yes; for he has robbed the treasury of Santa Margarita, murdered a goldsmith at Corleone, and burnt the village of Calaminia. Moreover, all this will be proved at the trial, and he shall not be shot without good reason."

"You think, then, that he will be shot?"

"I feel pretty sure of that! We were talking just now about the diligence having been held up last night; well, if two or three more similar events take place, our reactionary journals will tell us that from Catania to Trapani, and from Girgenti to the Faro, nobody can dare to put a foot outside his home in Sicily since the Bourbons have been driven out. My friend Garibaldi once ordered one of his soldiers to be shot at Rome because he had taken thirty sous from an old woman. Garibaldi has for his entire possessions two pairs of trousers, two red shirts, two neckties, a sabre, a revolver, and an old felt hat. Garibaldi has to borrow a *carlin* in order to give alms to some poor person, because he never has a *carlin* in his pocket; but this does not prevent Naples journals calling him a filibuster, and French ones describing him as a pirate. In times like the present we must be trebly pure, trebly brave, and trebly just, if we would incur but a moderate degree of calumny. If we act in this way, then at the end of ten or a dozen years we begin to be appreciated by our enemies; and scarcely double that time is needed before we begin to be appreciated by those whom we have served. Now go to *déjeuner*, for it is quite time; and send me along some *bouillon* which you have made yourself, and a spoonful of preserve, if you can find any."

I shook hands with this man, who is so true, so good, so compassionate, whose heart is half that of an angel, and half that of a lion, who laughs at bullets and weeps over misery. I went away, deep in thought, pondering upon the hard task undertaken by Garibaldi and this man, Türr, not only to deliver, but, what is more, to purify a country corrupted by four centuries of Spanish and Neapolitan dominion.

Right through the day the thought of Santo Meli's arrest, of which I had been the involuntary cause, troubled me. I spoke about him to most of the officers, but they were so indifferent that they seemed scarcely to understand what I meant. If I did succeed in getting them to realise that I was referring to their prisoner, they said: "Ah, yes; you mean that brigand who is going to be shot to-morrow morning? Oh! we shan't let him escape, as Santa Anna did: leave it to us."

Good heavens! how can one be a judge or a public prosecutor—a man who is required to demand the life of one of his fellow men daily—and yet keep a smiling countenance and eyes undimmed? I can understand the ardour of the hunter who, carried away by excitement, kills everything, from a quail to a wild boar, without the least pity for the weakness of the one, or any regard to the fierceness of the other; but I do not call him a sportsman who wrings a chicken's neck or cuts a pig's throat.

Count Tasca, like myself, appeared to be rather grave; and as I thought it might be for the same reason, I had a talk with him. I found that I was not mistaken.

Santo Meli comes from the village of Ciminna, only a few miles from Villafrati. He is both much feared and much admired in the country round about. Men of energy and resolution, even though energetic solely in the pursuit of evil-doing, always capture the popular imagination: witness the popularity of Nero at Rome, of Mandrin in France, and of Fra Diavolo in Sicily.

So the Count, and a young poet of Palermo, named di Maria, and myself resolved that after dinner we would contrive to draw the conversation on to the subject of Santo Meli, and try to influence the mind of Major Spangaro in his favour, as far as we could. But in Spangaro we found what you always find—or nearly always—in military judges, who are neither influenced by sense of their power on the one hand, nor by personal hatred to the accused on the other: that is to say, they are men who tell you that the line of justice is absolutely inflexible, and that you must never deviate ever so little, whether it be towards harshness or towards clemency.

At almost the very first word Spangaro interrupted us by saying:

"In the office which I am about to fulfil there are two things of which I must be particularly careful: my impartiality, and having any feelings which might affect that impartiality. I must beg you, therefore, to make no appeal to my sympathy; for, seeing that I am a man, I might be touched, and then I should no longer be a judge."

Seeing that I was about to make a last appeal, he rose and left the room. I admire this stoicism very much, but do not feel myself capable of it. Then, again, these men have a duty to perform; whereas on my part there was no duty to make that observation which attracted Türr's attention, which led to the prisoner's arrest, and which will probably lead to his death.

I, who am passing through this beautiful land of Italy, into which a man chosen by Providence is now breathing a new life, I have no mission but to plead for the unfortunate, to weep for the dead, to smile upon the living; why, then, should I leave the trace of one drop of blood upon my path?

Perhaps the voice that now speaks to me from within is not that of conscience, but only that of weakness. No matter: this voice tells me I ought to do all I can to save this man, even though he be an assassin and incendiary; and I shall do it.[1]

26th of June.

On rising this morning I was told that a woman dressed in black was waiting to see me in the next room. It was Santo Meli's mother,

[1] Dumas was not weak, but humane and generous.

an old peasant woman with hair turning grey, pale complexion, clear blue eyes, and an intelligent face. Now who could have told her to come and see me—a man whose name she had probably never heard of till this morning? Who could have told her to address a stranger who had come amongst her fellow-countrymen?

However that may be, the fact remains that as soon as she saw me approaching her, she took both my hands in hers, desiring to kiss them, in accordance with Sicilian custom. She then told me that she was relying on me to enable her to see General Türr. I declined to do what she requested, for two reasons: firstly, Türr believed Santo Meli to be guilty, and considered that, for the sake of Sicily, it was necessary to make an example of him. Secondly, that in Türr's weak state, due to his vomiting of blood, any sort of excitement might prove dangerous, for he certainly would not reject the prayer of a mother without feeling emotion.

This poor woman, however, did not realise the full extent of her son's danger. I told her that she could do something better, and that was to ask to see her son. As the court-martial was to sit that very morning, I recommended her to tell her son to choose di Maria to defend him. After giving her a paper with di Maria's name on it, I got from Major Spangaro the permit which would enable her to see her son. She then started on her journey to the prison.

The prison is a square building in the middle of the town. There is nothing about it to distinguish it from other houses, excepting bars over the windows. I watched the poor woman till I saw her reach the door, the threshold of which her son had crossed the day before, and probably would not cross again, except to start his last journey, with death at the end of the road. The mother entered the prison.

The court-martial met at ten o'clock. Santo Meli, following the advice I had given him through his mother, had chosen di Maria for his counsel. At five o'clock the court adjourned for the day. The prisoner answered with great firmness, declaring that since the 4th of April, the date of the proclamation of the revolution in Palermo, he had kept the field with the tricolour flag; that if he had annexed monies and burnt villages, he was authorised to do so by the revolutionary committee of Palermo; that if he had levied contributions on villages, firstly it was only when such villages were Royalist, and secondly, in order that his men should not leave him, he had to pay them and feed them. Now, the pay was four *taris* per day (one franc twenty-five centimes), and the keep of each was two *taris* (ninety centimes), and, as he had between 300 and 400 men under him, the average cost of their maintenance was from 1000 to 1200 francs a day, which had to be procured in one way or another. As to the charge of setting fire to houses, he had never set fire to any, except those from which his men had been fired on; incendiarism was then only in the nature of a reprisal.

Finally, he asked the court to weigh carefully the services he had rendered to the insurgent cause by keeping his men under arms, as against any harm done by necessities incidental to their maintenance. He only asked to be judged impartially.

These reasons would not count for much in a country like France and amongst a civilised community; but in Sicily, amongst a rude and illiterate peasantry, their soundness impressed the court. The evening and the next day were spent in examining witnesses. The court considered the matter a very serious one, not only on account of its issue as regards Santo Meli himself, but also because of the resultant moral effect of their decision.

Those who stood for the letter of the law said: "The greater the services this man may have rendered to the revolution, the more severe we should be, when we have before us a patriot who has not been able to keep himself undefiled by those excesses which are systematically laid to the charge of revolutionists."

The more moderate replied: "At the present time there are two peoples in Italy, differing as regards civilisation, country, and even race: the pure Latin race which has just crossed the sea to liberate Sicily finds this island inhabited by a cross-breed of Latins, Greeks, Saracens, and Normans. If we are too severe to Santo Meli, will not the Sicilians say that one of the first acts of their brethren from Northern Italy was to shoot a Sicilian patriot?"

At eleven o'clock in the evening, whilst I am engaged in writing this, the court-martial is still sitting.

27th June. Morning.

Yesterday, whilst witnesses were being examined, Santo Meli's mother came to me, on behalf of her son, to beg me to go and see him in prison, for he wished to thank me personally for all my interest in him in his misfortune, and to beg me to continue my exertions.

I complied with her request. The prisoner is confined in a cell the door of which opens at the foot of the staircase up which you ascend to the room where the court is sitting. He was awaiting my arrival with considerable anxiety. So much was conveyed to me by the expression of his eyes, that it was scarcely necessary for him to speak. He seized my hands, despite the bars, and kissed them, little as I desired it. His mother meanwhile stood close by.

I told him first of all to have confidence in his judges; and further, that the President, Major Spangaro, might be relied on to observe the utmost impartiality. As to the case, I recommended him to confess everything, and to plead the necessity of the times in justification. He told me that such was his intention. I remained about ten minutes with him. He was a young man whose massive hairy chest indicated deep and powerful lungs. He wore baggy trousers and boots turned down below the knee, like those worn by country gentlemen of France in the old time.

His arrest has caused great excitement in the country round about here—his native village, Ciminna, not being more than seven miles from Villafrati.

Türr's sufferings are steadily increasing. My letter to Garibaldi has produced the desired effect; but instead of sending his orders to Türr, he has sent an entreaty that he will return to Palermo. It is difficult to express the affectionate tenderness of Garibaldi for those whom he esteems and loves. A father could not have greater love for his children. He carried his regard for Türr so far as to give the command of our column to Colonel Eber, a friend of Türr's, and a countryman of his, with the idea of giving him no cause for taking umbrage at the temporary change. Eber was Colonel of the Foreign Legion in the Crimea, and is now correspondent of *The Times*, which pays him 30,000 francs per annum to go anywhere, when important events are happening, and to furnish reports thereon. He has entered the service of Italy for this emergency only. Eber is, as we have said, a Hungarian, but he speaks French, English, Italian, and Russian with equal ease and elegance. He arrived here last night. Garibaldi not knowing that I was as intimate with Eber as I was with Türr, and fearing that the passport given me by Major Cenni would not be sufficient, has sent me another.

The terms in which this passport is couched are another proof of that affectionate tenderness of Garibaldi, of which I spoke just now.

I give a translation of the Italian.

> *"General Headquarters of the National Army.*
> *"Palermo, 25th June,* 1860.

"I desire that free permission to pass through Sicily be given to an illustrious man and intimate friend of mine, Alexandre Dumas; and I shall be grateful for every attention which may be shown to him.

> "GARIBALDI."

Türr left at half-past three in the morning for Palermo; and at five o'clock this evening the column will continue the march towards Girgenti.

Letters received yesterday from Genoa announce that 40,000 muskets and a steam-boat have been bought; and that 45,000 volunteers have signed on, and are coming to Sicily to join the army of liberation.

As soon as that army is properly organised, we shall drive the Neapolitans out of Messina, and then march upon Naples by way of Calabria, where insurrection is already beginning to ferment.

When I left Palermo the last words of the General were: "You know that as soon as we reach Naples I shall have apartments prepared for you in the Royal Palace."

"Whilst you are about it," was my reply, "you might order a country-house to be prepared for me at Pompeii."

The court-martial only resumed its sitting at two o'clock in the morning. After three days' discussion, it does not consider itself to have adequate knowledge about this matter of Santo Meli; so the prisoner is to be sent to Palermo, where a fresh inquiry will be opened.

I stress this fact, just to show what a difference there is in the way of administering justice between the Royalists—those pillars of law and order—and the Revolutionaries—those "men of blood." In illustration of this let me make a comparison: In four hours, a court-martial held by the Royalists on the 5th of April in connection with Riso's rising, condemned fourteen people to death; whilst, after three days' sitting, the revolutionary court-martial, held at Villafrati, did not consider itself to have sufficient information about the facts of the case to justify condemning to death one man, who had confessed to having burnt half a village, imposed levies, and robbed banks and cash-boxes.

Whilst writing, I noticed Santo Meli and his six *guerrilleros* passing beneath my window, on the high road leading to Palermo. They were going on foot, with an escort of fifteen men.

We are leaving this evening at five o'clock for Sotto Vicari, on the road to Girgenti.

CHAPTER XXX

ALIA

TRANSLATE Alia by "Eagle's Eyry," and you will have an exact definition of the situation occupied by the village of Alia, at the summit of a peak.

We had left Villafrati at about two o'clock in the afternoon; by four we had rejoined our young companions, who had set out in the morning. They had set up their tents upon a rise, at some little distance from a village, almost hidden from view on the steep mountain-side, amid trees and rocks, and topped by the ruins of an old Norman castle. This village is called Sotto Vicari. There we halted, so as to rest our horses. When we started again, we left our companions there, promising to send them supplies of every kind, to make ready for the reception of Eber, who, it will be remembered, was taking the place of Türr as commander of the column.

We reached the foot of the mountain of Alia at dusk. Four or five horses were awaiting us. We got out of our carriages, which were then put into big sheds built at the foot of the mountain for this purpose. Our luggage was loaded on mules; we bestrode our horses and started the ascent of a slope, at an angle of 45 degrees and paved in a manner that resembled the Appian Way. This climb lasted more than three-quarters of an hour. At last we reached one of the model farms. All the walls are tiled. Count Tasca is the only possessor of such farms in Sicily—perhaps in the world. This farm is tenanted by the parish priest, who came out in a black coat, a three-cornered hat, riding-boots with spurs, and grasping a stick.

In Sicily—especially in the villages—as in Calabria and the Abruzzi, the priestly office does not exclude the following of other occupations. In all the places we have just named, the priesthood is not a vocation, it is a business. At Avezzano, among my friends, I know a good canon who runs a millinery business, and gravely attends to the trying on of hats and bonnets by his lady customers, be they young or old. He would be very much astonished if anyone were to suggest that this second profession might imperil his salvation in the first. We shall presently see how priests in Sicily observe the vow of chastity.

My first care, on my arrival, was to keep my promise to send to Sotto Vicari all the fresh meat I could get, together with my cook, Jean, who had now become cook to the General's staff. As for ourselves, thanks to Count Tasca, the hospitable man *par excellence*, we had nothing to trouble about. Salvator, his valet, was always at his destination two hours before ourselves; and when we arrived, we had nothing to do but wash off the layer of dust with which we were covered, and then sit down to table.

It was a delight to witness how Count Tasca was welcomed by his farmers. We slept in charming rooms, lined with porcelain, like Chinese pagodas, in which fleas and bugs could not find lodgings. Such rooms in Sicily, where paradise is everywhere, are the paradise of paradises.

Not seeing our companions at ten o'clock on the following morning, I feared that some misfortune might have happened to one of them. Urging the danger of meeting brigands as an excuse, each of them insisted on having his double-barrelled gun, and most of them did not know how to load or unload. About two in the afternoon the coachman, after making inquiries in vain all along the road, suddenly took it into his head to knock at the shutters of a house, closed like a jack-in-a-box. It was an inspiration. The shutter opened, revealing all the troupe battling with those insects, the absence of which I have just mentioned as being conspicuous at Tasca's farms. At the sight of our coachman, they uttered shouts of joy. They rushed pell-mell into the carriage, bitterly lamenting their hunger.

On the previous day, confident in my promise to send a waggon with provisions, they had calmly awaited its arrival, but in consequence of an accident to Lockroy, they had thought it best to shut themselves up in a barn and go to sleep. Meantime the column had passed by. Jean had met Colonel Eber personally; but the commander, not knowing that there were six travellers in the rear who had a claim on the provisions, took possession of the lot. Jean, who is not always on the best of terms with our young friends, whom we call "the militia," had not thought well to claim anything on their behalf. He had roasted and boiled, and whilst those in the rear, awake and scratching themselves, were awaiting beef, veal, mutton, *pesce spado*, and fowl, Eber and his staff were throwing the bones to the dogs, no doubt with the object of falsifying the proverb "tarde venientibus ossa" (the bones for late-comers). The result was that when the rear-guard, having learnt that the column had gone by, finally did arrive, they found that even the bones had disappeared.

Luckily, our young friends had stripped an almond tree and a pear tree, so that each had fifty almonds and thirty pears—please note the pears were as big as cherries. They had washed down this crude repast with three or four cups of black coffee—a beverage which, in memory of the Saracens, is never lacking. It was in vain that I tried to make the Sicilians understand that when their ancestors drove out the Arabs, the followers of the shepherd of Yemen had not yet discovered the joyous and stimulating properties of coffee; they still persisted in attributing to the Saracens the introduction of coffee into Sicily.

This frugal meal was not very succulent, so our travellers, badly ballasted as they were, did not desire to risk a march in the heat of the noon-tide. They had, therefore, shut themselves up, with the intention of putting into practice the proverb "He who sleeps, dines"; and if only the fleas and bugs and mosquitoes had not been there, they would doubtless have proved its truth. My coachman, however, cut short the trial when he scented them in their place of refuge.

They dashed into the dining-room, howling from hunger, and declaring that they could not possibly wait for dinner without collapsing. Thereupon I went down to the kitchen and made two omelettes, containing fifteen eggs each. These disappeared as miraculously as if Robert Houdin had sent them to China. Having received this much on account, the famished creatures promised to wait patiently for dinner.

I had heard some vague references to Lockroy's accident, which had led to the column being unnoticed when it passed, but I had not the inhumanity to ask for details during the repast. When it was over, I returned to the subject.

The accident was this (may it serve as a lesson to those who want to travel in Sicily between mid-day and two o'clock, when the thermometer registers near 100 degrees). Whilst four of the travellers were stripping the pear tree and the almond tree, Lockroy and Legray took it into their heads to climb Sotto Vicari, and speedily disappeared amongst its rocks and trees. Two hours slipped by without anything being heard of the two explorers. Thereupon the four others set out in search of them. When they had got half-way up, they noticed a crowd of people following a donkey led by the bridle by Legray. Lockroy was mounted on it, and had his head enveloped in an enormous white turban. On inquiry being made as to the reason for this masquerade, they were informed that the turban consisted of about two dozen napkins steeped in cold water and vinegar to allay the effects of sunstroke.

It seems that, on reaching the village of Sotto Vicari, Lockroy collapsed suddenly, much to the astonishment of Legray. He was taken to a neighbouring house, where, by resort to such measures as burning feathers beneath his nose and rubbing his temples with vinegar, he was brought back to consciousness. When he was himself again, he was decked with a head-dress like that of Lekain in Zaïre, placed astride a donkey, and led away.

For three days, instead of the sword of Damocles suspended above his head, he had the doctor's lancet suspended over his arm. But Fortune decreed that, like the one who flattered Denys the Tyrant, he should escape the threatening steel.

This and the succeeding nine chapters constitute the main "additions." *Vide* Introduction.

CHAPTER XXXI

VALLELUNGA

In the evening, the arrival of the Garibaldians was celebrated by an illumination which recalled that of Austerlitz. All along the road and on the mountain tops the peasants set fire to piles of faggots to betoken their joy. The red shirts, seen between the double row of fires, presented a strange appearance.

As the priest's house offered but limited accommodation, he sent our young people to the residence of his brother, who was also a priest. Four beds were improvised in the same room, and Paul, Lockroy, and the doctor were told to make themselves at home there. Just like schoolboys, they began to make an inventory of their room. The sacred was agreeably intermingled with the profane. Facing a portrait of the Madonna was a coloured lithograph, representing the young Adèle being carried off by an officer of hussars, habited in the costume of 1825. On one wall was a small collection of religious books; on the other a curtain of green serge discreetly veiled from view an assemblage of works of a much less orthodox character.

At Vallelunga we were to receive the hospitality of Count Tasca. All his farms vied, the one with the other, in their neatness and charm; only Vallelunga, as its name indicates, instead of being, like Villafrati and Alia, situated on mountain heights, occupies the bottom of a valley. On our arrival, we found all the village illuminated, and posters everywhere, bearing these words:

Vogliamo l'Annessione

al

Regno Constitutionale

di

Vittorio Emmanuele.

Our companions had set up their tents, and established themselves on the village square. It was one of the hottest days that we had had. The Count informed us that we were to spend the next day with him. He wanted to take us to see one of his properties, named Casabella, I think. As we had long been of opinion that the Count, in all that he did for us, only acted in our best interests, we consented.

The next day we started for Casabella, where an excellent dinner awaited us. When we were within about a quarter of a league of the village, we saw a procession coming along to meet us. It consisted of the whole village, headed by the parish priest and a band of music.

Casabella, a charming place, is one of the Count's favourite farms. To it he has had brought cows from England and Brittany; all kinds of inventions for improving agriculture have been introduced by him; there are three cheese factories tenanted by peasants from Switzerland and Dauphiny, who make sassenage and gruyère.

The notables of the district had been invited by the Count to a grand banquet. It had been arranged that we should return to Vallelunga after it; but the priest, thinking that we were quitting the table too soon, got hold of our young people and took them to his house, to start the festivities over again.

In justice to the priest, let us at once say that the fête lacked nothing. He invited the prettiest women in his parish to do the honours of his presbytery to the French volunteers. There was a ball, a supper, etc. No wonder our young friends are most enthusiastic about the Sicilian clergy.

The rest of us had already left Vallelunga, but I took care to leave a carriage for them. It was very welcome. Too hard a horse and too extensive hospitality have their drawbacks. We made only a brief halt at Santa Catarina, and maintained an even trot all the way to Caltanisetta.

It was there that we had to leave the column which was making for Catania, by way of Castrogiovanni. We had thought that Eber and our Garibaldians would go as far as Girgenti, so we had sent Captain Beaugrand there with the yacht.[1]

Caltanisetta is the limit of Count Tasca's estates; nevertheless, he wanted to take us there, and instal us at the house of one of his friends, Baron Trabonello, an excellent patriot and the syndic of his commune, which, by his proclamations, he had roused to revolt when Garibaldi was attacking Palermo.

We arrived during the evening, leaving the column two or three leagues in our rear. Next morning, we were scarcely awake when we heard the bugle call. We had only to go to our windows, which look upon the square, to see it enter. The column of foreign volunteers came first, with our young friends at its head and Captain Wolf in command.

A triumphant arch of greenery had been erected to receive the column; all the windows were crowded with women, and the streets

---

[1] Mr. Trevelyan says that Dumas returned to headquarters at Palermo. "Garibaldi and the Making of Italy."

packed with men. One heard nothing but cries of "Long live Garibaldi! Long live United Italy!" Flowers seemed to be falling from the sky, like a multicoloured and odoriferous shower.

A huge *déjeuner* had been prepared. It lasted till three in the afternoon. This naturally saved the guests the trouble of getting their dinners. In the evening the whole town spontaneously burst into illuminations, and a grand ball was given to the Garibaldian officers.

Now it chanced that the arrival of the column synchronised with one of the great fêtes of the country. St. Michael was making his entry into the town once again. He is the patron saint of Caltanisetta, just as St. Januarius is the patron saint of Naples; but instead of being an old growling saint, always in a bad humour from having been decapitated, and eternally threatening not to perform his miracle, St. Michael is a charming, fair-haired archangel, with the prettiest face in the world, and women—especially those that are *enceinte*—go to adore him, so that their children may resemble him.

Such is poetic Sicily—Greek, Saracen, and Norman. Here the worship of the beautiful is united with religious worship. It is a remnant of paganism, which requires not only that one adores, but also that one admires. This is why Palermo has her Santa Rosalia —a young, beautiful, and poetic recluse of Mount Pellegrino; a king's daughter who died a virgin. Her festival occurs in the month when flowers most abound. And it is to the cry "Viva Santa Rosalia!" that all the revolutions of Palermo have been made.

Just as all blasphemies against St. Januarius, every act of impiety against Santa Rosalia would be immediately punished at Naples and Palermo, so also at Caltanisetta—whose people are always so sweet, so hospitable, so tractable—misfortune would assuredly overtake anyone who showed any irreverence towards the holy archangel.

And it is only right for the people of Caltanisetta to be very grateful to the beautiful archangel, for he takes them under his very special protection. In 1837, when the wrath of God launched two scourges on Sicily, Del Carretto and the cholera, Saint Michael was seen, sword in hand, soaring above the town with wings outstretched, thus rendering it immune not merely from the Asiatic scourge, but also the Bourbon one.

Therefore the grateful people, with one accord, vowed a church to St. Michael, and chose for its site the most delightful spot that could be found—a smiling hill, about a quarter of a league from the town. This is the saint's summer abode.

17

CHAPTER XXXII

CALTANISETTA

As in the worship of St. Januarius at Naples, and in that of St. Rosalia at Palermo, so, in like manner, there is always a certain undercurrent of paganism in all Italian worship; or, at least, in that sensuous form of worship which we find in Southern Italy—formerly Greater Greece.

The Caltanisettois lay the blame for all calamities suffered by their town upon St. Michael; and in such eventualities put him in penitence in a dreadful convent of the Capuchins, dirty and ugly, which establishment contrasts cruelly with the beauty and elegance of the archangel himself.

This unpleasant experience was his lot not long ago; and it had bloody consequences.

In the spring of 1857, the grain did not germinate, in consequence of a complete absence of rain. A fortnight more of this drought, and all hopes of a harvest would be gone and the agricultural population of the province ruined.

The blame was put upon St. Michael.

According to custom, he had gone to spend the spring—that is, from the 18th of March till the 17th of May—at his country chapel. On the latter date he was to return to his cathedral.

But he reckoned without the Caltanisettois. There was a plot made to put him in penitence with the Capuchins, instead of allowing him to return to the cathedral. A rumour of this *coup d'état* got abroad, and reached the parish priest. The good man clearly foresaw peril of a loss of offerings to himself and the gain of them by the Capuchins, so he informed the police. The authorities sent a squad of soldiers to escort the saint, with orders to resist any attempt to take his shrine anywhere else than to the cathedral.

The people, on going to San Antonio, then found an armed force there for the purpose of keeping St. Michael on the right road. Not a sound was uttered. The bearers took the shrine on their shoulders, and the procession advanced towards the cathedral. All along the route the people piously cried:

"St. Michael for ever!"

But just as the bearers were about to enter the cathedral, they suddenly made a change of front, and began to run towards the convent. The priests and the soldiers at first stood still, quite astonished—the thing had been done so quickly and with such accord; but when they saw all the people leave them and follow the shrine, the priests began to cry "Treason!" The soldiers thereupon drew their swords. We must, however, do these latter justice, for they contented themselves, at first, with threatening the bearers, in order to make them retrace their steps; but seeing that the bearers only ran the faster, they began to cut at their hands. Here now was an opportunity for any who desired martyrdom! The mutilated bearers were replaced by others. Strike as the soldiers might and did, the shrine did not take a step backwards. The sabre-cuts only hastened the speed of the unhappy wretches who were bent on reaching their destination, even at the peril of their lives; for this destination meant, for them, the reward of their labours and bread for their families. Finally, in spite of the rage of the *sbirri*, the religious obstinacy of the people won. They reached the convent, entered the church, and whilst some laid the shrine on the altar, others forced the door to, and bolted it on the inside.

This done, the people's triumph was complete. The soldiers did not dare to carry their bloody and sacriligious conflict within the sacred edifice. Still, the victors were not entirely reassured by the sanctity of the place, and spent the night around the shrine, ready to defend it, if any enemy should try to carry it off. All whom the church would not hold remained outside, on their knees and praying.

In Sicily, besides, every man has his gun, and picks it up under the slightest provocation. A troop of 100 men quickly made its appearance in one of the streets, and came to take up its position in front of the church door, resolved to come to blows with the police, if necessary. But the police did not carry the matter any further, and retired. More than eighty persons had been wounded.

Towards three o'clock in the morning, the sky, which had been entirely cloudless, now grew black; the thunder rolled, lightning flashed, and at daybreak rain fell in torrents upon the people, who raised their hands to heaven, giving thanks to Almighty God, uttering cries of joy, and shedding tears of gratitude.

The wounded were offered treatment, but the only help they sought was bandages steeped in the miraculous water from heaven. I have seen some of these unfortunate beings with their arms literally hacked by sabre-cuts.

But St. Michael was soon to give the faithful an even stronger proof of his sympathy, not only with Caltanisetta, but with the whole of Sicily.

On the morning of the 27th of May, 1860, the sacristan ran, in a highly distracted state, through the town, calling out that though he had found the cathedral safely shut up, although not a window had been opened, St. Michael, who, at eight o'clock on the previous evening, had shown no intention of sleeping out, was no longer in his place.

The whole town rushed to the church, where, as a matter of fact, the niche of St. Michael was seen to be empty. All day long the cathedral was filled by an immense crowd, uttering the most lugubrious lamentations, and, with loud voice, supplicating St. Michael's return.

On the morrow, the 28th, St. Michael was found in his place again, without anybody having seen him re-enter.

On the 31st of May, it was known that Garibaldi had entered Palermo during the day of the 27th.

Where had St. Michael gone?

You do not guess? The answer is a very simple one: St. Michael had gone to fight, along with Garibaldi, against the Neapolitans.

Nobody in Caltanisetta doubted this; and certainly I, who, as will be seen later, am a citizen of the town, do not question that the warrior archangel played an important part in Garibaldi's victory.

Whilst I am busy giving you these details, the Municipal Council of Caltanisetta was in session, and passed this resolution:

"Caltanisetta, 3rd of July, 1860.

"The Civic Council of the town of Caltanisetta, capital of the province, has passed the following resolution, in session extraordinary, under the presidency of Advocate Don Vincenzo Minnichelli, and with the assistance of Secretary-Councillor Don Calogero Pugliese, the Secretary-Chancellor, who addressed the Council in the following terms—

" 'Respected fellow-citizens:—Monsieur Alexandre Dumas is amongst us. He comes from Paris to commit to history the glorious happenings of our regeneration —so great is the sympathy felt by civilised nations for the cause of Italian unity. Dumas merits the respect and veneration of the learned world. Italy owes him a tribute of sincere gratitude; for, an Italian of Italians by his principles, he has never ceased to work with the object of enlightening the minds of the peoples of the Peninsula by teaching them that only through the union of the Italian States can the power, grandeur, independence, and liberty of Italy be established.

" 'This great man is not new to our island: he has long studied this classic land. In 1835 he wrote upon our country. His romance, "Pascal Bruno," [1] met with as enthusiastic a reception in France as in Italy.

" 'This genius is with us; and it is a real joy to see him taking part in what is happening in our country. It is he who has drawn the masses together by his researches into the customs of our race, and by reminding us of all that this country offers in respect of antiquities and the fine arts. Finally, he has recorded on the roll of history the well-deserved welcome that our town gave the valorous champions of Calatafimi and Palermo, who, thence, sped on to Messina to root the enemy completely out. Every town of Sicily would feel itself fortunate if its soil were trodden by this great man.

---

[1] "Pascal Bruno" was first translated into English by Theodore Hook (London, 1837). It is when such early works of Dumas are read that one realises the absurdity of endeavouring to attribute the success of his later romances to his collaborators.

" 'We ourselves are gratified and happy to be able to grasp the hand of this genius. The memory of his sojourn here should be perpetuated amongst us, and a record of such an honour should be bequeathed to posterity. Let us therefore follow the example of our capital, Palermo; and let the Council accord him our citizenship.'

"The Council, in adopting the proposal of the Secretary-Councillor unanimously and with acclamation, passed the following resolution—

" 'That the citizenship of Caltanisetta be accorded to Monsieur Alexandre Dumas as a mark of gratitude and thanks to the French genius who, in contemporary history, has shed lustre on the glorious regeneration of this island and of Italy.'

" Enacted and resolved, the same day, month, and year as appearing above.

"The President of the Civic Council:
"VINCENTE MINICHELLI.
"The Chancellor-Secretary Councillor:
"CALOGERO PUGLIESE.

"The above is a correct copy.   3rd July, 1860.
"(Signed) The Secretary-Chancellor :
"CALOGERO PUGLIESE.
"Witnessed by us—
"President of the Council:
"V. MINICHELLI."

Clothed in my new dignity, I did not hesitate to ask a favour which I had been anxious to obtain, without daring to solicit it.

This was: to be presented to the archangel St. Michael.

The archangel had re-entered his niche behind the altar; and, unless it be for special reasons, he is not taken from that place, where, indeed, the light of day is never allowed to penetrate except on the great feasts of the year or the anniversary of some special incident in his own history. It was then against all precedent to disturb him for my sake, the more so as I had no pretension to his good graces, other than my quality of being a Frenchman. No sooner had I, as a citizen of Caltanisetta, expressed this desire than the matter was submitted to the priest, and he offered no opposition to the request. If I would proceed to the church at ten o'clock on the following morning, the picture which concealed St. Michael from the public eye would be removed, and the Saint would appear to me. Only, I was asked to give my permission to let the whole of the populace adore him at the same time. I was far from wishing to oppose so religious a desire; and replied that whether St. Michael appeared to me in public or in private, he would be doing me so great an honour that it was not for me to impose conditions. On the contrary, it was my place to submit to them.

Consequently, I went to the church at ten o'clock on the following morning. The populace, without knowing who I was, were aware that it was to me they owed the privilege and happiness of contemplating St. Michael at an unusual time; so they waited for me at my door and followed me to the church, having no doubt about my being a personage of the highest importance, seeing that St. Michael was granting me such a favour.

The faithful were massed so closely in the church that, seemingly, a pin could not be dropped between them; but hardly had I appeared on the threshold than a passage opened, as if by enchantment, all the way to the altar. I walked on, bowing to right and left, and followed by the crowd, which entered at my heels like the Macedonian phalanx into the Persian army.

I had hardly reached the altar steps when the picture turned of itself, and St. Michael appeared to me in all his glory.

I have never seen anything more charming than this life-sized statue; only, St. Michael seemed to me to touch paganism at one point: he looked as if he were own brother to that pretty damsel Marie Garnier, who played the part of Venus in *Orphée aux Enfers*.

I thought it my duty to address a little speech to him, so I called up all my eloquence on this occasion. I have spoken to princes, to kings, nay, even to emperors, but I had never yet spoken to an archangel. My embarrassment was increased by being obliged to speak to him in a strange tongue. Very certainly, St. Michael understands all languages, and it made no difference whether I spoke to him in Italian or in French; but it was not the same for my audience. I was speaking not only to St. Michael, but also to the people of Caltanisetta.

It would seem that I came through the ordeal covered with glory, for my discourse was received with universal applause. I was even assured that the general satisfaction had been shared by St. Michael; for he had deigned to make me an almost imperceptible inclination of the head, as a mark of his approbation. I must say that this sign was so imperceptible that I did not observe it; but the priest did, and, as a holy man cannot lie, I accept it that the sign was made.

The picture then turned again, and St. Michael was lost to view. I was escorted back as far as the house of Baron Trabonella, amid cries of "Long live St. Michael!"

CHAPTER XXXIII

SAN CATALDO

THE moment for *adieux* had come. We shook hands, we embraced, and embraced yet again. The column was starting for Caltanisetta, and we were leaving for Girgenti, which I was going to see again after an absence of twenty-five years.

It was arranged that we were to meet the column again at Catania. My intention was to proceed to Malta, which I did not know, then to return to say good-bye to our friends before continuing my voyage to the East. I have already said that the *Emma* was to await us at Girgenti.

During my sixty hours' stay with Baron Trabonella I had a continuous dispute with his son's tutor, a perfect specimen of the pious, greasy pedant. Differences began the very evening of my arrival. They opened with Dante, and continued successively through every topic of conversation—each of us taking diametrically opposite points of view.

Delighted with the reception which we had from Baron Trabonella, I wished to give him a souvenir of my stay. His son, aged about twelve or thirteen, was head of a company of youthful cadets. The children, pending the time that guns could be given to them, were armed with pikes. Now I had on board a splendid Persian pike, damascened with gold. I had the idea of offering this pike to the Baron, on condition that he could let a servant come with me and fetch it back. To my amazement, the tutor, who ought to have held me in execration, on account of the hard things I had said to him, asked to go, and permission was at once given.

So I found myself awarded the distinction of having the tutor of the heir of the barony of Trabonello thrust upon me, without my having in the least solicited the honour. He came triumphantly to tell me of his good fortune, and to claim a seat in our carriage. Fortunately, we had only a few hours to travel together.

Scarcely had we started than, throwing himself back, half-closing his eyes, and crossing his hands on his stomach whilst twiddling his thumbs, he asked me:

"What is your opinion about the formation of the globe?"

I was at first a little startled by such a question, put point-blank; but fortunately this antediluvian topic of discussion had always greatly interested me. I had devoured, as they appeared, the works of Cuvier and of Brongniart; and on board my yacht I had Zimmermann's fine work on the subject, which had appeared some little time previously. I was thus able to formulate to our tutor a geological theory which left little to be desired. The exposition of this theory, which covers developments from the lichens of Greenland to the oaks of Dodona, and from the polypi to the mastodons, kept us occupied till nightfall.

On reaching the top of a hill, we saw, about three-quarters of a league ahead, an immense illumination; and in the plain which separated us from it a great movement of men and animals, which, lit up as they were only by the first peeping stars, looked like beings from another world.

Suddenly, just when the silhouette of our carriages became visible on the top of the hill, loud cries rent the air, and we saw advancing towards us a frightful whirlwind of dust, from the midst of which came the noise of the galloping of a hundred horses. In five minutes, we found ourselves the centre of a troop of horsemen, each of whom bore a lance with a tricolour streamer. All shouted at the top of their voices: "Viva l'Italia una! Viva Vittorio Emmanuele! Viva Garibaldi!"

In an interval between these outbursts of cheering I was asked if M. Dumas was still far off. I was so far from thinking that it was in my honour that all this military display and frightful shouting was taking place, that I requested this man from San Cataldo to repeat his question.

Repetition of the question left no room for doubt: it was really for me that they had come, it was really for me that all this din was being made. In spite of my affrighted modesty, I was compelled to admit that M. Dumas had arrived, and that I was he.

Immediately three or four of the cavaliers started off at a gallop, leaving the rest of the band to act as an escort to me. These outriders, who faded into the darkness like spectres, bore to the town and to the populace spread over the plain the news of my arrival. Wheresoever they passed, the tidings gave rise to shouts similar to those which resounded around myself, and which steadily increased in volume as the two bodies drew nearer the one to the other.

The carriage had continued on its way, and rolling along amid the horsemen who formed a guard of honour, drew near to the main army, which was entirely composed of infantry and seemed to include all the men in the town. This body was coming to meet me, amid a dense cloud of dust, each man carrying a torch, the light of which seemed as feeble as a candle in a horn lantern.

The ringing of the bells told me that the outriders had reached the town. This immense multitude which rolled on towards us like a sea, finally reached us. I am not exaggerating when I say there were at least 6000 men, and that each one shouted with all the power of his lungs, in the hope of making himself heard above all the others: "Viva l'Italia una! Viva Vittorio Emmanuele! Viva Garibaldi!"

This would have been nothing, if all these good patriots had contented themselves with shouting; but, for fear of being thought a lukewarm supporter, I had to shout with them. The consequence was that I, too, began to call out like one possessed. It was the first time I had shouted "Long live," as applied to a king. Giddiness was now overtaking me; madness was seizing me, induced by breathing this dust, hearing these shouts, and witnessing all this sea of movement.

My carriage had become something impossible to describe. There were San Cataldians on the horses, on the pole, on the coachman's box, on the step, on the seat behind. No, I had never seen such a spectacle in my life, never had heard such shouts. I had to embrace, to shake hands, to shout, to wave flags, and to do them all at one and the same time.

Our pedant had become dumb; he made himself as small as he could. He was afraid.

Never had an Indian tribe dragging to execution an enemy chief who has been taken prisoner in a bloody struggle uttered such frightful sounds. Suddenly a band, composed of all the instruments which have been invented since the trumpets of Jericho, crashed out in most alarming fashion round my carriage.

We next saw, through the cloud of dust which was round about us, a strong light resembling that of a great fire. It was the town all lit up.

The carriage stopped. The way was barred by the clergy. All the bells rang as if bewitched and, like the men, caring for nothing but making the utmost noise possible. I got out of the carriage, or rather fell out into the arms of the parish priest. I was seized, raised up, carried off; I was borne through a population of women and children, who, as it were by the advent of some great cataclysm, had remained behind in the town, whilst every man capable of marching and bearing arms had dashed forward to meet me.

How was it that there were so many people in the plain, at the entrance to the town, in the streets, and at the windows? The explanation of this enigma was given to me: for ten leagues round, San Cataldo had been made a rendezvous; and thus the ordinary population of 10,000 souls had become 30,000 or 35,000. The streets, now become too narrow, were stifling. In a moment I had lost all my companions. Each of them had been seized and carried off, like myself.

I was now at the Syndic's. My mouth was opened, wine was poured into it and cakes were stuffed into it. I saw only too clearly that I was a dead man if I did not save myself by flight. But it is not easy to flee when you have the eyes of 50,000 people upon you. I had not a joint which did not ache, so much had I been pulled about. As to my voice, it had entirely gone, from shouting "Long live United Italy!" For three days after, I did nothing but expectorate dust.

Finally, a surging of the people brought me back the "Admiral," under the protection of Paul Parfait and Edouard Lockroy. We now found ourselves on a sort of plateau on a level with our carriage, so we slipped into it; and despite their cries, their prayers, and their supplications, we drove away, leaving as a prey to the San Cataldians the doctor, Legray, Vasili, Podimatas, our two Greeks, and our carriages. We did not see them again till two days later.

Brave and loyal country! dear Sicily of hospitable people! Palermo, Caltanisetta, Girgenti, San Cataldo, Catania, towns of enchantment and faëry art, you have left in my life a luminous track, by the aid of which I joyfully recapture the past. Lights, music, cries of joy, fraternal greetings, outstretched arms, cheeks offered, where shall I find you again? Never; nowhere; not even if I return to your very selves. Such festivals do not come twice: all the forces of the human heart would not suffice for such a purpose.

And never shall I consent to say: *Adieu.*

Au revoir, then, *au revoir!*

CHAPTER XXXIV

CANICATTI

An hour later, by a strange contrast, I came very near being arrested in the little village of Serra di Falco by the National Guard, who did not understand that honest men could be travelling, without escort, in a country infested by brigands. We assured the Guard that we believed their fears about brigands to be much exaggerated, that we had travelled throughout Sicily and had only met friends, and that if we had met any brigands we were well armed and could defend ourselves. In proof of what we had said, each of us produced a double-barrelled gun and a revolver.

On seeing these weapons, the Guard came to another conclusion; and this was that we were a gang of the Bourbon party, trying to reach Girgenti—a reactionary town—for the purpose of embarking there. In order to dissipate all these doubts, I had to produce Cenni's passport and my permit from Garibaldi, backed by the resolution passed by the Municipal Council of Caltanisetta, making me a freeman of the town.

The reaction was rapid and extreme. The officer in charge wanted to wake up the whole village, now in bed and asleep, by ordering his squad to fire a volley. With great difficulty I induced him to respect the repose of the citizens; but I had to accept his escort of four men as far as Canicatti, where we were going to enjoy the hospitality of one of Count Tasca's friends.

The extreme hoarseness of my voice did not admit of my discussing the honour that was done me. I accepted the escort, on condition that they woke up nobody, and that we should leave immediately. Four men then mounted their horses, carrying their guns across their saddle-bows; and with two on the right hand, two on the left of our carriage, we set out at a fast trot.

The honours paid us at San Cataldo, added to the difficulties we experienced at Serra di Falco, resulted in our knocking at the door of Count Tasca's friend just as the church clock was striking midnight. Everybody was asleep in the house. Our escort wanted to fire four shots to waken our host, and we had great difficulty in restraining them from carrying out their wish. At last someone came to parley with us through the door. We gave our names, surnames, and ranks; loud cries were heard on every floor, candle-lights were first visible in every window, and then came a rushing downstairs. The door opened, and our host appeared in his dressing-gown.

Truly it is only in Sicily where people awakened out of their first sleep, whom one does not know, whom one has never seen, at whose house one comes to lodge—and consequently to cause trouble and expense—receive one thus with open arms and a welcoming smile on their lips. We had been expected all day. Our dinner was still on the table, but we were not allowed to eat a cold meal. In vain I protested that I adored cold meat. My protestations were not listened to, and, in truth, they were made in too hoarse a voice to avail anything. The stoves were lit again, the best wines were taken from the cellar during the interval of waiting, and at the end of an hour we were served with an homeric supper.

Now that my voice has returned, I can thank my host to-day, and he can see that I have not forgotten any detail of the warm welcome he has given us.

Towards three in the morning, we went to bed, tired out, fatigued, knocked up. At ten o'clock, we were told that the *déjeuner* was ready: it was a worthy rival of the supper that had preceded it.

We did not even attempt to discuss leaving. The further south we went, the more scorching the sun became. We only arranged that our carriages should be ready about two o'clock. The desire to take a walk round Canicatti made us brave the dog-day's temperature; still, we did not spend much time out of doors. We were soon recognised, surrounded, and driven into a café, where we were stuffed with ices.

A great piece of news got abroad, which gave rise to all sorts of commentaries in Canicatti: a French schooner—evidently the *Emma*—had declared at Girgenti that she had met, out at sea, Neapolitan ships flying the Italian tricolour. What could have happened at Naples? Had that city also started its revolution? Had she joined the Italian cause? Had our campaign finished?

I must confess my first feeling was one of regret. I had never believed that the end would be so easy and commonplace. I was still dreaming of some fine battle such as Calatafimi; some splendid siege, like that of Palermo.

The solution of the problem was furnished by a little journal— *La Forbice*—which came from Palermo.

King Francis II, on the 26th of June, had given his people a new constitution.

Thenceforward there was less to fear. As this was the third constitution that had been given to the Neapolitan people, and the two previous ones had been withdrawn, it was probable that little trust could be placed in it.

The same journal contained a magnificent discourse by Hugo. Never had a condemnation been pronounced more eloquently. Its judgment will be irrevocable, because it will be that of posterity.

CHAPTER XXXV

GIRGENTI THE MAGNIFICENT

WE left Canicatti towards four o'clock in the afternoon, and we reached Girgenti at six. The municipality had been previously advised of our coming, and had quarters prepared for us. Twenty years had elapsed since my first visit to Girgenti—the ancient Agrigentum. Shadowed by the Neapolitan police, I went there then, provided with a false passport which I procured through the kindness of Monsieur Ingres, the great painter, who at that time was Director of the School of Art at Rome.

I had concealed myself in a wretched inn and remained a stranger to everybody, save an old antiquarian named Politi, a ruined man who welcomed me to his ruins—the ruins of Girgenti. To-day I re-entered the town, with a passport from Garibaldi; and the municipality made me their guest. Things had changed very much, you will notice.

We were not wrong in supposing that it was the *Emma* that had brought the news of the green, red, and white tricolour, floating over a Neapolitan vessel. The *Emma* had been awaiting us in port for three days.

We had arrived just in time to attend the procession of San Caloggiero—a saint probably unknown in the French calendar, but all-powerful in Girgenti, of which place he is the patron. Here, again, we have a saint of that curious type which is only to be found in the Italian almanack.

The statue of the saint was borne upon an immense platform, which was carried by forty men. At first sight I took him for a negro saint, and so the thing appeared to me all the more curious; but on coming closer, I was obliged to give up this picturesque aspect of the fête. St. Caloggiero has simply an iron head! As a matter of fact, a wooden head—even one made of teak—would not withstand the shower of varied objects which descends on it from every storey of the houses—bread, meat, sausage, game, vegetables. These are collected by a sort of showman, who stands close by the saint on the platform. This understrapper is charged with the duty of performing minor miracles which the Saint does not deign to deal with himself. He replaces dislocated arms and legs, restores speech to the mute, hearing to the deaf, and movement to the paralysed. Are all these people whom he cures really afflicted in the way alleged? I cannot tell you; but the incredulous doubt it very much.

Opposite to the house where we live is a chapel of ease to the Saint's church. At the door of this chapel stands a beadle, who bangs a big drum from morning till night. From time to time the beadle stops, and between the execution of two rolls he invites the faithful to enter. I know not why, but somehow I recognise in this beadle the counterfeit presentment of d'Odry in *Les Saltimbanques*.

What struck us on arriving in Girgenti was a slight breath of re-action, issuing from the houses of the rich and aristocratic inhabit-ants. It was the first time we had felt it in our faces since our arrival in Sicily. I must confess it made my flesh creep to some extent.

The day after my arrival at Girgenti, I received a letter from the Municipal Council, which, as at Palermo, and at Caltanisetta, would make me a freeman of the town. At first I felt inclined to refuse the honour. I was on the point of writing to Garibaldi to tell him of the painful impression that I had felt on entering the town, when I learnt that, on the evening of the 7th of July, Menotti was to arrive. So I resolved to wait for his impressions and to subordinate my own to them. If Garibaldi's son were content, I had no right to be dis-satisfied, I, who am only an amateur Italian.

The day was spent in paying a visit to the yacht for the purpose of telling the Captain to get ready for a cruise with Menotti, the follow-ing day, or the day after that.

The Captain handed me a bill on the Bank of Palermo for 2000 francs. It was the price of the ten revolvers that I had procured from the firm of Devismes for ten of our friends at Palermo. They were masterpieces of the gunsmith's craft. I record this detail for the pur-pose of stating a fact: the bill on the Bank of Palermo was worth fifty francs less at Girgenti.

Menotti's arrival was timed for five o'clock in the evening. At half-past four we went to take our stand at the gate of the town, which commands all the plain around, and whence the high road leads for a distance of three leagues. In the morning, we had been rejoined by the doctor, by Legray, Théodore, and the rest of the caravan. They told us fabulous stories about the hospitality of San Cataldo. They had no need to envy Antenor. Towards five o'clock, we saw, in the distance, a cloud of dust raised by carriages and horsemen. We had not the least doubt that this must be Menotti and his escort. The Syndic of the town also shared this view, as he came along in an open carriage for the purpose of going to meet the town's new guest.

I went down the hill on foot so as to be the first to embrace Menotti and to bid him welcome. I knew also that quarters had been pre-pared for him at the house of one who had been pointed out to me as the chief reactionary of the town, and I wished to forewarn him of this fact, which, in my opinion, was not without importance. When I reached the foot of the hill, I found myself, at a turning in the road, in front of the Syndic's carriage, which was on the way back into the town. Menotti was in this carriage, so he stopped it, and bade me get in; thus we entered Girgenti together. We had to get out at the gate of the town, for it was impossible for a carriage to move in the midst of such a crowd. As it could not see Garibaldi, it had to make shift with his son. It took more than an hour to get from the gate of the town to the house prepared for Menotti's reception. Before he went in, I had the opportunity of telling him what I wished, but he replied to the effect that the house had been chosen for him by his father, so he had no other course than to obey.

The next morning, I had a visit from my old friend Politi, the archæologist, who had, five-and-twenty years previously, as I have already mentioned, done me the honours of Girgenti—and that without knowing who I really was. One day, on reading the *Speronare*, he was greatly astonished to find that it was I whom he had received. He now came to thank me for the few lines I had written about him. When I left him in 1835, his age was sixty, and I may have thought that he would not grow older in appearance. I now saw my mistake. He was still the same little man, upright as a column, bald as a mile-stone, lined like a caryatide, but his little figure had diminished still further; the few hairs which were his, twenty-five years ago, had dis-appeared, one at a time; the furrows had deepened; the tendency to become petrified had become more marked. It was evident that the day was approaching when he would be found dead, leaning against the columns of one of his three temples.

Alas! his visit was not devoid of interest. The poor archæologist was not so steeped in the dust of the past that he did not understand that any stirring of this dust was indicative of something new taking place. He had come up from his caverns of Phalaris, and had heard people saying that two things, to him, unknown and unheard of, one called Independence, the other Italian Unity, personified in a man named Garibaldi, were advancing to overthrow the throne of the Bourbons. He had inquired whether this new Attila, when over-throwing thrones, would also throw down ruins, for in such event he had decided to bury himself beneath those of the Temple of the Giants; but, reassured as to the answer, he was coming to me, he said, just as he might have come to Parmenion, the friend of Alexander the Great.

Nothing touches me more than humility in old age, more than the poverty of men of science. Had this man been born in the department of the Ardennes, or of Côte d'Or; if he had spoken of the monuments of Girgenti without ever having seen them; if he had propounded some theory, however improbable, to prove that the ancient Agrigentum was not a colony of Rhodians and Cretans, but of Egyptians or Pelasgi; that the bull of Phalaris was made of brass and not of bronze; that Gelon, the tyrant of Syracuse, had not first been tyrant of Gela; it is probable that he would be a member of the Academy, would be decorated, would have 15,000 francs pension, for nothing but sleeping, and the double of that if he snored also; but as he was born at Girgenti, and has spent his life amid the ruins of the temples of Concord, of Hercules, of Castor and Pollux, of Apollo, of Diana, of Juno, of Ceres, of Proserpine, and of Jupiter Olympus, as he was a *sachant* and not a *savant*, the poor devil was dying of hunger in the same little retreat in which I had found him twenty-five years previously, surrounded by the same poor little collection, amassed by the labours of sixty years, and out of which he probably does not sell two items per year. So I promised him, with the utmost goodwill, that I would do all I could for him.[1]

Alas! two hours after the archæologist left me, twenty people came to me to denounce him as a reactionary and a spy; one or two even went so far as to say that he was a *sbirro*. And do you know why? Because during his sixty years of work, he had, by dint of importunities and petitions, obtained from the Bourbons some small assistance, by means of which he had had inscriptions placed on the pedestals of vases and statues found by him!

Pouah! as Monte-Cristo says, man is certainly an ugly toad!

The result is that I could do nothing for poor Politi, without the risk of being myself denounced as a reactionary and a spy, perhaps even —who knows?—as a *sbirro*.

God forgive me for my cowardice! I am not afraid of water, I am not afraid of fire, I am not afraid of bullets . . .

But I do fear calumny.

Homo, hominibus lupus!

If Politi still lives, and the Italian Government wishes to do a good deed, it will help to soothe the closing days of this poor old man, whose whole life has been one long excavation, both material and moral, into the past.

---

[1] Passages such as this one are scattered throughout Dumas' works. They explain the hostility of the *savants* towards him.

CHAPTER XXXVI

MALTA AND THE CHURCH OF THE KNIGHTS

THE next day we went for a sail with Menotti. Our captain had a day off, as Menotti, who is a fairly good sailor, took command of the yacht. In the evening the municipality gave us a grand banquet[1] at the house of Menotti's host, who, I ought to state, appeared to me to do the honours of his palace with a magnificence worthy of his Grecian ancestors. On the following morning, however, an officer arrived from headquarters to invite Menotti to choose another place of abode, and to order his host to leave Sicily—for a time, at least. On the 7th we said good-bye to our pedagogue, to whom I handed the pike for the baron's heir. I believe that, at the bottom of his heart, he was not sorry to get away. Our companions had made life a little hard for him.

When I took leave of Menotti, I gave him a double-barrelled carbine by Devisme which had accompanied me in all my travels, and of which I knew the accuracy and range. In the evening of the 7th, we returned to the yacht with the intention of continuing our journey to the East; but as adverse winds had been blowing all night, we postponed sailing. The following morning, the wind had changed, so we hoisted our anchor and left.

When we were off Licata, I saw that Vasili had left my travelling-case behind at Girgenti. This travelling-case had been made to my design, and contained not only my toilet requisites, but also everything necessary for my work or meals, and, in addition, a secret compartment which then contained 4000 francs. So I gave orders to stop at Licata. This we did at two o'clock in the afternoon. (Licata, or rather Alicata, is the ancient Phintias.) Théodore was told to return to Girgenti overland and to find my precious travelling-case.

Since the evening before, I had been filled with remorse for having left Sicily and abandoned Garibaldi in the midst of his struggles. I intensely regretted not being able to see him bring them to a conclusion by the complete overthrow of the throne of Naples—a work so well begun. I only needed some pretext for attaching myself to him again. I had the ambition to render a service of some kind to the Italian cause, so I entrusted Théodore with the following letter to Menotti, requesting him to see that it reached his father.[2]

[1] Dumas on these occasions—and they were numerous—must have been at his best.
[2] Compare this passage with the first version given in facsimile at the beginning of the book.

"MY FRIEND,

"I have just crossed Sicily from Palermo to Girgenti. Enthusiasm and good-will for the struggle everywhere, but no arms. Shall I leave for France and bring some back? Just a word from you to the poste-restante at Catania, and I shall give up my voyage to the East, in order that I may follow you to the finish. I shall not stop till you stop.

"Ex imo corde,
"A. DUMAS."

9th July, 1860.

Théodore left with this letter, and was told not to appear before me again without my travelling-case.

We could scarcely expect to see him back again before the next day, so we at once got ready for shooting and fishing. We could not have had a better opportunity for quail shooting, for these birds pass over from Africa into Italy throughout May. We were thus able to enjoy, off the coast of Sicily, the sport which we had believed we were going to have off the coast of Greece; indeed, it was very similar. As regards fishing, in these little-frequented spots it is almost always abundant. The most astonished members of our party were the two dogs. Accustomed in France to seeing seven or eight quails in the course of a day, here they no sooner left one bird than they came across the next. Besides, the poor birds were still so fatigued with their long flight that they preferred falling into our hands to struggling on further. Thus the day slipped by without boredom. Part of the night was spent by me in writing.

According to a verbal agreement, I reckoned on publishing the story of my voyage in the *Constitutionnel*, but the name of Garibaldi had frightened Mirès,[1] and the understanding had been mutually cancelled. I, however, ignored this, and worked my hardest.

The care taken by Paris journals to be badly informed is worth noting; and it may truly be said that such care is, as a rule, entirely successful.

The next morning, about eleven o'clock, Théodore returned, bringing back my travelling-case. He had also delivered the letter to Menotti. At six o'clock in the evening of the same day—Tuesday—we left for Malta. At ten o'clock next morning we made the acquaintance of the island of Gozo; and at two o'clock we cast anchor in the port of Valetta.

My resolution to return to Sicily and to continue the Italian campaign, if Garibaldi should judge that I could be of service to him, upset the projects of three of our friends, who wanted to go to the East, in any case. So when we reached Malta the break-up began. Legray, the doctor, and Lockroy insisted on leaving the *Emma*. I

[1] A brother of the great financier whom Dumas mentions in his chapter on Marseilles.

represented very strongly to Lockroy that he had been placed in my care by his father, and that it was with great regret I should see him go; but all that I said was without result.[1] These gentlemen landed and went their way. We went ours, and thus our caravan was reduced to the Admiral, Paul Parfait, and Théodore.

As we are spending but twenty-four hours at Malta, we can only speak to you of what little we have seen. Directly the Captain returned from the port with a clean bill of health, boats formed a large circle around us, some laden with fruit and vegetables, others empty and waiting to take us ashore when we had our permits.

We might have reached the quay in one of our own boats, but that would have meant getting into the bad books of all the natives at the very outset; we therefore went in a Maltese canoe to the famous landing-stage, known in the Frankish tongue under the notorious name of " Nix-Mangeare," where all that hungry rabble which lives on travellers salutes you with the eternal refrain that has given its name to this part of the harbour. So far as I know, it is only the beggars of Naples who, in the matter of boundless impudence and unconquerable perseverance, can vie with these bare-legged, yellow-skinned vultures, who fasten upon unfortunate strangers the instant they touch the soil of Valetta. We only got rid of them when we had the door of the hotel between us and them. I am sorry that I have forgotten the name of this hotel, which was an excellent one.

We had no time to lose if we wanted to see something of the town. Never had the events of Sicily seemed to me to merit so much interest as since I had left it; so I had decided to leave Malta the next day.

We asked our host for a carriage, and directed our coachman to drive to the Promenade St. Antoine. This we did on the recommendation of a Neapolitan refugee, who was only waiting for Francis II to quit Naples in order that he himself might return there. This man was the son of Martin Zir, the owner of the Hotel della Vittoria at Naples in 1835—but since deceased—who plays so important a part in my *Corricolo*. Here was only another proof that there is no place in the world where I am without acquaintances. I had only set foot on land five minutes previously, and had taken but ten steps in the street, when I heard my name called.

We took Andréa Zir for our guide; and at Malta the acceptance of the post needs courage—indeed, it was devotion on his part to ask for it. I do not know if there is a place in the world as hot as Malta—Algiers, Tunis, and Cairo not excepted. It was the 11th of July, so you may imagine how hot the sun was and how dusty the road, on both sides of which there was not so much as a blade of grass on which

---

[1] Lockroy soon fell in with Ernest Renan and went to Judæa with him.

the eye might rest. We proceeded for three or four kilometres, in a temperature which, two hours before, would have been unbearable; then, suddenly, in a dip in the ground, we saw a kind of oasis. It was the St. Antoine promenade. Wonderful result of water! A spring which gushes from the ground has converted a sun-scorched rock into a delightful Eden.

We might have supposed that we were going to meet all Malta on this promenade, admiring itself beside these waters and enjoying the shade of the foliage: not at all—the promenade was completely deserted. Malta gives, sells, buys, weighs, embarks and disembarks, but Malta has no use for promenades. We, who had no part in the doings of the Maltese, stretched ourselves out under the deepest shade that we could find, and waited the going down of the sun behind Gozo. Then we returned to Malta, where we bought complete suits of linen for thirty francs each,[1] and afterwards went to eat ices. These were all the delights that Malta could offer us.

At eight o'clock the next morning, we started out to see the Church of the Knights and the Armoury. The exterior of the church is mediocre, but this is compensated for by the beauty of the interior. Here lie the bones of the most valiant knights of the Order. Inscriptions are in all languages except English—no doubt because the Order ceased to receive English Knights after the Reformation. A Maltese tradition, which was recited once again for our delectation, is that, as the rails and balustrade of the high altar are of massive silver, it was feared that the French, when they took the island, would carry them off, in order to help to defray the cost of the war in Egypt. So they were bronzed over. Thus disguised, Bonaparte did not consider them worth consigning to the melting-pot.

In this church, as we have said, the bodies of the Knights sleep. The effigies of those who did the Order the most honour are sculptured on their tombs. Those who took part in the Crusades are represented with their legs crossed. We do not know the name of the sculptor who first had the idea of perpetrating this cynical jocularity.

At the Armoury, among a considerable collection of modern weapons, they have preserved the armour of the bravest Knights of the Order, including one set which must have fitted a hero, four feet six inches in height, at most. They could not tell me his name, but they assured me that the Turks found in him one of their most redoubtable enemies. At an interval of 1300 years, Virgil at Rome and Saadi at Chiraz have written lines which are applicable to this great little man.

Virgil says:

[1] A linen suit was Dumas' habitual wear on his travels.

"Ingentes animos angusto in pectore versant." (The loftiest courage dwells in a diminutive frame.)

Saadi says:

"Na har kits batamats mihtar bakimats behtar."[1] (The most valuable things are often in the smallest parcels.)

When we got back to our hotel, I found a family—father, mother, and child—who had been exiles from Palermo for twelve years. They had come to beg me to procure their passage home at a lower price than the *Messageries* boats charge, as their slender means did not admit of paying this fare. I answered by telling them that I would repatriate them for nothing, if they would consent to sit at my table during the crossing. They thanked me warmly, and asked by what time they should be ready. I told them to be so as soon as possible, for I had only one more visit to make, and was leaving immediately afterwards.

This visit was to the patriarch of Sicilian liberty, Ruggiero Settimo. He is descended from the princes of Fitalia, and is, at once, an honest man, an upright patriot, and a devoted citizen. Now more than eighty years of age, he has, in his long career, taken part in the four revolutions which have broken out in Sicily. The first was the diplomatic revolution of 1812, when Lord Bentinck, the representative of Great Britain, modified the old constitution of Sicily. In 1820, he was nominated a representative of the people; and in 1848, he was President of the Provisional Government of Sicily. When Sicily was reconquered by Ferdinand II, Ruggiero Settimo retired to Malta, where he has since remained in the dignity and silence of a proscribed gentleman.

I was the bearer of the duplicate of a letter from Garibaldi for him. In this letter—I regret I did not keep a copy—which was inspired by the admiration of a soldier for the man of affairs, he begged the illustrious exile to return to Sicily. But, whether Settimo feared a fresh return of the Bourbons, or whether, when one is eighty, one does not easily break with habits that have existed for twelve years, I do not know; but he emphatically refused to leave Malta, opposing all arguments by speaking of his failing health. I spent an hour with this worthy old man, and, entrusted with his good wishes for Sicily and his thanks for Garibaldi, I left, taking with me his blessing.

Two hours later, I received on board the Sicilian family—the child was a very charming little girl of four or five. Twice we tried to get out of the harbour, and failed, owing to a contrary wind. We decided to spend the night on board, in port, so that the Captain might profit by the first favourable wind. At four in the morning, we felt the wind

[1] Persian scholars may find something to correct.

change, and soon were out at sea. This wind continued to blow during the whole of the 13th and the morning of the 14th. Towards noon we saw the coast of Sicily, and at three o'clock, sped by the first gusts of a violent squall, we entered, full sail, into the harbour of Catania. Scarcely had we entered than the gale reached its maximum.

I returned to Catania, as will be remembered, to get from the *poste restante* a letter from Garibaldi, letting me know if he accepted my offer of going to France to buy arms for him. I at once sent the Captain on shore with my passport, so that he might get my letters at the post-office. An hour later he was back with this note:

"*Palermo, 10th July*, 1860.
"My dear Dumas,
      "I am awaiting both your own dear self and your splendid offer of arms.
                                             "Your most affectionate,
                                                       "Garibaldi."

There was no further need for hesitation. I must get to Palermo as quickly as possible. I offered to take the Sicilian exiles as far as Palermo, but the woman had been so sea-sick that, as soon as she saw land, neither gold nor silver would alter her resolution to leave the vessel. So they disembarked. I have never seen them again, or heard them spoken of.

CHAPTER XXXVII

CATANIA

So I found myself revisiting Catania, like Girgenti, after a lapse of twenty-five years. Five-and-twenty years before, I had ascended Mount Etna and peered to the bottom of its crater. Those who wish to accompany me in that first visit can do so, my *Speronare* in hand. I should much have liked to make a second visit to Syracuse, but it was in the power of the Neapolitans.

The Captain's visit to the post-office spread the news of my arrival. The French Consul and the English Consul at once came on board. It is true that the French Consul was an Italian. Through both of these I learnt an important piece of news—that General Bosco had left Messina with 6000 to 7000 men, to surprise Medici, who, with a column numbering 3000 to 4000, had left Palermo for Milazzo.[1] I also learnt that Eber had reached Catania with his column.

I asked the French Consul if he knew of a man who, for a reward to be fixed by himself, would take a message to Medici. On a good horse, and taking the road through Taormina and Castro, he could reach him in time. A man was produced who asked for eight ounces—that is, about 100 francs. I gave him four, promising him the four others on his return if he brought news from Medici. He took the eight piastres and promised me never to stop, neither to eat nor to sleep.

I at once went on shore and sought out Eber. He knew of Bosco's departure that morning. He had at first had the idea of going with his column to Medici's assistance, but map in hand he had calculated that he had four times further to go than the Royalists, and therefore would never arrive in time. So he had to hope everything from the courage of the Garibaldians for the fortune of Italy.

We dined with Eber, and it was only when night fell that we returned on board. Hardly had we done so, when we heard much noise on the Marina and saw a great moving illumination which stopped when it reached the edge of the sea. It consisted of 300 people bearing torches. A large skiff then left the shore full of musicians, whose brass instruments gleamed in the light from the torchbearers who made a circle of fire round them. Then numerous little boats came out in their turn and accompanied the big one. At the same moment, each window put out illuminations, candles or lamps, so that presently Catania resembled an amphitheatre of

[1] The rival forces were not nearly so large as Dumas states.

lights. I was wondering what was the cause of all this, when the Captain came and said—

"It is for you ; it is for you !"

At first I refused to believe it, but, as the fleet of fire continued to approach the yacht, I thought that I must honour the Catanians with a display of fireworks.

By chance, my friend Ruggieri [1] had, before I left, sent me a huge box of Roman candles, catherine wheels and Bengal lights. All colours were represented. I had the Bengal lights brought to me. I chose red, green and white ones, and while the Captain decorated the yacht with all her flags, the Italian tricolor predominant, I let off the Bengal lights, which, placed a metre apart, lit up the whole harbour. At this sight shouts burst from the flotilla, and fifty musicians produced the first bars of Garibaldi's hymn.

It was really to me that the fête was being given.

The boats neared us and enveloped the yacht in a circle of fire. The big skiff now lay alongside us. Then shouts of "Viva Garibaldi ! Viva l'Italia ! Viva Vittorio Emmanuele !" drowned the sound of the instruments and bore up to heaven one of those strange concerts which take to God the expression of thanks of a people. It was both beautiful and grand.

One boat was laden with fruit, ices, and all kinds of refreshments. A large table was spread on our deck, which was boarded in an instant, and the illuminations, the fête, the shouts, the music all went on there. Then there was dancing on deck : they danced on the tables, they danced in the shrouds, they danced on the skiff, in the boats, on the shore—they danced wherever any note of the music could be heard. The fête lasted until two o'clock in the morning. Then they left, or rather the illuminations did so. We shook hands, we embraced, we swore an eternal friendship and unalterable fraternity. And, what is rare, I believe the oath has been observed.

I remained on deck until the last boat had been secured on shore, until the last torchlight had disappeared ; then, in the midst of the silence that succeeded to all this noise, I recalled the strange vicissitudes of fortune which have been mine. Of a surety the memoirs of a man who, having been born with the nineteenth century, expired with it, would supply curious reading. [2]

The next day, while I made the most of the calm to continue my work in the yacht's library, I was told that a deputation was on its

[1] Ruggieri was the Brock of France. Dumas was extremely fond of fireworks, and devotes a whole *causerie* to him and his displays.

[2] It was believed that Dumas, who was born in 1802, and was in 1860 still like a young man, would live to be a centenarian.

way to the *Emma*. What had happened the evening before was a surprise and a joy, but anything of a prepared nature alarms and displeases me. I have never been able to reply to a discourse or even to a toast. What I like is the simple, the natural; and this is why, perhaps, I am not in the Academy, where I should have a discourse to make and to hear. On this occasion I had to do with an intelligent deputation. The three gentlemen of which it consisted each shook my hand and presented me with a paper.

I read—

"Copy of the deliberation of the Civic Council of Catania formulated in the Sitting of the 15th of July, 1860.

"The Council, wishing to perpetuate by a public declaration the happy arrival within our walls of the immortal Alexandre Dumas, and wishing at the same time to give him an expression of its admiration, as is the due of a European celebrity who with goodwill and wit has aimed through his books to instruct the citizens of the civilised world, unanimously confers on the aforesaid Dumas the Catanian citizenship. The Council delegates its President to communicate to the illustrious citizen the ardent wishes of the meeting. The present deliberation will be printed and sold to the public through the Secretary's office.

"A true copy.
"The Chancellor-Secretary,
"ZACCARIA NORBERTO.
"Witness for the President,
"The Vice-President,
"GIACOMO BELLIA."

I admit that this unexpected kindness, the true source of which was Garibaldi's friendship for me, touched me deeply.

Seeing that I was a citizen of four Sicilian towns it behoved me to be worthy of the honour done me and devote myself entirely to the Italian cause. I shall always find the East in the same place; but this opportunity of assisting in the triumph of a principle which has been and always will be the concern of my life—that of liberty—will never be found again. I decided then, if possible, to leave the same evening and to go to put myself at Garibaldi's disposal. So I went on shore with the deputation to take Eber's commissions for the General.

Eber had enrolled 2000 to 3000 volunteers, but in Catania, as all over Sicily, the same cry went up of "No arms!"

Eber gave me a letter for Garibaldi in which he pressed for red shirts for the backs of his volunteers and rifles to arm them withal. Red shirts were extravagantly dear, for Sicily was out of red material! Now a Garibaldian in a blue or a white shirt is no Garibaldian at all. I undertook to do all I could, and I returned to the yacht, but not before having taken leave of my old friends and my new friends. I say of my old friends, because I had found some acquaintances made on my first voyage.

In 1835 I had come to Catania with letters of introduction from poor Bellini. We were going, on my return, to make an opera together. I had left him—a young man—in the best of health. . . .

Alas! when I had reached Catania, when I had delivered his letters, and had embraced his old father, full of joy about his son's triumphs, Bellini was dead.

Two or three of his relations whom I had known as children five-and-twenty years before, shook my hand and took leave of me on the quay.

On nearing the *Emma*, I saw all on board staring at the water, and I climbed the ladder on the other side without anyone noticing me. I softly approached them, and I saw and heard Podimatas, the Captain, and Théodore exchanging remarks with a gentleman who was seated on the water like a Turk on his divan. He made no movement—he was just seated. I, for a moment, supposed that I had the glory of finding Nicolas Pesce, the subject of Schiller's famous ballad. The Captain presented me. He rose out of the water without moving his feet, but I begged him to resume his first posture. He told me in conversation that all depended on his head, which controlled everything. He then successively took every attitude without making any movement. He could remain for from seven to eight hours in the water without any fatigue. He could swim for a distance of four or five leagues; and, if he had provisions, could go as far as Malta. For my part, I think that his lungs must have had unusual properties. His name was Leonardi. I thanked him for having given me a wonderful exhibition, and for having so kindly answered all my questions.

CHAPTER XXXVIII

CHARYBDIS

WE spent the 15th and 16th of July trying to get out of the harbour, and only succeeded on the night of the 17th. In the course of the morning of the 18th, we sailed past Messina. The town was awaiting a bombardment from one moment to the next, and looked like a dying man. The greater part of the inhabitants had left the town and were concentrated on the shore between Messina and la Paci; some were under canvas, others in boats. Each person had his most precious household gods with him. These poor people were continually looking at the town, expecting to see the smoke from the first cannon shot. We passed without stopping, but, the wind being against us, we could not double the point, and were obliged to anchor before the Faro. While the Captain went to Messina for news, Paul Parfait and Théodore, without saying anything to anyone, got into the *youyou* and began to row towards Scylla. When we saw them they were already too far off to hear us. We made them signs, but they seemed not to see us and kept on. Presently, with our glasses, we saw them tie up their boat and get out. In the state of hostility existing between Calabria and Sicily, or rather between the Royalists and the Garibaldians, it was most imprudent to make an excursion in Calabria, especially as they were Frenchmen. As we could do nothing, we turned and watched for the Captain's return, but vainly. Our two young men, in the meantime, had reached the mountain and disappeared.

I went ashore near by the lighthouse along with the "Admiral," and we began to look for quails. But we were in the wrong spot, one in which they only rest for a moment before flying on into Calabria. We merely rose five or six in two hours.

No one has yet discovered how quails manage their migratory flight from Africa. All hypotheses on the subject are alike ridiculous. One simply does not know how it is done.

On our return on board, although we had been away for about two hours, there was nothing to be seen, either of Paul and Théodore, or of the Captain. At last, almost together, we saw appear the sail of the yawl, and from the foot of the rock of Scylla the *youyou* of the two men.

Podimatas made an exclamation on seeing the *youyou*. "*Diable!*" said he, "they are doing that just at the wrong time."

"Why?"

"The current will be at its strongest in half-an-hour, and if they do not manage to cross it, they will be swept to Stromboli, without saying anything of the dance the waves will give them near Charybdis."

"*Diable!*" said I in my turn.

And I riveted my gaze through my glasses on the two oarsmen.

For nearly a quarter of an hour all went well with them; they kept almost straight for us; but presently they began to be taken to the north. And as they had their backs to us they did not notice it. Besides, they were getting towards Charybdis, in the eyes of the ancients such a dangerous place, and in truth it is to a canoe. The nearer they got to it, the stronger did the current become. It forced them to give way. Podimatas was quite right: their situation was disquieting. What could we do for them? They had taken the *youyou*, the Captain had taken the yawl; we had only the canoe, which was little larger than their craft. It is true that we had the yacht, but as the Captain had taken two sailors and the apprentice, we had only two sailors and the boy. Nevertheless, I gave the order to Podimatas to go to the rescue of the oarsmen, who were being swept to the open sea. They now saw their danger and redoubled their efforts, but all in vain.

What would the Captain think when he saw us sailing away and thus abandoning him? But this could not be helped.

In the winking of an eye we had our anchor up and, with a good breeze, were rapidly and gracefully nearing the *youyou*. The two oarsmen, exhausted, had thrown down their oars and awaited our coming. The *youyou* danced on the waves like a cork, and it was only by throwing themselves from side to side in unison with the dancing that they escaped being wrecked. Luckily we rushed along.

But we could not stop; all we could do was to throw them a rope as we passed. Luckily, again, the yacht obeyed the helm to a hair. At the right instant we threw the rope; it was caught and we made our end fast. Then, hauling on the rope, they managed to reach us and seize the shrouds, and, with our assistance, climb the rail and fall exhausted on deck.

Then we turned our thoughts to the Captain. We were far from the lighthouse, and as the wind was favourable for Palermo, instead of entering the strait again, we ran along the coast.

An hour later, the Captain rejoined us. Then it appeared that with his excellent glass he had seen everything.

Paul Parfait and Théodore escaped the second edition of a rating. We had already given the first.

The *youyou* was hoisted up, and we headed for Palermo.

CHAPTER XXXIX

THE BAY OF MILAZZO

By the time we rounded the furthest point of the lighthouse it was afternoon; towards five o'clock, the wind dropped, and we could not expect its return until towards midnight. The month of July in the Mediterranean is the month of calms.

I stayed on deck until about one o'clock in the morning. I could not decide to go down to my room. For the second time, I found myself on these splendid Sicilian seas, where the air, the sky, the water—all is enchantment. We saw afar off in the transparent azure, which is not night, but only the absence of day, like floating clouds on the sea, Stromboli, Vulcano, Lipari—all the kingdom of Æolus, while the cape of Milazzo seemed, leaping from the land, to be trying to throw a bridge between Sicily and its archipelago. Instead of going below, I stretched myself on deck so that the first rays of dawn might awaken me.

Towards four o'clock, I opened my eyes. We had made little progress, and were about three miles from the Cape of Milazzo.

The Captain, seeing me awake, came to me and spoke of the necessity of stopping, either on the Sicilian coast, or at one of the islands, to get some fresh provisions. I told him to make for Lipari, where I had landed twenty-five years ago, and where I knew that we could get some excellent fish and poultry. Scarcely had he carried out the necessary manœuvre than the noise of a cannon-shot reached us, and near a village in the foreground we saw a cloud of smoke rising. A second shot followed, a second cloud floated above the trees and slowly upwards in the still and pure atmosphere. In all, we counted six shots and saw the smoke rise in different places. As this smoke then continued to rise without our hearing shots, we supposed that it proceeded from a fusillade too far off to be heard.

Evidently, the fighting was going on between Milazzo and the village, the name of which I did not know. I now ordered the Captain to go to Milazzo. Unfortunately, the breeze was so gentle that we could only sail at three miles an hour.

But the more we got into the eastern gulf of Milazzo the more, also, approached the fight, only it inclined towards the western gulf—that is to say, on the other side of the promontory. It was clear that if we remained on the eastern side of the isthmus, we should not see anything, the hill which extends from Milazzo to the end of the promontory, on which is the lighthouse, entirely cutting off the horizon.

I was so desirous of being present at this fight, which was evidently a hot one, that I wanted to land at Milazzo and get on foot to the other side of the village.

The Captain was just making some remarks about the danger to which I should be exposing myself when a light breeze came from land, carrying the smoke with it.

"If this breeze holds," said the Captain to me, "we shall find it shorter to double the cape."

"Do you think that we can do it, Captain?"

"With this breeze, we can do it in an hour."

"Well, then, double the cape."

And, in fact, within the hour we had reached the end of this point of Milazzo.

During all this time the cannon-shots came nearer and nearer, and had finished by bursting over our heads—that is to say, in the fort of Milazzo; only the shots were aimed towards the western gulf—that is to say, the point opposite where we were. This made us all the more anxious to double the cape: unfortunately the faint breeze was far from corresponding to our ardour.

At last we succeeded. This is how matters stood.

The battle still continued on land, and rapidly approached us, but what was drawing the fire of the fort was a big steam-boat flying the Italian flag with 200 to 300 red-shirted men on board, while a man astride the yard of the royals was examining the fort through a telescope and serving as a mark for the shots of the Royalists—for there was no doubt that the redshirts were Garibaldians and the men who fired on them Royalists.

But the men on the steam-boat were powerless against the men in the fort, whom their cannon-shots could not reach, while the fire from the fort, which plunged down on the boat, would have sunk it in five or six shots, had they been well aimed. Happily, the marksmanship was so bad that all the balls whistled over it and fell into the sea.

I gave the Captain the order to get as near the steam-boat as possible. But the wind favoured us still less than it had done on the eastern side of the gulf.

At last we were within forty or fifty metres. The firing continued on both sides. I had formed the idea a moment before that the man who served to draw the shots of the fort was no other than Garibaldi.

Now I clearly recognised him.

I hailed him. He turned towards me and in his turn recognised me. "What news?" I called to him.

"All goes well," he replied, coming down with a sailor's agility.

I let him do so, and when he had reached the deck,

"What shall we do?" I asked him.

"Keep as close to us as you can."

"You hear that, Captain?" said I to Beaugrand.

The Captain signified that he would do all that he could.

Our attention was then engaged by a new sight.

Seven to eight hundred Royalists had sallied out from the fort and formed up on the shore to oppose a landing, should such be attempted. Garibaldi steamed towards them, then when within five hundred paces of the shore turned his boat round and fired with a cannon—one of large calibre, I should say, if the noise it made goes for anything.

To our great astonishment, the shot, although fired so near, had no effect. I am in error; it had a great effect: the 700 to 800 men took to flight, or, rather, flew away like a cloud of birds. And this, although not a single one had fallen, nor—judging by the pace at which they went—had been wounded. In a second all had vanished.

In the meantime the fort had continued to fire on the steam-boat, but it seemed as tranquil as if powder only was being burst against it.

Suddenly we saw red specks appear on shore. It was the Garibaldians' advance-guard.

Directly Garibaldi saw them he steered towards them and signalled to us to come to him. We did all we could, but the breeze was nearly failing us.

The red specks were now increasing in number, and rallying to the steam-boat, which was nearing them. At this sight, the fire from the fort redoubled, and we saw the sand on the shore fly up.

The Garibaldians paid no attention to this detail. Some began to eat and others to play cards, while a few undressed and bathed.

The fort continued to fire on them and they continued to pay no heed.

When the steam-boat was within a cable length of the shore it put a boat in the sea. Garibaldi, as far as we could make out, got into it and reached the shore.

Then the red-shirts grouped themselves round him. A council, lasting ten minutes, was held, during which the boat went backwards and forwards between the shore and the steam-boat taking twenty men each time. Then the steam-boat made for the open sea.

Garibaldi and his little band of perhaps 200 men disappeared behind the aloes and cacti at the top of the beach.

I learnt subsequently that the fight had continued at Milazzo an hour longer when the Neapolitans, after being driven from house to house, withdrew into the castle. I landed, and in the midst of the last shots entered Milazzo.

It is difficult to give any idea of the disorder and terror which reigned there. None could tell me where Garibaldi and Medici were to be found until I saw Major Cenni. He and I discovered the General lying in the porch of the church, with his staff asleep around him. He was lying on the pavement with his saddle for a pillow, quite exhausted and fast asleep. Near him was his supper—a crust of bread and a pitcher of water. The sight took me, in imagination, back 2500 years.

I seemed to stand before Cincinnatus. May God preserve him! Should he perish, the whole world, my Sicilian friends, can never supply you with such another man.

The General awoke, and, on seeing me, desired me to spend the next day with him.

CHAPTER XL

GARIBALDI ON BOARD THE *EMMA*

Milazzo Roads, 23rd July

I MUST now tell you that the General left Palermo on the 18th, and reached the camp at Miri on the 19th. There, skirmishes had been going on for a couple of days. Immediately he arrived the General reviewed Medici's troops, who welcomed him with enthusiasm. Next morning, at daybreak, the whole force advanced to the attack of the Neapolitans, who had come out of the fort and the town of Milazzo. Malenchini commanded the extreme left; General Medici and Cosenz the centre; the right, which consisted simply of a few companies, was merely intended to cover the centre and left, in case of surprise. General Garibaldi took up his position in the centre, where he considered the engagement would be hottest. Firing opened on the left. About half-way between Miri and Milazzo they fell in with the advance-guard of the Neapolitans under cover of the reeds. After about a quarter of an hour's engagement on the left, the centre found itself face to face with the Neapolitan line, which it immediately attacked and dislodged from its first position.

Meanwhile the right wing drove the Neapolitans out of the houses they were occupying; but the difficulties of the ground prevented reinforcements arriving in time. Bosco, the Neapolitan General, rushed a mass of 6000 men[1] against 500 to 600 of his opponents, who at first drove him back, but, overwhelmed by numbers, they, in their turn, were forced to withdraw.

The General immediately sent for reinforcements. As soon as they arrived, a fresh attack was opened on the enemy, who were hidden amongst the reeds, or taking cover behind the Indian fig trees. The Garibaldians here found themselves at a disadvantage, for the situation precluded a bayonet attack.

Medici, at the head of his men, had his horse killed under him, and Cosenz received a spent ball in the neck. He fell, and was believed to be mortally wounded, when he sprang up again and cried:
"Long live Italy!"
The wound proved to be a slight one.

Garibaldi then placed himself, together with Missori and a few Guides, at the head of the Genoese Carabineers, with the intention of outflanking the Neapolitans. He hoped that this flank attack would enable him to cut off the retreat of a portion of their forces, but in

---

[1] Bosco had not as many men altogether.

advancing found himself faced by a battery of guns, which prevented his carrying out this manœuvre as intended.

Missori and Statella then pushed forward with fifty men, and Garibaldi, placing himself at their head, led them to the charge. When within twenty paces, the gun, loaded with grape-shot, opened fire. The result was terrible. Only five or six men remained standing. Garibaldi had the sole of his boot and his stirrups torn away. His horse was wounded, and became unmanageable; he was forced to dismount, leaving his revolver in its holster. Major Breda and his trumpeter were killed beside him. Missori fell beneath his horse, which had just been killed by a ball from a wall-piece. Statella remained erect amid a veritable hurricane of grape-shot; all the rest were either killed or wounded. At this point individual details necessarily cease; everybody fought, and fought well.

The General, seeing that it was impossible to take the gun which had caused all this carnage in a frontal attack, ordered Colonel Dunne to send him some companies, and with these troops directed a charge through the reeds. The plan entrusted to Missori and Statella was that, after clearing a way through the reeds, they should leap over a wall which would then face them, and thus find themselves close to the gun. Its capture should then be attempted.

This movement was carried out with perfect cohesion and great spirit by the two officers mentioned and fifty men whom they had with them; but when they got out on to the road the first person they met was Garibaldi himself, on foot, and sword in hand! The gun was fired instantly and some men were killed, but the others, in a brilliant charge, seized the piece and carried it off from the enemy. The Neapolitan infantry now opened their line to allow a squadron of cavalry to pass through and charge the captors of the gun. Colonel Dunne's men, who were little accustomed to fire, threw themselves to the ground on either side of the road, instead of meeting the charge at the point of the bayonet; but they were hemmed in on one side by the Indian fig trees, and on the other by a wall. The cavalry rushed past like a whirlwind, and then the Sicilians, who had quickly recovered from their sudden alarm, opened fire upon them from both sides. This fusillade from both right and left made the Neapolitan officer halt his men and endeavour to return; but he now found, in the middle of the road and barring his passage, Garibaldi, Missori, Statella, and five or six men. The General seized the bridle of the officer's horse, exclaiming: "Surrender!" but the Neapolitan's only answer was to aim a well-directed blow at Garibaldi with his sword which, however, the latter parried, and then by a dexterous back stroke, cut open the officer's cheek. The officer fell to the ground.

Immediately, three or four sabres were raised against the General, who wounded one of his assailants with a thrust. Missori killed two others, and brought down the horse of a third with a shot from his revolver. Statella disposed of another. A man who had been un-horsed sprang at Missori's throat, but the latter freed himself by smashing his adversary's skull with his revolver.

Whilst this formidable struggle was in progress, Garibaldi busied himself in rallying his scattered men. He now led a bayonet charge, and his men either killed or took prisoners the rest of the fifty horse-men. Then, with the support of the rest of his centre, he advanced against the combined enemy forces of Neapolitans, Bavarians, and Swiss. The Neapolitans fled before the advancing bayonets, the Bavarians and Swiss held their ground for a brief while, but soon fled also. The fate of the day was settled. Victory was not yet wholly secured, but soon would be in the grasp of the heroes of Italy.

The whole Neapolitan army then began to retreat on Milazzo, with ours in close pursuit till they reached the first houses. There, the guns of the fort now took part in the struggle, and I have already related what followed.

When the General expressed a wish that I should be his com-panion during the following day, he was unable to offer me any different bed from his own—and that was, the pavement of the streets, or the flagstones of the church porch. I preferred, however, the sands of the seashore. I had arranged with four of my sailors to meet me on the western side of the bay: they were to set up a tent for me and to await my coming, having a boat ready. They were on the spot when I arrived.

The General was expecting a sortie on the part of the Neapolitans during the night, and had consequently given orders that all the gates of the town leading to the Castle should be vigilantly guarded, and that barricades should be erected.

Before starting on the way down to the shore, I wanted to see for myself how these orders were being carried out, so I paid a visit to the gates of the town, near to the Castle. There I found a solitary sentinel, ready to drop with exhaustion, on guard, with fifteen of his comrades fast asleep on the ground near by. The sentinel was obliged to march briskly backwards and forwards in order to avoid going to sleep also, and even found it difficult to keep his eyes open whilst on the move.

As to the barricades, some tables, chairs, and planks had been placed across the street—an erection over which a child might jump. Those who were constructing the barricades had fallen asleep

over their work soon after starting it. These brave people, like the
Spartans of Leonidas, considered their bodies a sufficient rampart to
resist any enemy. I left the town, praying that General Bosco might
not take it into his head to try and make a breach through these
living but immovable ramparts.

About a mile from the town, I came across my sailors. I threw myself down in the boat and fell asleep, comforted with a profound faith
in human nature, which, for all its baseness, can be so sublimely
noble, and can point to Victor Emmanuel and Garibaldi in the same
generation as that of Francis II and Maniscalco.

Contrary to all expectation, the night passed off quietly. We rose as
soon as it was light. Dressing did not take long. After signalling to
the yacht to come as close to shore as possible—for she had not been
able to anchor in consequence of the depth of the soundings—we then
put out to sea.

About half-past five in the morning we were on board again. Firing
had just started anew, but the sounds came from the other side of the
peninsula—that is, from the direction of the harbour. The Captain
steered in the direction of north-east. There was only a very feeble
breeze blowing, and anxious though we were to reach the other side
quickly, we could not make more than two knots an hour. It was
therefore nine o'clock before we doubled the Cape of Milazzo. The
first thing we saw when we got to the other side of the lighthouse was
the steamer, *Tüköry*, being towed by some twenty boats. We en-
quired of a fisherman what had happened, and were informed that
the paddle-wheel had been broken during the previous evening. Thus
Garibaldi found himself deprived of one of his most powerful instruments of support.

The shores of the peninsula looked like a camp. A score of families
had taken refuge there, and were living under improvised tents;
others were in small boats anchored near to the shore—safely sheltered from the guns of the fort, thanks to the rapid declivity of the
mountain. Others, again, found an abode in the natural grottoes
formed by the sea. We boldly sailed out into the open and passed
beneath the guns of the fort. Out of regard for the susceptibilities of
my own Government, I had hauled down the tricolour flag and had
hoisted my own in its place. General Bosco apparently did not consider us worthy of his anger, and let us anchor at a distance of a
cable and a half from the fort. From this point we could distinguish
the Neapolitan, Bavarian, and Swiss soldiers crowded together in
the courtyard of the Castle. The vast buildings of the fort were filled
to overflowing, and the suffocating atmospheres within finally drove
masses into the square. The *Tüköry*, still towed by boats, passed with-

Milazzo 21 Luglio 1860

Le Journal que mon
ami Dumas veut instituer
a Palerme aura le beau
titre d'Indépendant et
il le méritera d'autant
plus - qu'il voudra com-
mencer par ne pas m'
épargner si jamais je
m'écarte de mon devoir
d'enfant du peuple, et
de mes principes humanitaires

G. Garibaldi

in fifty yards of us on its way to anchor in the harbour. The guns of the fort remained silent, and allowed the vessel to carry out this manœuvre without interference.

All this seemed to augur well for us. We thought that negotiations had been begun between the Garibaldians and the Neapolitans. This belief was founded not only on the silence of the big guns, but also on the cessation of the musketry fire. Scarcely had we anchored, when a shore-boat, conveying a "red-shirt"—all Sicily uses this term to denominate the Garibaldians—was seen making for our yacht. The General had sent a message to me requesting me to put into port and anchor astern of the *Tüköry*. A quarter of an hour later we were at the spot indicated, and I went aboard that vessel.

The General, who was awaiting me, looked cheerful and calm, as is his wont. It is difficult to picture a countenance so invariably serene as his: it is really that of the lion in repose, of which Dante speaks. No communication had as yet been opened between the fort and himself, but he felt reassured, by reason of the large number of the Neapolitans. He believed that the fort was not equipped for a long siege, and would speedily run short of victuals and ammunition.

After briefly dealing with the main events of the day, Garibaldi told me how gratified he was with my proposition to go and buy arms in France, and begged me to explain how I intended to put my plan into execution. I furnished him with all the details he required; and he, in his turn, gave me his instructions and advice in the matter. Finally he handed me an order instructing the municipality of Palermo to open a credit of 100,000 francs in my name to enable me to purchase arms.

"There," said he, on giving me the order: "Now get to work, and may good luck go with you!"

And, after a moment's reflection, he added:

"When you come back, Dumas, do you know what you ought to do?"

"What?"

"Found a journal."

"Well, to tell you the truth, General, I had already thought of doing it. Give me its name. That is really all I want in order to make a start."

Garibaldi picked up a pen and wrote:

"The journal which my friend Dumas is going to start at Palermo will bear the attractive title of '*L'Indépendant*'; and it will deserve its name all the more if it starts attacking myself, should I ever deviate from my duty to the people or my fidelity to humanitarian principles.

"G. GARIBALDI."

"Hurrah for *L'Indépendant!*" I exclaimed; "these lines shall serve for its motto." [1]

Just then a small boat rowed up to the *Tüköry*. The General, after exchanging a few words with the man in charge of it, gave certain orders to his *aides-de-camp*, whereupon one of these said to me:

"News from Messina! We shall have enough work to do to keep both hands busy."

As for the General, he made no further observation to me than, "Let us go and see your yacht."

Just then a paper was brought to him to sign. It was a credit for 500,000 francs opened in his name. After signing it, he cast a glance at my yacht and said:

"If I were rich enough, I should like to have such a yacht as yours."

Now, listen attentively to this, Sicilians, my fellow-countrymen, Italians, my brothers! This man who has at his disposal the blood and the wealth of Sicily, who is bestowing at this very moment 2,000,000 men on Piedmont, this man, I say, is not rich enough to buy a yacht which would cost 25,000 francs!

We then went on board my yacht. The contents of a bottle of champagne were poured into the glasses that I had brought from the royal palace at Palermo as my share of the booty taken from Francis II, and we drank to the welfare of Italy. Garibaldi drank water—his usual beverage. Whilst we were talking in the marquee on deck, he suddenly got up in order to survey a steam-boat coming from Palermo, which was just then doubling Cape Milazzo.

With the practised eye of the sailor, Garibaldi recognised it immediately.

"It is she!" he exclaimed.

Then, holding out his hand to me, he said:

"*Au revoir!* Come back to Palermo, and do your best for our cause. I must leave you, for I have business to attend to on board that steamer."

We took leave of one another, and Garibaldi went ashore. Here a horse was waiting for him. He mounted and then dashed off through the streets of Milazzo, but reappeared in a quarter of an hour upon the jetty. Meantime the newly-arrived steamer had come in and my yacht had got under weigh. All my sailors agreed that the new-comer was English, although it persisted in showing no flag.

At the sight of the steamer, all the Sicilian boatmen, expecting the usual landing of passengers, started rowing towards the mysterious vessel. Just when they were not more than 100 yards from it and we ourselves about fifty, a slight cloud of smoke arose from the platform

[1] Dumas' Prospectuses of his journal are given in translation in Appendix III.

of the Castle, and at the same time we heard the report of a gun and the whizzing of a ball as it sped along.

The ball fell between the Sicilian boats and the steamer into the sea, causing a waterspout as it sank. You would have laughed if you had seen how the boatmen scuttled off. Some of them sought refuge behind the *Emma*, a very poor shelter—little more than would protect them from a musket or revolver shot.

In the midst of this flying flotilla, which resembled a flight of scared birds, one boat alone continued its course, making straight for the ship, as inflexible as the man it bore. That man was Garibaldi. The fort continued to fire upon the steamer, but the balls fell either too high or too low: none of them touched it.

It was only after the eighth shot that the stranger ran up the English flag; but despite this English flag, yet another ball came from the fort—the last, however.

We were scarcely thirty yards from the vessel when it turned its prow to us and we were able to read: *City of Aberdeen*. Garibaldi went on board, came on deck, and mounted the paddle-box. Just then we crossed her course, and the General waved us his final good wishes for a prosperous voyage as he steamed away at full speed. Ten minutes later he had disappeared behind Cape Milazzo. The *Emma* continued her voyage; and to-morrow, or the day after, as it may please the caprice of the wind, I shall again behold that beautiful Palermo which has chosen me for one of its citizens.

Palermo, 25th July.

Immediately I landed, I went to the residence of the President of the Municipal Commission, and presented my letter of credit to him. Unfortunately, Garibaldi had forgotten to add to his signature the word "Dictator." The Duke of Verdura very judiciously remarked to me that if Garibaldi were killed during my absence, the Municipality of Palermo would be answerable for the money. Still, I thought the remark rather narrow-minded, seeing that the municipal councillors owed everything to Garibaldi, and if he did get killed, as the Duke of Verdura feared he might, nevertheless he would have laid down his life for Sicily.

It seemed to me that they might very well risk 100,000 francs for the conqueror of Calatafimi and of Milazzo; but then I am only a poet, and the Duke of Verdura is a syndic of the municipality, two states of life not in the least related to each other. I telegraphed to Garibaldi that the municipality had refused me the money. His answer was:

"Arrange the letter of credit with de Pretis."

I called upon M. de Pretis, who opened a credit in my favour for 60,000 francs.

I took with me to France a young artillery officer, named Rognetta, son of the celebrated physician of that name. It was arranged that he was to go to Liège to buy revolvers, whilst I would go to Marseilles to buy rifles and carbines.

We missed the steamer which goes direct from Palermo to Genoa, owing to the disinclination to be of service on the part of the French Consul, M. Fleury, who is the most whimsical Consul I have ever met—and God knows I have met some queer specimens amongst these officials in my time.

As we wished to lose as little time as possible, we immediately went on board the yacht again, and steered our course for Messina. If we have the good luck to reach there before the following Sunday, we shall be able to leave the same evening by the steamer going straight to Marseilles.

NOTE.—Colonel Dunne, whom Dumas mentions early in this chapter, was an ex-English soldier, who was opposed to the British Legion coming to Sicily. The regiment he commanded was composed of Sicilians. He rendered good service to Garibaldi. Dumas calls him "Colonel Donon."

CHAPTER XLI

THE TAKING OF MESSINA

Messina, 28th July

We made the passage from Palermo to Messina in thirty-two hours. When we were off Milazzo it was pitch dark and the weather frightful. We sent a boat to the shore to make inquiries about Garibaldi, and learnt that he had started two days previously for Messina. Sending to make inquiries meant a loss of two hours, during which, however, the weather became calm.

We were on the point of setting sail again, at two o'clock in the morning, when we saw the lanterns of a steamer coming round Cape Rasocolmo. The steersman accordingly signalled to the mate, and as a collision was scarcely to be feared in the vast bay of Milazzo, we took no further notice of the steamer, but continued our journey slowly, with our two lanterns lit. All of a sudden, a dark mass, enveloped in a cloud of smoke, approached within fifty yards of us, traced a semicircle round us after crossing our bows, then, putting about ship, came right across our starboard.

"The steamer! the steamer!" cried the sailor on the watch.

"Luff! luff!" shouted the mate.

This manœuvre was put into execution at once, but before it could be completed, the steamer was upon us. The scene that followed was indescribable.

The yacht was lifted up like a feather, and a sharp noise of cracking was heard. I was lying on the deck, and was covered with water. The steersman was thrown down, and the mate was tossed five or six feet into the air. Our cross-jacksail yard was broken, our spanker-boom bent like a reed, and our mainsail rent. The stern of the yacht plunged into the water, and emerged dripping wet. The steamer, believing that she had sent us to the bottom, went on her way. It was just a little Neapolitan joke! Our yacht had been recognised as having taken part in the affair at Milazzo, so it was determined to sink us.[1]

It took us till daybreak to repair the damage, for many things on board were broken, though fortunately nothing of vital importance. We replaced our mainsail by our trysail, and had duplicates on board for our jib and spanker-boom. The calm still continued; and it was not till towards midday that a light breeze sprang up, and, helped by the current, carried us towards the strait.

[1] Dumas must certainly be held to have borne a charmed life. Although continually in danger, he never came to any harm, and died peacefully in his bed.

On reaching the Faro of Messina, a fine sight met our gaze. A battery of three pieces of ordnance had been erected; and I counted 168 boats, all ready for landing men, each boat capable of holding twenty. Their number should have been quadrupled.

The nearer we approached Messina, the more clearly we discerned the Neapolitan sentinels pacing backwards and forwards on the ramparts of the fort facing the sea; whilst on a plain behind the citadel we saw bodies of infantry and cavalry manœuvring.

The Neapolitans, you know, are wonderfully good at manœuvres. In fact they have manœuvred so cleverly that they have finally managed to get shut up in the citadels of Messina and Syracuse.

As soon as we reached Messina, our first visit was to Garibaldi. Tears flowed down his face when I told him of the answer given by the Duke of Verdura. With a sigh, he remarked:

"When all is said and done, if I do get killed, it will not be for them, but for the liberty of the world."

Then addressing himself to me, he added:

"Start off now, Dumas, and come back as quickly as possible."

"General," I replied, "I can be back in a fortnight, but not much sooner."

"With the arms?"

"Yes, although I may have to pay a little dearer for them. I give you my word I shall be back here by the steamer of Tuesday fortnight."

"Very well. If it be so, I shall await your return before entering Calabria, and then we shall make our entry with your guns."

During my voyage to Palermo, the surrender of the fort of Milazzo and the capture of Messina had taken place. Here are some details which I gathered concerning the double event.

The day after our departure from Milazzo, a French screw steamer, the *Protis*, Captain Salvi, anchored in the roads. It was bringing provisions for the Neapolitan army; but the Captain knew nothing about the battle of Milazzo and the fact that the fort was now blockaded. To the boat which came along to hail him, he intimated his readiness to place himself at the disposition of the commandant at Milazzo, and likewise all his cargo. "But," said they, to his great astonishment, "it is Garibaldi who is in command here." As you may judge, the situation was rather embarrassing. The French flag, however, protected the vessel, so she remained at anchor, awaiting events.

On the evening of the same day, a big French screw clipper, the *Charles-Martel*, and another named the *Stella*, anchored before Milazzo, with the same intentions and purpose as the *Protis*. On the 23rd, at daybreak, the *Mouette*, a Government despatch-vessel, Commander

Boyer, coming from Naples, anchored in the harbour. An interview took place immediately between Garibaldi and Commander Boyer. The position of the French transports in the service of the King of Naples being fully guaranteed, this superior officer, who had despatches for Messina, was to proceed to his destination. He did not do so, however, without strongly urging the Captain of the *Protis* to offer his services, in the interests of humanity, in trying to open negotiations between General Garibaldi and the Commandant of the citadel.

The position of General Bosco was a very critical one. His garrison of 5500 men was shut up in a fort without any sort of provisions; consequently he could hardly hope for an honourable capitulation.

After interviewing Garibaldi and obtaining his assent, the Captain of the *Protis* proceeded to the citadel under a flag of truce, and after his eyes had been bandaged he was introduced into the presence of General Bosco. At first the General was very reserved, but when he knew that Captain Salvi was a Frenchman, he became more communicative, and did not conceal the fact that he was quite ready to enter into negotiations, provided that the conditions were honourable both to himself and to his troops.

The following is not the actual text, but is the substance of a letter to the Captain of the *Protis* for transmission to General Garibaldi:

"The General commanding the fortress of Milazzo, from motives of humanity, which he appreciates as much as General Garibaldi, and, above all, desiring to avoid useless bloodshed, would not be indisposed to surrender the fort on honourable terms, provided always that they met with the approval of his Government. He recognises that the position of the citadel is critical, although not desperate, for it still offers resources to a general and troops full of resolution."

General Bosco also entrusted to the Captain of the *Protis* a letter for the King of Naples. The Captain then retired, but, in pursuance of General Bosco's orders, his eyes were not bandaged, as was the case when he entered the citadel.

Immediately after the interview, the *Charles-Martel* and the *Stella* left for Messina; but the *Protis* remained at anchor, awaiting the issue of the negotiations which had been opened. The commander of the *Mouette*, feeling uneasy, only touched at Messina, and then steamed back immediately to Milazzo. On the way he crossed the *Charles-Martel* and the *Stella*, but held no communication with them.

It was about four o'clock when he came in sight of Milazzo again. Great was his astonishment when he saw four Neapolitan frigates, under steam, before the fort, and one of them bearing an Admiral's flag. The situation was open to all sorts of interpretations. Some on board thought that more troops were being landed, others believed that only foodstuffs were being brought; but all expected some sort of a cannonade.

With the assistance of a telescope it was not difficult to see that Garibaldi had made all necessary dispositions to resist any attempt at aggression. The General had ordered all troops to be summoned to arms. A battery of six guns, which made its appearance as if by enchantment, had been put in position on the quay at the foot of the citadel, whilst another of two pieces could be distinguished at the end of the bay, near to the mouth of the river. These two batteries were placed so as to give a cross-fire.

The two turrets which crown the heights of the peninsula had at the very outset fallen into the hands of Garibaldi; and now their four guns were also trained on the Neapolitan squadron. All this warlike array would surely not be in vain. The Admiral's frigate had a flag of truce hoisted at the mizzen-mast. The *Mouette* came and anchored very peaceably alongside of the *Protis*.

The Neapolitan squadron apparently had a plenipotentiary on board. At seven o'clock the negotiations were concluded; and the Captain of the *Protis* received orders to go to Messina at once in order to bring back the *Charles-Martel*, the *Stella*, the *Impératrice Eugénie*, etc., for the purpose of proceeding with the immediate evacuation of Milazzo. By two o'clock in the morning the *Mouette* was getting up steam for the return journey to Messina.

I am told that the conditions insisted on first of all by Garibaldi were that the garrison should be considered prisoners of war, but that the officers should be allowed to return to their homes with their arms and baggage. The conditions finally agreed upon were that the whole garrison should march out with their arms and baggage, but without cartridges; and that all stores and munitions in the citadel were to be divided equally between besiegers and besieged.

Now let us turn our attention to Messina.

The men-of-war stationed in the harbour of Messina were requested on the 22nd by General Clary to change their anchorage so as not to be in the way of offensive or defensive operations on the part of the citadel. This evacuation of the harbour by the war-vessels led to a precipitate flight from Messina of all those who had not already left.

The bulk of this unfortunate population was now herded together on the eastern coast of the Straits of Messina, partly in tents which were in rags and tatters, and partly in boats of every description. In these latter women and children were so crowded that in one small galley I counted twenty-eight women and a like number of children. The richer part of the population had fled into the country; and the town itself was as silent as the grave—a silence that was only broken by the challenges of the Neapolitan sentinels and the reports of musket shots which, without any justification, were aimed at anyone who dared to appear in the streets.

The harbour also was as deserted as the town, except for some Neapolitan corvettes which were ready to move off. The only vessel left was the *Mouette,* which, having to take in coal, was anchored off Terra-Nova.

The days of the 24th and 25th passed in a similar way, but it was pretty clear that a battle was imminent. Judging by such parts of General Clary's plans as were manifest, a desperate struggle was to be expected. As a matter of fact all the mountain crests which surrounded Messina were occupied by Neapolitan troops. Artillery, cavalry, engineers, were there: in fact, nothing was wanting for bringing into action all the forces at the disposal of the General of the Royalist army. Yet the mountain only brought forth a ridiculous mouse.

Towards seven o'clock in the evening of the 25th a slight skirmish took place between the advanced posts of the Neapolitans and the guerillas of a partisan chief named Interdonato, although orders had been issued to avoid coming to blows. This first brush, however, led to the expectation that on the following day a serious engagement would take place; but at sunrise it was found that the Neapolitans had re-entered the town, the *Picciotti* had withdrawn to the ravines, which they used to occupy whilst awaiting orders, and, finally, the evacuation of the harbour was beginning. This evacuation, the terms of which seemed rather puzzling, was undoubtedly the outcome of the capitulation of Milazzo.

By surrendering claims which he might have justly made, the General of the independent army had secured for himself the benefits accruing from the evacuation of Messina. The garrison of Milazzo was made the ransom for Messina—this in exchange for the demands first made by Garibaldi.

On the 26th the foreign men-of-war entered the harbour again, and the population, now reassured, began to return to the town. Several decrees, issued by General Garibaldi, restored public tranquillity. Any attempt to endanger personal safety was severely punished. A national guard was embodied, and took over the posts recently abandoned by the Neapolitans; and everybody, both victors and vanquished, embraced one another in the streets with emulous rapture.

The definite signing of the truce did not, however, take place till the 28th. The royal troops occupied the citadel and the Garibaldians occupied the town, each undertaking to abstain from hostilities against the other for a certain period of time, and to give notice, at least forty-eight hours beforehand, of any intention to resume.

CHAPTER XLII

THE NEAPOLITANS

The Bay of Naples, 31st July

I DO not know if you have ever been to Naples, but if you have, and should take it into your head to visit the city again, you would find it very much changed. Now, just listen to what happened to me—to me who had the honour of being condemned to four years in the galleys under the decree of his Majesty King Ferdinand.

Scarcely had the *Pausilippe* cast anchor in port, when some of the men of the town made their way on deck, and one of them, probably taking me for a patriot, to judge by my countenance, asked me in a loud voice:

"Where is Garibaldi, sir? When will Garibaldi be here? We are waiting for him."

You must know that I have all these Neapolitan tricks at my fingers' ends, so I concluded that my questioner was only a spy trying to draw me out, and that it were best to say nothing in reply. So I contented myself by replying with emphasis: "*Non capisco*" (I don't understand). The same man then turned to one of my fellow-passengers and repeated his question. Whilst I was about to listen to the reply which would be given, a gentleman took off his hat to me, and when I asked this polite gentleman why he did me that honour, he said:

"Are you not Monsieur Alexandre Dumas?"

"At your service, sir; but whom have I the honour of addressing?"

"Sir, I am ——, an agent of police."

In turn, I took off my hat, and remarked:

"Sir, I would point out to you that I have come here under the protection of the French flag, and that, if you have come to arrest me——"

"Arrest you, sir! you, the author of the 'Corricolo,' of the 'Speronare,' of 'Capitaine Arena'! Why, sir, my children learn French from your books. Arrest you! What an opinion you must have of us! On the contrary, sir, I thought it to be my duty to come here and invite you to land."

"And here is my boat at your service, my dear Monsieur Dumas," said a second gentleman, who took off his hat to me just as politely as the first.

"Pardon me, sir, but to whom am I indebted for this obliging offer?"

"I am the Commissioner of Police for the port, sir. Pray do not refuse my offer, for my wife is very anxious to know you. The other day your 'Monte-Cristo' was played at the Teatro Fiorentino, and was a very big success. Do come, I beg you."

"Gentlemen, there are two reasons why I am unable to avail myself of your very kind offer: firstly, because I have been sentenced to undergo four years in the galleys if I set foot in Naples again."

"Ah, sir, there is no need to trouble about that now. If it was known that you were in harbour now, people would come and take you and carry you off in triumph."

"The second reason," I continued, "is that I promised Garibaldi not to enter Naples without him."

"And when do you think he will be here, sir?" said the Commissioner, in his most charming manner.

"Oh, in a fortnight, or three weeks at the latest."

"So much the better! so much the better!" exclaimed the two police agents. "Everybody here is impatiently waiting for him."

I made no reply to this.

"You know, sir," continued one of the agents, "your letter about Milazzo came to us yesterday, by way of Leghorn. What a sensation it created! One printer struck off 10,000 copies, and if you land, you will hear it being cried about the streets of Naples."

I came down from my pedestal, and said in reply:

"Well, now, if you are such Garibaldian enthusiasts as you tell me, I will show you something that will please you immensely: a splendid portrait of Garibaldi."

I then showed him the photograph; and the sight of it almost brought tears to the eyes of my interlocutor.

"Oh, sir, we here have none but the most execrable portraits of the General, and even these sell at extravagant prices."

"Then," said I, "I should dearly love to have this one engraved, and present it as a patriotic gift to the city of Naples."

"But why make a gift of it, sir, when you are sure of selling it at any price you like?"

I was getting more and more bewildered; and finally could think of no other way of getting rid of the police agents than telling them that I was waiting to keep an appointment with someone, and I could not possibly land. The two then retired expressing their heart-felt regrets.

There you have the spirit of Naples at the present moment. Everybody is Garibaldian, even the police agents; and I go so far as to say that the most Garibaldian of all are the police agents, who, of course, want to keep their places when Garibaldi comes to Naples. In fact, the proclamation of the Constitution had a result which the one who proclaimed it little expected: everybody now spoke openly what he had previously only dared to think secretly. And that secret thought was: "We long for annexation to the Kingdom of Victor Emmanuel. Long live Garibaldi! Long live United Italy!" Such was the effect of proclaiming the Constitution. You see that Francis II was well advised when he granted it.

And it has had many other results too. It has created the National Guard, which, last Sunday, was fraternising with the army and raising the cry in the public streets:

"Long live Garibaldi! Long live United Italy!"

It has established the right of public meeting, and the citizens have met to conspire in favour of Victor Emmanuel.

It has led to the return of the exiles, and they, by relating the story of their sufferings in banishment, have only increased, if that indeed be possible, the detestation in which Francis II is held.

This petty tyrant did, indeed, at the instigation of the queen-mother, try to set on foot a reactionary movement on the 15th of July last. The grenadiers of the royal guard, who are allowed to wear their swords in the streets, made a sudden descent on the people and ordered them to shout: "Long live the King!", just as they did at Palermo; but the people of Naples, like the people of Palermo, answered with:

"Long live King Victor Emmanuel!"

The grenadiers thereupon drew their swords, and inflicted wounds upon some sixty citizens, whilst five or six were actually slain. The only punishment inflicted on the regiment was that of being transferred to Portici. But the King's punishment for this outrage will probably be his being sent to Trieste.

The news of the surrender of Messina arrived here yesterday and is being cried in the streets. Cannon are being fired round about here to-day in honour of the birthday of the queen-mother; and this, coupled with the news, has created a certain confusion in the public mind.

When the exiles returned, their instructions—given to them, we presume, by M. de Cavour—were to bring about a revolution without the aid of Garibaldi. It was at once seen that the thing was impossible; and M. de Cavour must be content to see the revolution effected by Garibaldi and with Garibaldi.

At Naples, as elsewhere, the effect of Garibaldi's name is magical. Soldiers who fought at Calatafimi say that the General is eight feet high, and that during the battle he received 150 balls in his red shirt, but that after the battle was over he shook his shirt and all the balls fell out at his feet!

When the Constitution was proclaimed, nobody believed in the good faith of the King of Naples; not a shout was raised, not a flag displayed, not a cockade saw the light of day. The lazzaroni were the first to rise; they immediately went to all the police offices, where they burnt the furniture and documents, but at the same time abstained from all looting. One of the lazzaroni was bringing out a straw mattress to feed the fire, when a poor old woman who was passing said:

"Instead of burning that paillasse, please do give it to me."

The lazzarone was about to accede to her request when his comrades drew his attention to the fact that the paillasse was to be burnt, not given away. So it was thrown into the flames, and those who were engaged in the work of destruction subscribed to buy the old woman a new one.

The exiles, on their return, were quite surprised to see the progress that the lazzaroni had made. One of these emigrants told me that, wishing to pay a porter for carrying two muskets from the guard-house to his lodgings, the man refused money, saying that he, too, wished to serve his country.

Within the memory of the oldest lazzarone such an answer had never been known to be given by any member of that honourable corporation.

These men had a little good sport in hunting out the *sbirri* when they knew that Francis II had abandoned his police to them; but it was not for the purpose of assassinating them, or roasting them, or eating them, as they are said to have done in 1798. They contented themselves with handing them over to the soldiers, and they were subsequently deported.

Two hundred and fifty of these *sbirri* were sent to Capri, along with the executioner of Palermo and his assistant. This assistant was nicknamed "pull-feet," because it was his duty to hang on to the feet of the condemned, as soon as he had been hanged by the neck.

It seems that a few collisions took place, but these only resulted in bringing out a better feeling amongst the people in general, and even in the army. At Avellino, the Swiss and the Bavarians attacked a post held by the National Guard, and drove them out in the first instance; but the Guard, after having received reinforcements not only of their comrades, but also of some mounted carabineers, took the offensive and drove the Swiss and Bavarians out of Avellino.

A few days ago a performance took place for the benefit of the returned exiles. The hall was packed, and the receipts amounted to 1800 francs.

At Naples seven or eight large papers have been started. Five of them are reprinting "Les Mémoires de Garibaldi," which I published originally in the *Siècle*, and each of these journals heads every instalment with the notice that these memoirs are its "exclusive property."

These news-sheets of yesterday are as accomplished liars as if they had existed for half a century. What a happy augury for the future of Neapolitan civilisation!

20

CHAPTER XLIII

RIFLES AND CARBINES

On the morning of the 31st July we awoke in the harbour of Civita Vecchia. If there is a place in the world where the sullen, grumbling god named *ennui* reigns, it is certainly Civita Vecchia. Happily, since my tour in Sicily and the publication of my brochure "Le Pape devant les Evangiles," I am forbidden to go ashore. My former proscription, removed by Gregory XVI, has been renewed by Pius IX.

Convicts on the chain, priests reading their breviaries, soldiers fishing with lines, a sentinel walking up and down on guard over a dungeon—such are the sights afforded by the place.

Would you like some archæology?

The harbour was the work of Trajan, as many inscriptions still to be read on the stones attest. The fortress was built by the orders and at the cost of the house of the Farnese, to the succession of which Naples owes its finest statues. The squares on which the city was rebuilt are by Michael Angelo, the basin, for the galleys, is by Rezzonico of the time of Clement XIII, the fountain is by Lambertini of the time of Benedict XIV; finally, the arsenal was built under the pontificate of Alexander VII. So much I write for the benefit of those who, like myself, are not allowed to land.

For those who have the permission, there are to be seen, three miles away, the *Thermæ* of Titus; four miles off, the woods of Cornato, where are wild boar; and, on the right bank of the river, Etruscan tombs which go back to the Porsena's invasion to restore Tarquin.

One has to stay in the harbour from six o'clock in the morning until three o'clock in the afternoon. These nine hours mean nothing to me, because I usually employ them in writing a sixth volume, but, for those who have not this resource, they are cruel. On this occasion I am employing them in writing my latest chapter. In the Gulf of Naples, the solicitations of the officers of the police of his Majesty Francis II to induce me to go on shore did not leave me time to write it.

At three o'clock we left for Marseilles which we reached on Tuesday evening at nine o'clock. I went to my friend Falquet, Hôtel du Louvre. Nothing could be done that evening: I only let the officer who had the distribution of the rifles and carbines know that I had arrived and wished to see him.

There was nothing indiscreet in such wish. Commander R—— and

I first met on 26th July, 1830. We did so as he was coming with
Charras from taking the Babylone barracks, and as I was coming
from taking the Artillery Museum. On the point of his bayonet he
had the sleeve of a Swiss Guard, and I, on my head, had the helmet
of Francis I.[1]

He was with me in the morning. I began by referring to the liberty
granted to ship owners to take carbines; but he merely said:

"You have not heard, then?"

"Heard what?"

"The leave is withdrawn."

The reason for this withdrawal was this: it was feared that the
arms would reach the Druses, and that French carbines would
assist in the massacre of the Christians in Syria.

My best hope had gone, but there remained Zaoué, who, as you
know, is the Devisme[2] of Marseilles. I went to him. He made all
kinds of difficulties before admitting that he had, outside the town,
at the Customs, "some cases" of arms. I had to make to him all
kinds of "marivaudages" to induce him to open the cases. He had
as great a wish to sell me guns as I had to buy them, only he is a
merchant and I am not. I stated my wish, he did not state his.
At last, I chose 500 English carbines, and 950 rifles. The carbines
cost eighty francs each, the rifles forty-five francs. I also got 100,000
cartridges and 300,000 caps. The bill came to 90,000 francs. I
cashed my bill of exchange for 60,000—I gave from 7000 to 8000
francs to Rognetta, for the purchase of revolvers at Liège, I dis-
counted my three drafts on Constantinople, Smyrna and Alexandria,
and I directed the cases to be put on the first Messageries boat leaving
for Messina.[3]

It was known at Marseilles that I had been in Sicily with Garibaldi,
so many questions were put to me.

In the evening, I went into a café for an ice. A gentleman recognised me, took his hat, made a collection, almost inaudibly, and
then emptied the result before me.

"For Garibaldi," he said.

There were 620 francs. Yes, at *Marseilles*, moreover! And from
one café. It seemed incredible.

I spent 10,000 francs in purchasing single-barrelled rifles at twenty
francs apiece, and double-barrelled ones at forty; pistols at six or
eight francs, and revolvers at seventy, and at eighty francs each.

[1] Dumas relates this adventure in his "Memoirs," and a very thrilling one it is.
[2] Devisme was the best gun-maker in Paris.
[3] See the accounts and documents given in Appendix IV. These papers were
recovered some years ago from a cellar in Milan.

On the eve of my departure, a refugee, whom a want of confidence in Francis II kept abroad, came to see me. He had known Liborio Romano, when an exile like himself, in 1848, and now that his old companion was Minister of the Interior, he wished to learn of him whether he could return to Naples. He gave me a confidential letter. According to what Romano replied, he would either return to Naples, or remain at Marseilles, which latter course seemed to him to be the safest for the time being.

On Monday, the 10th August, I got on board the boat—the *Pausilippe*—that had brought me. To my great regret, my cargo of arms had been refused; it must follow me or perhaps precede me to Messina on the direct boat.

On reaching Civita Vecchia the *Pausilippe* had dropped anchor half a cable length from its sister, the *Quirinal*.

The two boats of the *Messageries* presented a singular appearance. The *Quirinal*—that is to say, the one coming away from Naples—had on board Filangieri, the Duke of Sangro, Prince Zurlo, Vincenzo Zurlo—a great friend of the Prince of Aquila, the Sicilian reactionary Sabona, the Marquis Tommasi (who must not be confounded with Doctor Tommasi), the Prince of Centola Doria, the Duke of San Cesario, and, lastly, Madame Tadolini.

The *Pausilippe*, the ship which was proceeding to Naples, had on board, in addition to myself, Luigi Mezzacapo, a Piedmontese general; Francesco Materazzi, a Piedmontese colonel; Dr. Tommasi (not to be confused with the Marquis Tommasi); Cavaliere Andrea Aquaviva; Cavaliere Capecelatro; Giuseppe Rotoli, ex-Minister of the Sicilian Government; and, lastly, the historian and novelist La Cecilia. These flights and returns had been caused by the spreading of a report that Garibaldi had landed in Calabria.

Let us speak about the fugitives first. At Naples, they are leaving by sections and classifications. On the 28th of June, the lowest rascals, the *sbirri*, and the assassins headed the exodus. Sixteen or seventeen of them were killed, and the rest interned at Capri.

Then came the highly-placed rogues: Aïossa, the Minister for Police, whom public detestation has exiled from Paris—which city, however, is the metropolis of those with good political digestions; Merenda, the recruiting officer of the San Fédisti; Maniscalco, the Torquemada of Sicily; and, lastly, Campagna, the torturer of the Calabrian, Agésilas Milano, from whom the inquisition extracted cries which were heard at the Russian embassy, but failed to extract a confession.

Nunziante, a son of the general who ordered Murat to be shot, is now forced to give up his sulphur mines at Vulcano and his beautiful new palace at Santa Maria di Capella. It is, however, true that before leaving he wrote a letter in which he describes himself as a persecuted patriot—this by way of a parting shot at Filangieri, the Minister of War, who is a son of the famous publicist, Gaetano Filangieri, and a really first-rate man, whatever people may say or think about him.

After the massacres of 1799—events which we have already recorded for France, and which we will record afresh for Naples—Gaetano Filangieri and his brother came to Paris and were presented to the First Consul, Bonaparte, who ordered their free admission to the Prytanée. Gaetano was a captain at Austerlitz, and a major in Murat's army in Spain. He was wounded at Panaro, rose to the rank of general, and was decorated by Murat. In 1821, his star began to fade: clouds of suspicion were veiling its light. The officers of the Guards, who were then under his command, refused to fight against the Austrians; but he did not order them to be shot. He remained in disgrace till 1830, when he came into favour again. He tried to form a Liberal Ministry, and create a patriot king. He failed. This was in the first year of the reign of Ferdinand II.[1] King Bomba, that tiger-wolf, the personification of cunning and ferocity, cajoled him. He then resigned, retaining, however, the command of the engineers and of the artillery. The year 1848 finds him engaged in political manœuvring, till he finally joined the reactionaries, out of jealousy towards Pepe, who had been sent to Lombardy in place of himself.

The 15th of May, 1848, was the red-letter day of reaction in Paris, Vienna, and Naples; and from that time forward he openly declared himself in its favour, and always remained faithful to its principles. He was in command of the army corps ordered to retake Messina, and proceeded to bombard that city with the artillery which he had himself organised, thus earning for his king the surname of "Bomba." He reconquered Sicily in the following year, and became its viceroy. This post he held till 1855, when he was replaced by the Prince of Castelcicala, in whose room, as I have already told you, I wrote the story of Garibaldi's conquest.

The Prince of Castelcicala, who is the son of the inquisitor of 1799, is a brave soldier. As a consequence of a wound received at Waterloo, he is obliged to wear a silver cap on the top of his head.

Returning to the career of Filangieri: he became a Minister of State under Francis, but gave dissatisfaction to all parties. He, however, became celebrated, ministerially speaking, by his famous decree

[1] Ferdinand II, King of the Two Sicilies, 1830–1859. Nicknamed "King Bomba," after the bombardment of Messina in the reconquest by Naples.

against depositing filth in front of the San Carlo Theatre. Finally, he handed in his resignation over the rejection by the King—so he alleges—at the beginning of the year, of a proposed form of constitution. He carries this about with him, as a sort of safeguard. He has shown it to us, and says that it is the same as the one which the King threw in his face, exclaiming: "I would sooner die than grant it!"

The King has since granted a constitution, and is not dead yet; to tell the truth, however, he is feeling very ill as a consequence.

Well, gentlemen, we wish you a pleasant journey! We heartily commend your prudence. The day before yesterday Garibaldi slept at Reggio: and you all left Naples the day after!

In the midst of all these happenings, Naples, as you may imagine, is very excited.

There are four parties in Naples. The biggest is that which favours annexation through Garibaldi. A smaller party is the one that favours annexation through Cavour; and a still smaller one is the Murat party. Finally, there is another party so small as to be microscopic, and that is the one supporting Francis II.

This last party makes much noise and commotion, so that you may realise that it still exists. It orders the moving to and fro of soldiers between Cape Miceno and Salerno; it orders purchases of revolvers at Marseilles; it gets cases of arms sent to the Count of Aquila, under the disguise of being perfumery or hardware; it makes purchases of kepis—similar to those worn by the civic guard—so as to enable its Sicilian *sbirri* to mingle, at any given moment, with the national militia. The people see all this being done, and they laugh at it.

All eyes are now fixed on Garibaldi, the new Colossus of Rhodes, who has one foot on Vesuvius and the other on Mount Etna, and between whose legs pass all ships, whether they come from Rome or from Messina.

The strangest things are told about him. He is known to be capable of achieving anything. All Naples is convinced that he was in the harbour a week ago, on board the *Adelaide*, and that he had a conference, lasting six hours, with Villamarina. I believe this news to be untrue. If he had come into port a week ago, he would have landed, and from that moment there would no longer have been a King of Naples. His coming will cause this last phantom of Bourbon royalty to vanish.

This is all the news I have collected at half-past nine in the morning. But I am expecting a friend who lives at Naples; we are going to be informed at first hand.

CHAPTER XLIV

"RECENTISSIME"

Bay of Naples, 13th August, 1860. 11 p.m.

COTTEREAU is the friend in question. He is a music publisher, and a nephew of the well-known painter. Well, then, in the first place Garibaldi has kept his word. He has not landed personally, as these bulletin-makers pretend, but he has sent Missori, the Colonel of the Guides, to prepare the way. You know this brave man who saved the General's life at Milazzo.

Missori, after embarking at the Faro, crossed the straits, landed between Scylla and Villa San Giovanni with 153 men, and immediately made his way to the mountains. News of the landing was conveyed to the King by the Minister of War, Pianell, to whom it had been sent by telegraph from Reggio; but Francis II had already received the news, personally, by secret code. The young king, without in the least losing his composure, nevertheless exhibited much astonishment at the news. He had been positively assured, he said, by France and by Piedmont that Garibaldi would not be allowed to cross the straits, and it was because of the confidence he had in these promises that he had consented, or nearly so, to the abandonment of Sicily.

With all possible haste he sent for M. Brenier,[1] who declined to take any responsibility for the promises made to the King, declaring at the same time that he knew nothing about these promises.

Francis II reflected for a moment, and then, addressing M. Brenier, said:

"What would you advise me to do?"

"Sire," answered M. Brenier, "since Your Majesty does me the honour to ask my advice, I will tell you that, were I in your place, I would put myself at the head of my army and I would march against Garibaldi, entrusting the province of Salerno to General Pianell, and the city of Naples to the National Guard. The presence of Your Majesty in Calabria would prevent defection in the army, and would spur your troops on to fight. In case of defeat, the city of Naples would be spared, and the King could then leave for Trieste or Vienna, thus quitting Naples with a claim to the gratitude of its people, on the last page of its history."

The King reflected for a moment, and then said:

"After the first success, I will do as you advise me, but there must be an initial success."

[1] French Minister at Naples.

As for the Ministers, except Pianell, they learnt of the landing, along with everyone else, when the news became public property.

They met in council, and Liborio Romano, who was the first to speak, said:

"As the situation is serious, and cannot fail to become more so, we must, in our capacity of responsible Ministers, ask the King to agree that we be consulted and heard in all matters pertaining to the war."

Spinelli, the President, having been charged with the immediate transmission of this resolution to the King, went to the palace and set forth to Francis II the object of his mission.

"Tell the Ministers," said the King, "that the Constitution of 1848 gives me the right of making peace and war, and that I shall maintain that right."

On receipt of this answer, Liborio Romano proposed to tender his resignation, and Martino and Garofalo joined him, but Spinelli, Lanzilli, and Pianell were of a different opinion. Romano next proposed to draw up an address asking the King, at all events, not to let Naples and its neighbourhood become a theatre of war.

Romano was requested to draw up a rough draft of the proposed address, his colleagues declaring that they could not pronounce an opinion on such a matter until they had had the opportunity of reading the document, as the wording was of the utmost importance in all such cases.

"If you do not wish to sign the address," said Romano, "I shall sign it myself, take it to the palace myself, and hand it to the King myself."

Such is a fairly accurate account of what took place on the 12th of August.

When I saw Romano thus declare himself, I did not hesitate to send him the letter from his exiled friend. Cottereau, who took it, jumped into a boat, and half-an-hour later returned, telling me that in all probability Romano would come to see me on board the *Pausilippe* before it left. In any case, his friend could return to Naples. Having seen Romano, Cottereau reported to me the *recentissime*, as they call it in Italy.

On the morning of the same day, orders had been given to complete arrangements for the despatch of 30,000 men into Calabria. The merchants have all placed their goods and money on board the ships in the harbour, paying at the rate of two and a half per thousand for insurance premium.

For part of the day I awaited the coming of Liborio Romano on board the *Pausilippe*, having no desire to land, in spite of the gracious invitations extended to me by the police. I have been content to answer that, having promised Garibaldi not to land at Naples before he did, I would keep my word.

One of these police functionaries, who had been most pressing, having heard what I had said, came to me and asked:

"When do you think he will be here?"

"Who, my friend?"

"General Garibaldi, of course."

"Ah, my friend," said I, "you must not ask too much of a man, however fabulous his achievements may be. He has landed in Calabria at Reggio—that is to say, at the extremity of the 'boot,' on the night of the 19th or 20th. Give him a fortnight to cross Calabria, Cilento, and Basilicata, and an hour and a half to come from Salerno to Naples."

"Well, sir, let him hurry, for we are awaiting his arrival with much impatience."

And then the official retired.

General de Benedictis, father of the captain of engineers who was the first to go over to Garibaldi, has sent a despatch from Giulia Nova, saying that, having been advised by telegraph from Brindisi that an Italian squadron is cruising along the coast of Apulia and is moving towards the Abruzzi, he has changed his strategical positions by shifting his troops to Pescara and establishing his headquarters at Giulia Nova.

Another despatch of yesterday, dated from Palmi, and signed by General Melendez, announces that a Neapolitan cruiser, commanded by Salazao, by keeping between Villa San Giovanni and Reggio, has prevented 150 boats laden with troops from leaving the Faro. He adds that if it could be guaranteed that there would be no landing for the next two nights, he could, with the forces at his disposal, destroy the Garibaldians already landed, and also the Calabrian bands which yesterday were 200, to-day are 2000, and steadily increasing in this ratio. "Last night," he adds, "they consumed forty-three sheep."

A third despatch from the Captain of the merchantman, the *Vesuvio*, in the service of the Neapolitan Government, engaged for towing two large vessels laden with coal and bound for the citadel of Messina, states that he was obliged to fire three guns upon a flotilla proceeding towards the coast of Calabria in order to clear a passage through them.

I forgot to tell you that General Bartolo Marra, having published an order of the day in which he expresses his regret at having to command the same troops as he had commanded at Palermo, where they had behaved more like brigands than soldiers, has been arrested by the King's order and taken to fort Saint Elmo, where he now is. General Bartolo Marra used to command a division in Calabria.

The battery composed of the Bavarians—who have not been disbanded, in spite of Article X of the Constitution—was removed yesterday to the barracks at the gates of the town in the Granili quarter. This step has considerably increased public alarm. The 5000 men who compose the foreign legion are still at Nocera.

The elections are to take place, should the moment be favourable, on Sunday the 19th; but it is probable that the revolution will break out on Saturday, and that Garibaldi himself will head the electors. Meanwhile two electoral councils have been formed: one at the Calabritto Palace, with Pietro Leopardi as president; the other at Vico delle Campane alla Toledo, presided over by Orionzo Costa, the celebrated naturalist. The two committees have drawn up almost identical lists of candidates who support Italian unity; but that of Costa is perhaps the more advanced. The same committees have initiated a very active correspondence, and have sent commissioners to organise provincial committees. They make extensive use of the telegraph.

The Government has given up taking any part in the elections, and, on the 11th of August, has notified supervisors that it had no candidates to put forward.

The King is scared by the two committees, and especially by Costa's, which he regards as Garibaldian pure and simple. He went out yesterday, after shutting himself up in his palace for twenty days; but it was only for the purpose of cantering briskly up and down the Chiaïa.

It is probably his last ride here!

At four o'clock, Romano sent to tell me that he could not come, his every minute being occupied.

At five o'clock, we weigh our anchor and leave.

The next day, on awakening, we found ourselves between Scylla and the Faro. Both land and sea have a most war-like appearance. Nearly 200 boats lie side by side on the beach ready to leave. There are plenty of men, but they are under huts and are protected by a battery of formidable cannon. Above it floats the green, red and white flag. So much for the land.

Two Neapolitan steam-boats, the *Fulminante* and the *Tancredi*, are cruising in the strait at full speed, making curves like skaters to prevent embarkations. So much for the sea.

But how is it that the two steam-boats pass within two hundred paces of the battery without firing on it? And how is it that when they pass, the battery does not fire on them? I wonder whether the battery and the boats are not better friends in reality than they appear to be. With the help of God we shall see.

We drop anchor in the port of Messina at seven o'clock in the morning. I have kept my word to the day and to the hour. Garibaldi has kept his in waiting for me. Only, to announce himself in Calabria he has sent Missori and Cattabeni.

CHAPTER XLV

OLD ACQUAINTANCES

SCARCELY had we cast anchor, when the Captain of my yacht
hurried on board the *Pausilippe* to impart to me important news.
The important news was that an *aide-de-camp* of the King of Piedmont
had come to forbid Garibaldi to land in Calabria, and had ordered
him, in the name of Victor Emmanuel, to go to Turin to give an
account of his recent doings.

I laughed in the face of the Captain.

The Captain then assured me very seriously that the news was
absolutely reliable, for he had it from the French Consul, M. Boulard.
This, however, did not change my opinion in the least, seeing that I
find diplomatic agents are the last persons to get information, and
are always the worst informed.

"Well, M. Boulard is so well informed," answered Captain Beaugrand, "that he has even given me the name of the vessel on which
Garibaldi left, on his return to Genoa."

"And what is the name of the ship?"

"The *Washington*."

"My dear Captain, Garibaldi would never have chosen a ship with
such a name in which to make a retreat. I am still convinced that
Garibaldi has not gone to Genoa."

"At all events," continued the Captain, to whom it was painful to
cast a doubt upon news proceeding from official lips, "at all events,
no one knows where he is."

"Captain," I replied, "Suetonius, in speaking of Cæsar, says: 'He
did not give out on what days he would march, or on what days he
would fight; but requested everything to be ready for any moment.
He warned his troops not to lose sight of him, and then, all of a
sudden, would disappear, by day or by night, journeying a hundred
miles in twenty-four hours, only to make his presence known in some
place where he was least expected, like the bursting of a clap of
thunder.' My dear Captain, there is a good deal of Cæsar about
Garibaldi. And now, let us talk about the *Mersey*."

The *Mersey* was the vessel by which my arms were to be forwarded
direct to Messina. We could see the smoke of its funnel on the other
side of the Faro: it would therefore be in harbour in less than half-
an-hour.

I now left the *Pausilippe* and went on board my yacht, the *Emma*.

No sooner had my arrival become known, than all my acquaint-ances from Messina hastened one after another to communicate to me the "extraordinary news," but the more they repeated it, and the more they affirmed its authenticity, the less I was inclined to believe it.

One of my visitors, in order to overcome my obstinacy, ended by telling me that he had the fact from Garibaldi himself.

After this, if there was still any lingering doubt in my mind, that doubt vanished. It then began to dawn upon me that Garibaldi had put this rumour about in order to impose on the Neapolitan Govern-ment, so that he might land, without being interfered with, at any place that seemed good to him. Besides, I remembered that, at the time of my going to Genoa, Bertani told me that he was going to take 6000 men to Garibaldi, and, on the day following our con-versation, he had, as a matter of fact, left with 6000 men for Sardinia. I also called to mind that, two days after my arrival at Marseilles, I received a note from this same Bertani, a communication worded thus:

"I am just leaving. In my absence make any arrangements with my deputies."

In all probability Garibaldi had gone to meet this 6000 men either at Milazzo, or at Palermo, or even at Salerno. If he had really come to Naples, or rather to the bay of Naples, on board the Piedmontese vessel, the *Adelaide*, he had made himself acquainted with the spirit of the citizens, and in that case the odds were that, in order to avoid crossing Calabria with 6000 men, he would land at Sapri or Salerno. I, however, kept all these conjectures to myself. If I had guessed aright, Garibaldi would only desire the more that people should think he had gone to Genoa when he was drawing near to Cilento or the Basilicata.

The *Mersey* was now in port and had cast anchor. I sent a messenger on board. The arms were safely there.

I could not, however, get away from the fact that I was in an awkward position. You will recollect that I had given a bill of exchange for 40,000 francs; and this had still to be met. As I had barely 10,000 francs on board the *Emma*, I could not honour my signature, in Garibaldi's absence.

I made inquiries, and learnt that Medici was at Messina.

I was saved.

I hastened to him and informed him that I had brought with me 1000 rifles and 550 carbines.

"Have you any cartridges?" he inquired of me anxiously.

"Ten thousand."

"And percussion-caps?"

"Fifty thousand."

"Then we are all right," exclaimed Medici. "We are short of cartridges and our caps have got damp. We are going to pay you the 40,000 francs and take over the guns."

"You are going to land in Calabria then?" I asked.

"Why not?"

"Yes, but what about this order recalling Garibaldi to Genoa?"

"Did you believe it?" said Medici, looking me straight in the face.

"Not for a moment, thank goodness."

"That's all right, then."

"But where is the General?"

"Oh, as to that, nobody knows. The day before yesterday, he embarked on the *Washington*. He simply handed over the command to Sirtori and went away."

"And there is no news of him since then?"

"Absolutely none; only, I received, about half-an-hour ago, an order to be in readiness to leave this evening."

"For what place?"

"I have not the slightest idea."

"Well, let us lose no time. My carbines and rifles will be useful to you: they must be at the customs-house now."

We then called on M. Pié, agent for the *Messageries Impériales* at Messina, and there we met the correspondent authorised to present the bill for payment. He was taken to the office of the Minister for Finance, where the matter was settled: how, I do not know; that was not my affair. The essential thing for me was that the bill should be met.

Two hours later Medici had the arms collected from the customs-house.

As soon as this matter was ended, I called a carriage and told the coachman to drive to the Faro.

I did not expect to remain long at Messina, for I had a conviction that Garibaldi had designs on either Sapri or Salerno. I did not know when I should return here, but I had to pay two visits to friends before I left: the first, at Della Pace, to see Captain Arena, who commanded the little *speronare* upon which, in 1835, I made my voyage to Sicily; and the second, in the village of Faro, to my old friend Paul de Flotte, who had the command of the flotilla of boats which I had noticed when doubling the western cape of Messina.

On each of my preceding visits to this town I made inquiries about Captain Arena, but I only got very vague answers concerning him. Unfortunately, the news about his son and about our old pilot was more precise: the former died before reaching manhood, and Nunzio did not live to be an old man.

This time I put so much persistence and importunity into my inquiries that the inhabitants of this village Della Pace, after a good deal of cross-questioning of each other, finally informed me that Captain Giuseppe Arena lived with his wife, two sons and his daughter at a house called "Paradiso." As I had now passed a good quarter of a league beyond "Paradiso," I continued my journey, with the intention of paying my visit on the way back.

The Faro, with its camp of about 12,000 men, presented a singular appearance. The word "camp" is used, for lack of any other, to designate a large assemblage of armed men; still, "camp" presents to the mind the idea of an enclosure formed by trenches or palisades, containing a certain number of tents or huts, with straw beds inside.

Garibaldi's camp offered none of those comforts and conveniences which are to be seen in other camps. As the General always sleeps either on the bare ground or on the sands of the shore, or on the pavement of the streets, using his saddle for a pillow, he does not understand that the soldier can want anything other than what suffices for himself.

His 12,000 men are scattered about this spot, colouring the landscape with their red shirts, which, dotted amongst the trees, give the effect of poppies in a field of corn.

The water is brackish and there is none too much of it; but, what of that? they have the wines of the country to set things right.

I tried to find de Flotte amongst all these red-shirts. Everybody knows him, because he is always seen to be the first and foremost under fire. He, however, was not in the camp.

I wended my way back and called at "Paradiso" as I passed; but Giuseppe Arena was not at home, either. I was received by his wife, whom I had seen twenty-five years previously, suckling an infant of eight months. The woman is now getting old, and the child must be a fine big fellow.

Madame Arena promised me that her husband would come and see me next morning on board my yacht. And so it turned out: the very first person that my eyes fell on, when I went up on deck next morning, was my worthy Captain Arena. The lapse of twenty-five years had whitened his beard and hair, but his cheerful face was unaltered. It was ever serene, even in the midst of storms. And why should it have altered? He had been consistently lucky and prosperous. Instead of having one vessel, he was now master of three. His ambition had never soared higher than that. He brought with him one of the sailors of our old crew, Giovanni, who was after every pretty girl in those days and was a good dancer—he could even cook, if necessity arose. He was the sole survivor of our old crew.

Giovanni had not made a fortune—not he. Attired in torn trousers and a shirt in tatters, he picked up a living by doing the meaner commissions and odd jobs of the port in a patched-up old boat.

I listened to the history of his woes. One of his daughters had married, seven or eight months previously, a young fellow as poor as she was herself, so poor that they had not even a mattress to lie upon. I gave Giovanni a mattress and two louis.

Whilst in the midst of recounting these memories of old times and companions, I saw the gallant figure of Paul de Flotte approaching. I had not seen de Flotte since 1848.[1] His hair and beard were grey. He too had grown old in appearance, but not in the same way as Captain Arena. By the wrinkles which furrowed his forehead you readily understood that he had encountered more stormy than calm weather: proscription, exile, home-sickness, political deceptions, recurring despair had all left their marks on the brow of one who was ever loyal and lofty in character and ideals.—It is brows such as his that are scarred by the bolts of fate.

Poor de Flotte! he told me the story of all his mortifications. The General had been kindness itself to him; but the fact that he was a Frenchman was sufficient to arouse the antipathy of ignorant people towards him. Italy, in respect of fraternal feeling for other nations, has a long way to go. But let us continue to hope! The Italians have already overcome the greatest difficulty of all: they have ceased to hate one another.

What weighed on de Flotte's mind more than anything else was to find himself left in arrears for his men's pay. Even those who had money could not procure anything at the Faro camp, as I myself had seen clearly the evening before; how much worse then must be the plight of those who had no money?

De Flotte wanted 1000 francs to extricate himself from his difficulties. I, who have often been in want of twenty francs, happened to have 1000. Needless to say, I gave them to him. As I did so, a ray of unspeakable joy lit up his countenance; but as he feared that the municipal treasury of Messina or of Palermo might put difficulties in the way of repaying me, he handed me a draft on the committee founded in Paris to promote the cause of Italian independence, which had authorised him to have recourse to them in case of necessity. Nevertheless, he made no use of this credit, until he had devoted 3000 francs of his own money to the good of the cause. Such

[1] Dumas refers to the French Revolution of 1848, in which de Flotte took part.

are the profits which we Frenchmen reap when we wage war in
defence of a principle or to further the triumph of an idea.

Then he gripped my hand and said: "Farewell!"

"*Au revoir,*" I rejoined, stressing the words.

"It is not probable," said he, "so adieu."

A week later he fell mortally wounded at Selano, and Garibaldi in
his next order of the day made public the following tribute to his
memory:

"*Order of the Day, 24th August,* 1860.

"We have lost de Flotte.

"The epithets, brave, honest, and true democrat, are too feeble to do justice to
this matchless soul.

"De Flotte, a noble son of France, was one of those exceptional beings that no
one country is entitled to claim as its exclusive possession. No, de Flotte belongs
to the whole human race; for in his eyes that country was his country, wherever
there was an oppressed people fighting for its liberties. De Flotte died for Italy,
and fought for her as he would have fought for France. This illustrious man has
given us a precious pledge for that brotherhood of nations which is the ultimate
goal of humanity. Struck down in the ranks of the Alpine *Cacciatori,* he was,
with many another of his brave countrymen, a representative of that generous
nation which, although it may halt temporarily in its progress, is, nevertheless,
destined by Providence to march in the van of the peoples and civilisation of the
world.

"G. GARIBALDI."

It was in this fight at Selano that de Flotte touched a weapon for
the first time. In all the previous battles at which he had been
present he remained with his arms folded in the thick of the firing,
watching and encouraging his men. I had offered him both carbine
and revolver, but he refused them with these prophetic words:

"On the day that I kill, that same day I shall be killed myself."

In the attack on Selano he took a rifle and killed two Neapolitans,
but was himself killed on that battlefield. The big ball of a field-
musket hit him above the temple, inflicting a wound such as might
have been caused by a shell. He fell, muttering a few words, and
died without a struggle.[1]

On him was found a quarter of the sum of money which I had lent
him!

Let us conclude our tribute to de Flotte with one more illustration
of his wonderful *sangfroid* and bravery. It happened only a few days
before his lamented death. Feeling bored by the inaction at Messina
during Garibaldi's absence, he took a dozen men, all good fellows
ready for any enterprise, six Englishmen and six Frenchmen, and in
broad daylight set out to effect a spectacular landing on the Neapolitan coast. He was received by the fire of 300 to 400 Neapolitans.

---

[1] Paul de Flotte is the hero of "Souvenirs et Aventures d'un Volontaire
Garibaldien" (Paris, 1861). The spot where he was buried has been devastated
by earthquake.

This, however, did not prevent his setting foot on shore and opening fire on the enemy. The combat lasted two to three hours. Attracted by the firing of the Neapolitan platoon on shore, the three Neapolitan steam vessels which were cruising in the straits arrived to join in the fun, but when they saw a dozen men fighting against 400, they remained mere passive spectators of the fight.

After having killed or wounded ten of the enemy, de Flotte re-embarked his men, with one Englishman and one Frenchman wounded by the same bullet which passed through the thigh of the first and bruised the thigh of the second.

He now had to pass between the three Neapolitan cruisers. He steered straight for them. The cruisers, astonished at the bravery of this handful of men, opened a passage for them and saluted as they went through.

The Neapolitan navy is patriotic. Perhaps all its officers will not follow the example of Anguissola, but very few will give orders to fire upon us.[1]

[1] This adventure, which would otherwise seem almost incredible, is narrated at length in the book just cited.

Note.—The *Washington*, which is referred to in this chapter, had, together with two other steamers named the *Oregon* and the *Franklin*, been purchased from a French company and rechristened by their nominal owner, De Rohan, an American. They were destined to carry Medici and his men to Sicily.

CHAPTER XLVI

SALERNO

The "Emma," Bay of Salerno, 20th August, Noon

WE anchored off Salerno two hours ago. No news of Garibaldi yet, but his arrival is expected hourly. The Royalist troops keep on passing through Salerno on their way into Calabria. Two or three companies are all that now remain in the town. The National Guard is now organised. It consists of seven companies, commanded by patriotic officers chosen by their fellow-citizens, and is said to be well armed.

I expect to have some reliable news now; for my Captain and Brother John have both landed. The Bishop of Salerno was born at Marsala and happens to be not only a fellow-countryman of Brother John, but also a schoolfellow.

It is said that the young men of the seminary have risen in revolt, have driven out their teachers and taken up arms. If this is true, I shall put on red stockings and place myself at their head.

I am sending one of my secretaries to Naples to get news of what is going on in the capital, and also to bring back a friend, with whose help I can carry out some propaganda work on the road from Salerno to Naples.

2 o'clock.

Brother John has come back triumphant. Instead of the martyrdom which he expected, he received an ovation. He was followed by four boats so heavily laden that they were ready to sink. Thirty of these Salernitans have just drunk the health of Garibaldi in the King of Naples' champagne glasses.

The police and customs officers have ceased to exist: they died a natural death, so it is said; but would it not be more appropriate if we could say, like rats in a hole? As for the garrison, excepting two companies, it has left for Potenza, at which place, however, a revolt has taken place, involving the death of two or three gendarmes. So, you see, the Basilicata is following the example of Calabria.

We are now completely masters of Salerno. Only let Garibaldi come, and the shouts of joy which will welcome his appearance will resound even to Naples.

I have posted a sailor on the look-out in the shrouds, so sure am I that Garibaldi is at this very moment on the watery high-road that leads from Milazzo to Salerno.

4 o'clock.

News at last!

A rumour has got about that Garibaldi is on board my yacht. All the boats of the harbour are gliding in the direction of the *Emma* like a flight of sea-gulls. Women, too, are among the crowd. The *Emma* is completely surrounded; and I am compelled to pledge my word that I am alone. The Salernitans believe me; but General Scotti, the Neapolitan General, is not so credulous. He has brought out the whole garrison, and drawn it up in battle array in a semi-circle extending for a distance of two kilometres between the head-quarters and the railway. There is not more than half a rifle shot between us.

Loud cries are now heard in the town:

"Long live Garibaldi! Long live Victor Emmanuel!"

Meanwhile a deputation of the municipality makes its way to the *Emma* and solemnly declares its allegiance to the Italian cause. Salerno is illuminated like a fairy palace. General Romano lights up his house like the others; the headquarters, occupied by the troops, alone remaining in darkness. So I got out from my powder-magazine some Bengal lights and Roman candles in three colours, and with these the *Emma* was illuminated in her turn, amid great cheering from the townspeople.

The fête lasted till midnight. Ices and cakes were sent on board the *Emma*. I ordered up from the cellar some Folliet-Louis champagne and also some of Greno. The cries of "Viva l'Italia! Viva Garibaldi!" were loud enough to deafen the Neapolitan soldiers, who looked on at us quite dumbfounded, and listened quite scared.

My secretary returned at eleven o'clock by the last train. This is the news which he brings:

"A telegraphic despatch of yesterday's date announces that either Garibaldi or Medici has landed at Reggio."

The despatch, however, is wrong. It is neither Garibaldi nor Medici who has landed at Reggio; it is Bixio.

Medici and Garibaldi, Cæsar and Labienus, are elsewhere.

A despatch which arrived at four o'clock announces that fighting has been going on since ten o'clock this morning at Cape dell' Armi, which is near to Reggio.

General Florès, writing from Bari, says that on the 18th the in-habitants of Proggia and the 120 dragoons of the garrison united in crying "Viva Vittorio Emmanuele!" He sent two companies of the 13th against them, but they too joined the insurgents.

He is asking for Bavarians and Croatians to deal with the situation!

General Salazao, commandant of the naval station at Messina, also writes to the Government saying that Garibaldi has just been joined by the steamship, *Queen of England*, carrying eighteen guns and 18,000 rifles. He therefore demands prompt assistance. Orders were given to despatch the frigate, *Borbona;* but just as they were to get up steam, the engine-room men disappeared. So you see that on all sides the fall of the Bourbons is in process of being accomplished.

Here, however, we have the official version of the latest news from Potenza:

> "*To the Committee of National Unity of Naples.*
> "*Potenza, 18th August,* 1860.

"This morning, 18th of August, the gendarmes, numbering about 400, under the command of Captain Castagna assembled in the square at Potenza, and the populace compelled them to shout:

"'Long live Garibaldi! Long live United Italy!'

"Those who were in the front rank at once responded to the cry; but the captain shouted: 'Long live the King! death to the Nationalists!' and ordered his men to fire on the people and the national guard. The latter, although not very numerous, returned the fire instantly, and with admirable courage forced the gendarmerie to flee, with a loss of seven killed, three wounded, and fifteen prisoners. The rest of them are gradually giving themselves up.

"In the skirmish three of the national guard were slightly wounded, one of these being the brave Dominico Alcesta, who was injured on the temple. During the struggle some gendarmes entered the house of a poor couple of the working classes, and after killing a child, wounded both father and mother.

"At the present moment the revolution is in full tide, and masses are pouring in from all parts of the province.

"A provisional government will be proclaimed this evening.

"The arms expected have not yet arrived. We cannot understand this culpable delay, I do not say on your part, but on part of those who have made us so many promises. Fortunately, however, we have some sporting-guns, daggers, knives, and even nails are weapons in the hands of a people determined to win their liberty.

"And what, may I ask, are you doing at Naples? What is going on at Avellino, in the Abruzzi, at Campo-Basso, at Salerno? Rise up; imitate us; the supreme moment has arrived! In the name of Italy, to arms!

> "(*Signed*) COLONEL BOLDONI.
> "MAGNANA, Lawyer."

Tuesday, 21st August, 5 a.m.

On rising, I saw the quays of Salerno had been converted into a place for a bivouac. Four thousand Bavarians and Croatians had arrived during the night. A dozen pieces of ordnance placed in position in front of the Government offices do me the honour of turning their mouths towards my yacht.

If you were on board, my illustrious friend, Garibaldi, as was believed yesterday, these 4000 men would either present arms, or give them up to you, and these twelve guns would chant a fiery *Te Deum* in honour of King Victor Emmanuel.

8 o'clock a.m.

These 4000 Bavarians and Croats are intended to suppress the insurrection at Potenza; but they shall remain at Salerno as long as I remain here. And I shall remain long enough to give the messengers whom we are despatching to the mountains adequate time to warn our men of their arrival.

Ten thousand *Picciotti* are only awaiting a signal ; and they shall certainly get it, as long as I can keep the Bavarians and Croats in sight. It is a hundred to one that this column does not reach its destination.

I shall leave for Naples at about 2 o'clock in the afternoon.

2 o'clock p.m.

I am leaving, after having put into the hands of our brethren forty double-barrelled sporting guns, and a dozen carbines. You see it was well worth while for the customs officers and police to keep an eye on us.

CHAPTER XLVII

THE LANDING IN CALABRIA

The Bay of Naples, 24th of August, Morning

MATTERS at Salerno are steadily getting more serious. I went there, as I have already told you, to bring together the mountain chieftains, and to get them to post themselves and their men in echelons on the road leading from Salerno to Potenza. The opposition that was likely to be offered was such that General Scotti did not even attempt to force the passage; so, instead of continuing his march, he remained at Salerno. The revolution at Potenza was thus accomplished without any difficulties. But this hesitation on the part of General Scotti has led to something of a much more serious nature: the Bavarians and the Swiss who are under his command, being disheartened by the hostile attitude of the inhabitants of the country round about them, have made me an offer to desert with their arms and baggage, in consideration of a payment of five ducats per man. There are 5000 of them, so it is a matter of 25,000 ducats.

I have not, as you know, 25,000 ducats to give them; but I have just opened a subscription in Naples which will, I hope, yield one-fifth of that sum during the day.

Noon.

A courier, who has just arrived from Salerno, tells me that my men there have been denounced, and that my recruiting officer, a young man belonging to the town, has received a hundred blows with a stick by order of General Scotti. The whole town is in a ferment. On all hands applications are being made to me for arms.

I forgot to tell you that, just as I was leaving Salerno, the French vessel *Le Prony* entered the harbour. M. de Missiessi, the Captain of the vessel, was exasperated when he learnt of the reception which had been accorded to me on the previous day, and of the part I had taken in the insurrection which had penned up General Scotti and his 5000 men in Salerno. He was so angry that he went so far as to tell Dr. Wielandt that if he, the Captain of the *Prony*, had arrived whilst I was still in the harbour, he would have had me arrested and would have seized my yacht.

As soon as I heard this, I visited the flagship of Admiral Le Barbier de Tinan, who, however, was not on board.[1] In his absence, I

---

[1] Some French newspaper—a Marseilles journal, I believe—has said that the Admiral "refused to see me." Whatever paper is the author of this statement, it has uttered a falsehood. (Author's note.)

begged the Captain and the Admiral's *aide-de-camp* to receive my declaration.

This declaration was to the effect that I did not recognise the right of the Captain of the *Prony* to arrest me, or to seize my vessel, and that I would pledge my word to them to blow out the brains of the first officer or man who should endeavour to carry out the orders of the captain of the *Prony*. The views of the flagship officers were entirely in accord with mine upon this matter, and they suggested that the Captain's ill-humour was due to his Legitimist opinions. They, however, added that though they were quite ready to deny that the Captain of the *Prony* had any right to arrest me, they, nevertheless, felt bound to warn me that individual acts of hostility on my part against the King of Naples might prevent M. Le Barbier de Tinan affording me his protection, if the King of Naples should proceed to any act of violence against me.

I answered these gentlemen by saying that I had not come to claim protection at the hands of my own countrymen—in fact, I very heartily renounced it; and assured them that if I did have need of any protection—an event I did not believe likely—I should have recourse to the English Admiral. They then advised me to leave Naples, but I responded to this counsel by anchoring within half a pistol shot of the fort.

I have been trying to think out a plan for sailing under a flag which is banned by the Government, and I now think I have found it. It is possible that, as I am a citizen of Palermo, Caltanisetta, Girgenti, and Catania, you will see me arrive one day at Palermo flying the Sardinian flag.

And now let us talk a little of Naples. Naples is now in a state of inconceivable excitement. The news of the capture of Reggio has struck terror into the Government. The King is making a big show of bombs and shells at the castle of St. Elmo, and is swearing that he will not leave one stone standing upon another in Naples. Let us hope that this is only a drunken oath. Blood, it is said, causes drunkenness more quickly than wine, and his Majesty is still drunk with the blood of Palermo.

Going back to the events of a previous chapter, it will be remembered that we left Liborio Romano proposing two plans to his colleagues, both of which were rejected by them.

His first proposition was to send in his resignation; and the second was to send a message to the King urging him to spare Naples such a disaster as civil war. The day after that on which he put forward these proposals, Liborio Romano saw the King.

"What do you think of the situation?" asked Francis II.

"Sire," answered Liborio, " I think that the moment Garibaldi in person lands in Calabria and begins to march on Naples, defence of any description will be impossible, because it is not Garibaldi who is fighting against you, it is not Victor Emmanuel who is pressing you sorely, but because fatality attaches to your name and decrees that every Bourbon must abdicate. Sire, whether right or wrong, public opinion is now in such a state that it will never rally round you again."

"That is true," said the King; "but that is not my fault: it is the fault of those who reigned before me."

"And yet, sire," said Liborio Romano, "there was a time when you might have rallied men of all parties round you. If, on mounting the throne, you had given the people that very constitution which is now bringing about your downfall, you would have been saved."

The King then placing a hand on his Minister's shoulder said :

"I give you my word as a king that at one time I had such an intention, but I was prevented from carrying it out by Austria and by my advisers."

(These advisers were Ferdinando Troïa, Scousa, Rossica, and Carafa.)

"To-day the die is cast," the King went on to say, "and we must play the game to the finish."

"Will your Majesty allow me to ask what it is that you expect to accomplish?"

"War shall decide. Fortune cannot always be against me."

"Your Majesty knows how ill-disposed is your army towards you?"

"I believe that, at the very worst, I have 60,000 men upon whom I can rely."

Romano gave a significant movement of the head and shoulders which was as good as saying in reply : "I believe your Majesty is very much mistaken." The King, seeing and understanding Romano's gesture, did not wish to continue the discussion, so he extended his hand for the formal salutation, thus intimating that the interview was at an end.

Immediately after this came the news of the landing of Garibaldi in person, and of the battle and capture of Reggio.

This event happened whilst I was waiting for him at Salerno. Where was he then? Well, I am going to tell you.

Garibaldi had really gone on board the *Washington;* only, instead of proceeding to Turin to give an account of his conduct, he went to survey the coast of Sicily from Cape Vaticano as far as Paola. When this was concluded, he continued his journey, and landed at the Bay of Arancio in Sardinia, but did not find there what he had expected, that is, something like an army. The men who had been taken on board the *Iser* had mutinied, gone ashore, and then disbanded themselves. From the Bay of Arancio he went on to the island of Maddalena, where he coaled; and then, in a moment of doubt, maybe, of disgust, he went to spend a day at the isle of Caprera, on the granite soil of which the giant, worn out by the fatigues of strife, goes to recuperate his strength from time to time, and whither he will return, if ingratitude and exile overtake him.

Returning to the *Washington*, he touched at Cagliari, and from there sailed for Palermo, where he spent a day in arranging his plans and giving orders. After this, he changed from the *Washington*, and went on board the *Amazon*, in which he proceeded to Milazzo, doubtless wishing to come into contact with the land of victory, as an augury of future success. Here he changed his vessel once again, and went to Messina on board the *Black Fish*. He stayed there but a few minutes, and then proceeded to Taormina, where Bixio's column was. These troops were to be the principal factor in the landing operations.

Garibaldi had arrived at a rather awkward moment, as will be gathered from the following.

The *Torino*, which came from Genoa with part of Bertani's men, whom it had conveyed to Palermo, and the *Franklin*, with men taken on board at Palermo, had received orders to coast round Sicily, by way of Marsala and Girgenti, and then to await the General's arrival at Taormina, as he was expected to take the route of Cephala, the Faro, and Messina.

These two vessels started: the *Franklin* commanded by Orrigoni, an old companion of Garibaldi's exile, and the *Torino* captained by Berlingieri. They were to be escorted by the Sardinian steamer, the *Mozambano*. The last-named left the Gulf of Palermo along with them and escorted them for some time; but when night came on she disappeared off Cape San Vito. All, however, went well as far as Syracuse, where the *Torino* signalled to the *Franklin* to stop. The *Franklin* stopped. Then a boat from the *Torino* boarded her. It brought Colonel Eberhard, commander of the forces on board the *Torino*, who came to propose to Orrigoni that the landing should be at Nato instead of at Taormina, as he had learnt that all the coast between Scaletta and Taormina was guarded by Neapolitan cruisers.

As Orrigoni doubted the accuracy of this report, it was proposed to stop at Catania to seek information. Orrigoni seemed to agree to the proposal; but on reaching Catania, instead of steering for the town, he continued straight on for his destination. The *Torino* hesitated for a moment, and then followed the leader. Just as they arrived off the roadstead of Taormina, the *Franklin* broke the beam of her engine, and came to a standstill. At first, it was hoped that it would be possible to repair the damage out at sea, but Orrigoni, fearing that he might be driven ashore by the currents, anchored in twenty-three fathoms of water. The shock caused by dropping the anchor made the timbers of the old *Franklin* tremble; and in the morning it was discovered that the vessel had sprung a considerable leak. The captain immediately ordered all pumps to be brought into action, including those of the fire-engines, and hastened to Taormina to inform General Bixio of what had happened. Bixio, who was an able naval officer, immediately visited the *Franklin* in order to judge for himself as to the state of the vessel. In spite of the pumps, the water was gaining the upper hand, so it was decided that the *Franklin* should be taken in tow by the *Torino*, and, in order not to lose time, the anchor was attached to a buoy.

The *Franklin* thus towed, and also aided by her own canvas, succeeded in coming within half a cable's length of the shore. From there, all on board were disembarked in *felucci*, *speronari*, and other local boats which Bixio sent out. The pumps still continued to work, but the water was not mastered. Towards two o'clock the General suddenly made his appearance. On being informed of the state of affairs, he ordered someone to dive and find out the position of the leak; but as nobody seemed in a hurry to carry out the order he said: "Very well, I will dive myself." The captain and his lieutenants, however, immediately divested themselves of their clothing and took the plunge.

The situation of the leak was found to be in the middle of the ship. It was temporarily stopped with a mixture of mud and cow-dung spread on a lattice of osier twigs.[1] The pumping was then renewed, and it was soon seen that the water was diminishing.

"It is all right now," said the General; "all on board again."

But as the men who had been landed hesitated about again going aboard a vessel which had become very near sinking, the General exclaimed: "Captain Orrigoni, I am going to embark in your vessel."

No one hesitated any longer; in fact, everyone was anxious to go on the *Franklin;* so much so that 1200 men went on board, and this was 200 or 300 more than it would have been prudent to carry when she was in a perfectly sound state. Three thousand one hundred men were aboard the *Torino*. Garibaldi took command of the former, and Nino Bixio of the latter vessel.

They left Taormina on the evening of the 19th of August at ten o'clock, and made for Melito, a little town situated between Cape dell' Armi and Cape Spartivento, at the southern extremity of

---

[1] It was Garibaldi who devised this means of stopping the leak, and very proud he was of the achievement.

Calabria. Contrary to all expectation, this place was reached at two o'clock a.m., without any accident. In spite of her patch, the *Franklin* still continued to make water, and was finally so heavily water-logged that the men had to stand on the deck and balance themselves according to the rolling of the vessel.

On coming alongside, the *Torino*, which during the previous part of the journey had remained in the rear, now put on full speed, passed the *Franklin*, and then struck a rock. There was not a moment to be lost. The *Torino*, in her turn, had received a mortal wound. The *Franklin* got out her boats, and assisted in landing the troops from the *Torino*.

After two hours' work, the landing was finished; but, although relieved of her burden, the *Torino* could not put to sea again. The General ordered every effort to be made to effect this object, if possible, but the *Franklin* only wasted five hours in attempting the task. The General, being anxious not to lose his ships, decided to go to Messina himself, to see if he could get assistance from the Piedmontese squadron there. He therefore re-embarked on the *Franklin*, taking the second officer of the *Torino* with him, and steered towards the straits; but scarcely had he doubled Cape dell' Armi than he found himself between two Neapolitan cruisers, the *Fulminante* and the *Aquila*.

The *Franklin* hoisted the American flag, and affixed another, bearing the arms of the United States, on the deck ladder, to give warning that whosoever attempted to board the vessel would have his brains blown out. Moreover, the vessel was in a strait—that is to say, in free waters, where nobody had the right to board her. After tacking several times round the *Franklin*, now drawing close, now retiring, the *Fulminante* placed herself to larboard and the *Aquila* on the starboard side, with their portholes open and their gunners at their stations.

The captain of the *Fulminante* then took his megaphone, and hailed the *Franklin*: "Where do you come from?"

Orrigoni replied in English that he did not understand. He then slackened speed, and consequently let off steam, which, in escaping, caused a terrific noise. Orrigoni mounted on top of a paddle-box, the better to see what was going on around him. A boat now approached his vessel, and an officer on board repeated the question through a megaphone: "Where do you come from?"

Orrigoni, this time, had a two-fold excuse, not only for not hearing, but also for not understanding: and that was the noise made by the steam in escaping. So he made a sign to the effect that he did not understand. Finally, the two Neapolitan ships sheered off, quite convinced that they were dealing with a deaf man or an idiot. The *Franklin* now continued her journey to Messina.[1]

But the two cruisers made off in the direction of Cape dell' Armi, and scarcely had they passed that point than they caught sight of the *Torino*. On approaching her, they quickly recognised a Garibaldian vessel. They instantly opened fire, but soon perceiving that it was deserted, went on board and started pillaging. Finally they spread her sails, soaked them with turpentine and set them on fire.

The gunfire and the flames destroyed the poor ship, but they did no damage to the crew, seeing that all save one had left the ship. This man was one of the engineers, who did not seem anxious to leave with the others. He died of fright.

Garibaldi, judging by the cannonade he heard that it would be useless to try to do anything for the *Torino*, repassed the straits, and effected a landing in Calabria during the night of the 19th to 20th of August.[2] Reggio was attacked and captured on the 21st; and the news of this event was known in Naples on the 23rd—that is, on the day of my arrival.

3 p.m.

Fresh despatches have arrived from Calabria, and are adding to the general consternation of the Government. General Melendez writes to say that he has been beaten, after a strenuous resistance, and forced to give up the fortress of Reggio for lack of water.

Couriers have arrived from the Basilicata. Garibaldi has been proclaimed Dictator there, and a provisional Government has been formed. Colonel Boldoni is in command of the army; two pro-dictators, Mignola and Albini, sign all acts in connection with the organisation of the resistance. We know what became of the troops sent against them.

When this news arrived, the Ministers proposed to the King that Naples should be abandoned, and that the revolution should be left to follow its irresistible course. By way of an answer, the King drew from his pocket a letter written in Italian to the Emperor Louis Napoleon. In it he says:

"Your Majesty advised me to give constitutional institutions to a people that has not asked for them, and I acceded to your request. You have caused me to abandon Sicily *without fighting*, promising me that, by so doing, my kingdom would be guaranteed to me. *Up to now the Great Powers seem to have persisted in the idea of abandoning me.* I must, however, warn your Majesty that I have resolved *not to quit my throne without fighting for it.* I appeal to the *Justice* of Europe; and she shall know that I am going to defend Naples whenever I may be attacked."

---

[1] Mr. Trevelyan does not mention this incident of Garibaldi's effort to obtain assistance for the *Torino*.

[2] Mr. Trevelyan proves that the date was 18th–19th of August.

It was not till midnight that the Ministers separated; and at six o'clock this morning, Liborio Romano was again summoned to the palace.

25th August.

I watched all night, and made my men also watch, with their rifles loaded. I have never heard so many sentry-challenges, in German and in Italian, as I heard last night. The wind brought the echo of them as far as the middle of the bay. All this noise was caused by the return of General Melendez from Reggio with the remnants of his army. The wounded came first, then the effective troops, and lastly the artillery.

When the artillery arrived, the porters asked, "Where are your guns?"

"Well," answered an artilleryman, "you see *Don Peppino* had not any, so we gave him ours."

Yesterday I paid a visit to the English Admiral, and found his frigate encumbered with bags of money; for everybody, it would seem, is taking on board all the ready cash he possesses.

I have sent a courier to Garibaldi to inform him of the state of the town.

Last night, Pianell, the Minister of War, ordered two battalions of infantry and a battery of artillery to be in readiness to start. Three times have they embarked, and three times landed again. Now it is definitely settled that they remain at Naples.

My yacht has become quite a recruiting office. Both deserters and volunteers come in; I send them all to Garibaldi.

Nothing can be more extraordinary than what is now taking place before our eyes. This throne in dissolution does not fall or totter, it is simply collapsing. This poor little king does not understand how his person can be swallowed up in the quicksands of this strange revolution. He wonders what he has done, how it is that nobody stands by him, why nobody loves him. He seeks to discover the invisible hand which weighs him down.

Sire, it is the hand of God!

From the deck of my yacht, anchored just opposite the palace, I can see the King's room, which is easily recognisable by the awning stretched above the windows. From time to time, the little king comes to the window, and scans the horizon through a glass. He probably thinks that he can already see the avenger coming. The poor youth is so ignorant! He asked Liborio Romano, the day before yesterday, why it was that I hated him. He does not know that his grandfather had my father poisoned.

A newspaper, called *The Garibaldi*, has just appeared. It has reached the eighth number, and openly preaches the revolution. The town is in a state of siege.

Numerous arrests were ordered yesterday. I now have on board two of these suspects; one is from Cosenza, the other from Palermo. To-night, I am going to send away the one from Cosenza in a boat. He has fifty leagues of sea to cross. Heaven protect him!

A formerly proscribed politician, who is now a subaltern in the police, keeps us informed of all that is going on. His old sentence was one of forty-six years at the galleys for being a revolutionist. When Judge Navarra passed sentence on him, he said: "I shall do what I can, you shall do the rest."

He was released at the general amnesty, and obtained a position in the police. He makes good use of this office in preventing arrests by putting upon their guard those who are marked down. Once again I say, nothing can be more extraordinary than that which is taking place in front of our eyes.

Sunday, 26th of August, 2 p.m.

Luckily the steamer which was to take my letter has not yet left. Some important events have occurred since last night.

Firstly, then, General Vial returned yesterday from Calabria with his troops completely disbanded, and informed the King that any further attempts at resistance in Calabria was useless. The Government is uncertain whether it ought to make a final effort between Naples and Salerno, or whether it ought to renounce any further shedding of blood and recognise the triumph of our cause. Organising in favour of the cause still continues in Basilicata, and the prodictators have the support and sympathy of all citizens.

General Gallotti has capitulated, leaving in Garibaldi's hands all his horses and much of his artillery. Most of his soldiers, mindful of their native land, have come under the flag of United Italy.

At Spoggia an attempt at reaction has been attempted; but the dragoons fraternised with the people, and the Intendant and the Governor have fled.

In Calabria we can now number more than 100,000 rifles. A vast camp of insurgents is being organised at Cosenza, whither we have despatched Masciero, who has sacrificed his whole fortune in the Italian cause. In the district of Castrovillari the gendarmes have been disarmed, and a provisional Government has been proclaimed in the names of Garibaldi and Victor Emmanuel. But the most important event is another letter from the Count of Syracuse, of which the following is a translation:

"Sire—[1]

"If my words were ignored in the past when I sought to picture to your mind the dangers which threatened our house, now, when still bigger dangers threaten it, let me beg you not to turn a deaf ear to my advice, nor to reject it in order to follow that of evil counsellors. The change which has come over Italy, and the craving for national unity, now spread far and wide in the course of the few months following the taking of Palermo, have deprived your Majesty's Government of that power which can alone sustain a nation, and have rendered an alliance with Piedmont impossible.

"The people of Upper Italy, horrified at the news of the massacres in Sicily, have, by their avowed sympathy, rejected the ambassadors of Naples; and we are now reduced to so abject a plight as to be compelled to resort to the arbitrament of arms—alone, without alliances, exposed to the resentment of the masses, who everywhere have risen to the cry of extermination levelled against our house, which has now become an object of universal detestation.

"Civil war, already raging on the mainland of Italy, will inevitably drag down this dynasty into that abyss which the intrigues of perverse advisers have long since prepared for the descendants of Charles III of Bourbon. The blood of our citizens, uselessly shed, will again inundate the thousand cities of your kingdom; and you, in whom once centred the hope and love of your people, will be regarded with horror, as the sole cause of this fratricidal war. Sire, whilst there is yet time, save our house from the curses of all Italy.

"Follow the noble example of our royal kinsman of Parma, who, immediately civil war broke out, released his subjects from their allegiance, and let them become the arbiters of their own destiny. Europe and your people will honour so sublime a sacrifice; you will then be able to raise your eyes with confidence to God, who will reward this noble act on the part of your Majesty. Your heart, formerly steeped in direst misfortune, will expand with the noble aspirations of patriotism, and you will bless the day in which you so generously sacrificed yourself to the grandeur of Italy.

"In addressing you thus, Sire, I am only carrying out the sacred obligation that my experience imposes on me; and I pray that God may give you His wisdom, and make you worthy of His blessings.

"Your Majesty's affectionate uncle,
"LEOPOLD, COUNT OF SYRACUSE."

I have just received the following letter from one of the men who gave me the greatest assistance at the time of the Salerno movement: the one who put me into communication with the mountain chiefs, and whose prompt action prevented the Bavarian troops from entering the Basilicata.

"*Cava, 25th August*, 1860.

"MY DEAR DUMAS,

"I am writing to you in great haste to inform you that I have been suddenly obliged to leave Salerno and abandon what little I possess. I have been denounced as your agent, as being a purveyor of arms, and as trying to win over the Bavarians. Yesterday I had already been warned of what was being planned; to-day an officer of the National Guard came to confirm yesterday's report, and to advise me to flee immediately, if I valued my life. In fact, it meant nothing less than having to undergo the punishment awarded to the young man of whom I spoke in my last letter. He has already received an instalment of a hundred blows out of the two hundred to which he has been condemned.

"A few words about this martyr to our cause, upon whom the Royalists think they have not yet sufficiently satiated their vengeance. He is in prison, condemned to a death more painful than that to which his torturers have already led him half-way.

---

[1] This letter is referred to, but not quoted by Mr. Trevelyan.

General Scotti has forbidden the surgeons to dress his wounds, and his gaolers to give him anything to eat. For three days now, with his body a mass of wounds, he has been subjected to the additional torture of hunger. If Maniscalco were dead, it would be easy to believe that his soul has passed into General Scotti.

"All this, however, has not prevented a score of young people setting out for the Val di Diana.

"Telegraphic communication with Sala has been cut.

"You may always rely on me in every possible way. I am ever ready to sacrifice my life in the service of Garibaldi and yourself.

"Yesterday evening a battalion bivouacked outside the gate leading to Naples, another outside the gate leading to Calabria, a third outside the one leading to Avellino, and, lastly, one at the gate of the Offices of the Administration, where it guards the eleven guns which, you will remember, were once trained on you. A squadron of mounted men patrolled the town in all directions during the night. My hotel is full of Croats, from the ground floor to the third storey.

"Meanwhile, what can I do for the cause? There is a continuous demand for rifles and revolvers: fifty or even a hundred double-barrelled guns would be very welcome. I have received letters from all parts asking for them.

"Your most devoted fellow-countryman,
"WIELANDT."

"P.S.—The Commissioner of Police has just arrived, this morning—Sunday—at Cava, with his family. He tells us that Garibaldi's landing at Salerno is expected.

"A reinforcement of 3000 cavalry arrived last night. These men, urged on by their officers, have promised to fight. They have been assured that the town will have to pay by sack and pillage for exhibiting its sympathy towards you and for illuminating so brazenly in the presence of the Neapolitans.

"I have just learnt that the name of the man who denounced me is Peppino Troïano."

ALEXANDRE DUMAS

After an etching by Rajon

CHAPTER XLVIII

LIBORIO ROMANO

Bay of Naples, 2nd of September

I WILL now relate what has happened here since my arrival. I may say that until this moment, which is the culminating one—for the revolution must break out within the next three days—I have been unable to disclose the names of persons concerned in these secret events. Either the King leaves to-night, to-morrow night, or the night after, or we shall hear the gun-fire in the streets.

Well, then, the very day of my arrival here (23rd of August), Muratori, a delightful young fellow known to me in France, came to me from Liborio Romano, with whom I had been exchanging letters, about the arms I had caused Count Trani to seize.

In writing to Liborio Romano I had told him that I considered it impossible for an intelligent man such as himself to retain any hope of preserving the dynasty of the Bourbons in Naples, and I had stated the advantages that would be his as a statesman, the honour that would be his as a patriot, if he withdrew his most popular name, and thus his support, from Francis II, and, by declaring himself his enemy, become one of those causing his fall.

Liborio Romano's reply told me that he was expecting me during the evening at his own house. I answered that, my identity being well known in Naples, I should terribly compromise him by being seen there with him; and that, regard being had to our respective positions, it was rather for him to come to me, than for me to go to him. Muratori had taken him my answer. Two hours later, at nightfall and under cover of the darkness, a boat came alongside my yacht; in this boat were two men and two women; one of the men was wrapped up in a cloak and wore a wide-brimmed hat pulled down over his eyes. He was Liborio Romano. Our introduction was a brief one; we took each others hands and embraced.

Then I drew him into a corner, and we began to converse.

Romano's situation was this:

He had joined the constitutional Government, while reserving to himself his duty as an honest man and a good citizen. So long as he saw the King taking the right road which he had agreed to follow he would serve the King and the nation; when the King broke his oath he would leave him and serve the nation. His position of Minister of the Interior and Police had been accepted by him on this condition.

The events which brought about the state of siege are widely known; the two principal were the reaction of Prince Louis and the attempt made on the frigate of Castellammare.

Marshal Viglia was then appointed Commandant of the place.

But, thanks to Romano, never before was such a state of siege known: all the liberties guaranteed by the Constitution were preserved; the National Guard united with the troops in the performance of public duties; as for the liberty of the Press, only England enjoyed it to such an extent. Committees were organised, such as the "Committee of Order" and "Committee of Action." And, what is more, a newspaper called *The Garibaldi* sprang up. Having regard to all this, the police declared that they no longer needed *sbirri*. Any man who had been oppressed under the government of the King could, if he wished, enter the police.

Francis II felt that such a state of siege could by no means be allowed. He had sworn, at his father's death-bed to persist in the system which had gained for that monarch the nickname Bomba and for himself Bombetta—how then could he permit such unheard-of freedom?

He could not allow it; he took a reactionary course. The chiefs of his party were the Queen-Mother,—who resided at Gaeta by the advice of Romano—and the brothers and uncles of the King, the Count of Trani, the Count of Aquila, and the Princes Charles and Louis.

As for the Count of Syracuse, he was among the Liberals since the date of his first letter.

Romano's Liberal views irritated the King, but he had no choice but to keep in with him, seeing his popularity with the National Guard, the citizens and the people generally.

So matters stood when Garibaldi landed at Calabria.

This news destroyed the King's cherished hope that by surrendering his insular territory to Piedmont he had got free from the straits he was in. He had been sure that the Powers—the Emperor of the French in particular—would safeguard him his Continental territories. But no; though figuratively he stretched out imploring arms to them, they refused their aid. They thought of him sanctioning the destruction of lives and property at Palermo, and they were deaf. Then came the blow of the victory of Reggio. It was too much; he dissembled no longer, and began wrangling with Romano, the only one to dispute with in the Ministry, since he was its one veritable Constitutionalist.

Romano stood his ground; and, more, he caused the Queen-Mother to be banished from the Court. The King, in despair, had his plate, diamonds and a vast treasure taken to an Austrian frigate, and his attitude to Romano became almost menacing.

So matters stood when Romano came to me as Garibaldi's *intimate friend.*

No one at Naples was specially accredited by Garibaldi. His two agents, Carbonelli and Mignona, had already gone to the Basilicata to stir up a revolt. To the former I had given a revolver, Madame Ristori's [1] present to me. Brother John, also, had gone to Il Vallo with 200 francs from my purse and the revolver presented to *Alexandre Dumas premier,* by Émile de Girardin. I thus stood alone, with the two letters he had given me to serve as my credentials. I mention this to explain why Romano came to me.

This was what he wanted to tell me:

"I will fight for the constitutional cause as long as I can. When I can do so no longer, I will hand in my resignation, and I will come to you. I shall then either join Garibaldi or declare the King a traitor to the Constitution, and I shall so call him to the National Guard and the people."

"You mean that?" I asked him.

"Yes, on my word of honour."

"I accept it, but from what I gathered when on board the flagship of Admiral Le Barbier de Tinan my flag may well not get any protection. Permit me, therefore, to approach the English Admiral, so that you may find a refuge with him which would not be yours on my *boat,* as M. de Missiessi is so good as to call it."

"Do so, but I may have to leave the Ministry to-morrow."

"I shall go as soon as you do: how shall we communicate?"

"Either through Madame ——, who came with me, or through Cozzolongo, my secretary. Moreover, there is Muratori."

I was introduced to the two ladies, and the party left. I then went on board the *Hannibal* and asked for Admiral Parkings.[2] He was on shore, but was expected back shortly. I was received by the commander. Within ten minutes, however, the Admiral appeared. I explained my position, emphasising that, according to the two French officers, my yacht was no safe refuge for a dismissed Minister. I therefore asked him to shelter Romano in case of need.

The Admiral was most cordial, according to the traditions of the English navy. He at once sent for the commander. "Captain," said he, "have your cabin made ready to receive Liborio Romano."

The captain bowed and left. I thanked the Admiral and returned to my yacht.

---

[1] The great actress.
[2] Rear-Admiral Sir Rodney Mundy gives an account of this interview in his work: "H.M.S. 'Hannibal' at Palermo and Naples, during the Italian Revolution, 1859–1861."
Dumas however says: "Je me rendis à bord de l'*Annibal* et demandai l'amiral Parkings."

The following day Madame —— brought me Romano's portrait with a letter. I read as follows: "I beg of you to write under this likeness of me, 'the portrait of a coward,' if I fail to keep my promise to you of last night."

Romano's visit was on the 23rd of August.

Naples, though it appeared apathetic, indifferent, was really deeply agitated, among its citizens and nobility especially. Naples is like Vesuvius, which is strewn with flowers, until the fatal moment arrives and all is covered under streams of burning lava. There had already been two reactionary attempts, both of which were frustrated by Romano. The first had occurred on August the 5th, when the royal guard tried to compel all in the streets to shout "Long live the King," and had badly wounded several people; Prince Louis of Aquila had the credit of the second, the object of which was to overturn the Ministry, and also, it was thought, to make away with Romano and Muratori, thus enabling him to seize supreme power. A third attempt was obscurely throbbing among the lower orders of the city.

And while all this was going on, news kept coming from Calabria stimulating the general disquietude. Here is an example.

"Garibaldi the Dictator is advancing through Calabria leading 14,000 heroes. The royal troops either join him, or take to flight. The revolution is spreading from province to province. The chains of the hated Bourbons are severed for ever.

"Brothers, let us overthrow the enemies of Italy! Hasten, the moment has come; victory is certain, for our cause is just, and God is for us.

"CITIZEN GIUSEPPE DI MARCO."

Each night proclamations were mysteriously affixed to the walls to meet the eyes of all in the morning.

Then the second letter of the Count of Syracuse appeared. The effect was indescribable. A conspiracy, at the head of which was the King, was organised. Cutofiano was appointed commandant of the place, and Ischitella commandant of the National Guard. The Nuncio was a leading spirit, with the Bishops of Gaëta and Nola under him.

An extraordinary manifesto in support of the King was issued to the public, and burst like a shell on the head of Romano, whom it was hoped to crush. The following is the text:

" THE NEAPOLITAN PEOPLE TO THEIR KING, FRANCIS II.

" Sire,—When the country is in danger, the people have the right to call upon their King to defend it. Since kings are made for peoples and not peoples for kings, we ought to obey them; but they must be able to defend us. It is for that reason that God has given them not a sceptre only, but a sword also.

"To-day, Sire, the enemy is at our gates; the country is in danger. For the space of four months an adventurer, at the head of bands collected in every land, has invaded the kingdom and caused the blood of our brothers to be shed. The treason of some wretches has aided him, and a diplomacy even more wicked has seconded his culpable enterprises. In a few days this adventurer will impose upon us his odious yoke. His designs are known to us all, and you, also, know them, Sire. This man, moreover, makes no mystery of them. Under the pretence of uniting that which has never been united, he wishes to make us Piedmontese, in order the better to decatholicise us, and, religion destroyed, to establish on its ruins a republican government under the ferocious dictatorship of Mazzini, of whom he will be the arm and the sword.

" But, Sire, for centuries we have been Neapolitans. Charles III, your immortal ancestor, snatched us from the foreign yoke; we wish to remain, live, and die Neapolitans, in possession of that fine and wise civilization that that great King gave us. Shall it be said that the son of Ferdinand II could not grasp in a firm hand the sceptre inherited by him from his father of glorious memory, or that the son of the venerable Maria Christina is so cowardly as to abandon us to his enemy? Can it be that Francis II, our well-beloved sovereign, has not the courage and strength of the humblest of kings? No, Sire, no: it cannot be.

"Save your people then, Sire. We ask it of you in the name of the religion which has anointed you King, in the name of those hereditary laws which have put in your hand the sceptre of your ancestors, in the name of law and of justice which impose upon you the duty of watching continually over our safety, and, if need be, of dying to redeem your people.

"Sire, we tell you that the country is in danger, and loudly demands four things:

"1st. Your entire ministry is betraying you; its acts prove this, and its relations to Judas and Pilate bear witness to the fact. Turn out your ministry and place at the head of affairs one chosen from among honest men, devoted to your crown, your people, and the Constitution.

"2nd. Many foreigners are conspiring against your throne and our nationality. Let them be sent out of the kingdom.

" 3rd. Numerous depots of arms exist in your capital. Let a general disarmament be ordered.

"4th. The entire police is in league with your enemies. Let this police be replaced by an honourable and faithful body of men.

"Sire, these are the demands of your Neapolitan subjects. Your army is as devoted as it is brave. Draw your sword and save your country! Whoso has right and justice with him, has God with him also.

"God save King Francis II! God save our Country! Long live the Constitution! Long live the brave Neapolitan army!"

As I write, I have received an order to leave the bay within half-an-hour, failing which, I am to be fired on by the cannon of the fort.

Romano tells me that this morning, Sunday, the 2nd of September, at noon, the King having summoned M. Brenier, said, "M. Dumas obstructed General Scotti in his march to the aid of my troops in Basilicata; M. Dumas was the cause of the revolution in Salerno; M. Dumas then comes here, sends proclamations into the city, distributes arms and gives away red shirts. I insist that his flag shall not protect him and that he leaves the bay."

"Certainly, sire," M. Brenier replied, "your wishes shall be obeyed."

We weighed anchor at eleven o'clock and got under sail to join Garibaldi. In two or three days I, in my turn, shall give Francis II an order to leave not merely the bay of Naples, but his capital and kingdom likewise.

CHAPTER XLIX

THE GARIBALDIANS IN CALABRIA

BEFORE I got the order to leave, Muratori came to tell me that Garibaldi had landed in Calabria. Do you remember what I said to the Captain about Cæsar *à propos* of the General's disappearance?

Cæsar had reappeared, and, as Suetonius says, had signified his presence by a thunderclap. This Garibaldi did while I awaited him at Salerno. But before treating of Garibaldi, we are going to tell you what had become of Missori and Cattabeni.

The object of their expedition to Calabria was this:

A Calabrian Colonel named Musolino had offered the General to attempt to capture the fortress of Altifiumara if he could have 200 picked men. His idea was to climb up into the fortress and, in the morning, to signal the success of the enterprise. The General then put Missori and Cattabeni at the disposal of the Colonel, together with fifty Guides, a company of Sacchi's brigade, another of Bersaglieri and some artillerymen. And he attached such importance to the expedition that he personally directed the embarkation, which was to take place at ten o'clock at night, and to leave the lighthouse in thirty boats.

Musolino went in the first boat.[1] The night was a dark one; each boat contained twelve or thirteen men with four oarsmen and a captain. Garibaldi saw the boats pass him one after the other like a string of migrating birds; then he accompanied them in a yawl as far as the middle of the Strait, when he shouted, "Adieu until tomorrow," and left them.

As we have said, the night was a dark one; they could not see what was ahead of them; they landed without any hindrance, but without knowing where they were.

There they were on the beach, but whether at the spot chosen by the guide they could not tell. They had neither cartridges, ladders nor torches, for they were all in the boats, which, directly they had touched land, had rowed off again heedless of the plight of the little column.

Musolino sent a patrol in search of the guides. The rest of the column waited, lying on the ground. The sentinel's "*All'erta*" from the fortress was the only sound, but fifteen minutes had barely elapsed when four or five musket shots and a cannon shot, giving the alarm from the fortress, rang out. The Garibaldian patrol had

[1] On August 8th.

run against a Royalist one, and had taken two prisoners. It returned with them, but without having met the guides.

Everyone, with common accord, turned to Musolino and asked what was to be done. Now Musolino was as much at a loss as anyone. Before them was the black, shapeless mountain. Musolino began to climb it, but hardly had they gone fifty steps amongst the rocks than they reached the first of a series of walls, built for the vines, which were most difficult to get over. They managed it by making ladders of themselves, but some of their muskets went off, wounding three or four and killing one of their number; a few men fell exhausted on the ground, where, the next morning, they were made prisoners by the Royalists. They thus continued to struggle until three o'clock in the morning. Then a portion of the column, led by Musolino and Cattabeni, found itself near a little farm with a chapel attached to it. After a little hesitation they opened a little door and found a poor woman, who, taking the Garibaldians for brigands, asked for mercy, her hair standing on end from terror. They asked her if she had seen anyone else, and she told them that fifty men in red shirts had appeared and departed with her husband and son as guides. The little column followed in the tracks of their friends. Happily, there were no more vines and walls to conquer, and they reached the top of the hill, where, utterly exhausted, they lay down. An hour later, the intensity of the cold awoke them, for they had lain down bathed in sweat without covering of any kind. So they had a twofold reason for going on— to get warm, and to reach somewhere. Presently they met two mountaineers, one of whom agreed to serve as guide as far as Fiumara di Muro. So, under Musolino and Cattabeni, they proceeded. In an hour's time, as they descended the other side of the mountain, they found a convent built on a hillock. Musolino and Cattabeni halted the men and went on by themselves to explore.

From the hillock they could see the white houses of Messina on the other side of the Strait reflected in the mirror-like sea. Growing near the convent were cacti, palms, and tobacco plants; within, it all was of poor and ancient appearance. They went through the front door, passed through three or four corridors, entered a cell, where a young monk looked at them with a timid expression.

A little later, a jovial, fat, short, high-coloured individual appeared and, with outstretched hands, said to the officers:

"What can I do for you?"

The position was explained to him.

"You are our brothers," he went on, "and we will save you; here now, smoke a cigar and drink this coffee."

While they were taking advantage of this hospitality their host summoned the commander of the National Guard and the principal inhabitants. They came, procured the Garibaldians every help, and lent them guides.

A messenger arrived opportunely with news of Missori's column. They were camped near by. The two columns then joined one another.

Musolino, Missori and Cattabeni were anxious to inform Garibaldi of all that had happened; and on his side, Garibaldi, with his eye glued to his telescope, vainly waited on the *Aberdeen* for the agreed morning signal to appear on the fortress of Fiumara.

"There are always the same sentinels," he said in a vexed voice, turning to those who were by him.

Cattabeni offered himself to bear a message across the strait. Accompanied by a guide and a Greek, he descended the rocks. At last, overcome by heat and fatigue, they reached the convent and Cattabeni, after a meal, fell asleep. But alas! he was soon awakened by the monks, who told him that the Royalists were approaching, and that the convent was surrounded by sentinels. The guide offered to take the letter to the General, and Cattabeni contrived to rejoin his column.

CHAPTER L

THE DOVE FROM THE ARK

AT this news the column began its march, and, on the first day, reached a hunting resort on Aspromonte; some shepherds were there with their wives, and the Garibaldians spent a day and a half with them. The sister of one of the shepherds assumed the task of victualling the little column, and obtained for it bread, wine, eggs and fowls.

The next day the column was joined by the first Calabrian volunteers. For a moment, on seeing them appear, it was hoped that the whole province had risen, and that, in concert with Garibaldi, it would be possible to press an attack on the Royalists. But the volunteers never numbered more than 200 or 300.

Meanwhile, Reggio and the adjacent villages sent to the column mules laden with wine, so great, in those early days particularly, was the desire of the people to testify their sympathy with the Garibaldians.

The place is a most picturesque one, alike for its surroundings and the dress of its inhabitants: the peasants wear knee-breeches of black velvet and woollen stockings turned over the ankles. The well-to-do wear shoes with buckles; the poor *la ciocca*, a leather covering similar to the Roman cothurnus, laced to the leg. In summer-time a coarse and very white shirt suffices, which contrasts admirably with the black nether garments. In winter-time they wear a coat of black velvet with their knee-breeches. The women wear cloth petticoats of brilliant colours and usually ornament their hair with a bandeau of red silk. They are handsome, and their ancient custom of carrying pitchers of water on their heads makes their figures lissome and gives them an elegant carriage.

All went well in the daytime; but not so at night, when the volunteers suffered greatly from the cold.

It was necessary to leave Aspromonte; the Royalists were approaching in such superior force that there was no use in fighting them, especially with such a want of ammunition. They had to straggle from wood to wood. From time to time they started at the sound of a cannon-shot fired at random which echoed and re-echoed through the mountain.

Then the same news which had been given me when I got to Messina, reached the poor exiles: Garibaldi has left Messina for Turin by order of King Victor Emmanuel; others said to march against the Roman States. In either event the Garibaldians might consider themselves abandoned, and the situation became a very difficult one. The forced marches meant, most of the time, want of food. After a trying march in search of safety it was often necessary to make another similar march in search of something to eat. Musolino decided to reach Bagnara. The Calabrians protested, but, protesting, followed the column.

They had left the Casina dei Forestieri at midnight, reckoning before daybreak to be on the heights near Bagnara. Unfortunately, they mistook the way, and continually climbing and descending again by paths unworthy of the name, they only came in sight of Bagnara at eleven o'clock.

The column separated; a portion led by Musolino and Missori marched forward to the attack of the Royalists; the reserve was commanded by Cattabeni.

Hardly had they reached the plains than the enemy outposts fired all along the line; nevertheless, the attack of the Garibaldians was so fierce that the outposts were obliged to retreat. But the alarm had already been given in the town: the drums sounded the recall to 2000 or 3000 men, and after a desperate fight, the column, which only had sporting powder and bullets, had to retreat; worn out by the heat and fatigue, they had to climb the mountain again and follow the way by which they had come.[1]

A guide, in falling from a rock, had broken his leg. Two Calabrians who attempted many times to drag him or take him on their shoulders, were forced to desist, and to leave him, sorely against their will, in the hands of the enemy.

The column pressed on for the Casina through Solano, where de Flotte was to fall some days later. Solano is a little village situated on the side of a steep hill. A torrent, which falls into the village, has been diverted by the mountaineers and affords delicious icy water to the thirsty. Let us just add that the women here are charming.

Near this stream in the middle of the village the Garibaldians, who were still pursued, tried to make a moment's halt under the protection of the rearguard, but presently the women, who had constituted themselves sentinels on the roof-tops, perceived that the rearguard was in retreat and that the Royalists were coming on.

There was only just time to reach the wood near the village. Twenty times lost among the rocks, the thickets and the woods, the little column did not reach the Casina until the middle of the night.

[1] Mr. Trevelyan says that Bagnara was captured and held for a time.

The situation was more difficult than before. Three columns, one from Reggio, the two others from Bagnara and Scilla, pressed ever closer around the Garibaldians, who, almost abandoned by the Calabrians, would soon have no other resource than to reach the forests. They were on the point of deciding to do this, when, in answer to a sentinel's challenge, they heard a woman's voice reply, "Friend."

Everyone ran to her. The friend was a French amazon—her name discretion prevents our giving—who came, like the dove from the Ark, carrying, not the olive-branch, but instructions from Garibaldi.

She related the attempt made by de Flotte to come with fifty men to the Garibaldians, and announced the heroic death of our brave fellow-countryman. After a thousand difficulties, she had succeeded in reaching Calabria.

After some hours rest, spent among those to whom she had devoted herself, she undertook to return to Reggio to obtain relief for the column. She started, and the column, the same day, contrived to take up a position at the village of San Lorenzo.

It was there that, two days later, the volunteers heard the first cannon-shot announcing Garibaldi, and received a message which ordered them to proceed to join him in his march on Reggio.[1]

[1] Reggio was taken by Garibaldi on the 20th–21st August (see p. 332). The victory cost him about 150 men, killed or wounded.

CHAPTER LI

OPEN CONSPIRACY

Port de Castellammare, 3rd Sept.

I NOW resume my recital interrupted when in the harbour of Naples.

Two days before the attempted *coup d'état* by the reaction, a steamboat arrived, flying the Garibaldian flag, but with a truce flag at its mizzen. It was the *Franklin*, Captain Orrigoni,[1] with some of the prisoners made at Reggio.

Although he arrived as late as ten at night, Captain Orrigoni, nevertheless, was on board my yacht at six the next morning.

So original a character deserves a portrait, and I should like to present you with one. When events shall be less pressed on and less pressing, I will give myself the pleasure of doing so.

Let me now just say that Orrigoni is inseparable from Garibaldi; indeed when Orrigoni is absent something is wanting to the General.

Orrigoni followed him to Monte Video; he returned to make the campaign of 1848 with him; he was his companion in the dangerous retreat which cost the life of his Anita. Temporarily absent from Garibaldi, he rejoined him in Tangiers, went with him to North America, from there to the gulf of Mexico, and from there to Lima. He was with the General in the glorious campaign of 1859 in which each combat was a victory. He then came to rejoin him in Sicily, and here he is now with him in Calabria.

Brave Orrigoni! Exclamations of joy broke from me when I saw him, and it seemed to me that, on turning, Garibaldi would be there too.

But no; he is at Nicotera. He is passing through Calabria, effacing the footsteps of Cardinal Ruffo, and forcing startled Liberty to take the same road which, fifty years before, had been traced by Despotism.

It is through Orrigoni that I learnt of the death of poor de Flotte; the sad news broke my heart. It is difficult to realise that a human being whom one has seen five or six days before, alert, speaking, hoping, has become a motionless, quiet corpse, so one always tries to persuade oneself that the news of such a death is false. Unfortunately, the details were so precise that doubt was impossible.

Orrigoni spent the day with me. On my yacht he found the whole of Naples. Never has a king had in his ante-rooms and salons a crowd so large as the one which queued up in boats to shake my hand and

[1] Captain Orrigoni does not obtain mention in Mr. Trevelyan's works.

348

embrace me. Had Orrigoni so wished, he could have left with the *Franklin* more laden with passengers than he had come: everyone wanted to go with him; every day I refuse 300 volunteers.

During the afternoon the Committee of Action sent M. Agresti with two of its members. These gentlemen came to speak about the formation, in the event of the flight of the King from Naples, of a provisional government, of which M. Libertini would be President, and numbering among its members, Ricciardi, Agresti, etc., etc.

I replied that I was not empowered to discuss such weighty interests, but that if, nevertheless, the honour was done me of consulting me, I would reply that I did not consider the question of a provisional government an urgent one, that it was sufficient to name a prodictator; that, to my thinking, only one man was popular enough to guarantee, in holding this high position, the tranquillity of Naples, and that man was Liborio Romano. I added that as I never kept anything from the General I would write that very day to him.

This reply caused the deputation such great emotion that one of its members quitted the *Emma*, leaving his hat on board, and has not yet returned for it.

An hour after the departure of these gentlemen, Brother John's secretary, whom I had taken with Brother John himself to Messina, whom I had conducted to Naples, to whom I had given bed and board, came to tell me he had been chosen by the Committee of Action to be the bearer of a report to Garibaldi, and begged me to ask Orrigoni for his passage to Calabria.

I accepted the commission, thinking it a simple matter. But one of Orrigoni's singularities is to consider as *Jettatore* (having the evil eye) every priest, every brother of a priest, every cousin of a priest, every secretary, even, of a priest.

" Situated as is the *Franklin*, I would not embark Brother Jean's secretary if he were made of solid gold."

Such was his answer, and from it he would not budge. I was obliged to repeat it to the secretary, who left the yacht giving me his most evil-looking glance.

But, while refusing to take this secretary, Orrigoni accepted the offer of a patriotic Neapolitan, aged twenty-eight, named Alexander Salvati, who arranged to take a letter from me to the General. Here it is:—

23rd August, 1860.

'FRIEND,

"I am going to write to you at length and to speak to you about important matters; read carefully.

"In spite of my desire to rejoin you I am remaining at Naples, where I believe I am of use to your cause.

"This is what I am doing:

"Each night a new proclamation is posted up: without calling the Neapolitans to arms, which is unnecessary, it stiffens them in their hatred of the King.

"Each morning the journalists come for their instructions: they are easy to give, for all are devotedly—that is to say fanatically—attached to you.

"On my return from Messina I put myself into communication with Salerno; its spirit is excellent.

"I have been advised that, the moment Potenza revolted, 5000 Bavarians and Croats were sent with General Scotti to suppress the insurrection.

"I arrived at Salerno before General Scotti, and I at once, through the agency of Dr. Wielandt, entered into communication with the mountain chiefs. I distributed fifty double-barrelled guns among them, also carbines from my own supply. The defiles of the mountain have been guarded; Scotti and his 5000 Bavarians have not been able to cross the defile leading from Salerno to Potenza, and thus the Basilicata insurrection progresses undisturbed.

"This is not all: the Bavarians, realising that they cannot make a step in the mountains without risking as many shots as there are bushes and rocks on their route, have offered, for five ducats a man, to desert with arms and baggage.

"I have opened a subscription list: I have put myself at the head of it for 500 francs and I expect to get 10,000 francs together, that is to say, the fifth of the sum required; if I do so I will give it to our Bavarians on account; the balance will be payable at Messina.

"A young man of the town who recruited for us has been denounced and condemned to receive a hundred blows. This punishment has exasperated the Salernitans.

"Three Bavarians, arrested as they were in the act of deserting, have been shot.

"A hundred horsemen have this morning offered to desert with their horses, unfortunately I have no means of transporting them.

"We are sure of Salerno and of 10,000 men; if Menotti, Medici, Türr, or someone else wishes to land there, I will land the first to treat, and in an hour's time the town will be yours.

"Putting aside Salerno, too much *occupied* just now, one can land anywhere in the Cilento; all this coast is as good as the other, that of Amalfi is bad.

"I now speak of Naples.

"I have the word of a certain number of officers not to fire on the people if incited to rise; on seeing the first red shirt they will go over to your side.

"But this is the most important thing—

"Liborio Romano, the only popular member of the Ministry, is entirely at your disposal, with two at least of his colleagues, at the King's first attempt at reaction.

"At this first attempt, which will free him from his oath, Liborio Romano offers to leave Naples with two of his colleagues, to join you, to proclaim the fall of the King, and to recognise you as Dictator.

"To support him he has all the populace and the 12,000 men of the National Guard.

"If you make a landing in the Cilento, in the Gulf of Policastro, or in that of Salerno, he promises so greatly to alarm the King that he, who is easily alarmed, will quit Naples.

"Give us your written instructions; they shall be followed.

"M. Salvati, a member of the Garibaldian Committee, leaves with Orrigoni to rejoin you. Tell him everything, except about Romano's proposals—they are between four persons only; do not reply, therefore, except to me, on this subject.

"You know that for myself I shall never ask you for anything save a permission to shoot in the park of the Capo-di-Monti and the continuation of the excavations at Pompeii.

"Would you like all the journals, all the artists, all the painters, all the sculptors, all the architects to exclaim with joy? Issue a decree conceived in these terms:

"'In the name of the artistic world, the excavations at Pompeii will be resumed, and continued without interruption as soon as I arrive in Naples.

                                                          "'G. GARIBALDI,
                                                              "'*Dictator*.'

"You see, my friend, that I am doing what I can in publishing the great deeds that you are accomplishing. I praise you because I admire you, and I love you without any other desire than to be loved by you.

"Have I anything else to say to you? I do not think so. Do you want me? I leave to join you. Do you consider you have need of me here? I remain, although the French Admiral has had me informed that after all I have done and what I am doing each day, he cannot take me under his protection.

"I would tell you to take care of yourself if I did not know that such recommendations make you laugh; I will content myself, therefore, by telling you that I pray for you to the same God to Whom your Mother prayed.

"*Au revoir*, my friend; take the part of my heart which remained to me when I left France.

" ALEX. DUMAS."

Orrigoni departed on the night of the 25th to 26th, taking Salvati, who carried my letters with him. Let us follow him in his peregrination from the moment when he went on board the *Franklin* until that in which he found the General. Then, whilst Garibaldi is crossing torrents and mountains, we shall see what is happening in Naples.

The *Franklin* did not belie the reputation of being a slow boat which had been claimed for it by its Captain. By the evening of the 26th it had travelled only sixty miles; it had to stop during the night as the Royalists were patrolling the coast. At daybreak steam was got up, and, towards noon, it came alongside of San Lucido near Paola.

At San Lucido the revolution had taken place; the tricolor flag with the cross of Savoy had been hoisted, and the gendarmes had been disarmed. Garibaldi's victories were known; but no one could tell Salvati where he was to be found. The Committee came on board, and news of Naples was given it in exchange for news of Calabria; after which the *Franklin* set off again and continued along the coast in a southerly direction.

They reached Pizzo of bloody memory. There some definite news of the General was obtained. He was stated to be at Catanzaro.[1]

Salvati set off there that very moment, but the indefatigable scaler of mountains had already left for Mäida. Salvati reached Mäida. The General was no longer there; but he had quitted the place only about five or six hours before. Salvati continued his road and gained Tiriolo, where he found Nino Bixio only.

Bixio told Salvati that by putting on speed he would find the Dictator at Soveria-Mannelli, where he was engaging in battle with General Ghio's army.

And Salvati arrived there, in fact, just as the fight was beginning.

Garibaldi had surrounded the Royalists on all sides. They had fortified themselves in a plain before the village of Soveria, so that

[1] After taking Reggio, which event and some subsequent minor victories Dumas does not relate. Garibaldi was at Catanzaro on August 26th.

on arriving there from Tiriolo, the General had them in front of him. Then he had taken to the mountain, and after leaving some of his men along the heights, had returned to attack the enemy by the village.

When Salvati reached the spot where Garibaldi had left the road —that is to say, at the top of a hill—he was able to make out the General in the act of issuing from the side of the mountain opposite him, and descending towards the village. At half the distance of a gunshot, Garibaldi reached the church with his staff. Then the Royalists fired and the bullets crashed into the wall behind them; the General neither hastened nor slackened his pace. Not a single officer of his staff, not a single one of his soldiers answered the fire. He carried a carbine-revolver in a bandolier on his shoulder and held in his hand a pistol-revolver.

He entered the village, where he was lost to sight. In ten minutes time he reappeared at its further end. He was now only the distance of a pistol-shot from the enemy.

The order to fire was given, but Garibaldi's presence, his *sangfroid*, the prestige which accompanies him, produced their accustomed effect. Cavalry, artillery, infantry, 10,000 men or thereabouts, lowered their arms and dispersed.

It was four o'clock in the afternoon before Salvati could get to the General. He found him in Stocco's house,[1] worn out and lying on a bed. Salvati gave him my letter, which Garibaldi read twice, then he put a series of questions to Salvati respecting the attitude of the people, the opinions of the *bourgeoisie* and of the National Guard. No one could give better information than Salvati, he being a Neapolitan.

The General bade him return to Naples and to tell Liborio Romano to maintain the good feeling of the people, to prepare them, if need be, for insurrection, but to prevent them from doing anything decisive before he himself arrived.

"Above all," he repeated, "no fighting in the streets of Naples: Palermo has suffered too much from that."

Then he shook Salvati's hand, asking him to do the same for him in regard to Liborio Romano and myself.

Then, as he was leaving,

"The man whom I would best like to see at the head of affairs in Naples, is Cosenz. No man deserves it better than does he. Tell that to Dumas and Romano. Repeat to the latter that he ought to do all he can to induce the King to leave; but no rising in my absence; it would be too dangerous."[2]

---

[1] Francesco Stocco of the Thousand, the chief landowner of the district, who was wounded at Calatafimi.

[2] Mr. Trevelyan gives a similar account, and adds that Garibaldi set out to follow Dumas' messenger as fast as horses could carry him.

Having made this recommendation, he gave Salvati a free pass and three horses with which to return to Pizzo.

Salvati left, reached Pizzo safely, gave his three horses, which he no longer needed, to Colonel Agostino Marico, and then, not having any other means of returning to Naples, he took a six-oared boat and started for Messina, keeping near the shore. It was the 2nd September.

The day before that of the bursting of the little reactionary plot, the very day on which the letter of the Count of Syracuse had appeared, the Prince had sent me M. Testa, his doctor, to tell me that he had not forgotten our relations of 1835 and that he would be delighted to see me again. I replied that if he would do me the honour of coming on board the *Emma*, he would be doubly welcome as a friend and as a patriot.

The next day the Prince came on board.

We embraced each other; the Prince, looking at me, began to laugh.

"Well," he asked, "and what do you think of the position?"

"I think that if your Highness had accepted the proposition I made you fifteen years back much blood would have been spared to Sicily and Naples, and many misfortunes to your house."

"It is true," he said, "but who could foretell what would happen?"

"A prophet or a poet."

"And now, poet or prophet, what do you counsel me to do?"

"I counsel your Highness . . ."

He interrupted me, shrugging his shoulders. "Are there still to-day Princes and Highnesses of the house of Bourbon? We are all condemned, my dear Dumas; we roll irresistibly down the incline; Louis XVI has shown us the road to the scaffold, Charles X the road to exile; happy will be those who will reach exile."

"Well, my dear Prince, since you have reached such a degree of philosophy, historically speaking, why do you remain in Naples?"

"Because, up till to-day, I thought that I could fight against reaction; to-day, I feel my incapacity, and I retire."

"You can do so, you have shot your arrow."

"What do you think of my letter?"

"I find it all the more cruel, because it speaks relentless truth!"

"You know Liborio Romano?"

"Only for three days; but in that time he has become my friend."

"You choose your friends well. He is the only man in Naples. Warn him to keep on his guard."

"On your behalf?"

"If you like."

23

We then spoke of Paris, where we had met five or six times between our two political interviews, of the days of our vanished youth, of I can't tell what.

The Prince became sad and abstracted.

Suddenly, he returned to what we had first talked about.

"You advise me, then, to leave?"

"Yes, Prince."

"So I can do no good by staying?"

"You will only create the mistrust of all parties."

"Very good, I will come to see you again to-morrow."

He rose, embraced me a second time, went down to the boat which had brought him, and went on board the Sardinian Admiral's vessel.

Let me relate what had happened that same day.

A second vessel bearing a flag of truce had arrived bringing a hundred soldiers and thirty officers as prisoners.

With his admirable tact, Garibaldi understood the effect these ocular proofs of the Royalist defeats would produce on the Neapolitans. The ship was the *Ferruccio*, Captain Orlandini. I had known him when he was a child at Florence in 1840, when I lived in the house in the Via Rondinelli belonging to one of his aunts.

We had an equal desire to see each other, although I was unaware of his feelings, but I wished for news of the General. I sent my canoe with an invitation to come to *déjeuner* on board the *Emma*. He accepted, and, an hour later, he arrived.

Orlandini had left the General on the heights above Pizzo, continuing his march on Naples.

He had arranged to leave during the day.

"Remain," said I; "I will show you things this evening which will surprise you and which you will relate to the General: the words— *I have seen!* will be better than a long letter."

He promised to remain until midnight and returned to his ship to look after the landing of the prisoners.

Scarcely had he reached the *Ferruccio* than a young officer of about twenty-five, of fair complexion and a mild expression, though his eyes looked resolute, ascended the *Emma's* ladder.

He gave out that he had something particular to say to me.

We seated ourselves on the deck, where there was already seated a Neapolitan, whom Father Gavazzi had begged me to receive on board with one of his comrades; both of them, so Father Gavazzi said, were deserters who wanted to serve in Garibaldi's army and considered themselves in danger of arrest.

We did not pay any attention to the Neapolitan deserter, and, when we were seated, I asked the young officer to explain the object of his visit.

"I am an Englishman," he said, "but of Italian origin. My name is Pilotti; I command a little steam-boat. Here are my papers from Garibaldi; here is my muster-roll—fifty Englishmen, fifty Americans; total one hundred devils incarnate."

"Good; you are a pirate captain?"

"Just so. I have hired at Genoa a river steamer. I have stuck my men on it and—come what may!"

"Under what flag are you?"

"I have twenty on board and no preference for any!"

"But if you are taken, you and your men will be hanged."

"I will try not to be taken."

"*Diable!* . . . And what can I do for you?"

The young man pointed to one of three Neapolitan cruisers at anchor in the harbour which were doing duty for a circuit of four or five leagues as coastal police.

"You see that ship?" said he.

"Yes."

"Well, I want to capture it."

"A good idea, but how will you manage it?"

"With my boat."

"Have you cannon?"

"Not a single one."

"Well, then?"

"Well, then, this evening, in the still of night, I shall enter the port as if about to cast anchor near the boat; I shall make some stupid manœuvre, and, while crying 'Look out!' our men will leap on it, make the crew prisoners, tie it up to my boat, and take it out to sea; meanwhile we shall get up its steam. Directly that is done, *bonsoir!* it is the fastest of the three Neapolitan vessels: none is capable of catching it."

"And yours?"

"Mine is equal to thirteen knots in fine weather."

"And in bad?"

"Ah, that is another thing: it sinks. As I have said, it is a river boat which in stormy weather cannot ride the waves."

"All this does not tell me of what assistance I can be."

"Well, it is like this. My boat is hidden at Cumes. I am going to rejoin it and agree with your Captain on certain signals as to whether the Neapolitan boat is still where it is now; on others if it has left. I am out of coal, or, rather, I shall be so in twelve or fifteen hours. If the Neapolitan boat is at the same spot, all is well, for it has coal enough for both of us; but if it is cruising, it is otherwise, and the coal I shall then be needing I must get from you."

"How many tons will you want?"

"Forty or fifty."

"If the steamer leaves, look out for a lighter at half a cable's length from the *Emma;* the coal will be on it and waiting for you. You will then coal and leave."

"I have no money."

"It doesn't matter; I still have some."

"Then, all is arranged."

"All."

"I am going to return to my boat after having agreed on the signals with your Captain."

"You can arrange them . . . I am going to give you two men to add to your muster roll."

"What two men?"

"Two Neapolitan deserters who cannot go on land without being shot; you may be sure that they will not allow themselves to be captured."

"Where are they?"

"Here."

I showed him the man near us on the deck and his companion, who was conversing with my sailors.

Then, while he was arranging details with my captain, I explained to my two guests that I had found what they seemed to wish: an occasion to leave Naples.

The plan appeared but little to please the man near us on the deck; the other, on the contrary, embraced it warmly.

Pilotti had no time to lose. He had to take the little Ischian boat which plies between the island and Naples, and, at Ischia, a row-boat in which he could go to find his steam-boat.

We saw the smoke of the Ischian boat, which in a minute was within call of the *Emma*. We hailed it, it stopped. Pilotti got into the boat that had brought him, and was followed by the two Neapolitans.

But, in getting on board, the man who seemed unwilling to go, stumbled, and so clumsily that he fell into the sea. He was hauled out dripping with water. He made this the pretext for not going with Pilotti. He returned on board the yacht, made out that he must change his garments, and asked me to set him on shore as near to his hotel as possible.

On my reminding him of the danger he would incur of being arrested, he replied that he would adopt certain precautions against this misfortune.

I had no reason for keeping him dripping on deck; he did not inspire me with any special liking, little did it matter to me if he were hanged or not. So I let him get into a boat and go away.

In the meantime, Liborio Romano had sent me his secretary, Cozzolongo, through whom I had conveyed the advice of the Count of Syracuse to be watchful for his personal safety. I had added some details respecting Garibaldi's march which I told him I had received from the officer who bore the flag of truce.

An hour after Cozzolongo had left me Romano told Muratori to bring the Garibaldian captain to him. He invited me to accompany him, telling me that so long as he was Minister of Police I ran no risk in going on shore. I replied that any risk did not deter me from going, but what did so was my vow not to enter Naples except with Garibaldi, and that Muratori alone would accompany Orlandini to his Palazzo di Riviera-Chiaïa.

At the time agreed M. Orlandini came on board the *Emma*. The *Emma*, as I have said, was anchored two hundred yards from the King's windows, which were recognisable from the linen awnings hung above them to keep off the sun.

For two days past I had had fourteen tailors on deck making up red shirts to put, at a given moment, on the backs of the insurgent Neapolitans.

The previous day I had sent a hundred of these shirts to Salerno; four persons had taken them. Each of these individuals had put on five and twenty, one on the top of another. The thinnest of them looked enormous; the others had lost all human resemblance; fortunately it was night-time.

The truce officer only told us of what he had seen and heard. He had gone into the town and had everywhere seen portraits of Garibaldi and Victor Emmanuel. Around the *Emma* a number of swimmers cried, "Vive Garibaldi!" and young men in a boat sang the *Marseillaise* in *patois!*

I had got out my best champagne—Folliet-Louis and Greno; fifty young men who could not dine with us, seeing the limited dimensions of my table, drank the Dictator's health.

And all this, I repeat, within two hundred yards of the windows of the King, who could not look at the sea without running his eyes against the two masts of my yacht.

At eight o'clock, M. Orlandini had to go to Romano's. At the moment of his departure I drew out my Bengal lights, green, red and white, Roman candles and Catherine wheels. The treaty captain went down to his yawl in the midst of an eruption of fire; the *Emma* seemed to offer defiance to Vesuvius.

Two Roman candles were held by two *commissaires de police*.

Could we have conspired more openly than we did?

Two hours later Orlandini returned. Romano had renewed, for conveyance to Garibaldi, the promises that he had made me. It only remained for him, as Minister, to try to spare Naples the horrors of a bombardment. For the rest, he sensed something to happen that night, and had left, not to return until the next morning.

The treaty captain, who was curious to know what was going to occur, promised me not to leave until noon the next day, and to come and dine on board the *Emma*. What did happen was the attempt at reaction of which I have spoken to you.

Towards nine o'clock that evening, a young printer employed at the Ferranti works, named Francesco Diana, appeared before the *commissaire* Antonio Davino and told him that an hour previously a Frenchman named Hercule de Souchères had taken to his lodgings, largo Santa-Teresa, No. 6, a large quantity of printed matter which he, Diana, judged to be seditious; but, as the *commissaire* did not appear to attach much importance to what he stated, he insisted that the authorities should impound the papers, making a domiciliary visit for the purpose to Souchères', where they would certainly find them.

When the *commissaire* asked Diana what had been his connection with Souchères, and how it had occurred that the latter had gone to him, Diana, for the printing of the dangerous papers, he replied that he had known him for some time past, having printed for him an opuscule called "Naples and the Revolutionary Journals," and that, not having cared to print it himself, he had sent Souchères off to other printers, but had got an estimate of the cost of the work and had undertaken the proof correction, which Souchères, being unacquainted with the Italian language, could not do himself.

He, also, then declared that before having obtained the manifestoes printed by Carlo Zumachi he had realised, from what Souchères said when the manifestoes were handed to him for printing, that their aim was to incite a bloody reaction led by personages in the highest positions, and that this would take place the next day, the 30th August, at noon.

Diana signed this declaration.

Besides these proclamations certain papers were seized, among which was this letter, the only important one. It makes curious reading, inasmuch as it indicates the rôle played in the plot by the King, the royal family and the clergy.

"To the Reverend Father Giacinto, Reader in the College of Capucins, Rome.

"Naples, 29th August, 1860.

"My Dear Sir,

"You may accuse me of ingratitude, or, at least, of negligence; but I have often thought of you and your enjoyment of your retreat, and, if my prayers were answered, you would be as happy in your vocation as you merit to be.

"Since my sad departure from Rome, Providence has prevented me from executing all my projects. I have been obliged by circumstances to stop at Naples, where I have suffered greatly for some months. To defend the King and the Pope I have written a brochure which you ought to have received a month ago. In consequence I am on the point of being assassinated by miserable revolutionists.[1] One of them has already appeared here for the purpose. At the moment I was at mass: God has thus saved me. Shall I escape? I hope so. Happen what may, one thing only causes me grief: it will be to die before having paid my sacred debt; but you will pardon me. If I am so fortunate as to live and when politics are calmer I shall be, for some time at least, attached to the King's person. Already I am attached to one of the royal princes to write letters to some French journals; my devotion is recognised. The Emperor of Austria and the Duke of Modena have paid me compliments on my books. I hope that, thus, my financial position will much improve in a very short time. God has seen my sufferings and the humiliations I have been subjected to. I have confidence in Him. Sending me on a mission to Rome is spoken of. If that eventuated, I could clear my position. My first visit after those to Saint Peter and the Minerva,—where I was so happy in laying my misfortunes before God,—will be to you. I have many things to say to you.

"Here, we are on the eve of a frightful insurrection. All that I said in our private talks, this winter, is being accomplished. Garibaldi has now a powerful party favoured by Napoleon. The worst characters of all countries flock into the capital. The King is about to leave to put himself at the head of his army. He has courage, but is surrounded by so many traitors that he sometimes gives way to despair. As he is very virtuous and his people have only strayed because of his great ignorance of everything, I think that he will succeed in surmounting the obstacles which are created each day to destroy him; but it will not be without loss of blood. His entourage is faithful and very irritated against the Garibaldians; it wishes to make a massacre similar to that of St. Bartholomew. If God does not aid us there will be many victims, and that before many days are over.

"It is said that Lamorcière is with our army to command it in the first battle that takes place, and on which will depend the future of Neapolitan monarchy, of the Pope, of religion and of all Italy; for a great victory would encourage the audacity of our enemies and cast down for a long time the Royalists.

"What is said in Rome? Are you organising as the papers say? Is the Pope much loved? Have you powerful troops? Does the French element dominate? And . . . do the people hope?

"We are passing through such a crisis such as has not been seen for a long time, such as, I believe, has never existed; brains are diseased; it is a sort of madness which attacks even good Catholics, even priests and monks. Here, it is not that *all* has need to be reformed, but to be demolished and reconstructed anew, *all, without any exception*, were it not for some virtuous persons, among whom I number the King and Queen.

"I received your letter from Jerusalem; it gave me great pleasure; but I had no money for postage stamps, which is the chief cause of my silence; the second is that for the last three months or thereabouts I have not known what to do on

---

[1] Let us state here that not only have these revolutionists not assassinated M. de Souchères, but after having arrested him, after having convicted him of the crime of conspiring against the State, they have released him after eight days in prison. We ask whether Ferdinand II and Francis II would have acted likewise towards their enemies. (Author's note.)

account of being so very busy. To-day, the revolution leaves me some leisure, and I profit by it to send you my news and to ask for yours.

"If chance takes you to the Minerva, or you meet the Abbé Laprit, kindly tell him that he ought to have received my letter through the Neapolitan Embassy. Remember me to him, and express my thanks to M. Scuive.

"Believe me, etc.

"(*Signed*) De Souchères.

"As I do not know what may happen, you can write to me as follows: *Al reverendissimo padre Antonio del Carmello, per il signor de Souchères, convento di San-Pasquale, a Chiaïa, Napoli.*"

At midnight, the Minister waited on the King to announce this attempt at reaction, of which his Majesty knew perfectly well. Francis II listened to the recital with a certain bitterness, then, addressing himself to the Minister of the Interior and Police,

"Don Liborio," he said, "you are cleverer at discovering royalist plots than liberal conspiracies."

"Sire," replied Don Liborio, "it is because the royalist plots are woven at night between few people, and liberal conspiracies are woven in daylight among the whole populace!"

"I knew a French priest who conspired with a reactionary aim, but he has got away," said the King without replying to Romano.

"Your Majesty is mistaken," said Romano, "he is arrested."

"Well," said the King, with some momentary impatience, "send him to the Criminal Court and let him be tried."

They then separated.

The next day M. Brenier called on Romano. He came to demand the freedom of M. de Souchères.

"What good can it do to keep this miserable priest in prison?" he asked.

"Well," said Romano, "if he is a priest, he is all the more dangerous."

And he kept him in prison, in spite of M. Brenier's insistence.

The matter was, in truth, most serious; it compromised the Count di Trani and the Count di Caserta, who had dictated the proclamation. As to General Cutrofiano, he had contented himself with correcting the proofs.

The same day I received a message from Romano. It was this: "From this moment, war is declared between the King and me; he will leave Naples, or I will leave the ministry."

The next morning the Count di Syracuse was on board the *Emma*. He knew all that had passed during the night, the nomination of Cutrofiano to the command of the fort, that of Prince Ischitella to the chief command of the National Guard.

He asked whether I had news of Romano. He had been told that the

Minister had been arrested in his bed. I reassured him by saying that Romano had not slept at home.

The Prince left in an agitated state. He would leave Naples, he assured me, the next day at the latest.

I had spent the night, until four in the morning, on deck awaiting Pilotti. If he had come, he would have got his coal.

He returned by the Ischian boat without having found his own steam-boat; it is probable that he had been denounced and that the three cruisers had been after him.

Pilotti and the Neapolitan deserter who had gone with him left on the *Ferruccio* with Captain Orlandini.

Towards seven in the morning the man who had fallen into the sea returned to his post on the yacht.

During the day a person calling himself the Marquis di Lo Presti called on me, saying that he knew for certain that the King would go out that evening to judge the effect on the people of his *coup d'état;* that he, Lo Presti, and a friend of his, would take advantage of the occasion to throw a bomb into the King's carriage.

I called Muratori, and in front of the so-called Marquis,[1]

"My dear Muratori," cried I, "go at once on shore, hasten to the Count di Syracuse and tell him to warn his nephew not to go out this evening."

Then, returning to the man of the bomb,

"Sir," said I, "you have heard me; now there is only one thing for you to do, and that is to leave the *Emma* this very moment, or I will have you thrown into the water by my sailors!"

The false Marquis got into the boat which had brought him, and I saw no more of him.

The Count di Syracuse replied to me that after the *coup d'état* of the previous night the King was his nephew no longer, and that consequently all that might happen to Francis II was a matter of indifference to him.

One of our friends, Stefanone, the brother of the celebrated artist, happened to be by when this answer came.

I turned to him.

"You know the Duke of Laorito?" said I.

" Very well."

" Go and find him, my dear Stefanone, and ask him to warn the King."

In an hour's time, Stefanone returned; the King had been warned.

At noon, Liborio sent to tell me that all the Ministers had resigned,

[1] Let us say here that he was a spy who had taken the honourable name of the Marquis di Lo Presti. (Author's note.)

and that from this moment he considered himself free from all duty towards the King.

While these events were occurring, Dr. Wielandt arrived from Cava, where he had been obliged to take refuge. The most complete disorganisation reigned in the camp of Salerno; the soldiers were deserting, the officers declared that they would not fight. Bosco had returned to Naples ill from rage.

Avellino only waited for the order to declare the revolution. Dr. Wielandt knew the *intendant;* he offered to write a letter to him in his own name and in that of Romano.

The messenger only was wanting. We had him ready in the person of the deserter; he was just the man we wanted.

Muratori gave him the letter, his instructions, and thirty francs for the journey, and he left.

With Dr. Wielandt had arrived some of our friends from Salerno. They asked me whether I had received any arms. I had ten cases full on the *Pausilippe;* but the Captain, fearing, and with good reason, to compromise himself, had refused to send them to me. I gave the Salernitans three carbines and twelve revolvers; they were all that I had left.

All day long, Naples was in a state of great agitation: the officers of the National Guard protested against the *coup d'état,* and came to beg Romano to cancel his resignation, but he held firm to his resolution.

During the evening, patrols were to be found all over the city. The Commandant, Cutrofiano, when insulted by an officer of the National Guard, was obliged to put up with the affront.

At nine o'clock, Cozzolongo was bidden by the self-dismissed Minister to tell me that on the morrow he would probably come to dine with me, on his way to ask for the hospitality of the English Admiral. Cozzolongo was also told to go, on leaving me, and announce to the Captain responsible for the negotiations, who was starting that same evening, that as Romano now had his liberty in full, Garibaldi could rely on him, and that he would renew his engagement to hand over Naples to the General without the shedding of one drop of blood.

At ten o'clock the *Ferruccio* raised its anchor. It carried with it another letter from me to Garibaldi.

Here is a copy:

"In the name of Heaven, my friend, not another shot. It is unnecessary; Naples is yours.

"Come quickly to Salerno, and from there communicate with Liborio Romano; he will go to you with some of his colleagues or await you at the railway station.

"Come without losing a minute. An army is unnecessary to you; your name is worth an army.

"If I did not wish you to have the pleasure of a surprise, I could send you the transcript of a discourse which will be delivered on your arrival.

"Vale et me ama,
"Alex. Dumas."

Night passed in a very noisy and excited fashion, but towards three o'clock the noise died down, the excitement ceased. Only Vesuvius continued, with deep growlings, to throw out flames and to overflow its lava. Vesuvius is Naples' safety-valve.

The next morning (Sunday, 2nd September) passed off very quietly. I happened to express my astonishment in front of Romano's messenger.

"Nothing is ever done in Naples of a Sunday," he observed. And, in fact, Naples looked entirely different from what it had done the previous day; Naples appeared to be a thousand leagues from a revolution; of the resignation of the Ministers there was not the least discussion; of Garibaldi nobody seemed to have ever heard; of Liborio Romano, Ischitella, Cutrofiano, Frances II, all were alike ignorant of such people.

What Naples *did* know about were St. Januarius and the Madonna.

All day long squibs, I do not know in honour of what saint, were let off; every moment I trembled, believing the noise to be a fusillade. Ignorant fool that I was; had I not been already told that nothing is ever done in Naples of a Sunday?

The sole event of the day was the departure of the Sardinian steam-boat, the *Governor*, which fired eleven salutes, raised its anchor and steamed for Genoa. On board was the Count di Syracuse; he had followed my advice of two days previous.

During the evening our messenger returned; he brought back a very prudent letter from Avellino's *intendant* which engaged him to nothing. This reserve on his part was soon explained; we had sent, as messenger, one of the best-known spies of the former Government; so he had, as his letter proved, treated this man as an *agent provocateur*.

Happily for Seigneur don Julis, he was no longer there: had he been so, it would have been I who would have thrown him into the sea. Directly he had handed in his letter he had left the yacht, no doubt never to return. But the man who had accompanied him was still there.

I frankly put the question to him.

"Your comrade was a spy, and in all probability you are one also."

The poor devil swore by all his gods that he was not. He had never seen don Julis before that day.

"You know which is his hotel?"

"Yes."

"Very good."

I told Louis, one of my sailors, a kind of Colossus, capable, like Milo of Crotona, of carrying an ox on his back, and of killing and eating it the same day, I told Louis to keep watch on our prisoner and to strangle him if he moved.

Then Muratori jumped into a boat and went to find Cola-Cola. He is the police officer of low rank who replied to Judge Navarro, when condemning him to forty-six years hard labour: "Forty-six years is a long time; I will do what I can, you will do the rest."

Liborio had put him at our orders.

Half-an-hour later, Muratori returned with him, and we related the affair.

"It is a simple matter," he said, " I am going to arrest him as a reactionary, and put him in solitary confinement for two or three days; after that, all will be over, and I can either release him or have him tried, just as you like."

"Release him, Cola-Cola, I do not wish for the death of a sinner."

"Cola-Cola," I continued, "take this gentleman with you and watch him as closely as if he had swallowed diamonds belonging to the crown of Naples. He will take you to his companion's hotel, and he will assist you to arrest him; you will lock up the one you have captured, and you will release the other man in the middle of the strada di Toledo, inviting him to go and hang himself where he likes."

Cola-Cola beckoned to our guest to follow him, made him sit by his side in the boat, whispered two words in his ear, to which he seemed to agree, and silently disappeared into the night.

Half-an-hour later, Cola-Cola returned.

"Well?" we all asked at once.

"Well, he is locked up, accused of having wanted to assassinate the Minister."

Admit that it is a strange country—this—in which men who conspire, arrest the spies who spy on them.

It is true, however, that *we* are conspiring with the Prime Minister.

CHAPTER LII

THE PROSCRIPTION OF THE *EMMA*

Porto di Picciotta, 5th September

ON the morning of the 3rd September the Pope's Nuncio, a prime mover in the reaction, called on Liborio Romano, whose resignation was not yet accepted. He came to announce that there were serious uprisings in Benevento and asked for soldiers wherewith to repress them.

Liborio Romano began to laugh.

"Monseigneur," he said, "at the present time our soldiers refuse to fight for us; I doubt very much, as they decline to fight for us, whether they wish to fight for the Pope."

"But then," said the Nuncio, much flustered, "what is His Holiness to do?"

"His Holiness will do what King Francis is doing; he will resign himself to the loss of his temporal power, and, happier than King Francis, there will remain to him the most splendid heritage of Popes, since it is that which they hold from Jesus Christ,—his spiritual power."

"That is your answer?"

"Word for word."

"And what remains for me to do?"

"Only one thing."

"And that is?"

"To bless three persons—nothing else."

"Who are they?"

"King Victor Emmanuel, General Garibaldi, your servant Liborio Romano."

The Nuncio departed furious, muttering words which were far from resembling those of a benediction.

On Monday the agitation rose again to the height of Saturday: the Ministers sat with the King from eleven until five o'clock.

At half-past six, as we were finishing our dinner, an armed boat of war hailed the *Emma*, and a naval officer boarded us and asked for Captain Beaugrand. He was dining on the *Protis*, and had not returned. We answered, through Muratori, that the Captain was not there.

"Call the mate, then."

"We have no mate," said Muratori, "he is at Marseilles."

I came forward.

"In the absence of the Captain and the mate, will you tell me what brings you, monsieur," said I to the officer; "I am at once the fitter-out and the owner of the *Emma.*"

"I am ordered to address myself to one of the crew, and not to the fitter-out or owner."

"Then, Podimatas, my friend, show yourself and listen attentively to what the gentleman says."

Muratori and I returned to the table and finished our dinner.

The Neapolitan officer conferred with Podimatas for five minutes and then went down to his boat, which went away quickly.

"Well, Podimatas," I asked, "it is necessary to leave the harbour of Naples, is it not?"

"Just so."

"And when?"

"At once."

"Oh! oh! at once is too soon; we cannot leave our Captain in uneasiness about us."

"The order is peremptory."

"What worse can they do, Podimatas?"

"They can fire on us."

"Is that all? they fire so badly, they will miss us: you remember Milazzo?"

My reasoning appearing good to Podimatas, he went back to the table and finished his cup of coffee. As he was swallowing the last drop, Cozzolongo came on board.

"Well," said he, "you have received orders to leave the harbour?"

"Yes, tell me what has happened."

Cozzolongo related what I have already told you. The King, at noon, had summoned M. Brenier, and told him that I was the cause of all the troubles which had taken place for the last eight or ten days in Naples; that before my arrival Naples was tranquil, and that when I left it would become so again.

M. Brenier's ideas ran parallel to the King's, and he, in the name of the Government represented by him, gave his Majesty every power to make me leave the harbour.

As regards myself, M. Brenier wished me to have the pleasure of a surprise. Another man would have warned me that, having regard to the personal war which I was making against his Majesty Francis II, he could not oppose my departure.

After the advice tendered to him to depart, the King only received Pianell, Ischitella, Cutrofiano, and Capecelatro, the naval officer.

From the morning of the 4th, he accepted Romano's programme: not to make war around Naples, and, whatever might happen, to spare the city.

On the evening of the same day he decided to leave.

On the 5th he made his arrangements, saw the Spanish and French ambassadors, received the Generals and conversed quietly and calmly with them.

That day the Minister, Spinelli, was instructed to write the King's farewell to his people. Spinelli, however, called on Romano to beg him to do it for him; the task was not a difficult one, for, the departure having been foreseen, these good-byes were already on paper.[1]

During the evening of the 5th September Spinelli presented the proclamation to the King.

Francis II began to read it; but desisting after the second paragraph:

"It is not you who have written this proclamation, Spinelli," said he; "it is Romano. I recognise his style."

And he added:

"When he likes, he writes very well."

Then he signed the proclamation and directed Spinelli to have it printed.

Here it is:

"ROYAL PROCLAMATION"

"Among the duties ordained for kings, those that appertain to days of misfortune are the greatest and most solemn. These I intend to fulfil with resignation, free from all weakness, and with a serene and confident heart, as becomes the descendant of so many kings.

"With such feelings, I once again address the people of my kingdom, from whom I am now about to depart, deeply grieved at being unable to give my life for their happiness and glory.

"An unjust war, waged in defiance of the law of nations, has invaded my states, notwithstanding that I was at peace with all the European powers.

"The important changes which led to my adhesion to great national principles were not sufficient to stave off this evil; and the necessity of defending the integrity of the state forced upon me events which I have always deplored; therefore I protest solemnly against this invasion, and appeal to the justice of all civilized nations.

"The diplomatic corps, who are in close touch with me personally, are well aware of the sentiments I have ever expressed towards my people, as well as towards our noble metropolis. The desire to save this city from ruin and war, to secure her inhabitants and all their property, her churches, her monuments, her public buildings, her art collections, and all that forms the patrimony of her civilization and greatness and the inheritance of future generations, is an impulse which should rise above the passions of the day in which I live.

"The moment has come when I must make good these professions which I have declared. War is now approaching the walls of this city, and with unutterable grief I am now about to depart with a portion of my army to go whither the defence of my right calls me. The rest of my noble army will remain to insure the inviolability of the capital which I recommend as a sacred trust to the Ministry, to the Mayor, and to the Commandant of the National Guard. I feel that I can rely upon the honour and civic loyalty of all these to do everything to spare our

---

[1] I have the draft of this farewell, which, if one wanted to date it correctly, should bear that of 2nd September. The draft is written on paper with the impress of the Minister of State on it. (Author's note.)

most beloved country the horrors of internal discord and the disasters of civil war. For this purpose, I grant to the above-named functionaries the amplest necessary powers.

"As a descendant of a dynasty which has reigned over this country for 126 years, my affections are centred here. I am a Neapolitan, and cannot, without feelings of bitter grief, speak words of farewell to my dearly beloved people. Whatever may be my destiny, prosperous or the contrary, I shall always preserve for them a lasting and affectionate remembrance. I recommend to them concord and peace, and the observance of their civic duties. Do not let an immoderate zeal for my fate be made a pretext for disorder.

"Whether it may please the justice of God to restore me to the throne of my ancestors or not, all that I pray for is to behold my people once again united, strong, and happy.

"*Naples, 5th Sept.,* 1860."

On the morning of the 6th the King signed many decrees; at two o'clock he received the Ministers and said farewell to them.

"Gentlemen, I am forced to leave; I do so, calmly, because my fall is not caused by my fault, but by the decrees of Providence. Whatever may be my destiny, I will support it courageously. The only thing that breaks my heart is that Naples abandons its King's cause without striking a blow. I thank you for all you have done for the country and for me."

The Ministers then kissed hands.

Towards four o'clock the King went down from the palace to the dock. He was accompanied by MM. di Martino, di Capecelatro, di Carafa.

He embarked on the *Sajetta*,[1] commanded by Captain Criscuolo, a seaman who had had the confidence of King Ferdinand II.

At six o'clock the boat sailed, carrying towards Gaëta the last reigning son of Henri IV and Saint Louis.

---

[1] Mr. Trevelyan says the vessel was the *Messagero*, a small ship of 160 h.p. and four guns.

CHAPTER LIII

THE DEPARTURE OF KING FRANCIS II

M. Brenier did nothing,[1] and when I return to Naples with Garibaldi I will do myself the honour of calling and thanking him.

Captain Beaugrand did not return until ten o'clock, so we had plenty of time in which to learn what was going on in the city.

There was much agitation. Posters had been put up on which were the words:

"Long live Victor Emmanuel! long live Garibaldi! long live United Italy!"

The National Guard wanted to tear them down; the people wanted to keep them up. An officer tore down one of the posters with the point of his sabre; a man of the people, with a blow of his stick, killed him. The result was a conflict with the National Guard, in which the Guard was repulsed.

From the harbour were heard the cries of the *lazzaroni* and the beating of drums.

It was at this moment that we heaved up our anchor, while giving our friends a *rendezvous* at Castellammare.

Two journalists were then on board; on the morrow there must have been the devil to pay in the newspapers.

For the last week the *Emma* had been the hive where all the honey had been made—from her had radiated all news and from her had emanated all proclamations.

We left for Castellammare on the finest of calm days—in two hours we had not made a mile.

The *Emma* is so well known on all the coast for its enthusiastic Garibaldianism that hardly had the anchor dropped when visitors began to arrive. Everyone wanted the same thing—arms—but I had none.

Suddenly, as I was replying to my visitors' requests, a boat with a naval officer appeared.

The officer asked for the Captain.

The Captain rose.

"Captain," said the officer in very fair French, "it is forbidden to the *Emma* to sojourn off the coasts of Naples."

"Can you tell me, sir, to where at this moment the coasts of Naples extend?" I asked the officer.

[1] M. Brenier, the French Consul, did nothing to inform Dumas that he would have to leave the harbour.

The officer bit his lips.

"You have heard, Captain," said he.

"Yes, but it is impossible to leave just now," said the Captain.

"Why?"

"Because my papers are at the Consul's."

"Go for them at once."

"Monsieur," said I, "excuse another question, but I am very curious this evening, as is natural when one is leaving a country."

"Speak."

"Whose is that pretty little cutter dancing on the water over there in the harbour, half a mile off?"

"It is the King's, Monsieur."

"You are mistaken, it is mine."

"What! it is yours?"

"Yes, and the proof is that I will take it in passing by."

The officer then left without another word.

Our Captain had the yawl lowered and was rowed to land.

The port official was indeed unfortunate: the Consul's secretary had put the *Emma's* papers into a drawer, had locked it up and, having put the key into his pocket, had gone no one knew where.

So we could not leave.

Two armed war boats, each containing twenty men, came along and stationed themselves on either side of the *Emma*. This did not prevent Castellammare, which had learnt of my arrival, being illuminated as Salerno had been. This illumination frightened the commander of the place, he apparently having little faith in the cannon of his fortress.

At one in the morning he sent us this message:

Castellammare,
3rd Sept. 1860, Midnight.

"OFFICE OF THE HIGHER COMMAND
OF THE NAVAL DEPARTMENT.

"The commander of the yacht *Emma* is to sail immediately, and remain out at sea. In the morning the Captain only will go ashore to receive his papers, and that with the least possible delay. He will then leave."

You are going to see that it is I who have dethroned the King of Naples, and that I will be the Amerigo Vespucci of Garibaldi!

At nine o'clock only did the Consul's secretary return, as if a hint had been given him to enrage the senior officer of the naval department as much as possible.

Two hours previously, a messenger had left for Avellino with one of the free passes given me by Garibaldi. This pass will help him to make the province of Avellino revolt and establish a provisional government there.

At ten o'clock the Captain returned with our papers, and we left.

All day and during the ensuing night we were in a calm and with difficulty crossed the Gulf of Salerno.

On the 5th, at noon, we were in front of the village of Picciotta, waiting for a fishing-boat from which we wanted to glean information as to where Garibaldi was. The skipper told us that the latest news was of a landing at Sapri, and the arrival of Garibaldi at Cosenza.

As we were conversing with the skipper we were noticed by the villagers, and a boat full of men put off from shore and came to us.

All the men were greedy for news; we gave it to them up to date: we told them that Garibaldi was expected at Naples, and that he had only to show himself there to be welcomed with enthusiasm.

They themselves had not dared to do anything, but when they heard our news and realised who was giving it, they gave such shouts of *Viva Garibaldi! Viva l'Italia una!* that I saw my opportunity of finding backs for the red shirts I had had made on board—those red shirts which were so stared at by Francis II.

Let me here record that a thousand ducats voluntarily subscribed during my stay in the Bay of Naples, had enabled me to pay my agents who were sent out on all sides to spread the revolution, to help such of our friends as needed help, to supply arms gratis and to pay for the making of red shirts.

One person had given enough stuff for four hundred shirts. And what is surprising, these excellent patriots insisted, and insist still, that their names are not given. With my own resources I could not have accomplished half of what I have done.

The men, who were not expecting such gifts, passed from enthusiasm to frenzy. There being no looking-glass, each looked at his companion, literally howling with joy.

Seeing what was going on on the water, and without understanding the change effected in costume, two other boats brim-full of passengers came rowing out to us. The newcomers received their red shirts and mingled their hoorahs with those of their friends.

One of them—a young fellow of from eighteen to twenty—asked me for pen, ink and paper, and improvised a proclamation—a thing of which I should have thought him incapable. It was read aloud then and there, and hailed with applause.

We counted the men, and found that there were about fifty. The number was considered sufficient to make Cilento revolt. Muratori, partaking in the general enthusiasm, declared that he would quit me to take the command of these fifty volunteers. I made him Captain, a nomination which was confirmed unanimously; I made the author of the proclamation his lieutenant; I gave to each a carbine and twenty-five cartridges, and they left. Muratori took three or four hundred francs, leaving me his much-diminished purse.

The poor lad, who had come to me with over 300 louis, had now scarcely 1000 francs left. In his patriotism, he had lavished his money.[1]

I watched the boats row away. This time, M. Delamarre might truly have said that he saw filibusters. They landed, and a moment later Muratori and his men disappeared.

While all this was going on, a useful breeze from the north-east had sprung up, and under full sail we made for Messina. There, I hoped to gain sure intelligence and with the aid of the *Ferruccio* or the *Franklin* to go to rejoin the General.

In the afternoon of the next day we reached Messina: neither Orrigoni nor Orlandini was there. The *Orégon* was the only vessel in the harbour. I sent word of my arrival to the Captain and begged him to send me news when he got any. This he promised to do, but for the moment his only instructions were not to leave his anchorage and to await orders.

I busied myself over my arms, which were at the Customs. I had them taken on board the *Emma*, hastening the transport as much as possible, so convinced was I that it would be necessary to leave at any moment.

On the 8th September, at about four in the morning I heard my name called out on the deck at the head of the companion ladder. I asked who wanted me.

"Garibaldi has entered Naples," answered a voice which I recognised as the Captain's.

I was lying on a cushion. I leapt down and rushed upon deck.

But the Captain, while answering for the news, could not give me any details other than those transmitted by the telegraph, an instrument which we all know is very much averse from details.

Let me now relate what events had passed at Naples since my departure—that is to say, since the evening of the 3rd September.

---

[1] This money has never been reimbursed him, although on returning to Naples he found his friend Liborio Romano at the Ministry where he had left him. (Author's note.)

CHAPTER LIV

GARIBALDI AT NAPLES

DURING the evening of the 6th came the news of Garibaldi's arrival at Salerno.

The King, on leaving, had requested his Ministers to take measures for the preservation of public order. Anxious to fulfil the duty thus imposed on them, they met towards nine in the evening at the house of Spinelli, their president, and decided to send the Mayor of Naples with Prince d'Alessandria and General di Sazepono to Garibaldi to treat with him concerning his entry into the capital.

Further, it was agreed to have them preceded by the advocate Emilio Civitta, whose brother was in Garibaldi's army, and who was very intimate with Romano. Cozzolongo, who had recently been promoted to the post of Commissary of Police, was to go with Civitta.

And it was arranged that early the next morning they should reassemble in the usual meeting-room and then decide on any further steps.

The next day at six o'clock Romano, Lancilli and the Directors, di Cesare, Carafa, Giacchi and Miraglio met together, but Commander Spinelli, di Martino and Pianell failed to appear.

The Ministers decided to present an address to Garibaldi. Romano had already written one, and, being approved by all, it was signed by Romano, di Cesare and di Giacchi.

Here it is:—

"GENERAL,

"You have before you a ministry whose power was conferred on them by King Francis II. We accepted our duties as a sacrifice due to our country, and accepted them at a difficult period: at a time when the thought of the unity of Italy under the sceptre of Victor Emmanuel—a long-cherished hope of Neapolitans, and now already proclaimed in Sicily—had become an irresistible power, sustained as it was by the might of your sword; at a time when all confidence between the Government and the governed was at an end, when old wrongs and suppressed hatreds had come to light—thanks to recent constitutional liberties—when the country was profoundly agitated by the fear of a violent reaction. This was the state of the country when we accepted power, and we did so in order to maintain public order and to save the state from anarchy and civil war. This was the aim of all our efforts. The country understood our motives and appreciated our conduct. The confidence of our fellow-citizens has never wavered, and it is to their zeal that we owe the tranquillity which has saved the city amid so many conflicting parties.

"General, all the populations of the kingdom have manifested their desires, either by open insurrection, or through the voice of the Press, or by other means. They, too, wish to form a part of one great united Italy under the constitutional sceptre of Victor Emmanuel. You, General, are the highest expression of this aspiration. All eyes are turned towards you; all hopes are centred in you. And we, the trustees of power, as well as being Italian citizens, place this power in your hands, confident that you will use it worthily and lead the country toward that noble objective which you have ever had before you, which is not only inscribed on your standards but is enshrined in the hearts of all—ITALY AND VICTOR EMMANUEL.

"*Naples, 7th of September,* 1860."

Now let us return to Prince d'Alessandria and General di Sazepono, who had been sent to Salerno by the Council of Ministers.

The two first messengers, Emilio Civitta and Cozzolongo, found Garibaldi forewarned. He was at the palace of the Intendant, the only one, it will be recalled, which was not illuminated on the evening of my station in the port. The General received them, spoke with them about the King's departure, and sent the following telegram to Don Liborio Romano, Minister of the Interior and of the Police—

"ITALY AND VICTOR EMMANUEL.

"TO THE PEOPLE OF NAPLES.—As soon as the Syndic and the Commander of the National Guard, whom I am expecting, arrive, I shall present myself amongst you.

"At this solemn moment I recommend you to maintain that order and tranquillity which so much conduce to the dignity of a people which is about to reassume the exercise of its own rights.

"The Dictator of the Two Sicilies,

"G. GARIBALDI.

"*Salerno, 7th September,* 6.30 A.M."

Liborio Romano answered by the following dispatch:

"*From Liborio Romano, Minister of the Interior and Police, to the invincible General Garibaldi, Dictator of the Two Sicilies.*

"Naples awaits your arrival with the greatest impatience, that it may hail the redeemer of Italy, and place in his hands the powers of the state and its own destiny.

"Having this in view, I shall make myself responsible for the maintenance of order and of public tranquillity. Your own words which are known to all the people are the surest pledge of success in all such efforts.

"Awaiting your further commands I remain, with profound respect,

"LIBORIO ROMANO.

"*Naples, 7th September.*"

But, instead of sending his orders, Garibaldi thought it better to present himself.

He took the morning train at about half-past ten with ten of his officers, the deputation that had been sent him, and a few members of the National Guard.

The train reached Naples at about noon.

Liborio Romano awaited the General with Giacchi and di Cesare; and Liborio Romano read the address we have already cited.

Garibaldi gave him his hand and thanked him for *having saved the country*. These were the General's own words, and they expressed the truth. Indeed, that blood has not been shed at the doors and in the streets of Naples is due to Liborio Romano.

Carriages were in waiting outside the station: that in which Garibaldi took his seat moved off the first in the procession, on its way to Naples.

The forts were still guarded by the royal soldiers. As the General neared them, a hostile movement was made by the artillerymen.

Garibaldi, seeing it, stood up in his carriage, folded his arms, and looked fixedly at them.

The artillerymen then gave him the military salute.

At Grand'Guardin an officer gave the order to fire; the soldiers refused to fire.

It being the custom for every king, every prince or every conqueror who makes his entry into Naples so to do, the procession went on to the cathedral.

Brother John performed mass and thanked God. The *Te Deum* having been sung, Garibaldi invited Romano to go with him, and the carriage set off for the *Palazzo d'Angri*, which both Championnet and Masséna had once occupied. When they arrived there, the General left the first floors for the use of his *aides-de-camp*, his staff and his secretaries. He himself took possession of the attics.

The whole of Naples had followed him from the sea fort to the cathedral and from the cathedral to the palace.

An immense shout, which sounded as if from the throats of the 500,000 inhabitants of Naples, burst forth towards heaven—it was the hymn of vengeance against Francis II, it was the hosannah of gratitude for the Liberator:

"Long live Garibaldi!"

The General was forced to show himself at the window. The shouts then redoubled; hats and bouquets were thrown into the air. At every window looking on the palace the women waved handkerchiefs, leaning out at the risk of falling into the street. The revolution was accomplished, and, as I had promised Garibaldi, without the shedding of a drop of blood.

Such was the triumphant entry that the telegraph announced to me on the morning of the 8th at Messina through the mouth of the Captain of the *Orégon*.

PALAZZO DI CHIATAMONE

15th November, 1860

I AT once gave the order to heave up the anchor, but the loading of the arms was a tedious affair, and it was actually not until noon that the yacht got under way with a nice breeze from the south-south-west.

Once we were in the open sea the wind freshened, clouds covered the sky and thunder growled. The captain took in one reef, then two, and finally lowered the mizzen.

All night long the wind blew with sufficient violence to be somewhat dangerous. If the tempest had driven us towards Naples I should have been glad of it, but it tossed us about the triangle formed by the shores of Sicily and Calabria, and Stromboli.

For two whole days we had Stromboli in sight. During all this time we barely made six miles; on the night of the third day the wind got up, and slowly, mile by mile, we found ourselves making four or five knots.

During the day of the 12th we got within two cables length of Capri, but there we were overtaken by a dead calm, which kept us between the grotto of Arno and Cape Campanella. With despair I was watching evening drawing on without a breath of air, when I made out, hugging the coast of Sorrento, a steam-boat which the captain identified as being the *Pytheas.* We sent out signals and it came to us.

It was going to Capri for troops, but had also the orders, if it met me, to give me any help I wanted.

Strange to say, it was one of the boats which were let by King Francis II to the Altaras Company. It was commanded by Captain Faci.

I gratefully accepted the towing that he had been ordered by the Dictator to offer me. We threw him a cable which he made fast at his end, and at full steam ahead he took us to Naples in an hour and a half, casting us off in the midst of the French and British warships. Then, bidding us farewell simultaneously with our expression of thanks, he turned his boat round, headed again for Capri, and disappeared in the darkness.

It was about nine o'clock. There was a heavy swell on; we got under sail and anchored near the mole.

On waking the next morning I found Muratori awaiting me on deck with a telegram in his hand. Garibaldi had given orders for the *Emma* to be signalled to him directly she hove in sight, for, the evening of the previous day, the following telegram had been sent to the General and transmitted by him to Muratori:

"The steam-boat *Pytheas* is coming from Capri towing a French yacht believed to be the *Emma*."

Muratori had looked for us that same evening, but had failed to discover us. In the morning he had renewed his search, and had been more fortunate.

Garibaldi was expecting me immediately on my arrival, and it goes without saying that Liborio Romano awaited me also. We picked him up in passing.

Don Liborio was still all on fire with his victory; he ran rather than walked with me to the *Palazzo d'Angri*.

We found the General on the fourth floor, in the garret, according to his custom.

"Ah! here thou art," he cried, on seeing me. "God be thanked! Thou hast made me wait long enough."

It was the first time that he addressed me as "thou." I threw myself into his arms, weeping for joy.

"Come," said the General, "there is no time to lose. Don Liborio, now for our excavations and our liberty to hunt!"

It may be recalled that these were the two favours for which I had asked. Only, what I had not asked, and what the General gave me, was the conduct of the Excavations. Don Liborio was bidden to have signed, the following day, the decree which appointed me Director of the Museums and Excavations.

"And now," said Garibaldi, "show Dumas to his palace. Then, turning to me, he added, "I dare say thou hast had doubts whether I would keep the promise made thee at Palermo? Only, I have done better for thee than a room in the royal palace, from which it would be necessary to dislodge thee some day or other. I have chosen a little palace where thou canst stay as long as thou listest."

I thanked the General.

"And do they know at the palace?" I asked.

"Yes; besides, to-morrow I will send thee by Cattabeni an authorisation in due form."

We embraced each other again and we separated.

Don Liborio was so good as himself to take me to the *Palazzo di Chiatamone* and instal me there.

Orders had been given to the hôtel *des Crocelles* to bring me meals twice a day across the street until I should get comfortably installed. It was this that made certain people believe that I was being fed at the cost of the municipality. The municipality did not have the idea of offering me this charity; consequently, I did not have the necessity of refusing it. At the end of a week I owed the *Crocelles* 1000 francs. I considered I had had enough of this. I paid the 1000 francs, and sent for my cook from the *Emma*.

A great stir was made about this thousand francs spent in a week. The good people said that Naples was feeding me, and that I (I, who drink water only) was ruining Naples by my orgies.

Garibaldi was told that I was spending fifty piastres a day, and that I constantly had twenty diners at my table; but he merely replied in his melodious voice:

"If twenty people sit down at Dumas' table, I am sure of this, at least, that they are twenty good friends of mine."

M. N——, who wanted the position of Director of Excavations, and who probably was unaware that it was a purely honorary post, prepared a petition against me.

The General sent it on to me.

He was told that I had shot on two occasions in the Capo-di-Monte, that I had carried off my game in a waggon, and that I had even shot hens and chicks.

He replied:

"Dumas is a sportsman . . . I am sure of one thing—that he has shot only cocks."

The day following my installation in the *Palazzo di Chiatamone* the General, in pursuance of his promise, sent me my lease in due form.

The document reads as follows:

Naples, 14th September, 1860.

"M. Dumas is authorised to occupy for a year from now the little *Palazzo di Chiatamone* in his capacity of Director of the Excavation and Museums.

"G. GARIBALDI."

This decision produced great scandal at Naples. The journals cried out about it; one of them reproached me for having myself watched over like a king by the National Guard. When Garibaldi gave me, at the royal palace of Palermo, the apartments of the Viceroy Castelcicala, Palermo applauded the act, and made me a citizen of Palermo. It is true that I had done absolutely nothing for Palermo, having reached there when all was over; whilst, on the contrary, I had risked my life for Naples.

May God nevertheless protect Naples! And may I do for it all the good of which I dream, and for the accomplishment of which I will, if it be necessary, risk my life again.

FINIS

APPENDIX I

TEXT OF MÉRY'S POEM

A MES CONVIVES

Je veux vous raconter ce que peut faire un homme,
Mais je n'ose, messieurs, vous dire s'il se nomme
Alexandre ou César; entre amis, on se sert
De ces ménagements à la fin du dessert.
Je ne le nomme pas: si quelqu'un veut connaître
Son nom, il peut venir, là, près d'une fenêtre,
Et je vais le lui dire, à l'oreille, en sortant,
Comme un secret d'État, le secret d'un instant.

Il pouvait bien aussi chanter, après Horace:
"Mon travail est complet, mon pied a fait sa trace;
Voila mon monument; le repos m'est bien dû:
Dans un monde d'oisifs, je n'ai jamais perdu
Un seul jour; j'ai conduit une plume acharnée
Dans toutes les saisons qui forment une année,
Depuis l'heure où ma main hésitait, en traçant,
Sur une tombe illustre, un vers adolescent."

Et nous ajoutons, nous: "De sa plume féconde
Il avait fait la joie et l'entretien du monde;
Au théâtre, il avait suivi tous les chemins,
Rajeuni les vieux Grecs, restauré les Romains,
Animé de sa verve et de sa poésie
Les héros de la fable et de la fantaisie,
Emprunté, dans l'histoire aux mobiles couleurs,
Ou le succès du rire, ou le succès des pleurs;
Homme de tous les temps et de tous les usages,
Peint le monde moderne après les anciens âges,
Et créé de sa main, pour nos amusements,
Un peuple de théâtre, un peuple de romans.
Quand nous le contemplons penché sur sa fournaise,
L'Alcide du travail, le poète Farnèse,
Le conteur sans égal, le puissant romancier,
Labourant le vélin sous sa plume d'acier,
Nous disons: le repos n'est pas loin; notre athlète
Va connaître un loisir, car son œuvre est complète.
Il est temps! ses amis, autour de lui groupés,
Préparent l'édredon; les lauriers sont coupés."

Comme on parlait ainsi tout bas devant la porte,
En craignant de troubler son sommeil, on apporte
Un message daté de . . . je ne sais plus d'où,
D'un pays inconnu, voisin d'un fleuve indou.
Le Titan du travail, dans sa marche hâtée,
Escaladait le roc où mourut Prométhée,
Et tuait des vautours, comme à nos jeux de tir,
Pour venger son aïeul, le poëte martyr.
Il était au Caucase! et quand la nuit venue
Lui donnait un loisir, de quelque pierre nue
Il faisait un pupitre, et, la plume à la main,
Sans trop se soucier d'un douteux lendemain,
Il écrivait des vers, traduisait un poème,
Semait d'esprit joyeux ces beaux récits qu'on aime,

Créait tous les héros de deux romans promis,
Et, pour se reposer, écrivait aux amis.
Puis il a reconnu la zone fortunée
Où Caspys mit en lac sa Méditerranée,
La Perse, qui nous montre encore dans son jardin
Les oiseaux et les fleurs du poëte Azz-Eddin;
Le rivage où le flot du Pont-Euxin se brise,
Où Lucullus conquit la pêche et la cerise;
Où le grand Mithridate enseignait le chemin
Qui guidait les vengeurs chez le peuple romain.
Et toujours en courant, sans jamais perdre haleine,
De la ville au désert, du vallon à la plaine,
De la tente nomade au caravansérail,
L'illustre romancier, l'inventeur du travail,
Brûlé par le soleil, ou rafraîchi par l'ombre,
Ajoutait un volume à des aînés sans nombre,
Et redevenait jeune en voyant l'horizon
Du magique pays qui rajeunit Eson.

Ainsi, ne croyons plus que ce labeur immense
Ait entrevu sa fin; Henri Trois recommence;
Ce n'était qu'un prologue! A Paris arrivant,
Il va bientôt encore rendre sa voile au vent;
Il avait vu Sigée et son haut promontoire,
Son rivage, où la fable est mêlée à l'histoire,
Mais la vapeur, en vol si léger,
Trop vite, sur la mer, emporte un passager;
Il veut revoir Sigée, où le flot d'Ionie
Chante encore Ilium dans sa douce harmonie,
Où la vague d'azur, comme un sillon, guida
Les Grecs d'Agamemnon au pied du mont Ida;
Il veut revoir aussi la Grèce, notre mère,
Ce domaine divin de Virgile et d'Homère,
Ce pays du soleil et des arts, qui nous rend
Le pieux souvenir de tout ce qui fut grand;
Comme un digne filleul, il veut aussi descendre
Sur le môle africain que bâtit Alexandre,
Sur l'Egypte, qui garde encore dans l'oasis,
Les doctrines du mage et les secrets d'Isis;
Où la sagesse dort dans le puits des momies,
Gardant pour l'avenir des paroles amies;
Où les sphinx prodigues donnent à chaque pas
Des leçons à Cousin, car ils ne parlent pas.

Qu'il parte ou qu'il arrive, envoyons au poëte
Ou nos adieux d'amis, ou nos hymnes de fête!
S'il arrive, il apporte à nous qui l'écoutons,
D'harmonieux récits, notés sur tous les tons,
Au monde qui le lit, des histoires sans nombre,
A l'acteur qui le joue, une œuvre gaie ou sombre,
Trois assises de plus que l'architecte met
A cette pyramide, où manque le sommet.
S'il part, nous graverons sur sa corvette agile
Les vers que chante Horace au vaisseau de Virgile,
Nous le suivrons de loin, sur la mer, en priant
Le Dieu du bon retour, le soleil d'Orient,
Ce soleil qui toujours fut propice aux poëtes,
Et, quand il reviendra, nos coupes seront prêtes,
Et nous l'honorerons, parmi nous arrivant,
Quoiqu'il soit notre maître, et quoiqu'il soit vivant.

Paris, 2 avril, 1859.

APPENDIX II

ITINERARY DRAWN UP FOR M. ALEXANDRE DUMAS BY MM. AMÉDÉE JAUBERT,[1] ALEX. DE LABORDE,[2] AND ALPH. DE LAMARTINE

Corsica, Italy, Sicily

Go from Genoa to Bastia, Corte, and Porta Vecchio (M. Jaubert has visited this place and believes it will be found an interesting spot to explore); from Porta Vecchio, by crossing the mountains, reach Ajaccio; from there, resuming the route along the coast, visit Calvi and Saint Florent; and finally come back to Bastia. You will thus have seen the greater part of the sea-shore, and the southern part of the island which is the most interesting.

In this excursion you will be able to come across traces of Roman dominion, Saracen incursions, and Genoese institutions.

Study the customs of the inhabitants and their local features; and make research to find if there still exist amongst them some points of resemblance to the Greeks, or Romans, or Arabs.

From Corsica pass over into Italy, visiting on the way the Isle of Elba: here it is impossible to map out any special itinerary, we must therefore leave the choice of the route to the taste and fancy of the explorer. Only we would specially recommend him to visit what the ancients called Greater Greece, and to seek for ancient monuments and ancient pelasgic towns. Our colleague, M. Petit-Radel,[3] will give M. Dumas some detailed notes on these places, which will be of very great service to him.

In Sicily, M. Dumas will certainly not forget the ruins of Agrigentum, Syracuse, Taormina, and ancient Trepanum. He would, no doubt, like to visit the Æolian Islands, which are so interesting and yet so little frequented that no traveller, from the time of M. Dolomieu until M. Jaubert, has explored them. The islands of Lampedouza and Pantellaria seem equally to invite curiosity and merit the attention of travellers.

Then, cover historical ground as far as Venice, and pass rapidly through Illyria on the way to the Epirus.

Greece, Turkey, and Asia Minor

Visit the port of Actium and the town founded by Augustus to celebrate his victory; then the Ionian Islands—look for marks which English dominion must have left upon the Greek population. Push right up the Gulf of Corinth, and in the Morea follow the track of the last scientific expedition of Colonel Bory Saint-Vincent. Round the Peloponnesus, and come back to visit Megara on the isthmus, Salamis, Attica, Negropont, Calcis, and the Euripus; sail up the Ægean Sea along the coast of Thessaly, going as far as Macedonia, and stop at Salonika (consult "Travels in Macedonia," by M. Cousinéry, Paris, 1832). Touch at all the isles celebrated in history or story; hunt up souvenirs of the line of march of the first Crusaders. Return by the Hellespont to Troas, where you will most certainly find remains of ancient Ilium, visit the Archipelago. Set foot on land again at Smyrna, penetrate into the interior as far as Sardis, and then come down to Rhodes by way of Ephesus, Miletus, and Halicarnassus; end at Crete.

---

[1] P. A. E. P. Jaubert, peer of France and member of the Institute, author of "Géographie d'Edrisi," etc.

[2] Comte Alexandre de Laborde, member of the Academy, author of numerous works.

[3] The Abbé Louis Charles François Petit-Radel, member of the Academy, custodian of the Mazarine Library.

Syria, Palestine, and Egypt

Cyprus and Cilicia, Antioch, and Seleucia. Inland, visit Aleppo and Damascus; come back to Sidon, Tyre, Acre, Cæsarea. Enter Palestine by way of Samaria, visit the Holy Places, follow the track of the Crusaders and of the expedition into Syria. Cross the Isthmus of Suez, and get familiar with both ancient and modern achievements in that region. Go up the Nile as far as possible—consult Herodotus, Rüppel, Denon, de Laborde: in coming down again, follow the arm leading to Damietta, and round there seek anything connected with the expedition of Louis IX.

Malta, Sardinia, the Coast of Africa, and Spain

Stop at Malta, and hunt up historical and political memorials of the Order of the Knights; from there go on to Tripoli; keeping along the coast, visit Tunis and Carthage; sail for Sardinia, traverse it, using as guides the works of MM. de Mimant and d'Azuni; visit the provinces of the interior, and come back to put to sea again at Cagliari bound for Algiers, Bona, and Oran. Cross the Straits of Gibraltar, enter Spain, and follow in the footsteps of Carthaginians, Romans, and Arabs, touching also at the Balearic Isles.

Paris, 23rd March, 1835.

APPENDIX III (A)

SICILIAN PROSPECTUS OF DUMAS' JOURNAL, *L'INDEPENDANT*

DEAR FELLOW-CITIZENS,—Knowing, as you do, that four towns of Sicily—Palermo, Caltanisetta, Girgenti, and Catania—have conferred on me the rights of citizenship, I, therefore, have the privilege—one of which I am proud—of addressing you as "dear fellow-citizens."

I left Marseilles with the intention of visiting Greece, Turkey, Asia Minor, and Egypt. "Man proposes, but God disposes." I have landed in Sicily, and in Sicily I have remained. You have heard of those islands of fable, the shores of which the enchanted traveller could never leave, once he had landed upon them.

Well, the fable in my case has become a reality. Only, it is not Palermo's wooded shores, her azure sea, her perfumed air that have kept me captive; it is her misfortunes, her ruins, her tears. Palermo is beautiful when she smiles, she is still more so when she weeps.

Palermo was weeping when I set foot on quay which lay beneath the baleful shadow of Francis II's blood-stained banner. Palermo was weeping for her murdered citizens, for her houses destroyed by fire, and for her outraged convents. Could I leave her in her distress?

Now, the consoler of Palermo, he whom God has raised up for the freedom of the world, that man, unique and elect among men, who has made visible the hand of Providence in the land of Italy, was my friend. Four months ago, at Genoa, he had given me a rendezvous in Sicily. I repaired to that spot, whither he had preceded me. At Calatafimi he was revealed to you as the Messiah of Independence, whose precursor Rosolino del Pilo had been.

You have understood that I would speak to you of the conqueror of San Antonio, of Varese, of Como, of Treponti,—in a word, of Garibaldi.

But on the morrow of the battle of Milazzo, just as I was taking leave of him to continue my voyage to the East, he said to me: "Remain with us, my friend, you can be of service to us." From the moment these words were spoken, my voyage was indefinitely postponed.

"Found a journal at Palermo," he added, "in which you will uphold the cause of Sicilian independence before the face of European diplomacy. Strip bare and blast the tyranny of the Bourbons which has so long oppressed this unhappy country: in short, achieve with the pen what we are accomplishing with the sword."

I gave him my hand.

"You know," said I to him, "my profound admiration for you. I love you as a brother; and to tell me that I can be of service to the cause which you are defending is to make me the proudest of men. Give me a title and a foreword, I will do the rest."

"Call it *L'Indépendant*. It is in the cause of Independence that both of us have been fighting for thirty years. As for your epigraph, take these few lines which I am going to write, and put them at the head of your journal."

Milazzo, 21st July, 1860.

"The journal which my friend Dumas is going to found in Palermo will bear the brave title of 'L'Indépendant,' and it will deserve its name, if it does not hesitate to attack myself, should I deviate from my duties as a son of the people and from my humanitarian principles.
" G. GARIBALDI."

From that moment my resolution was taken, and my calculations made. My resolution was this: to return to Palermo and issue the following prospectus.

I call myself the *Indépendant* and I shall justify this title. I have been independent all my life, and I shall die independent.

This is what *L'Indépendant* will be like. It will be issued daily. It will contain, at least every second day, a leading article which will discuss the events of the day. This will be in Italian, as also will be the news. My *causeries* with the reader, the *feuilleton*, and the *variétés* will be in French. The *causeries* will turn either on political events, or on things of the imagination. The *feuilleton* will be the history of events in Sicily from the 4th April until to-day. The *variétés* will be the Memoirs of Garibaldi, either written by himself or under his dictation.

In addition, we shall have a correspondent at Messina, Catania, Naples, Rome, Milan, Genoa, Turin, Paris, London. We shall become subscribers to the "Times" and the "Morning Post"—the two journals of the banks and the aristocracy in England—and also to all the leading journals of Paris.

The paper will be issued for delivery at the subscriber's home, and also for sale in the streets. The respective prices appear at the end of the prospectus.

The journal will come out as soon as we have 6000 registered subscribers. No subscriptions need be paid till after the receipt of the first number. Subscriptions are requested for three months only at any one time, as the journal will be issued for the duration of the events which interest the reader. When Sicily is annexed to the Kingdom of Victor Emmanuel, when Naples has been conquered, Rome liberated, Venice delivered, the mission of Garibaldi accomplished, the journal will have done its work, and, in all probability, cease to appear.

The subscription for three months will be *two ducats*. The price in the streets will be *four bajoques*.

Au revoir, then, dear fellow-citizens. I am leaving for France, where I am going to work for you. Let those who love me, and who have confidence in my pen, second my project; and, on my return, *L'Indépendant* will appear.

Before a month is over, I shall be amongst you again. Love him a little who loves you so much.

Palermo, 24th *July*. Alex. Dumas.
My birthday.

APPENDIX III (B)

FRENCH PROSPECTUS OF *L'INDÉPENDANT*

L'INDÉPENDANT
JOURNAL FRANCO-ITALIEN
D'ALEXANDRE DUMAS

AT the present moment the eyes, not merely of Europe but of the world, are focussed upon two great events: Garibaldi's expedition to Sicily, and the massacres in Syria.

One of these will, in all probability, result in the downfall of the royal house of Naples. *L'Indépendant*, which comes out in Sicily, will be in a position to give the French public the latest news and the most detailed accounts of the progress of events both in Naples and in Syria.

We have already secured a correspondent in Beyrout. As for news of the expedition to Naples, we have it from Garibaldi himself. In addition, we have correspondents in Constantinople, Naples, Rome, Leghorn, and Turin. *L'Indépendant* may not be produced under the ægis of the Dictator, but it is inspired by him; nevertheless, it is not in any way bound to him, politically, as is proved by the following epigraph given to us by him for the purpose of publication.

"The journal which my friend Dumas is going to found in Palermo will bear the brave title of 'L'Indépendant,' and it will deserve its name if it does not hesitate to attack myself should I deviate from my duties as a son of the people, and from my humanitarian principles."

In these few lines you can sum up the man whose brilliant campaign we have recently described, and whom we are going to accompany in his march on Naples. The letters which we have written on Milazzo, and the one on Naples just published in *le Sémaphore*, are specimens of the form in which political news will reach our readers.

This journal will be written half in Italian and half in French. This is a necessity imposed upon us by the birthplace of the paper—Palermo. At present, Sicily is little familiar with the French language, but all Sicilians will speak it in ten years' time.

The journal, which will be similar in size to *l'Annexion* and *l'Italie Nouvelle*, will appear daily; but in France, it will only be delivered to those who are in correspondence with us. Naturally, we shall be pleased to hear from all who will communicate with us.

As the journal will only be issued for the duration of the events which have brought it into existence, subscriptions for three months only, at any one time, are requested.

The subscription for THREE MONTHS is SIX FRANCS (for any part of France), post-free. Subscriptions need not be paid till after the receipt of the first number.

All letters containing money, inquiries, subscriptions, and complaints should be addressed, post-paid, to M. Félix Valmont—sole agent *for France*—at Marseilles.

Marseilles, 7th August, 1860.
A. DUMAS.

APPENDIX IV

DUMAS' PURCHASE OF ARMS FOR GARIBALDI

(Copy of the original bill and documents connected with the transaction.)

Zaoué—Marseille.

MONSIEUR ALEXANDRE DUMAS Père a Zaoué les armes ci-après. Embarquées sur le vapeur fr^{caise} des Mess. Impe^{les} le Mercuryen destination de Messine.

Marseille, le 9 août, 1860.

(A.Z.—2402)

1 caisse — 19 carabines avec sabre bay^{tte} (2403–2463/2481–2561/2563).

23 caisses—   Chacune 20 carabines soit
    —460 carabines avec sabre bay^{tte} (2564).

1 caisse — 19 carabines (2404).

1 caisse — 9 carabines type Vincennes (10).

1 caisse — 5 carabines type Vincennes (2387/2387–2391/2399–2405/2441).

512 carabines à L. 87·50 · · · ·   L. 44,800

    52 caisses par 12 fusils chacune soit.

728 fusils de guerre avec la bay^{tte} avec hausse à 1000 m. (2388/2390).

    3 caisses chacune 20 fusils soit.

60 fusils avec hauses à 1000 mètres (6/9).

100 fusils Dite (4 caisses).

888 fusils de guerre avec bay^{tte} à L. 45 · · · · ·   39,960
(Les unes dans les autres.)

5 moules à balles pour les carabines dans chacune des caisses (2561/2564) soit 20 moules à balles F. 13 · · · ·   260

Dans la caisse 2560–2562/2564 n. 1 sous les 512 accessoires

512 accessoires pour les 512 carabines à L. 3·30 (A.Z. 902–903) .   1,689·60

    2 caisses—chacune 250 mille capsules soit 500,000 capsules
    (caisse frais compris) (7 A.Z. 2523–2524) · · ·   3,500

    2 caisses—chacune 2000 cartouches soit 4000 cartouches (2525)

1 caisse   1000 cartouches

5000   cartouches avec
balles prêtes à
charger · ·   L.   600

90 caisses emballage à L. 8 (Non-compris les caisses capsules) ·   ,,   720

Frais d'embarquem . . . a bord à . . . par caisse L. 2·25 · ·   ,,   180

Reçu de M. Dumas la somme de · · · · ·   F. 91,709·60
                                        ,, 51,518·40

Reste de   L. 40,191·20
G.^{ges} Zaoué

Zaoué—Marseille

Sur les soixante mille francs reçu de M. de Pretis :
J'ai payé a Zaoué armurier pour une portion de la facture ci-contre
la somme de . . . . 51,518·40
J'ai remis à Rognetta (Ci-joint le reçu) 7,000
J'ai payé décompte pour la lettre de change 300
J'ai dépensé bateau à vapeur aller et retour 880
Enfin j'ai payé à Messine pour erreur commise au moment du
débarquement 1,800

Total 61,498·40
Comme le général Medici en reçevant les fusils à payé les 40,191·20
1,498

Qui soustraits donnent une somme égale à 60,000

ALEX. DUMAS.

J'ai en outre avancé mille francs à . . . pour payer les hommes.
J'ai donné un révolver . . . 200 francs au Père Jean. Un révolver à Carbonelli.
Enfin . . . autres avances qui seront object d'un compte particulier pour lequel
M. de Pretis me dira ce que je dois faire.
Reçu de M. Dumas la somme de deux mille cinq cents francs pour nous désinté-
resser de l'erreur qui a été commise à notre détriment, trois caisses d'armes nous
appartenant ayant été prises lors du débarquement qui fut fait des fusils et des car-
bines rapportées par M. Dumas au dictateur et livrées au général Medici.

Messina, 8 settembre, 1860.

Riceviamo la somma di Franchi Mille ottocento per nostra parte d'interesse.

ANDREA BONO E F.

Ces trois caisses appartenaient à deux personnes—l'une était intéressée pour
1800 fr. l'autre pour six cents, une seule personne poursuivait le procès. Je l'ai
desintéressée quoique le reçu soit de 2400 F. Il n'y a donc eu que 1800 F. payés
par moi.

ALEX. DUMAS.

Marseille, 4 Août, 1860.

Reçu de M. Dumas sept mille francs devant servir à l'achat de cent révolvers,
avec cartouches et frais de transport et de voyage.

F. B. ROGNETTA.

BORDEREAU

1200		
1100		
1000	30 jours de date sur le trésorier général	
900	de Sicile. Palerme 12–23	F. 60,000
705·29		300
4905·29		59,700

Reçu de M. Alex. Dumas les effets ci-dessus sur Palerme contre notre payment
de cinquante neuf mille sept cents francs d'une lettre de crédit de Mess. Ig. et
Florio.

Palermo en date du 27 Août, 1860.

V. DROCENA ET TURTES.

PRINTED IN GREAT BRITAIN BY RICHARD CLAY & SONS, LIMITED,
BUNGAY, SUFFOLK.

IN ACTIVE PREPARATION

A Translation into English of

THE MEMOIRS OF GENERAL GIUSEPPE

GARIBALDI

WRITTEN BY HIMSELF

Edited, with considerable additions, by

ALEXANDRE DUMAS

Author of ' The Three Musketeers,' ' On Board the Emma,' etc., etc.

This translation of an enthrallingly interesting
book, which is being made by Mr. R. S. Garnett,
will be noteworthy for its inclusion of some 60,000
words written by Alexandre Dumas which have
never hitherto appeared in English.

London
ERNEST BENN LIMITED
1929